THE
EASTERN
EUROPE
COLLECTION

NATIONALISM AND WAR
IN THE
NEAR EAST

Edited by
Lord Courtney of Penwith

ARNO PRESS & THE NEW YORK TIMES
New York · 1971

Reprint Edition 1971 by Arno Press Inc.

Reprinted from a copy in
The University of Illinois Library

LC# 79-135800

ISBN 0-405-02742-7

The Eastern Europe Collection
ISBN for complete set: 0-405-02730-3

Manufactured in the United States of America

NATIONALISM AND WAR

IN THE NEAR EAST

PRINTED IN ENGLAND
AT THE OXFORD UNIVERSITY PRESS

1569·7

Carnegie Endowment for International Peace

DIVISION OF ECONOMICS AND HISTORY

John Bates Clark, Director

NATIONALISM AND WAR
IN THE NEAR EAST

(By a Diplomatist)

EDITED BY

LORD COURTNEY OF PENWITH

OXFORD: AT THE CLARENDON PRESS

London, Edinburgh, New York, Toronto, Melbourne and Bombay

HUMPHREY MILFORD

1915

INTRODUCTORY NOTE BY THE DIRECTOR

THE Division of Economics and History of the Carnegie Endowment for International Peace is organized to ' promote a thorough and scientific investigation of the causes and results of war '. In accordance with this purpose a conference of eminent statesmen, publicists, and economists was held in Berne, Switzerland, in August 1911, at which a plan of investigation was formed and an extensive list of topics was prepared. The programme of that Conference is presented in detail in an Appendix. It will be seen that an elaborate series of investigations has been undertaken, and the resulting reports may in due time be expected in printed form.

Of works so prepared some will aim to reveal direct and indirect consequences of warfare, and thus to furnish a basis for a judgement as to the reasonableness of the resort to it. If the evils are in reality larger and the benefits smaller than in the common view they appear to be, such studies should furnish convincing evidence of this fact and afford a basis for an enlightened policy whenever there is danger of international conflicts.

Studies of the causes of warfare will reveal, in particular, those economic influences which in time of peace bring about clashing interests and mutual suspicion and hostility. They will, it is believed, show what policies, as adopted by different nations, will reduce the conflicts of interest, inure to the common benefit, and afford a basis for international confidence and good will. They will further tend to reveal the natural economic influences which of themselves bring about more and more harmonious relations and tend to substitute general benefits for the mutual injuries that follow unintelligent self-seeking. Economic internationalism needs to be fortified by the mutual trust that just dealing creates ; but just conduct itself may be favoured by economic conditions. These, in turn, may be created partly by a natural evolution and partly by the conscious action of governments ; and both evolution and public action are among the important subjects of investigation.

An appeal to reason is in order when excited feelings render armed conflicts imminent ; but it is quite as surely called for when no excitement exists and when it may be forestalled and prevented from developing by sound national policies. To furnish a scientific basis for reasonable international policies is the purpose of some of the studies already in progress and of more that will hereafter be undertaken.

The publications of the Division of Economics and History are under the direction of a Committee of Research, the membership of which includes the statesmen, publicists, and economists who participated in the Conference at Berne in 1911, and two who have since been added. The list of members at present is as follows :

EUGÈNE BOREL, Professor of Public and International Law in the University of Geneva.

LUJO BRENTANO, Professor of Economics in the University of Munich ; Member of the Royal Bavarian Academy of Sciences.

CHARLES GIDE, Professor of Comparative Social Economics in the University of Paris.

H. B. GREVEN, Professor of Political Economy and Statistics in the University of Leiden.

FRANCIS W. HIRST, Editor of *The Economist*, London.

DAVID KINLEY, Vice-President of the University of Illinois.

HENRI LA FONTAINE, Senator of Belgium.

His Excellency LUIGI LUZZATTI, Professor of Constitutional Law in the University of Rome ; Secretary of the Treasury, 1891–3 ; Prime Minister of Italy, 1908–11.

GOTARO OGAWA, Professor of Finance at the University of Kioto, Japan.

Sir GEORGE PAISH, Joint Editor of *The Statist*, London.

MAFFEO PANTALEONI, Professor of Political Economy in the University of Rome.

EUGEN PHILIPPOVICH VON PHILIPPSBERG, Professor of Political Economy in the University of Vienna; Member of the Austrian Herrenhaus, Hofrat.

PAUL S. REINSCH, United States Minister to China.

His Excellency BARON Y. SAKATANI, recently Minister of Finance; Present Mayor of Tokio.

THEODOR SCHIEMANN, Professor of the History of Eastern Europe in the University of Berlin.

HARALD WESTERGAARD, Professor of Political Science and Statistics in the University of Copenhagen.

FRIEDRICH, FREIHERR VON WIESER, Professor of Political Economy at the University of Vienna.

The function of members of this Committee is to select collaborators competent to conduct investigations and present reports in the form of books or monographs; to consult with these writers as to plans of study; to read the completed manuscripts, and to inform the officers of the Endowment whether they merit publication in its series. This editorial function does not commit the members of the Committee to any opinions expressed by the writers. Like other editors, they are asked to vouch for the usefulness of the works, their scientific and literary merit, and the advisability of issuing them. In like manner the publication of the monographs does not commit the Endowment as a body or any of its officers to the opinions which may be expressed in them. The standing and attainments of the writers selected afford a guarantee of thoroughness of research and accuracy in the statement of facts, and the character of many of the works will be such that facts, statistical, historical, and descriptive, will constitute nearly the whole of their content. In so far as the opinions of the writers are revealed, they are neither approved nor condemned by the fact that the Endowment causes them to be published. For example, the publication of a work describing the attitude of various socialistic bodies on the subject of peace and war implies nothing as to the views of the officers of the Endowment on the subject of socialism ; neither will the issuing of a work, describing the attitude of business classes toward peace and war, imply any agreement or disagreement on the part of the officers of the Endowment with the views of men of these classes as to a protective policy, the control of monopoly, or the regulation of banking and currency. It is necessary to know how such men generally think and feel on the great issue of war, and it is one of the purposes of the Endowment to promote studies which will accurately reveal their attitude. Neither it nor its Committee of Research vouches for more than that the works issued by them contain such facts ; that their statements concerning them may generally be trusted, and that the works are, in a scientific way, of a quality that entitles them to a reading.

JOHN BATES CLARK,
Director.

EDITOR'S PREFACE

THIS is an original, thoughtful, and a thought-provoking book. It invites to inquiry and reflection. The author was asked a year ago by the Carnegie Endowment for International Peace to write this review of the conditions under which the last wars in the Balkans were begun and waged, of the situation in which they left the combatant States, and of the prospects of the future which might be anticipated as possible and probable. He is anonymous, but I may say he has had special qualifications for the task entrusted to him by the Endowment. He knows the Near East at first hand, yet he writes from a point of view sufficiently distant to enable him to see the relative value of forces with a more accurate perspective than could be commanded by one in the midst of the turmoil. Add to this the rare distinction that he has moved in and out among Chancelleries and knows their atmosphere without ever having succumbed to its asphyxiating influence. The result is this interesting study. The writer invites us to accompany him in his analysis of the confused experiences and training of the races and States of the Balkans, thence into an examination of the circumstances and promise of the Islamic revival, next into the negotiation of the webs of agreement which preceded the War of the Coalition, and finally in the never-to-be-sufficiently-hated War of Partition which reduced the well-wishers of the inhabitants of the Balkans almost to despair. The writer, however, takes his stand by the side of the situation as left at the end of this war. He sums up the gains and losses of Princes and States, economically, politically, and morally ; and, whilst bitterly condemning the mischief that has been done, attempts some suggestions by way of forecast of what may be expected in the near future. Readers who have been brought to this point must be conscious of the severe trial to which the author's work has been subjected. There are many indications that he was conscious and even expected that a conflict of the Great Powers might issue out of the recast but still unsettled Balkan situation, but his main attention was devoted to an inquiry how the future might be developed more or less domestically. His conclusions are still valuable, but like the gods of Olympus we may smile in secret when we see how some of them have been affected by the great struggle now in progress. His good words touching the position of the Prince of Wied must sound strangely in the ears of that potentate if they come to him in his present situation. Yet an Albania survives and must continue to arrest our attention. The most direct interference of the new war with the situation in the Near East raises the great question of Constantinople and the Straits between the Euxine and the Mediterranean; and here it will appear that our author's suggestions agree with those most recently formulated under the authority of the large experience of Sir Edwin Pears. It is enough, however, to mention such a topic to see in what troubled and difficult waters we are moving. As we said at the outset, we are forced to inquire and to reflect. The real student will be thankful for the lead he gets, but he will examine and re-examine the statements of facts and arguments submitted for his consideration. The book will thus prove its value, and it may be recommended to those who wish to learn, few perhaps rather than many, with the counsel long since given: ' Try all things. Hold fast to that which is good.'

COURTNEY OF PENWITH.

March, 1915.

AUTHOR'S PREFACE

THE following study of the connexion between nationalism and war, as exhibited in the recent events in the Near East, was written, shortly after the Treaty of Bucharest, in the hope that it might suggest some warnings to Western civilization as to the fool's paradise in which we were then living. But already, within a year, these Balkan Wars have had their anticipated result in a European War; and the deadly danger, to the holiest shrines of civilization, of the explosive forces liberated by infusing nationalism with war need no longer be proclaimed for it can no longer be prevented. When the conflagration has burned itself out : when the gains in conquest and *kudos* accruing to the victors from their ' insurances' in armaments and alliances have been cashed in : when the losses of capital and credit of both victor and vanquished have been cut ; and when civilization starts again to resume its interrupted activities—then let us remember the relationship between nationalism and war, which is at the root of the evil, and re-establish the international structure on a sounder foundation. This work will not have failed of its purpose if it reminds any European or American reader of the results of a ' crusade for civilization' in Eastern Europe a few months ago. In Western Europe there must be no wars of ' partition' or of ' extermination' : no arbitrary and anti-national amputations—aching wounds that will again fever nationalism into war : no diplomatic deals that will leave civilization precariously balanced over chaos : no more subordination of free States to militarist cliques, and no more subjugation of free citizens into mobilized conscripts.

A Balance of military Power abroad and a preponderance of militarist policy at home were treacherous foundations for European peace. But they might have lasted long enough to dissociate European nationalism finally from war, but for two factors. The first and most important of the two was the failure of European democracy to assert its control over diplomacy; with which, however, we have nothing directly to do here. The second was the failure of European diplomacy, largely owing to its undemocratic inspiration, so to further the growth of nationalism in the Near East that it might expand and express itself otherwise than by war.

Nationalism in Eastern Europe is naturally more prone to warlike expression than in Western Europe, for it is in an earlier stage of development. Western nationalism looked upon its armaments as a sort of inoculation or insurance, and was indeed probably beyond risk of infection with war from any other quarter than the Near East. There have been outbreaks of war in the West, but they have been dealt with. Thus we have just seen the democratic diplomacy of the United States successfully isolating for many years a civil war in Mexico that might have caused a race war between the leading Latin and Anglo-Saxon nations of North America as it did half a century ago. We have seen the diplomatic democracy of the United Kingdom negotiating one truce after another in the secular warfare between Irish nationalism and English imperialism. But while war in Ireland or in Mexico was a matter of far more direct import to culture and capital than war in the Balkans, yet the danger to the European system from such war was far less. How is it that war in Serbia outside the pale of the European polity instantly and irresistibly carried the contagion to London and Paris?

It may be that forty years of peace in Western Europe had reduced the moral resistance to war—but it is probable that the plague would have been stayed but for the commitments of European nations in the Near East and among themselves. Russia was committed to Serbia, Austria to Bulgaria, Germany to Turkey; while Germany was compromised with Austria, France with Russia, and Great Britain with France. This policy of counter-alliance, like that of competitive armament, received its popular sanction from the instinct of national self-preservation, that first law of nations; but alliances and armaments intended as defensive will always be interpreted as offensive. The English, French, Russians, and Serbs were brought together by the appalling military and political engine erected in their midst by the German race—while the Germans were deterred from dispatching their own Frankenstein by the vast and vague forces of the Eastern Slavs and Western Sea-Powers that encircled them. Having once accepted this social system of armaments and alliances the peoples of Europe found themselves mechanically and morally bound to take the consequences. The British have gone to war willingly because their honour had been pledged to defending France and Belgium by arms and they feared that otherwise they would lose them as buffer states against a German advance to the Channel. The French are fighting because their honour was pledged to take up arms with Russia and they feared that otherwise they would never recover Alsace-Lorraine and a bulwark against another German advance over the Rhine. Russian honour was pledged to the Serbs and Russia feared the destruction of the South Slav barrier against German expansion eastwards into Asia.

This brings us back again to the Serbs and suggests that it is the expansive force of South Slav nationality communicating itself to Russia that has exploded the mines and magazines with which diplomatists and militarists had sapped the foundations of the European social structure. The South Slavs have been the fighting slaves and the farming serfs of Central Europe for centuries, and it is their struggle for freedom that has upset the European equilibrium and set in motion the mobilization machines. It is in part a visitation for the sins of their fathers towards the nations of the Near East that to-day the freemen of Europe are being rounded up by millions, railroaded to the front, and fed to the machine guns.

The makers of wars, European or Balkan, will have to stand their trial before the Court of History, which in due course will deliver its final judgement; and any attempt to anticipate that judgement would be now contempt of court. But meanwhile the progress of making history continues, and is, to some extent, influenced by our attitude toward the makers. That attitude is, in its turn, affected by the reports of journalists and diplomatists who have special opportunities for observation; and, although neither journalists nor diplomatists can write history, they contribute very considerably to the making of history by their reports on what is happening. Governmental policy and public opinion give direction and driving power to the making of history; and depend for much of that driving power and direction on the reports of journalists and diplomats being from an impartial point of view and in correct historical perspective. The following journalistic review or diplomatic report may suggest some of the probable causes and possible consequences of the present war by showing the causes and consequences of the Balkan Wars of the last decade. The intention is, moreover, to show these happenings in such perspective as might be got from the vantage-ground of a century hence; since, in order to see the shoals and currents of a disturbed sea, the observer must get well above and away from the surface.

With regard to the facts and figures on which the opinions

here presented are based, the writer does not claim to have had access, either as journalist or diplomatist, to sources of information not available to any one who has been associated as he has with the Balkan peninsula. It is only an experience of some years' work on Balkan affairs, and of many more given to foreign affairs generally, that excuse any apparently authoritative statements that may hereafter be made.

The respective responsibilities of journalist and of diplomatist have been, of recent years, brought into closer relationship with each other, although possibly, so far, the contributions of journalists to diplomacy have been more notable than instances of successful journalism by diplomats.[1] The present purpose is journalistic, in so far as the object is to put before people whose lives are passed in circumstances very far removed from those of Eastern Europe some general idea of the meaning of the series of wars that have succeeded each other in the Balkans during the last five years ; while it is diplomatic, in so far as the object is to give the English-speaking peoples of the West a clearer understanding of, and a closer sympathy with, the Balkan peoples. As the wars in which the latter have been engaged mark an epoch in European history, a clear understanding of them will be valuable to a reading public, even though so far removed in circumstances and so remote in situation as that of North America ; while the sympathy and support of the great Atlantic peoples is of vital importance to the younger nations of the Aegean and Adriatic.

It is a fact that progress in Eastern Europe has been, and will be, for many years, dependent on the attitude adopted towards it by Western culture and by Western capital. The Balkans have long been the borderland between East and West, and their final annexation to Western civilization, effected by the Turkish Civil War and by the

---

[1] For an example of the former, see the part taken by a journalist in the negotiations for the Balkan Coalition, p. 181.

Balkan War of the Coalition, opens up to the older democracies of the West new opportunities for aiding these younger
peoples; for the diplomatic difficulties that have hitherto
hindered Western democracy in developing the domains
of an Eastern despotism now no longer exist. It is therefore very important that Western public opinion, especially
that of the United States, should inform itself from impartial
sources of the forces that are at work in Eastern Europe.
It is especially important that Western civilization should
not be prejudiced against the Balkan peoples by offences
on their part which are only incidental to their stage of
civilization, and should not turn away in discouragement
or disgust from a region where Western interest and Western
investment are both urgently required and would be amply
rewarded. Governments notoriously have no gratitude in
their diplomatic relations, but in the democratic relationship between peoples, the gratitude of the younger nation
for aid in its development is a real moral force, and often
a valuable commercial asset.

The indebtedness of the Near Eastern peoples to the
peoples of England and of Russia will be dealt with later
as a matter of history. But such indebtedness also exists
even when the democratic relationship is so remote that it
has been recognized only by the poor relation. For instance,
the relationship between the American democracies and
those of the Balkans is one that in the United States itself
is frequently overlooked and always undervalued. The
writer will be bold enough to assert, on the strength of many
years spent among both the American and the Balkan
peoples, that the American democratic relation to the
Balkans has, in the short time that it has existed, done more
for the emancipation of those peoples than the diplomatic
relation of any European Government with the Governments of the Balkan States. ' Ce qu'on voit '—in political
as well as in commercial relationships—is generally of less

importance than 'ce qu'on ne voit pas'; though the doctrine of the advantages of democratic relationships over diplomatic relations and the proof that balance of power is as misleading a half-truth as balance of trade still await their Bastiat.

One great need of the Balkans is capital. Not only the capital for large exploitations, which is in large part wasted, and which, in most cases, imposes servitudes and mortgages on the national liberties, but capital for the small enterprise, the shop, the school, or the farm. Such capital, no penny of which is wasted, and every penny of which represents emancipation from the usurer, local or international, is now annually poured into these poverty-stricken territories from the earnings of emigrants to the United States.[1] It is largely with American money that of late years Macedonians have been ousting the Moslem landlord from his property rights—a process which has had a most important effect on the extension of Balkan nationality to this province. Another requirement of the Balkan peoples, and a no less urgent one, is education. Not such education, moreover, as is entirely inspired by a patriotic propaganda and by a purely Balkan point of view, such as, to take an extreme instance, the education given in recent years to Macedonians by the various national propaganda, but an education of a more liberal character. In this respect no better education could be devised for the purpose of preserving peace in the Balkans than that provided by emigration to the New World; and it is found that the returned Balkan emigrants, whom the traveller now meets everywhere, have risen to a higher and wider plane of civilization, without losing more than is wholesome of their original primitivism, or of their newly acquired patriotism. Twenty years ago the outer world was represented to a Balkan villager by

---

[1] A good emigrant will in five years save £350, and the average seems to be as much as £200. In Greece the annual receipts from America have amounted to as much as £1,500,000 in 1910.

oleographs of the sovereigns and statesmen of the Powers
that solicited his suffrages, and by the occasional passage of
tourists and consuls—an event comparable to the arrival of
the circus in the villages of the West. The oleographs were,
like the eikons which they surrounded or replaced, ugly
objects of superstitious fear or affection; while the foreigners
on tour were, like the ' popes ' and monks, generally objects
of ridicule. Nowadays everywhere are to be met Balkan
men and women who can distinguish between democracy
and diplomacy; who know, for instance, that a Russian
vice-consul does not always represent the will of the Russian
people, and that an American tourist is not a ' lordos Ingles ',
but represents a power even more productive of good. The
young Bulgar who has braved the terrors of the Atlantic
and of Ellis Island, and who has seen the wonders of New
York and Chicago—the Mecca and Medina of the Western
Hadj—becomes a local prophet of progress, even as the old
Bosniak who has faced the Red Sea in a pilgrim ship becomes
a high priest of the mysteries which make life worth living
to the oriental. The outward and visible signs of the western
pilgrimage are less picturesque than the green turban, while
the philosophy of life it produces is unpleasingly cynical
and crude; but as the Balkan peasant has got to become
a European proletarian, and can never hope to be an Asiatic
prophet, the sooner he gets through his novitiate the better.

Besides this leavening from the bottom upwards, the
United States has for a quarter century been educating the
Balkans, from the top downwards, through Robert College.
There is probably no educational foundation in the world
which has rendered such special services to contemporary
progress, or which has kept so closely in touch with the
crisis of European politics as this American institution.
There is scarcely a Bulgar statesman who has not received his
education there—an education often continued long after the
pupil had become a ruling factor in his country's fortunes.

It was Robert College that alone afforded the Ottoman Greeks and the Armenians some relief from the mental starvation which was one of the worst privations imposed by Hamidian tyranny on those most intellectual races.[1] Under the new conditions the Near East will before long be able to provide sufficiently for the education of its own manhood, and it is therefore well that American beneficence has also taken up the task of educating the womanhood of the Near East. The American woman's college at Constantinople will no doubt play as important a part in the social emancipation of Near Eastern womanhood as did Robert College in the political emancipation of the men.

The author of this monograph is not an American, nor does he write especially for his American readers. He writes mainly for those whose attention has been drawn to the Balkans by recent events, and who have come in, so to say, at the third act; but he hopes that those who, like himself, have followed the plot with anxious interest, from the gallery or from the wings, will find, in the suggestions that follow, some new ideas as to its meaning and some useful indications as to its motive.

The meaning of the Balkan War can only be found by seeking evidence of the forces at work, either through excavation in the dry dust of 'Eastern Question' literature, in which lie buried a few significant facts, or else through personal contact with the peoples themselves. Even so it is not easy to put

[1] It is interesting how great work, however modest, nearly always succeeds in making a dramatic appeal to the imagination. Democratic influences on the fortunes of peoples have their *coups de théâtre* no less than diplomatic interventions. Such a dramatic challenge to the Hamidian régime was displayed by the American college before every visitor to the national capital. He had no sooner passed the gloomy valley where under a sky-line of barracks the last of the tyrants lurked in obscure lairs hidden among the trees, than there appeared standing up boldly on a bluff above the ruined castle of Mahmoud the Conqueror the four-square large-windowed buildings of Robert College. The lurking 'shadow' seemed to shrink deeper into the shrubberies of Yildiz before the straight-forward stare of those windows of the West.

the results together in a clear and consecutive account. For
this ' question ' is, in a political aspect, the so-called Eastern
Question: in an historical aspect it is the European ' nationality ' movement: in a geographical aspect it is the shifting
of the point of contact of Europe with Asia.

The main interest of the story of the Balkan wars lies
in the fact that the duel between East and West, which is
as old as history, and which has for five hundred years been
dragging along with no particular end in sight, has within
the last five years developed three distinct *dénouements*.
Each of these was a surprise in itself, and each, just when
it seemed to be accepted as final, was destroyed by an even
more surprising discomfiture of the forces making for progress. Thus the Anglo-Russian combination—which a year
or so before its conclusion seemed the least likely combination in the world—was, in 1908, on the point of establishing
a settlement on an international basis of Cretan and Macedonian liberty with a new European guarantee. But the
half-completed structure of autonomy was ruined by the
Ottoman revolution, and instead of the Empire being forced
to reform Macedonia, Macedonia forced reform upon the
Empire. Thereafter the establishment of a constitutional
Empire was considered as having solved the Eastern Question on an imperialistic basis of Ottoman equality, guaranteed
by new representative institutions. But the Ottoman
imperialist revolution proved to be a Turkish national
renascence, and as such, came into violent collision with
Balkan nationalism. The consequence was a coalition of
the Balkan nations against the Turkish nation, and the
expulsion of the latter from Europe. Then, lastly, as a result
of the War of the Balkan Coalition, the Eastern Question
seemed to have been settled for ever by a partition of Turkey
in Europe on a nationalist basis of Balkan fraternity,
guaranteed by a Balkan federation. But the war of the
Macedonian partition between the Balkan nations so greatly

injured the nationalist character of the settlement as to pre-judice its permanence. The attempt to frame a settlement on the basis of the balance of power rather than that of historical, geographical, and ethnological fact leaves the situation still in unstable equilibrium.

We have had already ample proof that in Balkan affairs, as elsewhere, a democratic movement cannot finally be brought to rest by a diplomatic settlement. The believers in human nature and in the humanity of nations—the adherents of democracy and progress, who found encourage-ment in the Macedonian millennium and in the Balkan coalitions, have been rudely and bitterly disappointed. Balkan diplomacy, after imposing itself on Europe by its solidarity and its soundness, and after extorting the admira-tion of Europe for its principles and its prudence, has relapsed into dependence and dissension. The Balkan peoples com-bined first against the youngest democracy, Turkey, which was probably in the circumstances, indispensable—then against the most primitive, Albania, which was perhaps not inexcusable—and finally against the most progressive, Bul-garia, which was almost unpardonable. European diplomacy successfully intervened to save for young Turkey and for young Albania their capital and a sufficient territory, but had not democratic inspiration and force enough to impose peace at the critical moment or to protect Bulgaria. As a result, South Slav and Greek nationalism were unduly favoured in the settlement. The peace of Bucharest was but a pre-lude to wars of Hellenes with Bulgars, of Hellenes with Turks, and of Serbs with Bulgars, Arnauts and Austro-Hungarians. It is the last of these which has made of the Balkan wars of yesterday a prelude to the European wars of to-day.

Happily the works of man are never wholly evil, and even Balkan wars must leave some good behind. It is due to the Turkish Civil War and to the Balkan Coalition War that Constantinople, if still corrupt, is no longer a cesspool, and that Macedonia, if still a *casus belli*, is no longer a cockpit.

Again it is very possible that one of the results of this European War may be a satisfactory re-arrangement of frontiers in the Balkans. It is true that Europe has now graver affairs to settle than whether the inhabitants of Monastir are Bulgars or Serbs, or whether a Greek occupation of Lemnos is a strategic menace to Turkey. But war in Europe can scarcely fail to reopen all such ill-regulated questions, and, either by conquest or in the congress that is bound to follow the general war, we may expect the Balkans to attain a more permanent peace than that promised by the Treaty of Bucharest. Perhaps also it may be that, as a result of two as bloody and barbarous wars as any which have afflicted the civilized world, Europe, even if it remains entrenched in armed camps, may be secured against being again embroiled by armed conspiracies.

When peace has again been established in Europe and the Balkans, and the time comes for the civilized peoples to reconstruct their international relationships, it will be well for the world if they have learnt one lesson—that national responsibilities may not be neglected with impunity in any region, however insignificant, or by any citizen, however ignorant. If Europe has now twice within five years failed in securing the requisite minimum of progress without ' crusades for civilization ', the responsibility for these failures must be borne by the more liberal and enlightened citizen of the civilized Western States. The European wars of to-day and the Balkan wars of yesterday are due to the failure of the electorates of Western Europe to impress on their Governments their own instincts of common sense and conscience. A foreign policy that has no weight of public opinion behind it has to get its force from strong action and the momentum that results therefrom, and it must take its direction from traditional formulae, from popular passion, or from interested influences. The British citizen who thinks diplomacy a mystery beyond him, and the American citizen who thinks it a mummery beneath him, are only right in so far as they themselves have made it so. International politics will suffer as much through being cut off from the common sense and conscience of citizens and committed entirely to professionals as do municipal politics. ' *Humani nil a me alienum puto*' should be translated by every intelligent citizen as, ' I will treat nothing of human import as a foreign question '.

Yesterday we Europeans sought peace by preparing war: to-day we seek peace by proclaiming war: to-morrow we shall seek peace by prosecuting war to the bitter end. But what has war to do with peace ? If only we had known, even we, in this our day, the things that belonged to our peace ! but now they are hid from our eyes.

August 30, 1914.

CONTENTS

CHAPTER I. INTRODUCTORY

Allons, whoever you are, come travel with me !
Travelling with me you find what never tires.
The earth never tires.
The earth is rude, silent, incomprehensible at first ;
Nature is rude and incomprehensible at first.
Be not discouraged, keep on,
        there are divine things well enveloped :
I swear to you there are divine things
        more beautiful than words can tell.

WALT WHITMAN.

§ 1. NATIONALISM AND PACIFICISM

TREATED as a political problem, the Eastern Question, or, as we should now call it, the Near Eastern Question, with its nucleus the Macedonian Question, is a regular maze in which, without a clue, one may wander indefinitely up innumerable blind alleys and in interminable vicious circles. Or, one may picture it as a deep-sea octopus with tentacles twisting away through the obscurity, an obscurity which it increases at critical moments with floods of self-secreted ink. But it is only when considered as a separate political problem that the ' Eastern Question ' is obscure and complicated. Treated as one volume of the history of European civilization, and as the first chapters in the histories of the youngest communities in that civilization, it becomes not only a clear and consecutive story, but even a drama of intense interest. For the clue to the maze, the motive of the drama, the key that gives meaning to the cipher, is ' nationalism '. The main motive of the history of Western Europe yesterday and of Eastern Europe to-day is the ' nationality ' movement ; that phase of adolescence in the cycle of birth, growth, decay, and death that every political organization must pass through.

If the European nations had all been born at the same time and had grown at the same pace, there would still have been

1569.7   B

a Near Eastern nationality movement, but there would
have been no Eastern Question for Europe and no Macedonian
Question for the Balkans; nor would Near Eastern nationalism have been so unfailing a source of war. The difficulties
that have in the end brought about the Balkan wars come
from the nations of Europe being in different stages of
development; the stage to which each must be assigned
being different again according to whether the standard is
a material or a moral one. Take, for instance, the relations
of Austria and Russia to Servia and Bulgaria. Russia or
Austria is, diplomatically and materially speaking, a strong
and stable Empire, while the Bulgarian or Servian State is,
by the same standard, a starveling and a weakling. What
better fate, one might think, could these smaller peoples
have than amalgamation with their co-religionists and
kindred races in one of the Empires. But if the lot of the
various peoples constituting the Austrian and Russian
Empires be compared with that of the Balkan peoples,
the independence of the latter seems worth the sacrifices
made for it. For in the Austrian Empire it has not yet been
decided whether the dominant type is to be German, Magyar,
or Yugo-Slav, and the Russian Empire is still slowly
assimilating to the Russian dominant type its raw and
often refractory materials; while the peoples of the
Balkan States are already perfect though primitive nations.
What worse fate, from this point of view, could there
be for young democracies which have just succeeded in
freeing themselves from one imperial autocracy than to
be subjected to another? Then again, if the moral and
material resources of Austria and Russia be compared with
those of Servia and Bulgaria, it is evident that the closer
the relations between the older and younger civilizations,
the swifter will be the moral and material progress of the
latter. International relationships between young and old
nations are not the simple equations in terms of population
and armaments that they are often stated as being.

A writer on the Eastern Question has the choice of either giving a chronicle of events, leaving the reader to infer the motive forces for himself, or else of taking the main motive force as an argument to the drama—in this case the nationality movement—and bringing the main events into relation with it. Fortunately the course of national development in the Balkans has followed a broad line of average advance which can be traced in its general direction both geographically and historically. But the progress of Balkan nationalism has been slow and subject to many set-backs and checks: for it has been forced to fight its way; and war is a primitive and unreliable means of progress.

It is very important for the reader of a treatise on present-day politics to have a clear idea at the start of the point of view from which it is written. In this treatise the point of view is that of a pacificist progressive—a point of view which permits of an impartial and critical trial of war-makers, and allows of any verdict on them from one of wilful murder to one of justifiable homicide. Such a point of view may also, perhaps, throw some new light on a question that has been investigated from almost every other aspect. The 'Eastern Question' may still have some teaching for us if examined from a standpoint which avoids the quietism of the Manchester school and the quixotism of the Midlothian campaign, while adopting the fundamental truths of both these political philosophies.

Although at the present moment West-European civilization is established on a basis of polemist alliances and armed populations—yet warfare is no longer an essential element in western nationalism.[1] It is a savage survival in the international relationship—a social relationship hitherto very impervious to progress. Nationalism is still unleavened by the spirit of civilization in proportion as international

[1] The above was written at a time when a general European war was no more than a risk and before it had become a reality. We have now no want of proof that war is a savage survival of an earlier phase of nationalism.

relations are unenlightened by the inspiration of democracy. But the West-European nations have, broadly speaking, outgrown war. Our progress is expressed in economic terms : our philosophers preach efficiency : our principles are inspired by an ethical expediency: whereas war has come to be recognized as being, under modern conditions, inefficient, uneconomic, non-ethical, and inexpedient. In international relations between Western Powers war has been a risk to be insured against and a remedy to which recourse would only be had in very special circumstances. In the ordinary diplomatic relations of civilized States even a reference to such a remedy has been considered as bad form and bad business. ' Pacificism ', though it has scarcely yet found a place in the dictionaries, has already been so much of a principle of popular government that the measure of pacificism in the diplomacy of a western civilized State is almost always the measure of its democracy. In imposing this policy on the institutions and ideas inherited from a more primitive society, democracy has created various institutions, political, judicial, commercial and scientific, international or individual. Such are administrative commissions like those that regulate the Great Lakes, the Danube, and the Suez Canal ; general judicial courts like those of the Hague, or special courts like that for arbitration of Anglo-American claims ; scientific conferences and technical congresses ; commercial conventions and labour unions: all are engaged in building up a corpus of international common law and an international social structure. Not the least important of these international institutions is that which proposes, by a scientific study of the physics and psychology of war, to prove that, in the present state of progress reached by the greater European peoples, war is an anachronism—an atavism.

A European war is either a crime against civilization or a crusade on behalf of it ; for we have become men, and should have put away such childish things as trial by battle. But there are young European communities who have still to fight their war of independence for liberty, adolescent communities that have still before them their civil war for equality, and adult communities that will have to face their social war for fraternity. Some European peoples are not yet democracies : others are not yet nations : none are yet Christian communities. War may be necessary to convert a democracy into a nation ; it may be noble when it is to raise a' people to a democracy ; and there are still Crusades for a Peter Hermit to preach and Holy Wars for a Bunyan to prophesy. Circumstances alter cases. And while the nations that have reached the status of national democracy are being driven by the forces both of peace and of war into international association, those democracies that have not yet reached the national stage may be forced by the same tendencies into destructive international antagonism ; and, finally, those communities that are not yet democracies may be driven by the same living and moving force into internal warfare. Civil war is the most uncivilized of all forms of war, but it is also generally the most defensible. Indeed, one may even go so far as to assert that the more internal and endemic the state of warfare is, the more morally justifiable it will be on general principles. But for the apparent paradox one might suggest that it is a principle of progress that the more hardships, even the more horrors, produced by a state of war, the more hope and healing does it bring. A civil war is more calamitous than a foreign war, but it holds more capabilities for good.[1]

If we apply this theory of war to international relations, beginning with these relations in their most highly civilized form, we shall find that it will explain why a war between the peoples of the United Kingdom and of the United States seems as criminal as a war between Essex and Wessex— a high treason against sovereign democracy. For an Anglo-American war only becomes defensible if we suppose the

[1] This was written before Europe found itself involved in war with the Prussian military power—a war which can be represented as a crusade for fraternity—a campaign for the equality of nations—or a civil war for liberty within the polity of Europe. It shows indeed many of the characteristics of a civil war, especially in its bitterness and brutality.

democratic sovereignty in either party to have been replaced by a despotism—when war of the nature of civil war might again become a means of progress. It is to be remembered that the war of the colonies against George III not only resulted in the foundation of the American Commonwealth, but also in the restoration of the British Constitution. A few years ago an Anglo-German war would have seemed scarcely less impossible. But Anglo-German relations were always a very different thing from the Anglo-American relationship; for the international relationship constituted by the alliances and antagonisms known as the Balance of Power, in which the factors are governments and armaments, is a social relationship of a lower order than the Bond of Peoples between the United Kingdom and the United States, in which there is a living force.

Unfortunately the moral issue in a war is seldom clear at first. Thus the African War was preached on the Afrikander side as a war in the cause of nationality—on the Outlander side as a war in the cause of liberty and equality. The event seems to indicate that South Africa did not become a nation, because it had still to become a democracy; and the more odious hardships of the war suggest also that it had much of the character of a civil or revolutionary war, in which the Outlander had the force of progress on his side. As another instance, at the other end of the scale, we may take such a war as the Soudanese campaigns against barbarism— a barbarism whose very virtues made it all the more a blot on civilization. If these African wars put an end to barbarism and obscurantism and made peace and progress possible, it is not inconceivable that a European war might put an end to the epoch of militarism and imperialism.

While war cannot create progress directly, it can cause it indirectly by breaking the bonds laid upon nationality or the barriers raised against democracy. As will be shown later, there is no human action which finds a swifter reward or a surer retribution than war-making. War is the act of a few, and the many pay for it or profit by it. If they pay more than they profit, the responsible few are made to pay in loss of power. A misguided war means a misgoverned people, and an unjustifiable war will justify itself on the war-makers.

It will be the purpose of this treatise to show that the war of the Balkan Coalition of 1912 is a war altogether justifiable. This war belongs to that early stage of civilization where freedom must be fought for, and to that stage of human society where a community is fighting its way to self-government. The second war, that between the allied Balkan States, the War of Macedonian Partition, is a war between national forces in a later stage of development, where other methods than those of war are possible, and a war for purposes of policy and aggrandizement. The war between Europe and Asia, between free nations and a military Empire, stands obviously on a different plane from a war over the partition of provinces and populations. Whether this second war is justified is a question which will be left open for the reader's judgement after a broad statement of the case. Approval must depend on whether the results are sound and whether war was necessary to achieve them.

But, if a war has become justifiable because inevitable, it is not to be inferred that it was always inevitable. Communities in an advanced stage of civilization may get into a warlike relation to one another through misguidance. Communities in a primitive stage of civilization will not easily get out of a warlike relation unless these relations are regulated for them by more civilized neighbours. The difficulty is that such regulation tends to check their natural growth, especially in respect to their national development; in which case regulation becomes an evil worse than war and itself productive of war. It can, unfortunately, be shown that the Balkan wars, though justifiable last year,[1] and inevitable for several years before, were not always inevitable, and might have been prevented by Europe up to a few years ago.

[1] Written in 1913.

§ 2. Near Eastern Nationality

Geographical history is to political history as geology is
to natural history. By tracing the Wars of the Ottoman
Revolution, of the Balkan Coalition, and of the Macedonian
Partition, back to geographical circumstances, we can at
least feel we are getting down to bedrock.

Now geographical history tells us that civilization flows
from east to west and is now returning from west to east. But
it is returning in a different form. Westward the Star of
Empire takes its way ; but it is eastward that the Star of
Emancipation has guided kings and shepherds. The nationality
movement, which is the main historic tendency of the nineteenth century, is a phase of the acquisition of political power
by the people, even as is the related movement for democratic
popular government. Near Eastern nationalism is a result of
the same renascence that took among western peoples the
form of a movement for democratic institutions. They are
both movements for government of the people by the people
to the exclusion of absolutism and autocracy. This movement
caused wars among the Anglo-American and Latin communities towards the end of the eighteenth century in the
regions bordering the Atlantic, and ever since has been
steadily making its way through the people of Europe and
Asia. After revitalizing the mid-European races, it has
passed into Asia with the beginning of this twentieth century ;
its successive invasions of the Iberian, Italian, and Balkan
peninsulas being specially instructive. Of course the movement was not uniform and on one front. The tide flowed
fast in the open channels or filtered underground : dykes
were built against it : Mrs. Partington was busy with her
mop. Its effect on the Balkan peninsula was exceptionally
erratic, for whereas the Greeks were reached by it even
before many of the Latin races, the Turks were affected
a full century later. Thus it comes about that the arrival
of the nationality movement among the Greeks and the

War of Emancipation of the beginning of the nineteenth century is the first historical cause of the Balkan war ; while its arrival among the Turks and the Ottoman revolution of a century later is the very last. It would be easy, though it would be too long, to explain this by the particular circumstances and character of each place and people. It would be of the greatest interest to examine in detail the political or social conditions under which, for instance, Greece, which had so long a start of Bulgaria, has been overtaken within our generation ; or why Servia as a national democracy is a higher political organism than autocratic Russia. But the geographical method of studying the movement makes such detailed inquiries unnecessary ; for these irregularities, if traced to their source, are to be explained either by direct geographical circumstances such as the checks opposed by mountains and deserts or the channels offered by seas and rivers, or else by indirect geographical influences working on national character. This brings us back again to the geographical origins of history. Balkan politics can only be understood through a knowledge of the stage of development of the Balkan peoples. The Balkan peoples can only be understood by a knowledge of the configurations and characteristics of the peninsula.

When, moreover, the main configurations and characteristics of the peninsula are observed it will be found that the character of the populations has a regional rather than a racial basis, and is indigenous to the locality rather than inherent in the stock. This can be illustrated in the case of every community in question. Greece is inhabited, and, so far as investigation shows, always has been inhabited, by people of the Greek type of character in spite of renewals or even removals of its inhabitants by Cretans, Dorians, Slavs, Albanians, and such alien types. The assertion can be advanced beyond this, and it might even be said that records suggest that the population of Boeotia, or of Sparta, or even of Athens, have maintained through all vicissitudes each their distinct sub-species. Again, Montenegrins and certain Albanian tribes are of very similar physical type; but their mental and moral character is distinct, and while one represents an essentially Slav culture, Albanian civilization is peculiar to itself and long antedated the advent of the Slavs. Bulgars are of Finnish stock, have a Slav tongue, and a Mongol name; but their national character is also peculiar to themselves, though it strongly resembles that of the Finland Finns. The Bulgar national type is evidently one which has had time to adapt itself perfectly to its surroundings, or, as suggested above, to have been perfectly assimilated by its surroundings, physical and political. Back through Byzantine history we find Bulgars playing the same political rôle and exhibiting the same peculiarities.[1] Roumanians are also a composite race of Latins and Vlachs with some borrowings from Jews and Gypsies; but the dominant characteristics of their culture cannot be accounted for from any of these sources.

It will help to explain much that is astonishing in the development of the Balkan nationality movements if we can account for the very marked and matured national characteristics of these very youthful nations by peculiarities in the natural conditions and configuration of the countries they inhabit. For instance, the most marked characteristic of the peninsula of Greece is that it has a deeply indented coastline and that the mainland is cut up into valleys by difficult ranges. These valleys are even more independent

---

[1] The Bulgars have played a very consistent rôle in the peninsula. The phenomenal development of the modern Bulgar State is paralleled by that of the mediaeval State of Boris and Simon (A.D. 892–927), which within half a century advanced from barbarism to the full culture of the time, and drove the Byzantine power behind the walls of Constantinople. This Bulgar State was broken up by the Russians and the Greeks under a Constantine Bulgaro-Ktonos with fearful ' atrocities '. When a Bulgar State reappears 150 years later, it is allied with Roumania in resisting Byzantine extortion and corruption. Under Kaloyan it reaches a high pitch of civilization, and plays off the Eastern against the Western Empire. The early history of the Serbs is also characteristic in respect of the effect on it of Hungarian hostility and of its own dynastic dissensions.

of and isolated from each other than the islands of which a large portion of the Greek national territory consists. Greek civilization centres in and surrounds the Aegean, just as Anglo-Saxon civilization surrounds the North Atlantic. The Hellenes, like the Anglo-Saxons, have in consequence always consisted of independent communities of valley or island folk in a sea-faring, that is a foreign, relation to each other, united only by a common culture and civilization. The course of the early development of the small Greek democracies was by competition rather than by combination. Consequently the natural characteristics of the Greeks in political and social relations are rather intelligence and independence than gregariousness and generosity. This Greek 'separatism' was due also in part to disadvantages attending the development of maritime communities in those days from which our later maritime civilizations have been free. In primitive times the sea was more of a barrier than now ; for while it was already the high road for culture it was also the open road for piracy, and the pirate of that age was as important a factor in regulating and restricting the free growth of a community as the wolf which kept prehistoric man to the hilltops.

But Greek national culture and character were due to more peculiar geographical advantages than an indented coastline and intersecting ranges. From its situation at the juncture of the three continents Greece became the first country in Europe to enjoy the stimulus of Egyptian culture and Phoenician commerce, and owing to its configuration it was especially well adapted for assimilating these advantages. Greece thus became a group of politically compact but socially complex urban communities. Compact because their political relationship to each other and to the outside world was a foreign and frequently hostile one ; complex socially because their situation demanded independent municipal life and commercial pursuits tend to sub-divide a community into social strata. Such a collection

of communities and such a category of classes Greece has
remained to this day ; for while the leading political feature
of Greece nowadays is the all-dominating idea of national
fraternity, yet this great motive principle of Greek public life
has not levelled out the local feeling and local characteristics
that differentiate the component Hellenic communities. So
also, while the dominant social note is democratic equality,
this again has not affected the essential classifications of
Greek society. Again, the principal pride of the individual
Greek is his liberty of thought, his independence of mind,
but no man is more dependent on the opinions of others
or on obtaining from abroad the raw material of culture for
the industry of his intellect. In a word, the typical Greek
is an islander, a townsman, and a brainworker. The
Greek is a cultivator of necessity, the Bulgar by choice ;
as appears in the fact that the Bulgars of Constantinople
are market gardeners and market their produce through
Greeks. The Greek village is a country town ; the Bulgar
village is a collection of farms. Greek nationalism may be
described perhaps rather as an imperial than a national
consciousness. The Greeks of Crete and Corfu are one as
the British of Montreal and Liverpool are one, but not as
the Serbs of Belgrade and Cettinje are one.

As we go north from the islands of the Morea the valleys
widen into plains. First the Boeotian valley : then the broad
vales or narrow plains of Thessaly and of Epirus : north of
them the wider Macedonian valley, until, across the Balkans,
Greek influence dies away in the vast Danubian plains. The
Greeks of these plain lands have throughout been the least
Greek in character. This Boeotian temperament we all
know from the Classics, and it is still the butt of the Kafeneion.
The Thessalian temperament was the basis of Alexander's
empire, which was as non-Greek in its constitution, its
phalanx, and its inspiration as the empire of Napoleon was
non-Latin. This national character explains why the
Greek has had so much difficulty in retaining the interior

of the Peninsula, although holding the coastline—contrary
to the usual rule that who holds the coast holds the
country. He has exploited the coasts of the Aegean
and of the Black Sea, while the Bulgars, Slavs, Turks,
and other plainsmen have exploited the plains. The Greek
has found the process of recovering Thessaly and Epirus
a long and laborious task; and Thessaly is the northernmost
plain country the acquisition of which can be justified as
ethnological. If the Greek national character had allowed
of the Greeks being plainsmen, there would have been no
'Eastern Question'.

Their northern neighbours, the Bulgars and Serbs, offer
very illustrative contrasts. The Serbs in their broken forest
country have retained in their character many more of the
mystic qualities of an earlier civilization. In their social
structure may still be found relics of early social institutions,
such as the 'zadruga', long lost elsewhere. Their main national
occupations are that pastoral pursuit which reformed the
prodigal son and the idyllic industry of making plum jam.
Their national character is best explained by the fact that
they are nearly all poets and pig dealers; and if their
national policy seems sometimes to be more inspired by
their trade than by their temperament, it is perhaps chiefly
the fault of modern civilization, which has given them cause
to seek a political rather than a poetical expression of their
woodland nature.

Bulgar nationalism is as different in character from that of
Greeks or Serbs as the Bulgar fertile plains and grassy downs
differ from the wooded hills of Servia or the stony ranges of
Greece; and the Bulgar ploughman and shepherd both have
the true plainsman's character. Rural life on open plains
and pastures develops character in its moral rather than
in its mental or mystical capacities. It is a common mistake
to assume that highlanders are more devoted to liberty
and more diligent in moral discipline than lowlanders.
Mountains have offered a refuge and a stronghold for tem-

porary resistance against oppression, but it is in the plain
that liberty, equality, and fraternity can best find the
air, the soil, and the springs necessary for their growth.
To their plains the Bulgarians owe the fraternity and
equality—the ethical solidarity, and the economic socialism—
which have made their moral and material renascence
so surprising in its swiftness and smoothness. The moral
qualities of the Bulgar character are in a different sphere
from that of the Greek mental qualities or from that of the
mysticism of the Slav. If the political position of the British
Isles in the sixteenth century were to be compared to that
of the Balkan peninsula of to-day, we should call the Bulgars
Lowland Scotch, the Serbs Irish, the Albanians Welsh, the
Greeks English,[1] and the Roumanians French. The analogy
is of course very imperfect, but may be a help in placing
these peoples politically.

While the Balkans offer an especially favourable field for
studying the effects of nature on nationality and of geographical conditions on the character of nations, the phenomenon is of course not peculiar to the Balkans. The same
thing can be observed in any country of marked configuration
and character. A Cromwellian, Englishman or an Angevin
Norman emigrating to Ireland becomes, in a few generations,
entirely assimilated by the Irish ' nationality ' ; indeed the
working of this spell is quite evident even in a few weeks.
The development of Irish ' nationalism ' in Saxon or Latin
immigrants into Ireland is as swift as its disappearance in
Celtic emigrants out of Ireland. The Irish-American is as
empty of Irish ' nationality ' in one sense as he is exuberant
in Irish 'nationalism' with another meaning. The same is
true of the Greeks. The Scotch, like the Bulgars, take their
name from one foreign stock, their culture from another, and
their central government from a third ; but are, and always

---

[1] The Englishman and the Greek of to-day would probably both find
this comparison odious. But the Englishman of the sixteenth century
has more points of likeness to the Greek of to-day than to the Englishman of the twentieth century.

will be, a ' nation '. The extent to which ' nationality ' can digest foreign material, the extent to which, in other words, the autochthonous character can assimilate the alien character, will depend, of course, on the relationship between the dominant and the subject race. ' Nationality ' will survive the extermination which was the foreign policy of the Hebrews, as their nationalist prophets bear indignant witness. ' Nationality ' will survive enslavement, as is shown by the eventual emancipation of the Balkan peoples. It is questionable, however, whether ' nationality ' can survive the ' pacific penetration ' of modern civilization, which either rejects it as barbarism and crowds it out, or raises it to internationalism and redistributes it in classes.

Although attention has only lately been directed to national consciousness as a moulding moral force, and to the possibility of its possessing subliminal qualities, the effects of this force have long been observed by the democratic diplomatist ; and nowhere are they more remarkable than in the Balkans. In Balkan politics, such a subliminal national consciousness can alone explain events which otherwise would be extraordinary but not enlightening. Events such as the sudden emergence of nations like Bulgaria, fully equipped for, and expert in, the difficult functions of national democracy, from an inchoate mass of corruption and degradation such as was Roumelia in the nineteenth century. Events such as the course taken and the centre chosen by the Greek renascence, which developed through the Moreote peasants instead of through the national culture centre in the Phanar. Events such as the postponement of the renascence of Turkish democracy until it was too late to save the Turkish predominance. These and many other phenomena require something more than an explanation drawn from current politics.

The striking persistence in the Balkan peninsula of national character and national culture, both through long periods of submergence and through operations such as the substitution of a new race for the old, suggests that this power of endurance

may stand in some relation to the period of duration of
culture before the submergence or the shock. We find
encouragement in this theory when we note that the Balkan
peninsula, with its two broken bridges thrust out towards
Africa and Asia—one being the Morea with Crete, the other
Thrace with the Troad—must always have been the European
port of entry and centre of production for supplying to
Europe the culture products of Egypt, Phoenicia, Mesopotamia, and Asia Minor. The Balkan valleys and plains
were the channels and reservoirs through which eastern
culture flowed into and fertilized the desert of European raw
humanity. The prototypes of those national cultures which
we call nowadays Greek or Latin can be dug out of the
Aegean islands or Balkan plains even as we dig out the
prototypes of our domestic animals. Still they are prototypes only; for Minoan 'nationality' is not Greek, any
more than the tree-climbing hipparion is a race-horse. To
these primitive prototypes of national character may be
assigned an intermediate place between, on the one hand,
unconscious habits and modes of expression common to all
mankind, formed during whole geological epochs of primaeval
darkness, and, on the other, the conscious civic functions
of the short noonday of civilization. It is the differences in
subconscious habits of religious and political thought, and of
artistic and literary expression, formed during the long dim
dawn of our modern social civilization, that constitute the
ineradicable and immutable atmosphere of nationality and
connect it indissolubly with the area in which it was born.
Those who oppose a nationality movement from arbitrary
policy, as do reactionaries, or from artificialities of reasoning,
as do some revolutionaries, are only one degree less foolish
than those who pervert the habits of man's body. Civilization has rendered our body independent of the natural
changes of sun, moon, and stars under which its habits
developed; but that does not permit us to ignore these
habits. We can live now as conveniently by night as by day,

but we must still have sleep and sunlight. Even so, political progress can civilize Russian or Bulgar serfdom into self-government and Russian or Turkish autocracy into a democracy, but did not and cannot civilize a Bulgar into either a South Russian or a North Hellene, a 'Young Turk' or—shall we add—an 'Old Servian'. The Balkan peninsula contains those regions where early European culture existed longest, where early European national civilizations were most completely extinguished, and where modern European national democracies have been most perfectly and speedily evolved. It is argued that there must be a relation between these facts ; a gospel of national resurrection full of hope to the worn and weak among the nations.[1]

If this conjecture be permitted us, a corollary to it suggests itself which will carry us still further into an understanding of Balkan events. These early Balkan civilizations, some of which were more completely extinguished than others, seem to have revived with a completeness and quickness proportionate to the severity of their suppression. Bulgaria is by far the most perfect national democracy in the Balkans, and in its case all traditions of nationality and self-government were so completely wiped out that intelligent travellers, such as Kinglake in mid-nineteenth century, ignored even the existence of the Bulgar as a distinct race stock. The Serb, the Rouman, the Greek, the Turk, take rank for perfection of national democracy in the order named, and that order also represents the degree of suppression suffered by their cultures and civilizations. On the reflux of the Turkish inundation the Bulgar reappeared a Bulgar, and all the more Bulgarian for having so long been a Greek rayah and an Ottoman subject ; the Serb reappeared as the most Slav of Slavs, and all the more Slavonic for having been a Turk, an Austrian, or

---

[1] ' In the collapse of all human resources, in the return of the nation to that elemental form of life in which the creatures of human skill and industry no longer come between man and his Maker, it will become plain that there is a God in Israel.' Cf. *The Hebrew Prophets*, Robertson Smith.

C

a Hungarian, according to the vicissitudes of the time. It would seem as though the deeper the submergence and the more sweeping the inundation the more does anything atrophied or alien get purged out of the national character, leaving only the efficient and essential elements. The virtues of Balkan nationalities suggest the good qualities peculiar to the original national temperament, but deepened and broadened ; whereas their vices seem to be the general evil effects of their temporary subjection. For this reason perhaps the vices of the Balkan nationalities are all the same sort of servile vices, dissimilar only in the same respects that the national characters are different. Thus the Balkan races, like all subject races, are cruel to their inferiors with a cruelty somewhat different in each case. The cruelty of the Slav is the emotional cruelty of a certain class of poet or of pork butcher. That of the Greek is the logical cruelty of the student and the sweater. That of the Bulgar is the moral cruelty of the diplomatist and the drover. The cruelty of the Turk, on the other hand, is that of a ruling class. The lovable Turkish kindness to inferiors—domestic animals or Christian rayahs —changes in a moment to the cruelty of a class fighting for its privileges. Even in an English landed estate or in an American factory it is but a short step from this sort of kindness to that sort of cruelty. Thus also the Balkan races have all the servile vices of crookedness in dealing with superiors. But the Greeks will be tortuous from mere mental exuberance and the joy of running rings round a slow-witted adversary. The Serb will be crooked from natural incapacity, because he loses his way in the arbitrary moral conventions of a complicated and uncongenial civilization. The Bulgar will give the effect of crookedness from a love of working out for himself the line of least moral resistance towards a goal he has chosen for and keeps to himself. Since we Anglo-Saxons are apt to adopt a moral standpoint in dealing with younger nations—as we do with our so-called social inferiors —the result is that we find the Bulgars most worthy of our approbation. Indeed, whether the standards of modern morality by which they are tried are those of Nietzsche or of Kipling, under either the Bulgars will be almost in a class by themselves, as ' supermen ' of energy and efficiency or as ' legionaries of the law '. This, it is argued, is partly due to their original national character, but principally to the purgatory of oppression through which the nation has passed.

If, as must be admitted, a war may be a phase of progress towards the emergence of a nationality or the emancipation of a democracy, then, to go a step further back, a war which submerges a nationality and suppresses popular rights may serve a social purpose under certain conditions. This is a hard saying, but if nations that have sinned are to be saved, they perhaps can only be saved as by fire. It does not follow that oppression is not an offence or that arbitrary alien rule is not an anomaly for which the penalty will be paid by the party responsible. The partition of Poland was a crime for which the penalty has been paid and is being paid both by the accomplices, at the price of a century of antagonisms and armaments, and by the civilization which permitted it, in the loss of the Polish national contribution to the arts. But the Poland that succumbed as an aristocracy has been helped by its submergence to become, as it is now becoming, a democracy. A people must be a democracy before it can be a nation; though it can, as Bulgaria has done, combine in one effort the achievement of both grades.

If the Bulgar, as he has evolved, is to the Anglo-Saxon the least antipathetic of the Balkan nations, the Serb, including the Montenegrin, has emerged so intensely a Slav that probably the Russian people alone are capable of properly appreciating his national qualities. This, quite as much as present-day political considerations, accounts for the Russo-Serb relationship which has been a ruling factor in the late Balkan war.

The Greek is most sympathetic to the Latin races. But the general mistake which western peoples are apt to make in judging the Balkan peoples is that of expecting from the latter the principles and point of view peculiar to the more advanced civilization of the West; and the further west the point of observation is placed, the more likely is this mistake to be made. American or English public opinion is harder in its judgements of the Balkan peoples, even as it is warmer in its sympathies, than the public opinion of central Europe.

§ 3. NEAR EASTERN CIVILIZATION

Our western civilization has both a moral and a material basis: it is both an ethical and an economical system: its strength is the strength of accumulated civic experience equivalent in some respects to Christianity, and of accumulated prosperity expressed in some of its forms as Capital. From this system comes a social solidarity which fuses differences of race, religion, or region in one common crust of custom and convention. The crust may be thin in places, but it holds, except during the greater eruptions of the vital energies of humanity. In Anglo-Saxon countries this crust of civilization has been so long undisturbed that only a trained eye can see the extinct volcano or the remains of past civilizations beneath the undulations of grassy down. But eastern Europe is still like the volcanic islands of the Aegean, which yesterday were devastated by lava and to-morrow may be submerged by salt water. ' Trust the Turk and trust the deep sea,' said the Greeks whose lives were spent in choosing between one and the other. ' Grass dies under the Turkish hoof,' say the Bulgars whose lives were spent under that hoof. It is indeed difficult to convey to a western mind what is meant when it is said that civilization did not exist in European lands under Turkish authority. A traveller passing through European Turkey in Hamidian times received a general impression of misery and squalor:

his railway carriage, his cab, his hotel, his sight-seeing, or
his money-making, were all curiously depressing; but still
there was the machinery—the outward and visible sign of
civilization. So he inferred from these symbols the system
they would elsewhere have implied, and he even accepted this
inference against the evidence of sights or stories that seemed
impossible to reconcile with so drab, dull, and dead-alive
a scene. If, however, he ever succeeded in escaping out of
the railway carriage, the café, or the club into the real life
of the land—and it was not easy to escape—his sensations
were those sometimes felt in a bad dream. He found himself
in a dreadful underworld—in a new moral dimension—where
foulest vices were the only way to honours: where acts of the
most noble virtue were punished worse than our gravest
crimes: where the machinery of civilization—the railway,
the telegraph, the police—were instruments for the destruction of all that makes for civilization: where the only hopes
of progress lay in the success of dynamitards and banditti.[1]
He came back from his excursion a sadder and a wiser man,
and set to work to revise his views on the Eastern Question
and the Lower Regions. He learnt that the symbols of
civilization may have either a plus or a minus sign, and that
the cable between Capetown and London is a different sort

[1] A very strange and daunting experience is the sensation of fear as
an objective and oppressive presence, which the writer, for one, always
felt while down in the real life of Turkey in Europe. This, after a time,
seemed to awaken an extreme sensitiveness, almost an extra sense,
such as animals have. For instance, once when resting on the sand in
a remote cove of the Chalcidic peninsula, after several days' hard riding
in which all spies and escort had been shaken off, the sense of oppression came with such force that the brilliant sunshine seemed to darken.
On looking up, the red fezzes of spying zaptiehs appeared peering
over the furze on the undercliff. It was this spell of fear that distorted
the whole underworld of Macedonia. The writer is tempted to refer the
reader to a description of a child in such an underworld, as giving some
idea of the imprisonment of a young national consciousness by fear.
' It was not so much a nonsense world—it was too alarming for that—
as a world of nightmare wherein everything was distorted. The spirit
of disorder, monstrous, uncouth, terrifying—reigned supreme ' (*Jimbo:
A Fantasy*, by Algernon Blackwood, p. 207).

of imperial bond from the private wire between Yildiz Kiosk and the Salonica Konak.[1]

Where *Homo Faber* has no control over the results of his industry there can be no accumulation of capital, and where *Homo Sapiens* cannot exercise his intellect there can be neither currency of thought nor community of mind. Civilization cannot exist without both such ethical and economic components, and both of them were impossible under the unholy alliance between Orthodox obscurantism and Asiatic autocracy. We ourselves, products of a western civilization established by the Catholic Church—whose national renascence was engendered by the Protestant Reformation—whose national development has been inspired by subsequent religious revivals, can scarcely realize the disadvantage to the growth of a community whose progressive forces get no inspiration from Protestantism and whose conservative forces are not firmly founded in Catholicity.

Religion in eastern Europe is convicted of a complete failure either to exercise a unifying influence on rival races as does Islam, or to assimilate itself with the common life of one race as does Judaism, or with the civilization of an epoch as does Protestantism. The reason for this failure is perhaps to be found in that close association of national life and culture with the soil that has already been remarked as explaining much else in the Balkans. It will serve to give some idea of the backwardness of culture and civilization in the Balkans

[1] There shall be no chain
    Save underneath the sea,
    Where wires murmur through the main
    Sweet songs of liberty.

So wrote Emerson of the newly-laid Atlantic cable, and the prophecy has on the whole proved true. But the interdependence of communities resulting from such developments of intercommunication as the telegraph does, of course, lay chains on nationalism as well as open channels for it. The net result will be considered to be in favour of progress and civilization, or against it, according to whether the point of view taken is that of Mr. Norman Angell or of Mr. Brailsford—hope in the strength of the international commonalty or fear of the strength of international capital.

if it be boldly asserted that there the religious standpoint is still so deeply rooted in the soil that it is in spirit pagan and pantheist.

The history of early Christianity is that of a struggle of local Christian cults to absorb local pagan cults and of the central church to absorb the local cults. The activities of the early churches were chiefly occupied in adapting pagan and pantheistic local religions to catholic and orthodox rituals. In this task the Orthodox Church was materially helped by the culture of classical Greece, which had already transferred religion to some extent from the soil to the State, and had converted the rural nature-worship into an urban and national cult. The classical Greek State religion had already developed the original Greek religions of local deities of wood, spring, and mountain into more artistic and anthropomorphic conceptions; still retaining in many cases their local associations. These classical deities later became the conventional saints and virgins of Byzantine Orthodoxy. But although the State religion of Pericles and that of the Patriarchate have borrowed freely from the preceding cult and based their authority firmly on its ruins, yet at each remove the hold of religion has been weakened. The relics of paganism that survive to-day reproduce the old wood and spring gods rather than the dignified deities of the classical State religion. This is partly owing to their closer association with the local community; partly owing to the fact that such creations, like the national character that created them, survive by strength of their age-long persistence rather than by virtue of any aesthetic perfection.[1] The Orthodox Panaya is a sympathetic personification; the classical Pallas Athene a striking one: but these *prime donne* of the State religions will have left the stage when the local Centaur, that rude relic of a monstrous

---

[1] The ' Klephtic ' Madonna of the island of Grabouza, off Crete, to which the pirates paid their vows, and the ' drunken St. George ', at whose feasts Dionysian ritual is still observed, are examples.

paganism, will still, as to-day, defend his Thessalian haunts
with uncanny horror and uncouth horseplay. There is a
church in Athens built round a pillar of the temple to
Aesculapeius, which in turn, no doubt, marks the shrine of
a deity of a healing spring or grove; but the church plays
a small part compared to the temple, and no doubt the
temple held a lower spiritual authority than the shrine.
The universalism and uniformity of a Catholic Church make
no appeal to the Greeks, and so, with their usual mental
acuteness, they have analysed out of it such lay element of
universality and uniformity as their peculiar character
requires, and that is the idea of Greek national unity. The
' megáli idéa ', the consciousness of nationality, is to the
Greeks what monotheism is to the Jews.

That the religion of eastern Europe has never received
any reform or revival from official Puritans or from revolutionary Prophets is due to the Orthodox Church having
fallen entirely under the control of the Greeks, the least
religious and most rationalist race in Europe. The Greeks
have always exploited the Orthodox Church as a political
expression of their national unity, instead of allowing it to
express the spiritual catholicity of eastern Christianity.
In order to retain their own control of the Church, the Greeks
were compelled to suppress all revivalism or protestantism,
and did so by a free use of the metropolitan authority and
of the civil arm, whether Christian, Pagan, or Mohammedan.
They also played off the different points of view in the
Church against one another. Thus the image-breaking
movement in the eighth century—that protestant reform
inspired by the same Asiatic point of view that inspired
Islam—was suppressed by European Orthodoxy, which
used as its chief instruments two Greek empresses, Theodora
and Irene. Coming almost within range of modern history
we find the Slav revivalist movement of the Bogomils, or
Old Believers, as ruthlessly suppressed by an alliance between
the Greek and Asiatic authority. The contributions of the

Greeks themselves to religious thought will be found in the controversies on dogma with the ensuing decisions of the Councils which closed the life of the Orthodox Church in the early Middle Ages. Such controversies as those over the monophysite and monothelite heresies, and the schism with Rome on the *filioque* clause, are merely Greek and mediaeval methods of dealing with very real political conflicts.[1] Their modern equivalent is the competition for bishoprics in Macedonia, which, it need scarcely be said, in no way represents any increase there of religious feeling.

Nothing could better prove the utter deadness of the Orthodox Church and its utter incapacity to draw fresh life from the overflowing wells and springs of the Balkan renascence than the relations of the Greek Patriarchate to the Greek national movement. It is, in fact, in the writer's opinion, a considerable though very common mistake to overrate the advantage to the Greek war of emancipation of association with the Orthodox Church. It is true that what the movement especially wanted was anything that would give it cohesion and concentration; but the cohesion and concentration given by the Church was not of the character required. The movement for self-government required a local centre, a civic tradition, and a common constructive purpose. But none of these could be supplied by the Church centred in Constantinople, trained in Byzantinism, and entirely without spiritual life or liberty of thought. It did indeed contribute the fire of fanaticism to the movement for liberty; but the spirit of revolt against Turkish tyranny and the consciousness of Greek nationality would have been quite enough motive power. Moreover, while the identification of the orthodox patriarchate with the Greek national movement was not of any decisive, or even of any determining importance to that movement, such identification was

[1] As Professor Beecher points out (*Cambridge Mediaeval History*, vol. ii), the monophysite heresy was an early expression of ethnical separatist tendencies. It corresponded to the patriarchist and exarchist schism caused by Bulgar national separatism a few years ago.

disastrously injurious to the general religious influence and catholicity of the Orthodox Church. The result of this association was that the political system of the Ottoman Empire which identified ecclesiastical institutions with civil rights was reproduced in the political systems of the Balkan States that were to replace that Empire in Europe. Instead of the Patriarchate becoming, like the Papacy, an institution independent of temporal governments and representing a moral civilizing force with which such governments must reckon, the Orthodox Church lost all catholicity and central control and became divided into different political propaganda in support of the national movements of the Balkan races. The Papacy may perhaps ·be described as the first political institution of western civilization as a whole. The Patriarchate never was more than the last political institution left to Byzantine civilization; and as the extent of the new Balkan nationalities grows, the Patriarchate diminishes. It is now not different in point of catholicity and central control from the national patriarchates of Armenians and Syrians, or the autocephalous churches of Serbs and Bulgars.

The Ottoman Government had found it politic to leave the Christian races, on their coming under the Turkish yoke, a certain measure of self-government as ' millets ', or ecclesiastical communities. And when in due course the time came for these races to assert their rights to autonomy again, it was found convenient to avoid the appearance of Home Rule by giving an ecclesiastical expression to any independent political institutions that might be required. Whenever some race had so far thrown off the Turkish yoke as to be no longer amenable to political control through its ecclesiastical head and hostage in Stamboul, an autonomous charter was given it in the form of an autocephalous church. But this concession of political rights in the form of ecclesiastical privileges, destroyed, as it was no doubt intended to, all forms of religious unity among the Christian races. Not that the form of Christian unity as represented in the Orthodox

Patriarchate mattered much, for the spirit had long been killed by the association of the Orthodox Church with the Ottoman Government in suppression of the rayah. The rayah revolted quite as much against the extortion and corruption of the Orthodox bishop and priest as against those vices in the Ottoman official.

The Orthodox Patriarchate was an obstacle to Balkan national progress. As an instrument of Turkish imperialism it was an obstacle to all nationalism, including even that of the Greeks. To the Patriarchate and the Phanariote oligarchy the 'great idea' was a restoration of the Greek Empire, not a renascence of the Greek nationality. Nothing could have been more disastrous to the growth of the Greek nation than the restoration of the Greek Empire over the Balkan nations through the Patriarchate. Consequently it is quite natural that the nationality movement has ended in dethroning the Patriarchate by destroying its claim to catholicity and its metropolitan control. This came about, as stated above, by the Ottoman Government giving political concessions an ecclesiastical form, so that the young nationalities fought with mitre and crozier until they could arm themselves with helmet and sword. In this way, the establishment of an autocephalous church became equivalent to a recognition of national self-government; while a Berat for a new Macedonian bishopric meant recognition of a claim to establish a political party there, and, so to say, regularized the status of a new party 'machine' in that province. But the most serious result was that the autocephalous Christian Churches of Eastern Europe have contributed nothing as evangelizing influences to the maintenance there of peace and goodwill; while, as educational influences, they have contributed only to the growth of nationality, and have failed to exercise any influence on the new spiritual life of the Balkan peninsula. That they have so failed will be clear if we compare with the silence and sloth of the Orthodox Church the controversies that keep the catholicity of Rome in contact with the thought of the time, or the constructive energies developed by Rome in assimilating new movements. There are no signs of a Loisy in the Orthodox Church, nor has there yet been a Loyola.

The entire failure of the Orthodox Church to keep alive any consciousness of common Christianity, to say nothing of any common Christian conscience, is largely responsible for the calamities of Macedonia and for the catastrophe of the War of Partition. Moreover, as national political institutions, the Churches have probably done the national causes they represent more harm than good, for they have offered the enemies of peace and progress in the Balkans easy channels for exercising disturbing and disruptive influences. Unfortunately, such enemies have been found, not only among the Moslem patrons of the Orthodox Church, but also among its Christian protectors. The substitution of pan-orthodoxy for Panslavism as the *mot d'ordre* of Russian policy in the Balkans was, for this reason, a development of sinister import to the liberties of the orthodox peoples in the Balkans, and an omen of war rather than of peace. The idea of Panslavism was a confederation of free democracies on a basis of the rights of man ; [1] the ideal of pan-orthodoxy is control of a congregation comprising all orthodox individuals on the basis of the divine right of a War Lord.

The Orthodox Patriarchate and the Phanar represented to the other Balkan peoples so much that was odious in their past and obnoxious to their future that a century of political separation of the Hellenic State from the Greek Church, and a half-century of ecclesiastical separation, had to elapse before any general political alliance of the Balkan peoples became possible. As to ecclesiastical reunion, even in the year of grace 1912, after the dissociation of the autocephalous

[1] Danilewsky, whose work was considered as the authoritative exposition of Panslavism, proposed a Slav Confederation, composed of (1) the Russian Empire, (2) a Slovak-Tchek-Moravian kingdom, (3) a Serbo-Croat-Slovene kingdom, (4, 5, 6, and 7) Bulgarian, Roumanian, Greek, Hungarian kingdoms, (8) a province of Constantinople.

churches of the Balkan peoples, after the disestablish-
ment policy of the young Turk, and after the undenomina-
tional influences of a European education on the emancipated
peoples, it was none the less obvious that no revival of the
catholicity of Orthodoxy was possible. The political schisms
in the Orthodox Church are quite beyond fusion by anything
less than a revival of religious feeling, of which there are no
symptoms at present. A few tentative efforts made recently
by well-meaning western friends to consolidate the Balkan
alliance by regularizing the relations between the churches
showed, in the words of one of them, Mr. Bourchier, *The Times*
correspondent, ' that it would be better to let well alone '.
The fact is that there is as little prospect of reuniting the
Greeks and Bulgars in one Church as in one Chamber, and
for the same reasons.

The War of Coalition and the subsequent partition of
Macedonia have, to a large extent, terminated the political
struggles between the Orthodox Church and the Ottoman
State ; for it is better to avoid using the terms Christianity
or even Islam in relation to secular strife. But it will be long
before the War of Partition between Patriarchist and Exarchist follows into obscurity the factious fighting between
Monophysite and Monothelite, or between Iconoclast and
Iconodule. The relations between the Bulgar Exarchate
and the Serb Autocephalous Church have been perverted
into bitter hostility by the political struggle between Bulgar
and Serb for Macedonia. For this struggle, after being decided, as the result of a quarter-century of Bulgar educational
penetration, in favour of Bulgaria by the Treaty of Alliance
of 1912, has now been decided, as a result of the War of
Partition, in favour of Serbia by the Treaty of Bucharest.
The consequence of this will be a forced conformity of the
Bulgarized Macedonian to the Serb State Church ; for the
Treaty of Bucharest contains no guarantees for religious
toleration. Already a movement has been started for the
revival of the Orthodox Uniate Church of Macedonia ; that

is to say, for the transfer of the Macedo-Bulgar from the protection of the Patriarch to that of the Pope. The object of this movement is, of course, to preserve the Bulgar nationality of the Macedonians by securing to them a separate Church. It is also intended, no doubt, to bring pressure on Russia to protect these co-religionists as an alternative to their transfer; and a similar movement in the 'sixties was largely responsible in obtaining from the Turk and from the Russian the establishment of the Bulgar Exarchate. Moreover, the removal of the Bulgar Exarchate from Constantinople to Sofia, and its termination as an Ottoman institution as the result of the partition of Macedonia, deprive the Bulgars of Macedonia of their Church. A Uniate Bulgar Church in Macedonia would keep alive Bulgar nationality there under Graeco-Serb domination much as a Uniate Church preserves Poland from denationalization under the Russo-German partition. Failing this or some other protection of their ecclesiastical entity, the Macedo-Bulgars will resubmit themselves to the Patriarchate and become Serbified, very much as their fathers joined the Bulgar Exarchate and were Bulgarized.[1]

The truculencies and treacheries of Balkan warfare are not to be criticized by us from the superior standpoint of a civilization built up by past generations. Barbarisms and bigotries are inevitable when people, whose religious cult is no more than a simple superstition and whose civil experience is still at the tribal stage, are forced to fight their way to better things. It may well be that such better things will be attained all the easier in that the new life in the Balkans will be able to interpret Christianity for itself without much

---

[1] The political and geographical position of the Bulgars caused them to vacillate in early days between the Pope and the Patriarch. King Boris, in the ninth century, finally decided for the latter after some wavering; but Kaloyan, the third of the Asen dynasty, went over to Rome in the thirteenth century. The Uniate movement in the 'sixties ended with the accomplishment of its political purpose and the removal of the head of the community to a Russian monastery.

interference from the authority of the Orthodox Church. Life in the Balkans, with all its barbarities, is after all on the whole a truer expression of Christian principles than is ours. There has been no failure there of Christianity, but only a failure of the Church.

With this we arrive at the last link in the argument and may boldly assert that the only basis of European culture and the only bias towards European civilization to be found in the Balkans, after centuries of subjection to Asiatic Byzantinism, is the consciousness of nationality. To that consciousness in a subliminal state may be ascribed the survival of such civic virtues as formed the small moral capital of each community on emancipation. And this is the reason why the Bulgar komitadji hiding dynamite bombs in a Messageries mailboat in Salonika harbour was an emissary of European civilization, while Hilmi Pasha, that courteous, cultivated gentleman, administering 'Macedonian reforms' and 'Mürzsteg programmes' from his study in the Salonika Konak, was not.

Wherever and whenever in the Balkans national feeling became conscious, then, to that extent, does civilization begin ; and as such consciousness could best come through war, war in the Balkans was the only road to peace. Nor would this war be restricted by any lines of race or religion ; for each nation would strive to save itself foremost and let the devil take the hindmost. Where national consciousness is only awaking there cannot be much activity of the national conscience. Birth is a brutal business, and babies are not generous or far-sighted about their bottles.

> It is very nice to think
> The world is full of meat and drink,
> With little children saying grace
> In every Christian kind of place.

But the Balkan nursery is not that kind of place.

CHAPTER II

THE EASTERN QUESTION

§ 4. Byzantinism.
§ 5. Hellenism.
§ 6. Panslavism and Philhellenism.

Clime of the unforgotten brave!
Whose land from plain to mountain cave
Was Freedom's home or Glory's grave.
Shrine of the mighty, can it bè
That this is all remains of thee ? . . .
Enough—no foreign foe could quell
Thy soul, till from itself it fell.—BYRON.

§ 4. BYZANTINISM

HISTORICALLY considered the Balkan War of the Coalition is a perfectly normal development of the nationalist movement. Not so inspiring perhaps as the Italian *risorgimento* that first showed our fathers the meaning of the historical movements of the nineteenth century in Europe, nor yet so important perhaps as the Chinese revolution that may teach our sons the meaning of the historical movements of the twentieth century in Asia; but more epoch-making than either in that it rounds off the last chapter in the current volume of the story of the nations. The chapter is the history of the ' Eastern Question ', or, as we should say now with our wider horizon, of the Near Eastern Question. The volume is that of the nationality movement of the eighteenth and nineteenth centuries—the history of the epoch of national democracy.

The Balkan settlement by war is not a mere corollary to national and international history of the nineteenth century ; but may be described as its culmination, and might, under better human guidance, have become its crown. It is a culmination in that these wars have won for the European system of national self-government the last territories in Europe still subjected to an Asiatic military occupation. It

has been no crown to this work because not only has it not
been final, but its inherent instability may probably give the
impetus to overthrow European political equilibrium. The
settlements effected by the Treaties of London and Bucharest
were imperfect ; in the former case in regard to execution,
and in the latter case in regard to equity. War settlements
generally are imperfect, and thus does war breed war.

But this brings us to a necessary distinction between the
Balkan wars. The War of the Coalition can claim to have
been both progressive and epoch-making. The succeeding
War of Partition was rather predatory and ended no epoch,
though possibly it may have begun one : it is interesting
not as a settlement but as a symptom. Although the second
war succeeded the first almost without a pause, they none
the less belong to different historical epochs. The War of
Coalition was a good ending to the nineteenth century, the
War of Partition a bad beginning to the twentieth.

The War of the Coalition is best understood if considered
as the last scene of a second act ; just as the succeeding
War of Partition can be considered as the first scene of the
third act. It is indeed evident that the War of Coalition
presents all the features of a closing rather than an opening
scene. Political like geological epochs show their age by the
cooling off of the volcanic forces : the levelling down of
prominent peaks : the specialization and speeding up of
organic growth. When we find a campaign in common by
different communities—moved by no universal passion or
panic—encouraged by no symbolic heroisms—inspired by no
great personality, one may safely infer an overdue and long
discounted liquidation in international affairs. The political
revolution that is effected by a government, the war that
is won by pitched battles and by plans of campaign—both
belong to the second act of the national drama. The first
act will be filled with mistakes and misunderstandings—with
sacrifices to causes that seem to be lost and ideals looked
upon as impossible. The political principle of the Balkan

peninsula for the Balkan peoples could not have forced itself
so promptly on a coercive empire—even one so rotten as
Turkey proved to be—or on a conservative Europe—even
so ready to accept it as Europe proved to be—if it had not
been a *dénouement* already long overdue. The enterprise of
expelling Asia from Europe would not have proceeded so
swiftly and smoothly if the driving power had not been long-
pent-up forces of progress.

It is assumed here, and it is now generally admitted, that
the nationality movements of the Balkan peoples were incompatible with the maintenance of the Turkish Empire in
Europe. But generations of statesmen who poured out
European blood and treasure for ' the maintenance of the
integrity of the Ottoman Empire ' did not think so ; and it
is only bitter experience that has proved the Ottoman
Empire incapable of converting itself into a democratic
Federation. This incapacity is, however, peculiar to itself
and does not necessarily follow from the fact that the empire
consists of different races, religions, and cultures. Its next-
door neighbour, the Austrian Empire, combines in one organization Germans, Slavs, Magyars, Roumanians, Italians ;
Catholics, Protestants, Uniates, Mussulmans, Kingdoms,
Principalities, &c., all on a basis of universal manhood
suffrage and universal military service. Why could not the
Ottoman Empire do the same ? The leadership of eastern
Europe lay for fifteen hundred years between the two empires ;
why have the German successors to the Western Empire
succeeded and the Ottoman successors to the Eastern Empire
failed ? Both were founded on conquest and organized on
a feudal basis ; both were established in conflict with the
Church which was the main power for progress in the early
Middle Ages ; and both arrived at a concordat which converted respectively the Pope and the Patriarch into an
imperial institution. But there was one difference which
must be borne in mind : Charlemagne did not establish the
centre of the Holy Roman Empire at Rome ; Mahomet the

Conqueror did establish the seat of the Islamic Empire at Constantinople. This false step decided from the first the fate of the empire. Rome it was and 'Roum' it is to all Asiatics to this day, and none of its conquerors, western crusaders or eastern Caliphs, have succeeded in making it other than the centre and seat of Byzantinism.

The first cause of the Balkan wars is the failure of the Turks to keep their empire alive. This failure is generally attributed to the physical and intellectual decay of the Turkish ruling class and to the spiritual and intellectual decay entailed by the Islamic religion. It is true that the ruling class of the Turkish race have shown themselves utterly incapable of keeping the empire together and of even keeping themselves going. The result of their five hundred years of power has been that the government was entirely divorced from all vital forces in the governed, so that the measure of development was the measure of decentralization. On the other hand the Turkish peasantry, still on the land, retained their racial health and strength of character, but remained peasants. Their sound stock never became available to revitalize the dying ruling class. So the power fell altogether out of Turkish hands into those of ever lower racial types, as the follies and failures of the ruling Turks brought the government into less worthy hands. The Greek and Roumanian nobles who administered the empire for the Turks, as Hospodars in the provinces or as Dragomans in the capital, threw the Turks over or were overthrown by them. The Armenian or Turkish officials of the middle class that took their place became in turn suspect and were replaced in turn under the Hamidian régime by Levantines, landless men, renegades, and rapscallions, and all the outlaws that haunt the borderland of East and West.

But why was this so? The four estates of the early empire—the provincial nobility, the landed gentry, the city burghers, and the farmers on a feudal tenure—were originally prosperous and fairly progressive. The Turkish feudal and

judicial system was not unlike that out of which Anglo-
Saxon democracy and the British Empire developed : in
some respects it was superior. Oddly enough its principal
superiority was in its superior democracy. The great weakness of the English system, as of most of the European
systems, has been land monopoly, from which arose excessive
ecclesiastical and feudal privilege and thence hereditary class
privilege. But the very elements in the early Turkish polity
which are generally blamed for its failure—the nomadic
traditions of the race and the system of land tenure—should
have made for its success ; for to them was due the democratic
fluidity and flexibility of Turkish society.[1] The origin of the
great hereditary landed families mostly antedated the Ottoman
conquest—they having been allowed to subsist on sufferance
in Asia and on the European border in Bosnia because their

---

[1] Khosrew Pasha, the seraskir (commander-in-chief) of the reforming
sultan Mahmoud II, was the instrument and inspiration of his master
in his two great undertakings, the destruction of the provincial pashas
and of the janizaries. Khosrew was a Georgian, bought in the Stamboul
slave market—a minion of Selim III and a typical Byzantine beggar-
on-horseback—corrupt, cunning, and cruel. But there was at this time
a shameless simplicity in Ottoman society, which showed that the new
blood brought by the Turks was not as yet completely corrupted, and
which is in refreshing contrast to the shamefaced snobbery which is our
besetting social sin. Here is Khosrew, in his old age, talking to Slade
(*Travels in Turkey*) : ' *Khosrew* : " It is wonderful. Halid is going as
ambassador. God is great. I bought him, now behold him an elchi.
A sweet child, a charming boy, he cost me 1,500 piastres." *Slade* : " That
is not dear for such merit—surely Your Excellency cost more." *Khosrew* :
" I ? That 's quite another thing, truly. I was worth more. I cost my
master 25,000 piastres." ' We owe, oddly enough, to this Turkish simplicity
—in an earlier and more admirable form—the most scathing satire on
its own snobbery that the West has produced. In the year 1669 a Turkish
embassy had come to Versailles, and the Roi Soleil had set his mind on
impressing the envoy with his glory. Accordingly, after keeping him
waiting some months, he received the Turk in robes covered with diamonds,
while his brother was similarly bedizened with pearls. To Louis's mortifica-
tion, the envoy appeared dressed with the utmost simplicity, and apparently quite unmoved by the splendours of Versailles and the king. Louis
determined on a curious revenge, and commissioned Molière to write
a comedy, stipulating that a burlesque Turkish ceremony should be
introduced. *Le Bourgeois Gentilhomme* was the result. It is to be hoped
that the Turkish envoy saw the point of the play.

presence there was no menace to the Sultan. The feudal family of the Turkish system, the Timariot, had little or no fixity of tenure. Career was open to talents in the land system of Mahomet the Conqueror as in that of William the Conqueror, but the ultimate result in the two cases was different. By the nineteenth century William's land settlement had cut up the British people into classes with little or no intercommunication—gentry, farmers, and labourers; but Mahomet's had reduced the Turkish people to labourers only. Why was this so? Mohammedanism will not explain it. For though Mohammedanism is of as much less social value than Christianity as the Koran is of less spiritual value than the Gospels, yet, as a political institution, the Kaliphate is less of an obstacle to new thought than the Orthodox Church. Islam has found room both for orthodox puritanism such as Wahabism, for the very broadest protestantism such as Babism, and for multifarious mysticisms such as the Bektashi and other Dervish sects. This intellectual toleration, which is extended to religions quite distinct from Islam, such as Christianity and Judaism, is in no way incompatible with the political intolerance which makes conformity to the faith of the ruling race a qualification for civil equality. A Turkish Mohammedan had always complete religious freedom of thought; and if at one time wine-drinking or smoking was a capital offence under the religious law, this was a sanitary enactment for the physical preservation of the race. If the Mussulman is a fatalist and a pessimist, so is his Christian fellow-subject; and for the same reasons. Indeed, in the matter of intellectual liberty the Christian was worse off, because both such self-government as the Empire allowed his ecclesiastical authorities, and such as he hoped for from emancipation, were conditional on his adhesion to his European orthodoxy; whereas the Turk, so long as he professed Islam, might indulge in any Asiatic nonconformity he pleased. Moreover, as a matter of fact the national domestic and social life of the Turk, where it still exists, unspoilt either

by unnatural luxury or misery, or by unnatural hatreds or
hopes, is far closer to Christianity both in its principles and
its practice than is the life of ' Christian ' civilization. The
Turk is a good father and husband, a good neighbour, a good
master, a good landlord, even a good governor ; whereas the
Greek is none of these. Travel with the Turkish muleteer,
and at the end of the longest day the baggage mule will
roll away his cares and start again at dawn a new animal.
Travel with the Greek, and the moment your back is turned
he will jump on the heaviest load on the rawest back ; and
your journey will be a weariness from the start and end at
half-way. Walk through the steerage of a Levantine coaster
and compare your observations on the domesticities of the
Turkish and Greek families. As to the Turk being a good
landlord and governor, it is difficult for the traveller to form
an opinion, for the Turkish patrician is almost extinct. But
there are good records of him in his prime, and he still survives in Bosnia to prove that his destruction is attributable
to something that is neither inherent in the Turkish race
nor in the Islamic religion. It is no answer that the Bosnian
is not of pure Turkish stock, for no Turk is ; any more than
is any English county family pure English. If by chance
the traveller should find one of the old Turkish Derebeys, the
old landed gentry, still living on his land—as the writer has
done—he could not fail to be struck by the likeness between
the Turkish squire and an English or, still more, a Virginian
country gentleman, both in the men themselves and in their
position. If he ever meets such a man in the position
and with the powers of a Pasha, he will be irresistibly
reminded of British colonial governors of the past who
attempted by administrative reform to stop the disruptive
workings of nationality movements ; and he will perhaps
remember that if the Liberal reforms of Midhat Pasha did
not save Bulgaria to the Ottoman Empire, no more did those
of Gladstone retain the Ionian Islands for the British Empire.
If again the traveller should meet one of the Turkish gentle-

men in power under the new régime, he will be as irresistibly reminded of the American colonial administrators of the present day, who are also approaching the difficult problems of colonial government hampered by a home government that makes no provision for its problems. The failure of the Young Turk in Macedonia had some elements of the failure in Persia of a certain energetic and enthusiastic American reformer. Why, then, did the Turk fail so utterly that we Anglo-Saxons, who have so much in common with him in character and political circumstances as to have a real sympathy for his difficulties, find ourselves to-day with no choice but to welcome as a boon to humanity the end of his empire in Europe?

What is the cause of this failure of the Asiatic in Europe? Is it present in the rule of Anglo-Saxons in Asia? Will Chinese and Japanese civilization some centuries hence welcome with thanksgiving the ignominious expulsion of the last vestiges of the British occupation in India or the American occupation of the Philippines?

It is suggested in accordance with the argument of the first chapter that his failure does not lie in any moral or mental inferiority of Asiatics to Europeans. The origins of our Christianity and of our civilization are after all Asiatic. Nor does it lie in any unsoundness in a system by which a strong and stupid race governs a weak and clever one. The success of the British rule in India forbids us to think so. But it does lie in the impossibility of Asiatics governing Europeans or of the British governing the Babu unless each retains his alien character and constantly renews his strength from his own homeland. Let us imagine the seat of government transferred from the United Kingdom to Delhi, or from the United States to Manila. Let us suppose the government be left in the hands of Eurasians, inheritors of the Mogul or of Malay culture, with such assistance as they could get from the native races; and that a half-caste government at Delhi or Manila could, by acquired authority of religious and racial tradition and by arbitrary power of money and militarism, impose their imperial yoke on native nationalism. The result would be the same as that which the establishment of the Turkish government in Constantinople has had upon the Ottoman Empire and its races. The ruling urban class would be unable to renew its strength from the rural stock, which would exist only to supply the country with men and money; the ruling class would sink morally and physically lower while the rural mass would be in no way educated but merely exploited. After a few centuries the Eurasian Empire would fall before vigorous young native kingdoms, and the moral would be drawn that Europeans are incapable of governing Asiatics.[1]

In a word, the failure of the Turks is due to Byzantinism. Their corruption and impotence were inherited with their national capital—not inherent in their national character. When they reached their promised land they would have done better to have followed the Hebrew policy of smiting the Amalekites hip and thigh until not one of them was saved. But they spared what was most pleasing in their own eyes and ran after strange gods. Byzantine civilization was overflowed, not flooded out, by the Turkish invasion; and all the worst features of the decadent Byzantine social system emerged, and flourished in the soil refertilized by new blood. No democracy, no simple virtues, and no sound vitality could grow in such soil without a more thorough purification than even Mahomet could give it. The decadence of the Turk dates from the day when Constantinople was taken and not destroyed; and the writer has the authority of more than one Turk for the opinion. Constantinople is indeed regarded with very mixed feelings by most provincial Turks. It is difficult for us younger nations of Europe, whose urban civilizations date at most from a few centuries, to understand the power over the minds and lives of rural man

[1] 'Turkey is perishing for want of Turks' (Lamartine, in a pro-Turk speech in the French Chamber, 1834).

acquired by the ancient Asiatic urban centres of civilization. Something in this attitude of mind is familiar to us in the abuse of Babylon by those sound nationalists the Hebrew prophets, and in the hatred Rome inspired in our Saxon ancestors. To them the culpability of a city for the corruption of a race would have been nothing new or strange. We of the newer lands have had as yet but few and short opportunities to experience the evil spell worked upon humanity by long-established centres of urban civilization. But we, too, may have noticed sensations in ourselves and circumstances in our surroundings which give a new meaning to ' God made the country and man the city '. It may seem a long way from the feeling that makes us take our holiday in the country to the feeling that made the Balkan wars against Byzantinism ; but it is the same instinct.

It would be easy, if it did not take us too far, to show how Byzantinism, that daughter of the horse leech, having in a few years reconquered the capital, proceeded to drain the life out of every Turkish or Slav institution and to turn to its own advantage every struggle for freedom of Turks or Christians and every effort of Asia and Europe to make her loose hold. Thus at the beginning of the last century the centralizing and Europeanizing reforms of Mahmoud II, which broke the power of the janizaries and the derebeys, destroyed in the first case all independence in the capital and the only check on the absolutism of the Palace ; and in the second case destroyed all local government and the only check on the arbitrary extortions of the Porte. Those pashas who were big enough, like Mehemet Ali in Egypt, broke away ; those that were not, like Ali Pasha in Epirus or Pasvanoglou on the Danube, were eaten up, one by one, down to the smallest derebey. The municipal franchises—the guild and communal liberties of the Christian millet—even the Islamic law, the Cheriat itself, were all drained of their vitality. In this process the moral and material support of the European Powers was exhausted in turn ; first France, then England, then Germany succeeded each other, leaving each a load of foreign debt. This debt itself brought Byzantinism new resources of capital and credit from the efficiency of the foreign administration of the debt and from the surplus of the revenues assigned to it. In the same way every imported mechanism was perverted into an instrument against progress—French legislative systems, from the *Lois des Vilayets* down to the Constitution of 1876—British administrative supervision from that of the great Elchi over the whole empire in the 'fifties, down to the services of financial and naval advisers of yesterday—German military reorganizations—railroads and telegraphs—financial reconstructions and political reforms—all were perverted into sewers for draining the life of the country into the Constantinopolitan cesspit.

It has been said that Byzantinism was especially deadly to the development of the Turk and the Slav; and it is to be noted that the nationality movements by which its strangle hold was shaken off began in regions remote from Byzantium —with one exception. That exception was not the Turkish nationality movement; for the Young Turk began in Macedonia, the farthest Turkish settlement from the capital. It was the Greek. The Greek Phanar and Patriarchate not only survived but thrived, in so far as anything could thrive, in the decay of all other communities. The Greek ' Nation ' even retained enough life to revolt in the very heart of the empire, and the Sacred Legion of Phanariote Greeks put up a better fight at Dragashani than any corps drawn from Stambouli Turks could have done. The Greek may be enervated and often emasculated by Byzantinism, but he seems to be immune to the mortal effects of the malady. He has been born and bred in the briar bush. The city that is the Babylon of one race may be the Jerusalem of another.

§ 5. HELLENISM

The primary cause of the Balkan wars is the decay of the Ottoman Empire—a decay due to Byzantinism. Secondary causes of these wars can be found in the course taken by the Balkan nationality movements when expanding to fill the void created by Ottoman decay. These secondary causes, in the more important case of the War of Coalition, are to be sought in the circumstances of the nationality movement among the Greeks and among the Turks; while those of the War of Partition can be traced to similar circumstances of the Slav and Bulgar movements. A review of the Greek and Turkish nationality movements should therefore give us an explanation of the War of Coalition, which is the more important of the two wars; and the Greek movement alone will require any considerable space, for this movement became a political fact with the beginning of the nineteenth century, while the Turkish dates as such only from the beginning of the twentieth.

The process by which the Greek nation came into its birthright by temporarily renouncing its inheritance is extra-ordinarily interesting as an instance of a nation being forced by the law of national regeneration into saving its national soul alive by sacrificing such material belongings as remained to it. At the end of the eighteenth century the Greeks were the undisputed heirs of the Ottoman Empire; or rather, they were still the rightful holders whose title had been usurped. Moreover, they still governed all the non-Greek provinces. Greece itself they had lost; for the Turks knew enough statecraft to keep the mother country of the Greeks, that is the Peloponnese, from getting any corporate organiza-tion or national consciousness such as would enable it to combine with the culture centre of the Greeks in the Phanar. Consequently, the Greek 'Stammland' in the Peloponnese was not allowed such local self-government as was permitted to the Danubian and Anatolian provinces. The only participation in the imperial government allowed to the Moreote peasant was the supply of tribute, in money or male children ; and the janizaries, although all of Christian birth, never developed any connexion with the rayah races from which they were recruited, but remained to the end a Praetorian guard, loyal to the Empire though often faithless to the person of the Sultan. On the other hand, the educated Phanariote Greeks, being under close supervision, could be employed without risk as responsible agents of Turkish oppression. It was the Phanariotes who maintained in the Ottoman Empire a standard of civilization which for long misled those who did not know how superficial it was in substance and how servile was its source. By this clever arrangement the Greeks, whether as Janizaries or Hospodars, were made to keep the Byzantine Empire going for the benefit of the Ottoman garrison, and were thereby diverted from developing their own national life.

Whatever sphere we examine, civil, military, or religious, we find such civilization as there is in the early Ottoman Empire to be really Greek. If we take armaments as the criterion of national power (as being generally the first charge on a country's revenues, the last word in a country's science, and the first and last consideration of foreign policy) we find that in the first quarter of the last century the Turkish fleet contained what was admittedly the most powerful battleship and the fastest cruiser in the world—both built by Greeks. In the big gun competition of those days the stone ball shooting cannon of the Dardanelles were as intimidating and ineffective as were the dynamite guns of New York harbour. Or, if we take administration, the next most important symbol of power, we find the Greek was omnipresent if not omnipotent. It was the Greek hospodar, the Greek bishop, the Greek tax-farmer, who were the indispensable instruments of Turkish rule. *Experto crede* : and we find that to the Bulgar and Serb the Greek was no fellow-sufferer ; he was an agent of the oppressor. Besides being the brains of both the military and the civil government of the Empire the Greeks were the bankers and merchants, with only some competition from their successors the Armenians and the Jews. Further, the Greek ' Nation ' of the capital was the only Christian political institution in the Empire; and after the suppression in 1766 of the last relics of the Bulgar and Serb autocephalous churches, the Greek Patriarchate enjoyed for a century complete control of the whole religious life of the eastern European churches. This involved in those days control of almost the whole sphere of mental and moral activity. But besides and beyond this, the Greek language was the only medium of intellectual intercourse ; and Greek culture was the only channel of communication between western civilization and the submerged nationalities. Thus the first Roumanian codes were written in Greek, and business correspondence throughout the Empire was conducted in that language.

Small wonder that Europe considered Christian rayahs as synonymous with Greeks, and that the Christian rayah considered the Greeks rather as synonymous with Turks. While the whole of eastern Europe was administered by the Phanar for the Turks, the Morea itself, the Greek homeland, remained passive under direct palace rule,[1] and there was only one small corner, the Maina, where Greek clans enjoyed an independence comparable to that of the Arnauts or Montenegrins.

Consequently, when Pitt of England and Catherine of Russia accepted the Greek Phanar and Patriarchate as the heirs of the Turkish Porte and of the Islamic Padishah, and proposed to restore the Greek Empire, this seemed to be a sound and obvious solution of the embryo Eastern Question. From an international standpoint it was sound enough, and it was only those who knew the internal relations of Greeks and Slavs within the Empire who would have questioned its feasibility. But there would have been few, if any such, so early in the history of the Balkan nationality movements as

---

[1] Athens itself was an appanage of the office of chief eunuch. ' Slaves— nay the bondsmen of a slave,' wrote Byron.

the latter part of the eighteenth century. Nor would this solution have been so unfavourable to the peaceable development of these movements as was the substitution for it of a policy of maintenance of the Ottoman Empire.[1]

While a restoration of the Greek Empire in Constantinople was, then as now, the true remedy for Byzantinism, this restoration of Greek imperialism had to be preceded by a renovation of Greek nationality. Before Greece could recover the imperial city it had to become a nation; before it could become a nation it had to become a self-governing community in a self-contained country. It would have seemed a mere absurdity to statesmen of the eighteenth century that the purely Greek and highly cultured aristocracy of the Phanar should be rejected as the culture centre and corporate embryo of the new nation; and that it should centre in the Graeco-Albanian and Graeco-Slav seamen or peasants of the peninsula and islands, whose claim to be Greeks was based on a debased dialect and a dead dogma. Still less would it then have seemed an advantage to the new nation, as we now know it to have been, that its capital should be set up in a mud village with a few interesting ruins, such as was eighteenth-century Athens, rather than in the capital of eastern Europe. But the Greek fishermen and peasants were chosen and the Greek hospodars and Phanariotes were left. Even as the Piedmontese took pre-

---

[1] A Greek Empire might, depending on British and Russian support, have resisted the Slav, Roumanian, and Arnaut nationality movements by force of arms, but would not have imposed on these movements such a war of extermination as they were forced to wage with the Turk. On the other hand, the protected Greek Empire might have become an empire something like its neighbour, the Austrian Empire, in which the Greeks would have taken the rôle of the Germans and the Bulgars of the Magyars, while the Serbs would have filled a similar place in both. In this latter case, no doubt by the middle of last century Russia would have had to intervene to preserve peace between Greek and Bulgar, even as, at that time, the Russian forces were called in to settle between German and Magyar; and, no doubt, by now, the result would have been a federation not unlike the Austrian Empire, and still more like that planned by Panslavists.

cedence of the Romans and the Galilean fishermen and
peasants were preferred to the Scribes and Pharisees of
Jerusalem ; for this is one of the laws that regulate the
regeneration of races.

After the failure of the scheme of England and Russia
for reviving the Greek Empire there was no further question
of such a policy; and the development of other Balkan
nationality movements soon rendered any such plan impossible of execution. Thereafter, the forces making for change
moved on the lines of political partition of the peninsula.
The internal nationality movements aimed at a partition
between the Balkan peoples ; the external pressures due to
the national expansion of the neighbouring Powers aimed at
partition between the Powers. In either case partition could
only have been effected through war ; but the war would
not probably have been prolonged if the partition had been
on purely nationalist or imperialist lines. The complications
which were the consequence of imperialism being first
counteracted by nationalism, and thereafter of nationalism
being checked by imperialism, caused a century of wars,
many of them barren of real result. The first partition
proposal was produced when all the European Governments
and frontiers of Europe had been melted down in the eruptions of the Napoleonic epoch. The design of Napoleon,
inspired by Talleyrand, was to divide the peninsula with
Russia, the division following roughly the ethnographical
frontier of the Greeks ; the southern half, including Constantinople, being under French protection. This policy,
which would have restored the Greek nation at one stroke,
came into being at the Treaty of Pressburg in 1805 and
lasted until that of Tilsit in 1809. The opportunity was
a short one and it was lost, largely owing to the Greek
Patriarchate foolishly making common cause with Slav
opposition to the French advance from Dalmatia. The
Patriarchate, like the Papacy in the unification of Italy,
had its chance of heading the Greek national movement

and associating itself permanently with it. A Napoleonic protectorate, if only for a few years, would have given time for the Greek national movement to consolidate itself at a period when no European power would have wished to restore the Turks. Metternich and the Holy Alliance would, at the fall of the Napoleonic Empire, have been faced with the *fait accompli* of a Greek nation. As it was, the Greek national movement had to make a bad beginning and thereafter to fight its way inch by inch against both the Empire and Europe.[1]

The Greek national movement thereafter was left to develop without outside help and from four separate centres. First of all there was the Patriarchate and the Phanar

[1] Napoleon's plan was to bring the Greek portions of the peninsula within the direct control of his empire, so that it might form a barrier to English extension eastward and to Russian extension southward. Napoleon's policies were always strategically sound, and a Graeco-Latin power, based on Italy and France, with its right flank in the Egyptian isthmus, would have been strong enough. But there were three insuperable obstacles : the world power of Constantinople and the question which partitioning Power should possess it, English sea power in the Mediterranean, and Greek Church power. It is not clear which of these obstacles caused the abandonment of the scheme, though in the following remark, reported by Las Cases, Napoleon ascribes the failure to the Constantinople difficulty. ' L'idée de chasser les Turcs de l'Europe me sourit, mais je savais ce que valait la possession de Constantinople et j'ai abandonné l'empire de la moitié du monde, plutôt que de donner à la Russie ce mince détroit.' The French footing in the Balkans—their occupation of Dalmatia—remained no more than a footing, for all penetration inland was repulsed by an impermeable barrier of Slavdom and superstition. Had the French attempt been made in the Greek regions further south, more sympathetic to the French character and more susceptible of modern ideas, it might have been successful. The Greeks, even at that early date, might have used a French occupation for their national developments even as they since used British or international occupations. As it was, the flowing tide of European civilization, like the ebbing tide of Asiatic conquest, found the Black Mountain, with its Prince-Bishop, an insuperable barbican, and the Orthodox Church, with its Patriarch, an impregnable Bastille. It is interesting to fix—by noting when French administrative policy in Dalmatia changed from a policy of development to one of exploitation for conscription—the exact time at which this French partition project was abandoned in view of the resistance of the Slav tribes and of the Greek Church.

representing the Byzantine tradition. This centre, as we
have shown, contained little that was valuable and much
that was detrimental to the national development. After
the failure to restore a Greek Empire the chief service of the
Patriarchate and the Phanar to Greek nationalism has been
that of keeping alive the Greek claim to Constantinople as
their national capital. While Greek nationalism had its goal
in the extreme north of Magna Graecia, it had its genesis
in the extreme south, where Maina, and later the whole
Morea, became a second focus of it owing to the revolt
of the Peloponnesian peasants and Aegean seamen. From
this focus came the fighting force of Greek nationalism
that conquered for itself a citadel of self-government. A
third focus was in the commercial communities of the Aegean
and Asia Minor, who brought to the movement the resources
of capital and commerce. The fourth and last focus lay in
western Greece and was represented by the embryo culture
centre in Epirus and the adjoining school of citizenship
afforded by Ionian autonomy. This latter was the channel
through which Western civilization and civic education came
to the Hellenic State. These four national constituencies
are still the component parts of that State, and on them it
will continue to rest even when the completed edifice has
entirely concealed them within its structure—as the dome
of St. Sophia covers its four supporting massifs.

The first result of the Greeks' national movement a century
ago was the complete and final loss of their imperial inheritance ; for if they ever recover their lost capital and their
lost compatriots of Anatolia, it will be as a nation and not
as an empire. But the distinction between a national
revival and an imperial restoration was not of course recognized ; and it was hoped at first that the two might be
synonymous. The movement, as planned, was to be a double
one, representing both the national and the imperial aims
of the Greeks. The insurrection of the Greek clans in the
Morea, the national rising, was to be combined with a rising

of the Bulgar and Slav peasants of the Danubian provinces
led by the Phanariote 'imperialist' nobles. Both were
failures. But the peasant rising in the Peloponnese had an
inherent vitality which could defy defeat; whereas the
Bulgar and Rouman peasants refused to follow their Greek
persecutors against their Turkish oppressors. The defeat of
the Sacred Battalion at Dragashani was the end, and no
unworthy end, of the 'imperialist' claims of the Phanariote
ruling class. Moreover, the elimination of this upper-class
element from a prominent place in the nationality movement
was soon followed by that of the middle-class element. The
depopulation of Chios was the melancholy end of any leading
part that might have been played in the renaissance by the
commercial communities of the islands. The execution of
the Patriarch and of the leading Phanariotes was a characteristic and conclusive declaration of war between the two races,
and the end of Turkish toleration. Like the expulsion of
the Protestants from France or of the Jews from Spain,
it portended ruin to the persecutor; for the dissolution
of the Turko-Greek partnership was a deadly blow to the
Ottoman Empire. The Turko-Greek alliance in imperialism
was shattered by the first touch of Greek nationalism, and
the divorce was final. Nationalism converted the Greek
âme damnée of the Empire into its avenging angel; and
from that day to this there has been a holy war between
Turks and Greeks. This does not mean that there have been
since then no Greeks in high position in the Turkish service,
any more than that Greek and Turkish villages have not
since then been peaceable neighbours. Greek and Turkish
villagers have in Macedonia allied themselves against
Bulgars, and Greeks have held high office. But we are
using here a broad brush. The Phanar is now a mere
faubourg: the Patriarch is no more than a bishop *in
partibus infidelium*: and the Young Turk has revived the
Empire on quasi-constitutional lines which offer the Greek
elements in it a means of political expression if they choose

to co-operate again. But between Greek nationalism and and the new Turkish nationalism there can be peace only when both have become more politically independent of each other and have developed a higher degree of economic interdependence.

We now begin to see that the Graeco-Turkish War of 1912 was only a pitched battle in the hostilities that began a century before, since the expulsion of the focus of the new Greek nation from the Propontis to the Peloponnese could only result in its return by armed force. The history of the Greek nationality movement will have written itself in three Books : the Book of the reconquest of the European mainland and islands, the Book of the recovery of Constantinople, and the Book of the reconstitution of the Greek Empire. The first we saw finished yesterday, the second we have seen begun to-day, the third is altogether a thing of to-morrow. The reconquest of Europe and the Aegean from the Old Turk took a whole century ; though there was never any question but that the Young Greek of the Peloponnese would in time, as he did, win back his national inheritance field by field. The war that began with the siege of Tripolitza, the Turkish capital of Macedonia, in 1821, and that brought about the taking of Salonika, the capital of Macedonia, last year, can only end with the taking of Constantinople. This is as inevitable as the Italian progress from Turin through Naples to Rome. It is only a question of time. If the first Book took a century, let us hope that the second, the recovery of Constantinople, will not take as long. If Byzantinism is the source of the difficulties of the Eastern Question, let us hope Hellenism is their solution.

It may be objected that this presentment of the Near Eastern Question as a duel between the Greeks and Turks ignores overmuch the historic and military claims of the Slav, Bulgar, Roumanian, and Albanian races. But it is not contended that these races did not contribute to the final settlement on national lines. The difference between them and the Greek in the present connexion is that their culture, development, and political position in the Empire never made possible a pacific reconstruction of the Empire by their means, as would have been possible by means of the Greek Patriarchate and Phanar. The Serb and Bulgar culture was extinct and their Patriarchate abolished ; the Roumans were never integral inhabitants of the Empire ; and the Albanians, although they contributed later to keeping the Empire going, were not capable of giving it a fresh start. Besides, all these stocks were essentially provincial as being concentrated in certain regions ; and none was maritime and metropolitan like the Greeks. The existence of the other embryo European nationalities made almost impossible a pacific settlement through a Greek Empire ; but offered no alternative to that settlement in a restoration of a Serb or Bulgar Empire.

A restored Greek Empire would have fought its own battles with the other Balkan peoples, and would have been, in due course, defeated ; but the intervention of European Powers for maintaining its integrity or monopolizing its inheritance would not have subordinated progress in the Balkans to the peace of Europe. As it was, the Turk was kept in his all-corrupting capital city, and the whole force of European civilization was put at his disposal in his resistance to the nationality movements of the Balkan peoples. In this resistance there were only two possible policies, which may be designated, for convenience only, as the ' diplomatic ' and the ' democratic ' methods. The ' democratic ' method is so called because it represented popular action rather than any personal guidance ; and meant resisting the nationality movements by destroying or driving off the subject peoples affected by such movements. This democratic policy of extermination has been put in force by the stronger Ottoman governments ; as, for instance, by the reforming Sultan, Mahmoud II, when he attempted to suppress the Greek movement in the Morea, and by the Young Turk reformers in dealing with the Macedonian movements. The defect of the policy lies in the fact that it unites all the discontented elements against the Empire; and also in the fact that, even in the early nineteenth century, in virtue of divine right, or in the twentieth century, in the name of constitutional government, it is difficult of thorough execution. The other policy, the 'diplomatic' method, was that affected by Abdul Hamid, and since his fall, by Turkish liberals such as Kiamil Pasha. It consists in playing off one movement against the other; and its defect is that, though a balance of weakness between the movements may be obtained, the general level of their strength must be continually raised by concessions to the weaker. Thus, while the result of the 'democratic' policy is that the separatist nationality movements develop spasmodically in overreachings and recoilings-back with a general condition of more or less open warfare, under the 'diplomatic' policy these movements develop slowly and steadily in a condition of more or less suppressed warfare. For instance, Abdul Hamid, by the 'diplomatic' method, was slowly losing Macedonia while he kept hold of Thrace; whereas the Young Turk, by the 'democratic' method, lost at one fell Bulgar swoop, both Macedonia and Thrace, but then recovered Thrace. The net result is probably to-day the same, so far as the Empire is concerned, as if Abdul Hamid had been in power. So far as Europe is concerned, the fact that European governments could guide and control 'diplomatic' developments in eastern Europe, but are apparently helpless in dealing with developments on 'democratic' lines, has been disastrous for the influence of western civilization in eastern Europe and for the establishment of a lasting peace.

The 'democratic' policy of the extermination of the Balkan nationalities by the Ottoman Empire has been carried at various times to such a pitch that the student is puzzled to explain its undoubted failure. It is barely a hundred years ago since the proposal for a general massacre of all Christians was rejected by the Islamic Empire as too expensive; and since then the Ottoman Government have permitted themselves considerable expenditures of Greeks, Bulgars, and Armenians. Chios, Batak, and Urfa [1] represent earnest efforts to deal faithfully with sedition, conspiracy, and rebellion; and the curse of Cromwell fell no more heavily on the Irish than did the constitutionalism of the Committee on the Macedonians in 1910. Why was it that such affairs as that of Kochana did not dispose of the Macedonian question any more than the Drogheda affair settled the Irish question? If European civilization had given a free hand to this ' democratic ' policy of extermination, would not the Eastern Question have been settled long ago without any international war by the Moslemizing of Macedonia? Would not the contending Slav claimants have been driven over the frontier to their respective compatriots in the free Balkan States, leaving the Turkish and Albanian peasants as cultivators of the soil, with the Kutso-Vlachs as traders and the Jews and Greeks as townsmen? The solution would have been pacific in a sense and undoubtedly permanent; and it is curious that the problem was not then anticipated, and that a nucleus of nationality in the free Slav states was ever allowed to develop. Again and again, in the days before foreign frontiers offered any refuge, misery and massacre forced the Serb and Bulgar peasants to islamize, and those converts, the Serbo-Bosniaks and the Bulgaro-Pomaks, have been the bitterest enemies of their Serb and Bulgar kindred, even as the janizaries were. But the Bosniaks and Pomaks have shown no capacity for taking advantage of their privileged position to get a start of or even to keep pace with the development, moral or material, of their Christian compatriots, and have merely

[1] Chios, 23,000 Greeks killed and 47,000 sold into slavery in 1821. Batak, 5,000 Bulgars killed in 1876, the total number massacred being over 12,000. Urfa, 3,000 Armenians killed in 1895, the total number massacred being over 50,000, of whom 6,000 were killed in Constantinople in 1896.

remained as Islamic colonies in a Christian country. Again
and again, since the establishment of the Christian principalities, misery and massacre have driven the Macedonians in
thousands over the frontier, but they have invariably come
back to bury their dead, rebuild their houses, replant their
orchards, and to resent further oppression all the more for
a breath of free air. It is true that the Turkish government
has not been able to make progress easy even for its Islamic
subjects, and that the Balkan governments have not wished
to encourage an emigration which would defeat their own
future territorial expansion ; but the explanation probably
lies deeper than questions of progress or of policy. The
association between a peasant people and the land is a relation
deeper and stronger even than the relation between the
people and its religion. For even an English peasant who has
little permanent interest in any particular land, and who is
in perpetual association with interests other than the land,
emigration is an event to be faced only by the boldest and
least bucolic. The Irish peasants who were driven out from
a famine-stricken and impoverished country to a land of
boundless promise have never forgiven the injury. It is in
the bond between the land and its labourer, born of long
association, that lie the elements of national character.
Where that bond exists, there is or may be national life;
and its destruction is the death of all that is national in the
individual. Indeed, if he be a true man of the land he will
prefer death to such destruction.

Even in Macedonia such an association between the
labourer and the land not only exists but alone explains the
survival and eventual supremacy of the persecuted section
of the population. This section represents those elements
we know as Christian, though it includes the seceding
communities of Christian stock that have islamized. These
Christians represent the Macedonians, that is to say the
races that have become indigenous to Macedonia. Although
they have not, as has already been pointed out, enough racial

definition, or enough regional delimitation, to enable them
to constitute themselves a nation, yet they rooted strongly
enough in the soil to enable them to survive even Turkish
and Albanian domination.

If ancient association with the soil is necessary to ensure
the survival of a race under conditions of oppression or
isolation, we may perhaps see, in the absence of all such
association, the reason why the Asiatic stock introduced into
European Turkey cannot survive there. For a thousand
years Asiatics have been pouring into Macedonia and
Roumelia: Petchenegues and Komans invited by Byzantine
emperors, invading Turks or Turkomans, and, in present
times, Asiatic stocks of all sorts moving eastward before
the Slav renascence in Servia and Bulgaria, and Georgian
or Circassian refugees moving westward before the Slav
advance across the Caucasus. Of all these Asiatic settlers
practically none have taken root, for the settlements of
Turks that still subsist are mostly of islamized European
stock. Of the thousands of Circassians settled on the best
land of Roumelia in the 'sixties, scarcely one remains. The
Osmanli Turks themselves are steadily decreasing, in spite
of every advantage ; a decline scarcely to be accounted for
by racial degeneration or by any of its moral and physical
diseases—for no man can degenerate much while he lives
directly by the land. But the Osmanli Turk in Europe,
while he lives by the land, is not for the most part a peasant,
and has never become associated with his Roumelian holding
as he has with the soil of Anatolia. Consequently when his
privileged position is taken from him, he leaves European
soil and neither regrets it nor returns to it. Europe for the
Europeans is a law written into the soil and the races of
Europe even more deeply than is the law that the Balkan
peninsula belongs to the Balkan peoples. Against such
natural laws of property, peoples offend only on peril of
gaining worlds and losing their own souls.

§ 6. PANSLAVISM AND PHILHELLENISM

It has been indicated that the primary causes of the Balkan wars are to be sought in the failure of the Ottoman Empire, and the secondary causes in the consequent separatist nationality movements of the Balkan peoples. It does not, however, necessarily follow that these nationality movements could not have been carried through without war if Europe had supported them against the Empire. The motive force of each nationality movement is made up of two factors—a native force of revolt and a foreign force of sympathy and support. At an early stage of the movement the foreign force is the more important factor, as when Russia freed Bulgaria, or Great Britain freed Greece. But gradually this foreign factor diminishes and is replaced by the growing native force developed by the free or partly freed nation. In the case of Balkan nationalism the measure of European intervention was the measure of Balkan pacific progress. For while the foreign Powers could give effect to Balkan nationalism at best by peaceable coercion of the Empire, and, at worst, by a formal and probably decisive war, the Balkan nations alone could only realize their national movement by long-protracted civil warfare—the most terrible of all wars. If Europe had done its duty by the Balkans in carrying eastward, when it could, the cause of liberty and civilization, there would have been few Balkan massacres and wars, if any. It will be well worth while to examine how it is that the default of Europe is as much to be blamed for the Balkan wars as the decadence of the Empire or dissension between the Balkan peoples.

Hitherto we have been dealing with the natural forces that make and unmake nations and that man cannot control ; though he may conduct his affairs wisely or unwisely accordingly as he understands and uses the opportunities they give him. But here we have to do with the responsibility attaching to a position of trust and to the exercise of power over the growth of younger nations, a responsibility that still rests on western civilizations. This responsibility is specially imposed on Great Britain, to whose policy the survival of the evil to the present day will be shown to have been mainly due. It will be shown that it was the failure of Europe in general and of the English in particular to realize this responsibility that was, if not a principal cause, yet certainly a condition precedent to both Balkan wars. This is not an indictment to make lightly, but all impartial examination of the causes of the Balkan wars will make it most indubitably and lamentably plain.

In order to give an idea in a few words of the part played by Europe in the Eastern Question it will be convenient to represent the relationship of each Great Power to each Balkan people as a double one. Such relationship is to be divided into two factors, which, for want of better terms, will be distinguished as ' diplomatic ' and ' democratic '. It is also suggested that the longer a government has been established—or the larger a State is in extent—or the less representative those in power are of public opinion—or the lower their ideals and sympathies—then the wider will grow the difference between national conduct and national conscience, and between the diplomatic foreign *Realpolitik* and the democratic foreign relationship. In a Balkan State this difference between democratic and diplomatic foreign relations is as yet small; though, in the events of these recent years it is already noticeable. But in the case of great powers, such as Great Britain and Russia, the difference is very great. Owing to the control over public opinion of the Cabinet and of the ruling class—even in so democratic a makeshift as the British Constitution—and owing to the force of public opinion over a bureaucracy—even when it is as despotic as that of Russia—it will be found that the foreign policy of either country is in a state of perpetual oscillation between democratic action and diplomatic reaction, between progressives and conservatives, between the 'tender-minded' radical and the 'tough-minded' *Realpolitiker*.

It may seem to be adding an unnecessary complication to the already sufficiently complicated Eastern Question to duplicate the relationship of each Great Power with the Balkan peoples into a 'democratic' and a 'diplomatic' relation. But these factors in the foreign policy of at least two of the Great Powers, England and Russia, must be clearly grasped by any one who would attempt to understand the vacillations and vagaries of their policy and the curious contradictions which complicated the notable contributions of each Power to the progress of civilization in eastern Europe.

The 'democratic' factor no doubt exists in the relations of France, Germany, Italy, and Austria to the Balkan peninsula; but these relations may, for our present purpose, be considered as purely diplomatic, and may be left alone until we have passed altogether from the region of underlying political forces to that of superficial foreign politics. France, in the early nineteenth century, when the democratic impetus of the Revolution was still felt, and before the interest of the French public in European democracies was made conservative by its investments, rendered chivalrous service to Greece. Italy also, under the impulse of the Garibaldian tradition, with its fellow-feeling for a war of liberation, has furnished volunteers to the Greek wars; but the feeling is not strong enough to affect its foreign policy. The German Empire has a dynastic connexion with Greece and Roumania, but no 'democratic' relation at present with any Balkan state, except perhaps a somewhat mercenary middle-class interest in Young Turkey. The Austrian Empire, on the other hand, has no less than three public opinions with regard to the Peninsula. That of the Hungarians is contrary to any 'democratic' progress there, and that of the Austro-Slavs in favour of it; so that these two roughly cancel each other, though the former is the stronger.

The third, Austro-German public opinion, is indifferent,
so that the general result is diplomatic and vacillating.
There remain, therefore, England and Russia as the powers
in which ' democratic ' feeling is strong enough to influence
foreign policy at critical periods in the development of the
Balkan peoples. Nor is it hard to explain why in these two
cases the relationship is double, and why their relations with
England or Russia have an importance for the Balkan peoples
that those with the rest of Europe do not possess.

The ' democratic ' foreign relationship between two peoples
depends on the extent and force of the ' definite connexion'
between them, to borrow a phrase from pragmatism. The
' definite connexion ' between England and Greece one
hundred years ago was the association of modern Greece
with the free thought and free institutions of ancient Greece ;
an association which assured to Greek nationalism the
sympathy and support of the classically educated ruling
class in Great Britain. This would have been enough in
itself to influence British foreign policy, but Philhellenism
was made a popular sentiment and became a democratic
relationship between Great Britain and Greece for a time
by the appeal to the national love of romance made by
Canning and Byron. Fifty years later, when the centre of
political power in Great Britain had shifted towards the
middle class, the appeal was converted from one of romance
into one of religion by the evangelical prophets of the middle
class, Gladstone and Bright. The first appeal was perhaps
the more admirable, asserting as it did a purely abstract
moral idea, that of freedom. In the second—the religious
appeal—Christianity is recommended rather as a means of
progress and prosperity ; so that, though the language in
which it expressed itself was biblical, and the policy it inspired
was rather philanthropic than political, the resulting relationship seems more material and interested. ' Give freedom to the
Greeks ', said the Philhellenes, ' because it is their right and
your responsibility.' ' Free the Bulgars ', said Exeter Hall,

'because it is to their advantage and yours.' The difference is somewhat like that between the First and Fourth Crusades.

It is curious that so unreal and dubiously ' democratic ' a connexion as Philhellenism—a romantic relation between the English ruling class and the Greek rayah—should have done so much good as it did, and lasted so long. It was unreal because there was no real resemblance between the Klephts and Armatoles of the Greek rising and the Athenians and Spartans of classical literature— the Odysseus who retook Athens being a very different person from the Odysseus who took Troy. It was ' undemocratic ' because there was no real relationship between the classically educated highly civilized English Philhellene and the Greek peasant. The result was in the end a reaction which has lasted to the present day ; for the Philhellenes led British opinion to look for an Alexander and an Aristotle, and the discovery that none were or would be forthcoming caused a disillusionment and disappointment from which the sympathy for Greece of the British ruling class has never recovered. This is one reason why English opinion has never realized the true qualities of the modern Greek. Another reason for the breach of sympathy between the British ruling class and the Greek nation was that, owing to party politics, the British aristocracy became Turcophil as soon as they stopped being Philhellene. The ' definite connexion ' of the British ruling class with the Turks was indeed far more substantial ; being based on the fellow-feeling of the former with a landed gentry threatened by dispossession through the political aspirations of a peasantry, and with a ruling class possessed of very similar virtues to the English. The English ruling class of to-day no longer goes to the Greek classics for its political philosophy ; like the Turkish ruling class it has replaced the Greeks by the Jews, and seeks its minds of light and leading among the Ashkenazim rather than among the Athenians. The English aristocracy is no longer led by a Canning or a Byron any more than the democracy is led by a Gladstone or a Bright. But in these days, when the ' classes ' and the ' classics ' are ordinary objects of attack, this one notable occasion when a ' liberal ' education did actually create a liberal foreign policy should be remembered.

Another connexion of value to the Greeks was caused by the British occupation and cession of the Ionian Islands. This political connexion produced a relationship which was no less disinterested and was far closer to realities than the romantic or religious connexion inspired by classical or middle-class sentiment. The experience acquired in the attempt to administer these islands gave the British nation a realization of what the force of the Greek ' Great Idea ' was; and of what the failure of Turkish rule in Europe meant.[1] It is largely owing to the lesson learnt by Gladstone in Corfu that Great Britain can claim to have made some considerable contributions to peace and progress in the Balkan peninsula.

In the latter part of the nineteenth century the British middle class had become the predominant influence in British politics ; though foreign policy remained, as it does to this day, exclusively conducted and almost entirely controlled by the upper class. The ' definite connexion' between the British middle class and the Balkan peoples was rooted in the two strongest characteristics of the former—business instinct and religious enthusiasm. The business connexion was a somewhat stronger bond with the Greeks, who were

[1] The retrocession of Parga to the Turk—the first consequence of the British occupation of the Islands—and the dramatic destruction of the Suliotes, made a profound impression on the British public of the day. The engraving of the fate of the women of Suli, hanging over the parlour chimney-piece, became a fact of life not to be effaced by any anti-Russian panics or pro-Turkish policies. Never again has St. George's Cross given place to the Crescent ; and if the British Government has since then more than once restored Turkish misrule over emancipated territory, it is safe to assert that such diplomacies have never had the support of British democracy. The British people are not hostile to the Turk, as their welcome of the Young Turk shows, but, having a strong instinctive grasp of political principle, they have often shown a truer appreciation than their rulers of what is practical politics in foreign affairs.

the leading mercantile business race of the Levant. The religious factor was stronger in the case of the Slav peoples, still engaged with the Turks in a war of races, which, as shown above, took the form of a war of religions. In the business relations between England and Greece, two notable links were the establishment of a prosperous Greek colony in London, dating from the expulsion of the Phanariotes, and the peculiar taste acquired by the British public for dried currants. The Greek banker in the city and the currant bun in the village shop were both powerful ambassadors and benefactors of Greece.

The religious connexion between Great Britain and the Slav principalities was of a less definite character, and consequently less reliable. It was inspired by broad principles of Christianity and common sense, but had in consequence difficulties in getting a practical expression in foreign policy. The economic expression given it by Cobden could excite no great energy of public opinion. Bright could give it expression in terms of simple religious feeling which went straight to the heart, but brought no practical convictions to the head. Molesworth and many others could give the popular point of view expression in policy but produced no effect on public opinion. It remained for Gladstone to unite all these in one ' Potent Head ',[1] and thereby to influence British foreign policy in favour of ' democratic ' intervention in the Balkans whenever opportunity offered ; although, unfortunately, antiquated constitutional machinery generally delayed the realization of Gladstone's foreign policy until the critical moment was past and the occasion lost. This is why Gladstonian principles of foreign policy still express the link between the British and Balkan peoples better than any other, and have, for the most part, become axioms of British policy ; even though the business and religious point of view of the Victorian middle class no longer inspires our

---

[1] ' As for the Commons, there is little danger from them except when they have Potent Heads.'—*Bacon's Essays*.

policy, and the old connexions with the Balkan peoples have changed. For the currants now appear liquefied in a Hamburg bottle instead of dry in a British bun : the Phanariote *émigrés* have become county families : the humanitarians have learnt that massacres are much oftener due to the illogical diplomacy of Christian Europe than to any inborn devilry in the Islamic Empire : and the evangelicals have learnt that the Christian Churches of Macedonia are of ethnological rather than of ethical importance. Nowadays the links between western democracies and the peoples of Eastern Europe are to be sought in large financial and industrial exploitations ; and these belong to the most ' diplomatic ' and least ' democratic ' category of relationships between peoples. Fortunately, as has already been noted in the prefatory chapter, a new ' democratic ' relationship between Eastern Europe and western civilization has been created by emigration to America—a development which promises to create a strong democratic bond between the English-speaking peoples and those of the Balkans.

We now come to the relationship between the Russian and the Balkan peoples. It will be unnecessary to enlarge upon the ' definite connexions ' between the Slavonic, Finnish, German, and Mongol stocks which constitute the Russian people, and the same stocks which go to make up the northern Balkan peoples. Russian civilization is itself Eastern European both in character and degree of development, and consequently its culture connexion with the Balkans is based upon intellectual sympathy, which is a far stronger connexion than the moral sympathy felt for the Balkan peoples by British altruists. Indeed, had the Russian people been a democracy, the Balkan peoples would have had little need of help from any ' definite connexion ' between themselves and the British people.

It has been the worst misfortune of the Balkan people that British and Russian diplomacy should have been in collision with only rare exceptions during the whole period

of their development. The consequence has been that most
of the time Anglo-Russian influence has been as little effective
for progress in the Balkans as has Austrian influence ; for
in both cases the democratic progressive factors have cancelled each other out, and left the diplomatic conservative
factors to make such history as they could. The short
periods when British public opinion was adequately represented by Canning or Gladstone, and Russian public opinion,
under Catherine or Alexander, was truly represented by
a Russian government, were the periods when all progress
in the Balkans was achieved. When these two influences
pulled together, barbarism and Byzantinism ebbed ; and
when Great Britain and Russia came into opposition the
ebbing Empire held its ground or even regained territory.
It was an Anglo-Russian alliance that freed Greece at
Navarino : it was an Anglo-Russian arrangement that freed
Bulgaria at Berlin : it is an Anglo-Russian agreement on
the Eastern Question, even though it be no more than an
agreement not to fight about it, that now, in the twentieth
century, has made possible another step towards a final
settlement. It is to be observed, however, that their joint
action has progressively become more and more disjointed
and less and less decisive.

In the eighteenth and early nineteenth century there was
little sympathy between British democracy and the Balkans
other than the classical interest of the then ruling class ;
but there was, on the other hand, as yet no diplomatic
policy based on balance of power to counteract it. Moreover there was no party difference of opinion in regard to
the treatment of the Eastern Question. Under these conditions, the scheme of Pitt and Catherine to settle that
question by restoration of the Greek Empire was a constructive proposal for dealing with a difficulty as yet not
beyond solution by western statesmanship. The Austrian
Empire had not yet been forced by Prussia into expansion
eastward, and recovery of the Slav provinces it had adminis-

tered early in the century was the limit of its interest. The
great difficulty of jealousy as to Constantinople was dealt
with by making Duke Constantine, a Russian prince who
had been specially trained for the purpose, emperor of an
independent empire. Putting on one side the difficulty
that the majority of rayahs hated the Greeks worse than
the Turks, this first Anglo-Russian settlement of the Eastern
Question was a bold constructive policy which compared
well with subsequent compromises and futilities. That
it was a bold conception was well realized by its promoters; although it could be recommended to reactionaries
as a restoration. No time was lost and few mistakes were
made in putting it into execution. A propaganda was started
in Roumelia, and risings were excited without difficulty in
Montenegro and the Morea—the respective centres of Slav
and Greek national consciousness. Sea power next came into
play, and a Russian fleet, commanded by British officers,
dealt the first mortal thrust at the heart of the Ottoman
Empire. The treaty of Kutchuk-Kainardji that closed this
first campaign in 1769 went fully half-way to realizing the
scheme, in establishing what was practically a Russian protectorate over the Ottoman rayahs. This treaty, which was
confirmed and completed by that of Ainali-Kavak ten years
later, amounted in effect to a declaration of independence
by proxy of the Balkan peoples. It was a blow to the
integrity of the Ottoman Empire from which it never
recovered; although the retirement into Asia and the reform
in administration now in progress may yet remedy its
worst inroads into the sovereignty of the Ottoman State.
This subversion of Ottoman sovereignty was the most
difficult initial step in putting the Anglo-Russian policy into
execution: the next step, the substitution of the Greek
Phanar for the Ottoman Porte, would have been no more
formidable than was the framing of the American Constitution after the Declaration of Independence; for the government was already as Greek in the one case as it was colonial

in the other. But this second step was never to be taken. There is an inherent weakness in any Anglo-Russian association that prevents it lasting long; and when the next Russo-Turkish war broke out, the two Powers had already revolved into opposition. As a result, the ensuing Napoleonic epoch introduced a new point of view into the foreign policy of the two Powers towards the Near East, and one moreover that was less favourable to Balkan liberties.

At the next crisis of any great importance in the Eastern Question we again find Great Britain and Russia in association—an association the result of alliance against the French Revolution and against the Napoleonic rearrangement of Europe. The failure of Europe to take advantage of the general Napoleonic liquidation to do anything for the eastern Christians, especially the Greeks, Roumanians, and Servians, had caused these races to take matters into their own hands. The reaction in Europe from the principles of the French Revolution to those of the Holy Alliance, and the misrepresentation of European public opinion by such councils as the Congresses of Vienna and Laibach, or by such counsellors as Wellington and Talleyrand, was not likely to favour the Balkan nationality movements. These movements therefore were driven back upon themselves and began to seek independence in local insurrection rather than from foreign intervention. Henceforward it is the Balkan peoples that supply the initiative impulse and the constructive idea, while the Powers, that is to say, Great Britain and Russia, sometimes ratify, sometimes stultify, and sometimes amplify the results. The relationship of the Balkan peoples with the Concert can roughly be compared to that of a Lower with an Upper Chamber; the Upper Chamber, having been once as constructive as the Lower, has become conservative, and having once been predominant, to the exclusion of the will of the Lower House, is now subservient to it. It is a far cry from Magna Charta to the Parliament Act; it is quite as far, internationally speaking, from the Treaty of London of the year 1827, by which Great Britain, Russia, and France undertook to intervene in behalf of Greek independence, to the Treaty of London of 1913, in which the Balkan States rearranged the map of eastern Europe for themselves.

The intervention of Great Britain and Russia that freed Greece was a naval demonstration at Navarino that ended in the destruction of the Ottoman fleet, the expulsion of the Egyptian auxiliaries from the Morea, and a Russian invasion that penetrated to the suburbs of Constantinople under Diébitsch and ended in the Treaty of Adrianople, September 14, 1829. The Treaty of London was the beginning of Greek independence, the Treaty of Adrianople was the beginning of that of Roumania and of Servia. But no more than a beginning, for, as the 'democratic' forces in Great Britain and Russia exhausted themselves in getting the principle of nationality recognized, 'diplomatic' fears recovered control and restricted, as far as possible, its practical realization. The fears of the Russian government lest Greece, Servia, and Roumania should become too independent of Russia caused Russian diplomacy to restrict their political independence and national entity as far as possible.[1] In every case Russia tried to introduce a constitution which would weaken the new nation by either territorial or political divisions. In every case, except that of Greece, this policy was ruthlessly carried out, as will be seen later. On the other hand, Great Britain, fearing they would be mere dependents of Russia, cut down the territory of these States to the merest corner

---

[1] The Russian fears of Balkan independence led to the Russian proposal of July 1824, when the Greek War of Independence showed signs of success, that the Greek countries should be divided into three, or rather four, vassal States—Thessaly, Epirus, and Crete—the Aegean islands to have autonomy. It is a pity, perhaps, that these proposals were not accepted. The division would not have long delayed Greek unity, as is shown by the successful suppression of similar splittings up of Roumania and Bulgaria ; for such political fictions can be modified, or even abolished, without calling in the Concert or creating a Balkan war, although political frontiers cannot. The difference becomes clear in the peaceful annexation by Bulgaria of eastern Roumelia, and in the fact that it has cost two, and will probably cos? three, wars to settle Bulgarian Macedonia.

of their proper ethnographical and geographical extent.[1] Consequently the new nations were given only just as much independence and resources as would make it possible for them to fight for more, and would give them every reason to do so. No combination of principles could have been better conceived for the creation of Balkan wars. Yet this futile and foolish policy is that which, throughout the nineteenth century, resulted from the double character of the relationship of Great Britain and Russia to Balkan nationalism whenever there was a disagreement between the diplomacies of the two governments.

The first three-quarters of the nineteenth century were occupied by the struggles of the Balkan peoples for self-government, against the Turkish Empire; in which they were supported by democratic public opinion in Great Britain and Russia. But British diplomacy wished to maintain Turkey so strong as to be able to resist Russia, and Russian diplomacy wished to maintain the Balkan States so weak as not to be able to do so.

A necessary result of the British mistake in trying to erect a barrier against Russia out of the Ottoman Empire, and not out of the new nations that were bound to replace it, and of the consequent collision in British foreign policy between the pro-Turk party in power and anti-Turk popular opinion, was to give Russia a preponderating position. Moreover, as a result of Greek independence, the British ' democratic '

---

[1] British diplomacy, of course, should have adopted a strong pro-Balkan attitude ; and, before the delusion of maintaining the Ottoman Empire misled British policy, British bias against Russia had this effect. ' Twenty-four years after the Treaty of London, Lord Aberdeen, the Duke of Wellington's Foreign Secretary, confessed that Greece owed her escape from vassalage and her independence solely to the impression created by the Treaty of Adrianople. The Duke believed the end of Turkey was at hand, and that it was therefore useless to place Greece beneath a suzerain too feeble to protect that country against Russia. On the other hand, he foresaw the further aggrandizement of Russia, and was accordingly anxious that Greece, believed to be Russophil, should not be too large. What the British Cabinet wanted was a small independent State.'—Miller, *The Ottoman Empire*, p. 106.

interest in Balkan nationalism had declined. Therefore, in the further developments of the nineteenth century, it is Russia that takes the initiative, while Great Britain either thwarts it diplomatically, or supports it democratically.

The third opportunity that was lost by the Anglo-Russian association of settling the Eastern Question peaceably, was one which extended over many years, and one which, by its failure, excited several Balkan wars. To this failure were due successively the Crimean War, which was engendered in the Balkans and in the end embroiled Europe, and the Balkan wars, which led to the Russo-Turkish War a quarter-century later, as well as these recent Balkan wars by which the peace of Europe is still imperilled.

This third opportunity of a pacific settlement came with the second quarter of the century, and lasted roughly over the end of the third quarter. By 1832 the Ottoman Empire had been reduced to international impotence by the civil war with Egypt and by the acceptance of Russian protection under the treaty of Hunkiar Iskelessi. The reforming régime of Mahmoud II caused both internal disorganization and discontent, and the first instalment of Balkan independence. It was then that—encouraged by the position acquired in England by the pacificists of the Manchester school, Cobden and Bright, and by their declarations of the principles of democratic internationalism—the Tsar Alexander proposed as a personal suggestion a scheme for partition based on an Anglo-Russian understanding. This partition was to recognize the principle of nationality, and to divide the peninsula between the Balkan peoples; but Russia was to take Constantinople with the northern straits and isthmus, leaving Great Britain Egypt and Crete, with the control of the southern isthmus. It was a statesmanlike conception, in that it separated those territories of Turkey in which all developments must finally be decided by Balkan nationalism, from those in which the deciding factor was the general interest of the powers, and which might be dealt with by diplomacy; and in that it partitioned these latter non-national territories between the principal land power, Russia, and the principal sea power, Great Britain. Such a settlement offered a prospect of peaceful progress, for no other foreign power would have challenged it, and it would not have come into collision with the development of the Balkan peoples. But British diplomacy could not believe, in spite of the examples of Greece and Roumania, that the Balkan peoples could develop independently of Russia; nor was it prepared then to cede Constantinople to a rival. Cairo and the control of the southern isthmus and the Canal had not yet counterbalanced Constantinople and the command of the northern isthmus and the Straits. So the offer was refused. Russia, overrating the influence of liberal public opinion in British foreign affairs, and underestimating the effect of Panslavism in the Balkan States on their future relations with Russia, persisted in its pro-Balkan and anti-Ottoman policy. Having no clear idea of their national responsibilities in the Near East or of their real relationship to each other in respect of them, the two governments drifted into war.

This war, which was eventually fought out in the Crimea, was partly a Balkan and partly a European war. Its only effect, so far as the Eastern Question was concerned, was an exhaustion of the three more progressive Powers, such as hindered them from intervening again for a quarter-century. When the next opening for a settlement was given to Great Britain, it was still the same opportunity, though presented from a new point of view. Thus in the offer made to Sir H. Seymour by the Tsar, already described, the partition of the strategic points between the two Powers was the primary consideration; while the partition of the Balkan peninsula between the peoples was left undefined as a minor point. But during the quarter-century between the Treaty of Paris and the Treaty of Berlin, the centre of gravity of the Eastern Question had

passed still more under control of the Balkan nationality
movement. Consequently, in the Treaty of San Stefano
that closed the Russo-Turkish War of 1877–8, the partition
of Macedonia was the main point, and the frontiers of the
Slav peoples were laid down with great particularity, and
a close and conscientious regard for ethnographical and
geographical considerations. Thessaly, Epirus, the Roumlouk, Salonica, and Athos were to be left to Greece : Albania,
Bosnia, and Herzegovina, to such disposition as Austria
chose to make : Adrianople and Constantinople to a Russian
protectorate : Egypt and the islands to a British protectorate. The Russian proposal was, it will be noted, still
the same in principle but adapted to the development of the
nationality movement since the pre-Crimean period. Inspired by a Panslavist ideal of a Federation of mutually
reconciled Balkan principalities under Slav protection, Russia
proposed partition of Roumelia *irredenta* on racial and regional
lines of least resistance, such as could not be bettered to-day.
Indeed, such a partition could probably not have been peacefully imposed to-day after the political propaganda of the
Balkan States in Macedonia, and the growth in the rivalry of
Bulgaria and Greece for the hegemony of the peninsula. The
fact that the Russian settlement of the Macedonian question
was both complete and conformable to all the interests
concerned has been obscured or overlooked through the
opposition to it of Disraeli and the ' diplomatic ' policy of
the Government. It is generally considered as having been
a disguised encroachment by Russia, a falsification of the
weights in the balance of power, and a mine dug under the
buffer states which serve as a natural bulwark to Constantinople. This may indeed have been the intention of Russian
diplomacy ; and if Russian diplomats, with their superior
advantages for ascertaining facts, made the mistake of
thinking they could Russify Bulgars—the same mistake that
they had made with regard to Serbs and Greeks—British
diplomats may be excused for not having learnt the same

lesson. But the point of use to us is that if British and Russian diplomacy had been contented with the simple policy dictated by common sense and Christianity, and advocated by their respective democracies (for in the 'seventies there was a democratic party in Russia), it would have been better both for their own countries and for civilization. There would have been no quarter-century of religious and race wars in Macedonia : no regular wars such as the Serbo-Bulgar, the Graeco-Turkish, the War of Coalition, and the War of Partition : a lesser risk of European war, and a lighter load of European armament. All these calamities were the direct or indirect consequences of British diplomacy at Berlin taking a reactionary line for various diplomatic reasons, not in themselves reactionary. A reaction which reverses an accomplished fact in the main movement of the century—the nationality movement—is likely to cause trouble. The first trouble might well have been another Anglo-Russian war ; for a reversal of the Russian peace provisions imposed by the Russian army under the walls of Constantinople was a more serious matter than the refusal of pacific overtures diplomatically advanced before the Crimean War. But British diplomacy had only been confirmed in its pro-Turk policy by that war and the ensuing quarter-century ; and, although British democracy, under the aggressive leadership of Gladstone and the impression made by the Bulgarian atrocities, was much stronger than it had been under the negative guidance of the Manchester School, yet the diplomatic party were in power, and could not be evicted in time.

Disraeli led his party to the brink of an Anglo-Russian war, and then made terms with Russia ; but his bargain was not a good one from any point of view. The two main defects in it were the partitioning between the Powers of some of the territories of the Balkan peoples, and the restoration of Turkish rule in the more debatable regions. This aggravated instead of appeasing all the elements of conflict

in the Balkans. The Great Powers were brought into collision
with the Balkan peoples, and the latter were left in conflict
with themselves and with Turkey.

The results of British ' diplomatic ' opposition to the
'democratic ' policy of Russia were no more fortunate as
regards the settlement outside the Balkan peninsula, where
no nationality movement was concerned. Having refused
the opportunity of securing British interests in Egypt by
international arrangement, Great Britain was within a few
months compelled by force of circumstances to armed
intervention, which became, in obedience to the same force,
a permanent occupation. If the sanction of Europe had
been secured for the British occupation of Egypt as part
of a general settlement, it would have saved much friction
in Anglo-French relations, much delay in the development
of Egypt, and some searchings of heart among the more
' tender-minded ' elements of the British national consciousness. As it is, the sanction of France has had to be
bought by the sacrifice of Morocco—also a trying transaction
to the ' tender-minded '. Crete, which was also to have
been allowed to Great Britain, would have passed to Greece
more peacefully through a British occupation than through
the insurrections and international occupations which have
made it for a quarter-century a stone of offence to civilization and a stumbling-block to diplomacy. Cyprus, taken
in its place, still belongs to Great Britain—a monument
to a threefold breach of trust in respect of the Turkish,
Greek, and Armenian protégés of the British Government.

Great Britain got eventually in Egypt and Cyprus almost
all that had been offered by Russia as the price of Constantinople, and yet saved Constantinople from Russia. This
was, no doubt, a diplomatic success, and a service, perhaps,
to international interests of commerce and finance. But it
was only effected, as we have seen, at a heavy material
and moral loss to the Balkan peoples. The moral cost to
the British people is a matter of opinion ; the material cost

is represented by the barren wars in the Crimea and in Afghanistan, the latter being the indirect consequence of British opposition to Russia in the Balkans.

We are not now concerned with the considerations of balance of power and high policy which inspired the official diplomacies of Great Britain and Russia. These will be given due weight later when we come to deal with those contemporary and more ephemeral conditions to which they belong. It is important to note, however, that till the present century, whenever democratic public opinion, whether in Great Britain, in Russia, or in both jointly, got command long enough to achieve a step towards Balkan self-government, official diplomacy sooner or later regained control and, as far as possible, counteracted what had been accomplished.[1] British official policy coerced or consternated its democracy into reaction by the view that every loss of strength to the Ottoman Empire was a corresponding gain to an aggressive Russia. Russian official policy was led into reaction by the discovery, in the case of each Balkan people in turn, that every loss of strength to the Ottoman Empire was a gain to the Balkan nations and a corresponding loss to Russia. Thus Great Britain and Russia joined to free the Greeks at Navarino, and immediately afterwards the Duke of Wellington joined Russia in reducing the limits of free soil to a minimum. The British democracy was in favour of Russia freeing Roumania and Bulgaria, but no sooner was this done than Palmerston and Disraeli joined Russian diplomacy in undoing the greater part of the work. The British statesmen, thinking in terms of balance of power, were out of touch with the whole

---

[1] ' The work of ministers and diplomatists is not to be set aside by popular emotion. But, on the other hand, to suppose that the world either is or ought to be governed by ministers and diplomatists is a delusion —a graver delusion. The world goes by motive power, and the motive power is supplied, not by the business of statesmen, but by the convictions and desires of populations.'—Llewellyn Davies, *Pamphlet on the Bulgarian Atrocities.*

meaning and movement of the century as we now see it. If they had themselves believed in democracy, they would have seen, as did Gladstone,[1] that a national self-government is the best barrier to autocratic aggression, and that the neighbourhood of a corrupt and coercive autocracy, such as that of Turkey, is not a barrier but a bridge to Russian expansion.

Russian diplomacy, being better instructed as to conditions and circumstances, made no such elementary blunders. Russian foreign policy aimed at replacing the Ottoman Empire by a Russian protectorate, or at best, by Russian provinces. This required extinction of the Empire and erection in its place of Principalities too weak to stand by themselves. It was especially necessary that Roumania should be under Russian control, because the main difficulty of Russian diplomacy has always been that this non-Slav race intervenes between Russia and the Slavs of Montenegro, Servia, Bulgaria, and Macedonia. But for Roumania, these southern Slavs would almost certainly have been, for a time at any rate, absorbed into Russia as Ruthenian Poles and Baltic Letts have been in spite of desperate resistance, and as Croats, Slovaks, and Slovenes might have been but for Hungary. The Russian policy was to encircle and partition Roumania, keeping it politically weak and in two pieces, so that each could in turn be swallowed. But Roumania refused to be partitioned. The two Principalities, Moldavia and Wallachia, were kept politically separate—a diplomatic device previously tried upon Greece and subsequently imposed as a check on Bulgarian nationalism.[2] Moreover, though

[1] On the occasion when the House of Commons, in fear of Russia, voted against the reunion of the Roumanian principalities, proposed by France and opposed by Austria, Gladstone's speech in favour of union contained the well-known passage : ' Surely the best resistance to Russia is by the strength and freedom of those countries that will have to resist her. . . . There is no barrier like the breast of freemen.'

[2] Bulgaria was divided at Berlin into three sections, a principality with national self-government, a province, eastern Roumelia, with local government, and a promised land in Macedonia restored to the mercies

France opposed this, Great Britain supported it under the influence of Lord Palmerston and Disraeli and against the advice of Lord Salisbury and Mr. Gladstone. The two Principalities, instead of coming into collision, shortly after constituted the Roumanian nation by the counter device of electing the same prince. Russia was foiled, but for long lost no opportunity of weakening Roumania. Every Russo-Turkish war was an occasion for Russia to exhaust and encroach on its auxiliary, whose reward for its assistance in the last war of 1877 was, first to be enclosed between Russia and the big Bulgaria of San Stefano, and then to pay for the cutting up of Bulgaria by British diplomacy by being cut up to compensate Russia. Disraeli really played into the hands of Russian diplomacy by breaking up the big Bulgaria forced on it by Russian Panslav democracy, and by handing over Bessarabia, the richest province of Roumania, to Russia.

The subsequent discovery by Russian Panslav democracy, that Bulgars are rather Finns than Slavs, made it easier for Russian diplomacy to pursue a weakening policy towards them under a cover of protection. There now remain only Serbia and Montenegro, to whose independent development both Russian democracy and Russian diplomacy are favourable. But Russian relations with these Slav peoples are complicated by the interposition of Hungary and by the proximity and predominance of the Austrian Empire on that side of the Balkan peninsula. Indeed, the fate of the Serbs has always been bound up rather with that of the Austrian than with that of the Turkish Empire.

of the Turk. But to make assurance of a weak Bulgaria sure, Russia imposed a Bulgarian constitution calculated to produce collisions between the prince and the people, and maintained a military government of the country for several years. Bulgarian democracy defeated both these conspiracies to some extent ; Eastern Roumelia was reunited and the country remained constitutionally compact. Russian diplomacy did, however, in the end turn the scale against the Bulgarian national movement in regard to the recovery of Western Macedonia.

It is to be noted that there has been no reversal of the
views of Russian diplomacy as there has been of British. The
British began to see their mistakes even before Germany
shifted the balance of power and brought British and Russian
diplomacy on the same side in the Balkans. Whereas British
diplomacy of the nineteenth century was doing its best to
weaken Russia by keeping the Balkan States weak, it would
probably now be prepared to strengthen them all it could
without thereby weakening Russia. But fundamentally
Russian policy in the Balkans has been as mistaken as was
British. If Russia had made the development of the Balkan
States as rapid as its full support and frank sympathy
might have done, the Russian position in Eastern Europe
would to-day be very much more favourable and the much-
coveted Constantinople might to-day be hers. Weakness
and backwardness in buffer nations is not an advantage to
their more powerful and progressive neighbours. When the
small nations are democracies, and when the weakness is due
to the deliberate policy of the large neighbour, then, the closer
the relationship the worse the relations. Grievances of Irish
against English, of Servian against Austrian, of Bulgarian
against Russian, of Greek against Turk, these are the *casus belli*
that no Hague Convention or Arbitration Treaty can provide
against. But, on the other hand, two neighbouring States in
prosperity soon create common interests which assure to
either the co-operation of the other for any progressive purpose. While the British Colonies were poor and discontented
there was no Imperial ' definite connexion ' and no common
co-operation. It is the material prosperity and moral progress of the United States that has made the present Anglo-
American relationship a very different thing from the relations
between the United Kingdom and the United States of
a century ago. The New England colonies were saved from
France by the Mother Country, and thereby enabled to assert
their independence and acquire a national status. But until
their growth had entirely removed them from the conditions

in which they were when still dependent, the friction caused by this dependence falsified the Anglo-American relationship. Russia might by now have formed a relationship of business and sentiment with Bulgaria that would have assured the two peoples as much control for peaceful purposes of the Aegean and the Balkan peninsula as is assured to the Anglo-American association over the North American Continent and the Atlantic. Even apart from such considerations of *Weltpolitik*, to a progressive country a strong neighbour is better than a weak dependent. It is Irish prosperity that will make a settlement of the Anglo-Irish disputes possible ; a settlement that will make Ireland a strength instead of a weakness to England. The loss of Cuba brought prosperity to Cuba, but still more to Spain. Nowadays the loss of one nation is not the gain of another ; and if a Great Power weakens a small neighbour it weakens itself internationally, while if it absorbs a hostile community it weakens itself internally. The mistake of both British and Russian diplomacy in regard to the Balkans was that in its calculations of the balance of power it put the factor of Balkan nationality on the wrong side of the account.

British and Russian diplomacy had proved by a *reductio ad absurdum* that it was incapable of making use of the long opportunity for settling the Eastern Question that lasted for sixty years from about 1820 to about 1880. It is not, therefore, surprising that the young diplomacy of the Balkans should have taken up the burden of settling the Eastern Question with the conviction that European diplomacy was as serious a difficulty for them as was Asiatic despotism. Bulgar diplomacy, which for the last twenty years has been the dominant factor in the Balkans, has been based on the decision of Stambouloff that Asia was less dangerous than Europe as a guardian for the minority of a young civilization. With this growing distrust of the Balkan peoples for the policy of the Powers went the diminishing influence on that policy of such democratic interest in the Balkan nations as was retained by the British and Russian peoples. This influence went on diminishing until a ' democratic ' relationship that had once inspired the most chivalrous actions of which the Russian and British peoples can boast was contented to second Austria-Hungary in producing such a merely conservative policy as the Mürzsteg programme. Even when a release from their respective embarrassments in Eastern Asia and South Africa and a rearrangement of the European balance of power again brought Great Britain and Russia into association on the Eastern Question, this association was almost entirely a diplomatic one. In recent Anglo-Russian action in the Balkans there has been little popular feeling on the British side, other than the desire for peace, and little on the Russian side beyond some general sympathy with Balkan co-religionists. Even so, the Anglo-Russian association will be found to have been the factor in European politics that made possible the settlement brought about by the War of Coalition. Had there been a little more ' democratic ' force in it, this association might also have prevented the War of Partition.

The reader who has followed this melancholy record of lost opportunities so far, will recognize that he has before him a series of lessons as to the loss to the world when the citizens of the great democratic Powers let slip from their hands all control over foreign policy. Diplomacy only gets so far off the true course when it has to steer by its own dead reckonings over the invisible tides of the affairs of men, through the fogs of ignorance and the storms of passion.

CHAPTER III

THE MACEDONIAN QUESTION

§ 7. The Macedonian Question to 1891.
§ 8. The Macedonian Question, 1891–1903.
§ 9. The Macedonian Question, 1903–8.

Thessalica infelix, quo tanto crimine, tellus,
laesisti superos, ut te tot mortibus unam,
tot scelerum fatis premerent ? quod sufficit aevum
immemor ut donet belli tibi damna vetustas?

LUCAN, *Pharsalia.*

§ 7. THE MACEDONIAN QUESTION TO 1891

THE Balkan nationality movements left certain debatable lands and remainder regions after the more national territories had been developed into States. The most important of these was Macedonia, for it was both the most extensive and the most bitterly disputed; and thus Macedonia became the arena for Balkan racial and social warfare and a focus of infection for European political war fever. But while the *scandalum magnatum* became more and more unsupportable, it became more and more indispensable to support the *status quo* ; for the peace of Europe rested on a counterpoise of pressures in Macedonia. The pressures from outside all centred on Macedonia, and the heaviest were those of Austria and Russia which had disturbed and displaced the frontiers from their true ethnological lines ; while inner rings of pressures were due to the rival Balkan claims to Macedonia. The historical and geographical claims were both such as to cause a maximum of difficulty in deciding between them. The result was a deadlock ; for there was no external or internal force capable of forcing a solution of the problem against competitive and conservative opposition. The Balkan States could not effect a partition and the Powers would not enforce a protectorate—and this was the only alternative.

The manner in which each of the Balkan peoples, Serbia,

G

Roumania, and Bulgaria, attained self-government and national status is very interesting, but not directly important to our pacificist point of view; for once the rupture between Turks and Greeks had decided that the Empire could not be reconciled with the European movement for national self-government, the separation of these peoples by war from the Empire was bound to follow. The only question remaining was whether separation would come by internal or by international war—by a prolonged state of insurrectionary and revolutionary warfare or by periodic wars between the States concerned. All Near-Eastern wars originate in Near-Eastern nationalism, and the kind of war is decided by the character of the nationalist movement. But this movement fell into some confusion and even into collision with itself in certain remainder regions of the Near East such as Macedonia and Thrace and with certain more refractory races such as the Albanians and Turks : and hence the peculiar character of these Balkan wars—confused in their development and compounded of civil and foreign war. Let us see how this happened; for it is out of this condition of affairs that the recent Balkan wars came about.

By the end of the nineteenth century the movement for national self-government had roughly partitioned the Balkan peninsula among the Balkan peoples. This apportionment had naturally begun in such regions as were especially and entirely appropriated by a particular race ; and around each nucleus of nationality thus formed was a region of debatable borderland. Even so the germ of life in an egg is surrounded by matter which will serve as food to the organism when sufficiently developed. This intervening common land was more or less broad in dimension and more or less bitterly disputed as the races which it separated were more or less closely related. Between Bulgar and Greek the whole extent of Macedonia was in dispute : between Bulgar and Turk the narrower Thracian region. Greeks and Albanians disputed the comparatively unimportant Epirus.

Serbs and Albanians struggled with each other for the
narrow isthmus of Old Serbia and the Sanjak of Novi-
Bazar. All these disputed regions were inhabited by a mixed
population which had no common consciousness or sentiment
of solidarity such as might have served as the motive force
for a separate nationality. In all of them their political
subjection and their racial subdivisions had kept them at
a very low stage of civilization. Moreover, these debatable
lands were little more than the battlefields in which the life-
and-death struggle between the neighbouring national movements were fought out. The two bitterest of these wars was
that between Bulgars and Greeks in Macedonia and that
between Serbs and Albanians in Old Serbia. The collisions
between Greeks and Albanians in Epirus and between Greeks
and Bulgars in Thrace were less violent; and in Macedonia,
as well as the main duel between Greeks and Bulgars, there
were other milder feuds. Such complicating claims were
those of Serbs, Albanians, Vlachs or Roumanians, and
last but not least, Moslems. In Thrace the Greeks had
a better ethnological claim than the Bulgars to the southern
and eastern coasts; but distance from the Greek base and
nearness to the Turkish and Bulgar bases had checked the
Greeks from making or maintaining any strong bid for
Thrace.

As a consequence of this condition of things, by the
last decade of the nineteenth century the state of Macedonia was such that it was a menace to European peace and
a disgrace to European civilization. *Res nolunt diu male
administrari* : something was bound to happen soon. But
the great Land Powers, Russia and Austria, had for reasons
of their own combined to prevent all change. The Sea
Powers, England and France, had lost interest in the fate
of East-European Christians and could not press reforms
on the Ottoman Empire against the opposition of Germany
and Russia. The 'Old' Turks preferred that Macedonia
should remain indigent, ignorant, and insurgent, a condition

which, they supposed, offered them the best hope of retaining it. In any case the régime of Abdul Hamid could not, if it would, improve a condition in Macedonia which was caused by circumstances beyond its control. The only dynamic force sufficient to overcome the *vis inertiae* of Ottoman despotism and to get out of the vicious circle of European diplomacy was to be found in the Balkan nationalities ; but they were divided by their rivalries.

Macedonia fell deeper and deeper into barbarism. No serious attempt can be made here to describe what the ordinary conditions of life in Macedonia were during the last quarter of the nineteenth century, and within a few hours by rail of Vienna. An attempt has already been made in the first chapter to give an idea of the effect produced by these conditions on the civilized observer. The bare facts themselves are to be found in files upon files of government publications, all in different coloured covers, blue, white, yellow, &c., and all equally colourless in their contents ; or in more attractive and less accurate private publications.[1] Here was a province of Europe, the seat of the most ancient continuous civilization of the West, inhabited by the most progressive and promising western races, subjected by the deliberate policy of western governments to an eastern obscurantism such as even the fellaheen of Egypt had thrown off. A province where the whole social structure consisted of two classes, a peasantry unprotected by law or order, and a predatory proletariat. This latter class was composed of Ottoman officials, Moslem beys, Greek ecclesiastics, Bulgar bands, Albanian brigands, and the human vermin that misery always collects to prey upon itself. The Jew merchants of

---

[1] The pessimism of official publications and the partiality of private reports are two serious difficulties to the student. Official pessimism is probably to be accounted for by a toughening of the sensibilities in self-defence when the natural outlet of disgust and despair in active protest is denied. The partiality of the views of those who are not so restricted from expressing their indignation is generally due to the obvious outlet being some form of violent partisanship.

Salonica, the Vlach traders, and the Moslem peasant did
enjoy some measure of protection and of prosperity; but
even the moslemized Bulgar or Slav, combining the patience
of his race with the privileges of his religion, was driven to
the verge of revolt.

The three burdens which broke the back of the Bulgar or
Serb peasant and the Greek townsman, inured as they all
were to misery and maltreatment, were the Ottoman official,
the Albanian freebooter, and the Macedonian partisan. The
object of the Ottoman official, whether a truculent gendarme,
a half-starved clerk, or a plethoric pasha, was to get as much
money as would pay his superior enough to secure him in
his position and leave him enough to live on. The higher
his position the greater his plunder. If, in the process, the
Macedonian who paid for all was ruined, his house raided,
his women raped, what matter? That had always been the
way of it—*eskisi gibi*: with luck, *Inshallah!* it will last
our time. The object of the Albanian, whether as bekji
(village watchman) in times of truce, or as bashi-bazouk
(freebooter) in times of disturbance, was to get what he could
by force in a world which gave him no other means of earning
his livelihood. If the Macedonian was exterminated the
Albanian could at the worst take his place and cultivate his
land. The object of the partisan Bulgar, Greek, or Serb was
to strengthen the cause for which he was risking his life by
making life, if possible, more intolerable to any one who was
not of his party.

It is not necessary to examine the various methods by
which their extortions were effected or the various outrages
on reason and humanity by which they were enforced. Each
petty tyranny, as a rule, had different methods of extortion
by law, by fraud, and by force. The official extorted in the
name of the law, though he generally did not take the trouble
to apply it or even to learn what it was. The amount and the
administration of some taxes was elaborately prescribed in
laws borrowed wholesale from the French; others were

assessed by rule of thumb and levied by rule of thumbscrew. In both cases the result was much the same ; and the flock of Angora goats was killed off or the cherry trees were cut down as the most economic way of avoiding the penalties of prosperity. It is perhaps expressive of the situation that the taxation most resented was that which was collected with the most conscientious observance of the law—the revenues assigned to payment of the Ottoman debt and administered by the agents of the Turkish bondholders. This resentment was not because the raising of these revenues for the benefit of the foreign creditors and of the imperial credit was morally the most objectionable of all the imposts on the peasant—in that it made him pay for moneys lent by European civilization to keep him in subjection to Asiatic barbarism ; but because the money paid to the agent of the Ottoman debt brought the peasant no return either in a present protection or in a promise of better things. On the other hand, the least legal of the calls made on him, that of the partisan organization, was the most willingly met ; for this at least secured him some small protection of life and some faint hope of liberty.

Enough has been said to show that while the Ottoman Porte, the European Powers, and even the Balkan Principalities' drowned the clamour from Macedonia with antiphones of Peace! Peace!—there was no peace. War entered into every relation of life ; and it was a warfare so intimate and inherent to all social relations that it was more ruinous morally and materially than a formal state of war. Warfare such as that in Macedonia means a moratorium of law and order, not merely of business and financial operations ; and the longer it lasts the lower it reduces the standard of civilization. To a country in such circumstances as Macedonia formal and final war comes as a blessing and not a curse. The Bulgar popular saying has been for many years, ' Better an end with horrors than horrors without end '.

It was on such a rotten and restless foundation as this that the peace of Europe reposed. The balance of power in Europe, the balance of powerlessness in the Balkans—both rested on an ' existing order ' in Macedonia where order in no respect and in no relation existed. Such a Temple of Peace must have collapsed at once but for the various counter-strains and complications that propped up and pinned together the absurd edifice. Even as the collapse of a great engineering enterprise will leave vast weights in an equipoise more delicate than any engineer could attempt, and in an equilibrium so unstable as to make the least touch a danger.

It was in the valley of the Vardar—that is, in southern Macedonia and Salonica—that all these counter-strains con-centred. Some of the heaviest stresses were set up by the pressures inward of the outer ring of great Land Powers, Austria, Russia, and Italy, which were passed on and aug-mented by the inner ring of Balkan States. These pressures were all directed upon the vacuum caused by the collapse of the Ottoman Empire on Macedonia ; and on intervening peoples they had both a penetrating and a pushing effect. The most formidable of them was the penetration of Austria through Old Serbia towards Salonica, which had secured an international sanction at Berlin and was for some years represented by Austrian garrisons in the Sanjak of Novi-Bazar. The Russian penetration towards Scutari and the Adriatic had less diplomatic authority but more democratic acceptance ; and was reinforced by a subservient dynasty at Belgrade and a subsidized one at Cettinje. Both penetra-tions had a serious breach of continuity ; that of Austria in the Russophil Serbs, that of Russia in the Austrophil Roumanians. On the other hand, the effect of the pushing pressures of Austria and Russia are seen in the serious encroachment of those empires on the ethnological domains of the Balkan States. These encroachments, by crushing the Balkan States together and compelling them to expand at the expense of one another, have contributed perhaps more than anything else to the deplorable War of Partition. Thus the pressure of Austria and Russia on Roumania, by depriving it of the purely Roumanian Bukovina and Bessarabia in the west and north, drove the Roumanians east and south, first into the Bulgarian Dobrudcha by the Treaty of Berlin, and now by the Treaty of Bucharest into Bulgaria proper up to the Turtukai-Baltchik line. Again, the pressure of Austria on the Serbs has left only a numerically and geographically insignificant part of the Serb race to the independent States of Serbia and Montenegro. It has also forced the frontier of Serbia east and south, first over the Bulgar districts of Pirot and now, as a result of the War of Partition, over those of Macedonia. It has also forced the Montenegrin frontier southward; though the sublime disregard of the Albanian highlanders for treaties that trade off their mountains has checked this process in the interior, while the equally fortunate disregard of European statesmen for international appearances has twice, by a naval demonstration, saved Scutari and its seaboard to a future Albania. It is obvious that the result of both pushing and penetrative pressures in Macedonia must have been greatly to increase the friction there between the rival races and the difficulty of composing their rival claims.

In the racial struggle for Macedonia good ink and bad blood have been poured out without stint. No ink has been more wasted than the floods expended on the historic and ethnic claims of each party. The historic claim has at least this advantage, that some facts can be definitely fixed, such as the duration of the Macedonian Empires known as Bulgar and Serb. Macedonia, broadly speaking, was held by the Byzantine Empire against Slavs and Bulgars from Basil the Macedonian to Basil the Bulgar-Slayer. There was a Bulgar Empire from 963 to 1018 under Samuel, a Bulgar Vlach Empire from 1196 to 1241, and a short but brilliant Serb Empire under Dushan from 1430 to 1458. In the intervals, Byzantine, that is to say, Greek, rule was more or less established. Such political facts as the hegemony of one or other of the rival races in the early Middle Ages have no doubt a sentimental value in stimulating national feeling; but the extreme use of such appeals and special pleadings by Greek and Servian advocates before the tribunal of European public opinion rather suggests a weak case in more practical and more present respects. The historical claim does not carry conviction, and when we come to such more practical matters as ethnological and ethnographical claims we find ourselves at sea amongst specious statistics of no real value at all. Only a few broad facts are ascertainable either by study or by travel. Such a one is the fact that the population of Macedonia consists in part of those who are really Greeks, Bulgars, and Serbs, and who are to be found in the border districts of their respective frontiers : Greeks in Epirus and the Roumlouk, Serbs in Old Servia, and Bulgars east of the Vardar; and that the remainder is a mixed medley which, with the exception of the Vlachs or Roumanians, Jews, and Albanians, may be called Macedonian. These Macedonians have a character and a dialect of their own, such as would justify their being considered one of the many distinct Yugo-Slav types. Their dialect is rather more Bulgar than Serb, but lacks the most distinctive Bulgar characteristics ; and the same might be said of their character. What is, however, of most present and practical importance is that this population, at one time without national consciousness, has by the educational efforts of the Bulgar people been to a very large extent Bulgarized in its sympathies. They have for a quarter-century been educated as Bulgars ; have fought as Bulgars in 1895, 1903, and 1912 ; were annexed to Bulgaria by the Russians in 1878 and by the Serbs in 1912 ; were assigned to the Bulgar Church by the Turks in 1872 and 1897 ; and are to-day, many of them, perhaps most of them, protesting against being treated other than as Bulgars. The claims of other countries were less obvious and often suspect of being based on gerrymandered constituencies or jugglings between the methods of counting votes. The Greek relied on the religious test and the statistics of the priests : the Serbs relied on grammar and the statistics of Mr. Goptchevitch : the Roumanians or Kutzo-Vlach relied on Turkey and Austria and Mr. Apostolos Margerides. Many permutations were possible when a Bulgar Serbophone Patriarchist might be reckoned as either a Bulgar, or a Serb, or a Greek, or all three. He would very likely call himself a Roumanian because it had been made worth his while ; or on the other hand he would fail in being counted at all because he was exercising the only real manhood suffrage open to him with a Bulgar ' komitet ' in the mountains.

The main lines of the constituencies of the principal races in Macedonia have, however, a distinct relation to their race-character and will be readily grasped by any one who has read what precedes on the subject. A glance at any ethnographical map of the peninsula shows that the Greeks, as might be expected, hold the coast and the principal towns ; though they share Salonica with the Jews—Adrianople with Bulgars and Turks—and Constantinople with Jews, Armenians, and Turks. Behind them the Bulgars hold the fertile plains and to the north of them are the Albanians and Serbs.[1] It will be noticed at once that the ethnographical division of this territory—the national frontiers—run east and west transversely to the peninsula ; while the geographic divisions of ranges and valleys—the natural frontiers—run north and south, or vertically. This is a very important contributory cause of the Macedonian question and of both the Balkan wars. It caused the first war, the coalition for the expulsion of Turkey, because there was in Macedonia no one sufficient

---

[1] No such map can be accepted as an accurate or authoritative partition of Macedonia. It would be hopeless to attempt to reconcile an Athenian ethnographic map, where only a few pale-pink cloudlets stain the blue Hellenic empyrean, with a Bulgar map where all is *couleur de rose* except for some unwholesome-looking blue spots. The only general rule seems to be to mark as Turkish what cannot safely be claimed or conceded. This gives an impression of impartiality, and does no harm.

fulcrum, either in race or religion, either in national or in
' neighbourhood ' interest, upon which the force of nationality
could so work as to decide the fate of this debatable land.
The Greeks, in spite of their sea power in the Aegean and
the national idea that drove them along the land route
towards Constantinople, could not hope to make good and
maintain their claim to the coast-strip against the right of
the Bulgars to some sea front on the Aegean and against the
military occupation of the Turks. The Serbs, cut off from
the Adriatic by the Austrian claim on the Sanjak and by
the Austrian coast-strip of Dalmatia, were driven to demand
an access to the Aegean across both the Bulgar and the
Greek claims. The Bulgars, who had the largest unredeemed
population, could not expect to make good their ethnographic
claim to the interior of Macedonia and their economic claim
to a seaport, against the opposition of Turks, Greeks, and
Serbs. The Albanians were ready on general principles to
attack the flank or rear of any movement against the Turk.
In short, no one Balkan State could pursue its legitimate
national development in Macedonia either by turning out
the Ottoman Empire or by standing off the Austro-
Hungarian Empire, without also having all the three other
Balkan peoples on its back. Thus the Albanians supported
by Austria prevented Greece getting Epirus at the Treaty of
Berlin. The Serbs supported by Austria would have prevented the Bulgars getting eastern Roumelia in 1885 if they
had not been defeated as they deserved. The Bulgars
supported morally the Ottoman government in defeating
the Greek invasion of the Roumlouk in 1897, and supported
morally the Austrian government in disregarding Serbian
aspirations in Bosnia in 1908.

In a situation of such difficulty and delicacy as that created
by the rivalries of the Great Powers and of the Balkan
nations, it is obvious that conservative interests would be
strong enough to check any influence for change that was
not driven by the full dynamic force of some national

movement. No such national democratic energy was forthcoming from public opinion in the Great Powers ; and the
reversionary interests of the European Governments were
as much served by the maintenance of the existing status
as were the vested interests of the Turk and his European
creditors. The diplomacy of the Sea Powers was passively
deprecatory, that of the Land Powers predatorily passive.
Nor was there any national energy for change forthcoming
at this time from the two youngest and most vigorous of
the Balkan peoples—Albania and Bulgaria. Albania for
democratic, and Bulgaria for diplomatic reasons, were anxious
to keep things much as they were. There remained, therefore, only the Serbs and Greeks : and they were the most
strategically remote, the least racially interested, and at the
end of the nineteenth century the least militarily effective
of the Balkan States. For after the rout at Slivnitza in
1885 and the flight from Larissa in 1897, Serbia and Greece
could scarcely undertake a military initiative against the
wishes of Bulgaria or Turkey.

Nevertheless there were not wanting signs that a pacific
solution was still possible either by agreement of the Balkan
peoples or by authority of the European Powers. There
was a period—from the proposal of Tricoupis in 1891 for
a Balkan partition of Macedonia until the Young Turk
revolution in 1908—when practical politics still permitted of
a choice of two solutions of the Macedonian Question. One
solution, that of nationalism, was a partition of spheres of
influence by arrangement between the Balkan States ; the
other solution, that of internationalism, was the establishment of an autonomous province under the guarantee of the
Powers. The choice was now between partition or protection,
for the old imperialist solution by regeneration of the Ottoman
Empire was almost dead ; though it still survived among
a few British conservatives.

§ 8. THE MACEDONIAN QUESTION, 1891–1903

The War of Partition cannot fairly be ascribed altogether to such remissness as there was on the part of the Balkan nations in not agreeing among themselves as to a division of European Turkey before going to war. Nor can the War of Coalition be attributed in any way to a refusal, on their part, to give the Powers plenty of time to put an end to Turkish misrule there. Moreover, their failure in both respects—in that, after a War of Coalition, Turkey still holds Thrace, and in that, after a War of Partition, there is still a Macedonian question—is not entirely their fault. If, after expelling the Turks and opening Turkey in Europe to peaceful exploitation, they brought them back again and made the peninsula an armed camp—this is only what the Great Powers had done at San Stefano or Berlin a generation before. Moreover, the deficiencies of the Treaty of Bucharest that falsify the Balkan situation are due to far more vital and inveterate difficulties than those which defaced the Treaty of Berlin.

The first practical expression of the principle that the Balkan peoples should alone dispose as to the Balkan Peninsula, was given by the proposal of Tricoupis, the Greek Premier, in 1891 ; and, thereafter, the possibility of a coalition on the basis of an agreement as to spheres of influence was always a political possibility. But nothing could be done on these lines because it was not in the real interests of the national movement either of Bulgaria or Albania, that the Greeks and Serbs should be admitted to so large a share of Macedonia and Albania as would have been necessary. It was, indeed, neither Turkish military strength nor Austrian diplomatic combinations that postponed a settlement by partition until the twentieth century ; but the opposition brought against such a settlement by Albania and Bulgaria.

The reasons for Albanian opposition are not far to seek ; for this youngest of the Balkan peoples had obviously nothing to hope from the break-up of the Empire. The Albanian was the spoilt child and the *enfant terrible* of the Balkan nursery. His barbarous independent institutions contained little that was subversive of Ottoman sovereignty, though they were generally a sufficient safeguard against Turkish tyranny. He was satisfied if he were let alone and did not require that his autonomy should be regularized in formal Ottoman edicts or guaranteed by European recognition. In return he was always ready to do yeoman's service—Irish yeoman's service—in repressing the other Balkan races, in supporting the Palace against the Porte, and generally in combining for Abdul Hamid all the duties of a highland cateran for his chief. He was the Kurd of Roumelia. The Albanian body-guard of Yildiz and the Albanian bekji in the Macedonian village were the left hand of the Turkish grasp of Macedonia. The right hand, of course, was the Anatolian regular soldiers. The guerrilla war carried on by the Albanians against the Serbs, the Bulgars, and the Greeks was incessant, although it was not waged equally at all times and along the whole line. In the north, against the Montenegrins, it was a war of extermination in which an equality of impregnable mountains and indefatigable manslaughter on either side prevented any definite result; but in Old Serbia the Albanian was steadily driving the softer Serb out of a less rugged country. In the Bulgars of West Macedonia the Albanian met his match, and on them he could make no permanent impression; though with the help of the Ottoman Government he was able to keep in check the Bulgar national movement there by preventing any increase in the numbers or prosperity of the Bulgar population. The South Albanian, the Tosk, was of milder mood than the Gheg mountaineer; and this, with a more open and fertile soil, gave the struggles between Greeks and Albanians for Epirus a more civilized form. Scutari fought Cettinje with long-barrelled rifles and bell-mouthed blunderbusses; Koritza fought Athens with Skipitar grammars and Latin alphabets. But both national culture and national consciousness are still somewhat forced and exotic growths in Albania. It was obvious that they would not avail to secure from the Balkan States much recognition for Albanian independence in a general break-up of the Empire. It is, indeed, a very interesting instance of the devious lines of least resistance along which a nationality movement advances that Albania, by the very fact of its primitive civilization and of its predatory relationships with surrounding civilizations, should have been led to contribute to the prolongation of the Ottoman Empire, and thereby to the preservation of its own independence. The Albanians kept the Ottoman Empire going until the revolution of 1908, because to the Albanians the unregenerate régime of Abdul Hamid meant licence to plunder in Macedonia, liberal pay in Constantinople, and a *laisser faire* policy in Albania. Their support of the Empire meant that any enemy of it in Macedonia would be placed between two fires, that of the Turkish garrisons from the east, and that of the Albanian guerrilla from the west. Further, the mere existence of their untamed barbarism discouraged the penetrations of European civilization from the west and complicated all schemes of reform. The result of Albanian policy seems to show that a democracy free to follow its own foreign policy, however unprogressive that policy may seem, is not likely to make a mistake prejudicial to its progress. By force of no movement other than its restless and reactionary guerrilla, with no dynastic or diplomatic representation, Albania has now not only obtained full independence, but an independence that has the coveted international guarantee. Albania in 1909, 1910, and 1911 fought the Turks single-handed, and not without success; for the terms accorded to Albania after the campaign of pacification, conducted by Torgut Pasha, compare favourably with those obtained by Serbia after its first insurrection. By one of the inimitable ironies of the diplomatic drama Albania owes its present position, more favourable in some respects than that of many of the Balkan States, to the self-interested intervention of its two hereditary enemies. The Serb drove the Turk out of Albania and then was driven out by the Austrian. The Albanian highlander has capped Cavour ; and the instinctive diplomacy of the Albanian democracy in supporting the Ottoman Empire has been amply justified by results. Bulgarian support of the Empire was, on the other hand, entirely diplomatic. The Bulgarian position at the end of the nineteenth century was almost as isolated as that of Albania. The short quarter-century following Bulgarian emancipation had been made use of in making up arrears of progress at a pace such as can be paralleled only in the development of newly opened reservations in the Western States. Besides this, the recovery of Eastern Roumelia had restored to Bulgaria about half the unredeemed territory which the Treaty of Berlin had taken away, and had raised Bulgarian military prestige to the first place in the peninsula by the notable feat of arms against Serbia and Russia. But these civil and military achievements, while securing to Bulgaria predominance in the Balkans and independence of the Great Powers, had left her without a friend. None the less an ally was indispensable, for there was no prospect at all that Bulgaria could repeat, in regard to Macedonia, the *coup de main* by which Eastern Roumelia had been recovered. Even in 1885 the risk had been great. On that occasion, Austria and Russia had assumed that a sudden Serbian invasion supported by Austria, combined with an equally unexpected withdrawal of Russian support from Bulgaria leaving the Bulgar army officerless, would assure the punishment of the principality for its independent initiative. If the conspiracy had not been promptly defeated by the flight of the Serb army from the soldier's battle of Slivnitza, the same policy would no doubt have launched Roumania, Greece, and Turkey against the presumptuous principality. But it took time to persuade Roumania to take up her future rôle as gendarme for the Powers that had robbed her of the Bukowina and of Bessarabia. Meantime Greece, to whom England had just given Thessaly, was kept quiet by a naval

demonstration of the Sea Powers, and Turkey was cowed by
a single-handed ambassadorial demonstration on the part of
Sir William White. In 1885 the Balkan democracies had
not yet been abandoned altogether by the democratic Sea
Powers to the diplomacies of the Land Powers; but ten
years later Balkan matters had been left wholly to the dual
control of Austria and Russia, and from them Bulgaria could
expect little quarter if an attempt were made to annex
Macedonia. There was, however, far more Bulgarian pressure
as to annexation of Macedonia, which was still under direct
Ottoman administration and exposed to the propaganda of
the other races, than there had been as to the self-governed
and segregated Eastern Roumelia. The whole of Southern
Macedonia and Northern Thrace was a Bulgaria *irredenta*
where the kinsmen of a free folk and fierce fighters were
being subjected, almost in sight, to a most cruel and shameful
ill-usage. In Stambouloff Bulgaria found a statesman who
could deal with the dilemma both diplomatically and democratically. The Stamboulovist policy was to give relief to
Macedonia by conciliating the sultan and to create a Macedonian national consciousness such as would enable it to
annex itself to Bulgaria eventually by force of its own nationality
movement. The Ottoman Empire was to be maintained in
Macedonia and Thrace· until all danger from the ambitions of
Austria or Russia, Serbia or Greece, was over. The Macedo-
Bulgar population were to be educated and encouraged in a
national consciousness until some form of guaranteed local
government became necessary. Then at some future favourable
conjuncture the coup of 1885 might be safely repeated. Secured
from Russian interference by a good understanding with
Roumania, and from Austria-Hungary by a friendship with
Serbia, Bulgaria could hold the balance between Greece and
Turkey, isolate Macedonia and Thrace, and leave the rest to
the force of circumstances and the fortune of the circumspect.

It was on this rock that the first attempt at a Balkan coalition
split when Tricoupis, the Greek Premier, proposed in 1891 to

Bulgaria and Serbia an aggressive alliance against Turkey on
the basis of an agreement as to partition. The proposal was
neither premature nor inopportune. Tricoupis and Stambouloff
were the two strongest Balkan statesmen of the last century,
and in the last decade of that century Bulgaria and Greece were
already strong enough to impose a joint policy both upon
Europe and upon Asia ; while the political and practical
difficulty of a Graeco-Bulgar partition would have been much
less then than it was in the succeeding century. But the
programme broke down. The Turkish Minister at Belgrade
by an ' indiscretion ' of the Serbs got wind of the matter.
Stambouloff, scorning such subterfuges, betrayed the proposal
to the Porte, and bargained on the strength of it for Macedonian bishoprics. Tricoupis resigned and Greece drifted
single-handed into a disastrous war. Stambouloff's policy
seemed likely to be justified, for it brought Macedonia well
within reach of Bulgaria. But this Bismarck of the Balkans with
a Louis Napoleon for a sovereign, was not to have the chance
of proving that his Fabian policy might have prevented both
the Balkan wars and the loss of Macedonia to Bulgaria.

Stambouloff's assertion of the principle of the Balkan peninsula for the Balkan peoples, went to the length of including
Turkey as a Balkan State the better to exclude Austria and
Russia. This required a great renunciation both from the
people and their prince. It seemed to deny the people all hope
of liberating their Macedonian kindred, whose lot daily became
worse ; it seemed to deny to the prince all hope of regularizing
his position through the recognition of the emperors—of the Tsar
especially. It might well seem to the Bulgars that a policy of
educating the Macedonians to insurrection, while supporting
their tyrants, was suicidal ; while Ferdinand might reasonably
think that the promotion of Bulgaria to be a sovereign state
and recognition of its prince was better than a Turkish vassalage with the risk of repeating the catastrophe of Alexander's
deposition by Russia. The superiority of democratic over
diplomatic foreign policy both in instinct and in intention

becomes evident when we see the Bulgar people prepared to trust Stambouloff with the Bulgar succession in Macedonia, while the Bulgar prince was not prepared to trust him with the Coburg succession in Bulgaria. Stambouloff was driven from power in 1892 and assassinated in 1894. Ten years later the shadow of Bulgarian kingship was won by diplomatizing, and five years later the bone of contention, Bulgar-Macedonia, was lost by it.

After the death of Stambouloff, during the years immediately preceding the Balkan wars, Bulgarian foreign policy becomes confused and contradictory between its two objectives: the dynastic objective to be pursued through relations with Austria and Russia, and the democratic objective in Macedonia to be pursued through relations with the Turks and other Balkan peoples. It loses principle and strategic design and becomes tactical and opportunist. The Bulgarian policy no longer controls the Balkan developments, but is controlled by them. The Roumanian alliance is lost, and Roumania under Bratiano is understood in 1897 to have an alliance with Austria promising Roumania a slice of Bulgaria. The offer by Greece, on going to war with Turkey, of a portion of Macedonia is refused under Russian pressure. Attempts at a Serbo-Bulgar Customs union in 1905 break down under Austrian pressure. Bulgarian foreign policy has lost force and principle, and has become diplomacy.

The preponderance of dynastic influence in Bulgar policy led to democratic elements detaching themselves from the government policy and acting for themselves in that 'foreign' question which concerned them most—the relations with the Macedo-Bulgars. The organization of the Bulgar movement in Macedonia was carried by the fighting section, and the relations with Macedonia were no longer under the complete control of the Bulgarian Government. The Macedonian organization was split into a fighting faction and a Fabian faction, the Government supporting the latter but not strong enough to suppress the former. Indeed Stambouloff himself would have found it difficult to restrain the *saeva indignatio* of a young generation of educated Bulgars divided by a treaty-line into bond and free. The result of these divided councils was that the party of action came more and more into control of Macedonian relations, and that its policy was guided by desperate men determined at all costs to raise the necessary national impetus for an isolated Bulgar action. The Bulgar insurrections of 1893 and the massacres that followed, the Bulgar dynamite outrages on Salonica, and the desultory but desperate fights between Bulgar bands and the Turks even in Constantinople itself, made a rupture between Bulgaria and Turkey inevitable. This made Bulgarian diplomacy all the more anxious to keep in with those powers which controlled the policy of Turkey and Roumania—that is to say, the Triple Alliance. While a section of the Bulgar democracy was forcing a forward policy which would leave Bulgaria diplomatically isolated to struggle single-handed with Turkey like Greece in 1908, Bulgarian diplomacy was desperately trying to play the waiting game of Stambouloff without enjoying the national confidence that was an essential factor in it. In such circumstances as those of Bulgaria in regard to Macedonia a Fabian policy requires a forceful personality.

Bulgarian diplomacy still thought that patience might win all Bulgar Macedonia and save the sacrifices of partition; but Bulgar democracy was losing patience and forced on insurrection, without troubling about agreements with the other Balkan peoples as to spheres of influence or even as to military support. It was clear that war between Bulgaria and Turkey, under very unfavourable conditions for the former, could only be avoided if the more liberal Powers, Great Britain and France, perhaps with support from Russia, pressed on provincial autonomy for Macedonia. Unsuccessful insurrections by the party of action with the resulting ' atrocities ' would stimulate such intervention and might cure the evil by the remedy of a European pacification before the crisis of a war with Turkey was reached. In 1903 the insurrections began. The division in the Macedo-Bulgar revolutionary organization sufficiently accounted for their failure, while the Turkish repressions did move Europe to interest and a very mild form of intervention.

Therewith the alternative policy to Macedonian partition—guaranteed provincial autonomy—came to the front until it in turn failed.

§ 9. THE MACEDONIAN QUESTION, 1903–8

Partition of Turkey in Europe could not be effected owing to the opposition of Albania and Bulgaria; while on the other hand the *status quo* could not be long preserved owing to the insurrectionary force that the Bulgars and Macedo-Bulgars were developing in Macedonia. Consequently the peace of the Balkans and indirectly the peace of Europe depended on establishing some form of administrative autonomy for the disturbed European provinces of the Empire. It was now a matter for the Concert of Europe to decide whether the territories of Epirus, Macedonia, and Thrace should obtain self-government by European intervention or by a war of the Balkan States against Turkey, and whether the future nationality of these territories should be decided between the Balkan States by war or pacifically by Europe. What the Concert of Europe could effect by a joint naval demonstration the Balkan States could effect only by a coalition and a successful campaign. The working partners of the Concert in the business of the Balkan settlement have been shown to be Great Britain and Russia, the leading Sea and Land Powers, on whose agreement all progress in settlement of the Eastern Question depends; and a previous chapter reviewed the failure of these Powers to take advantage of the long opportunity of settlement offered between the years 1820–80. The main responsibility for that failure was assigned to Great Britain; but in this final opportunity, which was much shorter, lasting only for about a decade, 1898–1908, the responsibility for failure must be borne chiefly by Russia.

The general alignment of the Powers during this period was favourable to joint action by these two Powers or to independent action by either of them. The old feud between Great

Britain and Russia was almost dead in the Near East, although in the Far East it still affected the relations between the Governments. It did not disappear until later, when the Dual Alliance of France and Russia was converted by the accession of Great Britain into the Triple Agreement, so as to restore the balance of power disturbed by the destruction of the Russian naval power in the Far East and the development of the German naval power in the too near West. But in the decade we are now dealing with, 1898–1908, London still could have acted in Eastern Europe independently of Petersburg, and could have forced Russia into action and agreement by an initiative in favour of Bulgaria. France, the ally of Russia and a Sea Power with liberal dispositions, would have joined in, and Italy would not have opposed. The opposition would have come from the reactionary Land Powers, Berlin, which had interests in Asia Minor, and was prepared consequently to go considerable lengths in support of the Hamidian régime, and Vienna, whose ambitions in Macedonia imposed an irremediable hostility to progress there in any form.   Vienna might, however, have been bought off with formal recognition of the *de facto* occupation of Bosnia and Herzegovina, and Berlin by recognition of the interests attaching to German railway rights in Anatolia. Greece and Serbia, the former discredited by defeat, the latter by dynastic dissensions, would have necessarily acquiesced in an autonomy for Macedonia even though this might well have secured the Bulgar succession there. Turkey, under Abdul Hamid, could have been dealt with by naval demonstration in the 'nineties without risk of the revolutionary results that attended this action ten years later.

But the only motive powers for progress were the democracies of Bulgaria and Great Britain, and the link between them was a very remote and abstract one. It consisted of a dim recognition by the better informed of the British democracy that a prompt realization of the Bulgar national claim to South Macedonia and Thrace was the only basis of permanent peace in the Balkans, and that Great Britain was responsible for this not having been accomplished a quarter of a century before;

and by a dim recognition on the part of the Bulgar people that
Great Britain was the only Power disinterested and democratic
enough to take trouble to get them autonomy without wanting
to be paid for it.   There was little business connexion between
Great Britain and Bulgaria—for the city, the heart of the Empire,
was interested only in the Ottoman debt; and where the
treasure is there will the heart be also.   There was no sentimental
connexion as there had been in the case of the Greeks; for
neither the Bulgars nor the British are an emotional people,
and neither had anything to give the other.   Nor was there any
direct advantage to Great Britain in an extension of Bulgaria
such as might be held to justify an adventurous diplomacy.
There was merely the indirect advantage to a maritime people
exporting capital and manufactures, in developing its business
relations with an inland industrious people, and in removing
a menace to the general peace.   These moral responsibilities and
far-sighted foreign policies might have been converted into a
force of public opinion by Gladstone, but Gladstone died before
the crisis came.   Moreover the British democratic demand for
reform was largely diverted to Asia Minor and Crete by the
Armenian atrocities, and by the Greek activities of the middle
'nineties.   On the whole, therefore, it is very creditable to
British diplomacy if so much quiet pressure for reform was
applied to the ' steam roller' of the European Concert that it
did actually begin to move.   An independent initiative would
perhaps in the end have been safer because quicker; and we
can now see that it would probably have succeeded where the
more cautious indirect procedure failed.   But the diplomatic
advantage of concerted action in dealings with Abdul Hamid
when all the European governments took different views was
undeniable; while the democratic danger of too deliberate an
advance were not so obvious.   It was indeed much to expect of
the British Government that it should take an independent
initiative in the general interests of Europe as a whole, but
against the wishes of the most interested European governments, and without any special mandate from public opinion.

It is too much to expect, even of the most enlightened diplomacy, that it should strain its relations with its most powerful neighbours by practising towards its poor dependants the precepts of Christian ethics and common-sense equity. Therefore, none could well blame the British Government for pressing Macedonian autonomy through the agency of the interested Land Powers, Austria and Russia. But the result was that it could not get them to move until the wars in South Africa and Manchuria had deprived Great Britain and Russia of any driving force in the Balkans. Anglo-German relations had, moreover, become so strained over the Boer war that the risk of a collision in respect of German protection of the Ottoman Empire was to be avoided, in the interests of European peace, at almost any cost to Balkan humanity. Besides this, Anglo-Russian relations were too strained by the Anglo-Japanese Alliance to allow of close co-operation over Balkan policy.

While the state of Macedonia became annually worse, the Austro-Russian ' diplomatic ' agreement to keep things as they were in the Balkans, in combination with German protection of the Porte, blocked British and Russian ' democratic ' demands for reform. The Bulgar-Macedonian organization continued, *pro forma*, to make futile appeals for a European guarantee of autonomy, and to work up the conditions of Macedonia to a pitch at which insurrections and repressions could be produced whenever the political situation took a favourable turn. On the other hand the Greek, Vlach, and Serb complications grew annually as their propaganda tried to make up for lost time in Macedonia, and intrigued with Austria and Turkey against an autonomy which would favour the Bulgar cause. The Turks on their side further confused matters by continually introducing reforms which were in themselves reactions, but which were none the less accepted by the reactionary Land Powers who were acting as the mandatories of Europe.

It has been argued that Byzantinism is the *fons et origo*

mali in the decline and fall of the Ottoman Empire. If this
be so, then the one essential of a reform that is to keep
Turkish rule going, is the separation of the province from the
metropolis. Once a sufficient measure of separation has been
secured, the various factors of disturbance in the autonomous
province can be left safely to work out a permanent *modus
vivendi* for themselves. Where a ' nationality ' movement
supplies no force of gravitation to draw the autonomous
province into a neighbouring nation it remains a part of the
Empire, as the Lebanon has—and as Armenia would ; otherwise it is drawn quietly away as Crete and Eastern Roumelia
have been. The only essentials for this peaceful settlement
by autonomy are that separation be sufficient and secure;
sufficient in providing independent power of the purse, and
secure in providing a European guarantee. Given these two
conditions it does not much matter how the independent
authority is constituted, or what form the guarantee takes.
The province would follow its own line of least resistance
no matter whether it was given an elaborate paper constitution as was Eastern Roumelia which was absorbed in three
years ; or a short international statute such as that of
Samos which after repeated modifications in a democratic
sense by agreement between the islanders and the Sultan,
lasted over half a century. Indeed Samos has undoubtedly
enjoyed itself more in its own Greek way under the
Sultan's rule, as filtered through this long obsolete statute,
than has Cyprus under the conscientious and cast-iron constitutionalism of the British. Above all else the European
guarantee is indispensable because without it there can be
no local government capable of resisting the centralizing and
corrupting influences of Constantinople. With a guarantee,
the rather anomalous autonomy of the Lebanon prospered
in spite of a mixture of hostile races and religions, with no
particular regional *raison d'être* ; indeed it would be difficult
to find a district with fewer components of a nation than the
Lebanon. Without a guarantee the ancient autonomies of

the Aegean islands were absorbed in spite of the uniformity and unanimity of their Greek population.

The one and only essential in a Macedonian reform scheme was an administrative authority, such as a governor, disposing of the revenues of the province subject to a fixed imperial contribution and responsible to, and removable by, Europe alone. Such an independence would have satisfied all parties : the Powers because it would have maintained the *status quo* while checking atrocities, and the Powers are all for procrastination and peace at any price: the Bulgars because any measure of autonomy promised them in time a peaceable succession, and the Bulgars are a patient and provident race : the Greeks and Serbs because their claim could not be in a worse position than they were and postponement might possibly bring things their way : the Palace because such a form of separation from the top was most easily reconcilable superficially with Ottoman supremacy though in substance it struck at the root of it. Abdul Hamid could have played the democratic suzerain in Macedonia as well as in Samos ; no doubt to the considerable embarrassment of the guaranteed governor. So also the Macedonian Moslem, while enjoying the benefits of the independent fisc, would have continued to enjoy the sense of social superiority even more indispensable to him than his political privileges. In Bosnia or in India the Christian is as free as the Moslem, but the latter need not consider him an equal.

The weak point of so many paper reform schemes was that they assumed social equality and fraternity to be an essential element of liberty in a society still in a mediaeval state of civilization and under a military dominion ; whereas making the Christians of the Ottoman Empire equals of the Moslems did not necessarily increase their liberty, while it quite destroyed any possibility of fraternity. Giving the vote to the negroes of the Southern States did not improve their position in any way. Christian and Moslem, black and white, men and women, cannot be made free, equal, and fraternal by law ; though when they are so in any respect, the law cannot long deny their equality in that respect. Another weak point on which reform schemes broke down was that the source of disorder and discontent was considered as being in the provinces where the symptoms broke out, instead of in the Byzantinism of the capital. This caused a great waste of time and trouble on elaborate local institutions such as foreign gendarmerie, financial assessors, local judicial reforms, and such like. These could only be local palliatives from the point of view of the Christian communities, while from the point of view of the Ottoman Empire they were far more prejudicial to its integrity than an administrative separation of the province from the capital, for they struck at the individual social supremacy that every Moslem expects as a right while under the Sultan and Khalif. The first mistake, that of over-elaborating administrative reforms instead of guaranteeing some simple system of self-government, enabled the Old Turk to stultify the efforts of the Powers in the nineteenth century. The second mistake, that of attacking Moslem supremacy instead of Ottoman sovereignty, enabled the Young Turk to stop Macedonian autonomy just as it was on the point of achievement.

The method by which the Old Turk dealt with the well-meant efforts of his friends to reform the more unsatisfactory portions of his Empire was to choke the cat with cream. Provincial reforms were by the clemency of the Sultan enlarged into Imperial revolutions ; that is to say, they would have been revolutions if they had been or could have been realized. As it was they were deprived of all significance and value, while Constantinople claimed the credit of having been more radical than the radicals. But this was not all ; for measures intended to decentralize became thereby an excuse for strengthening the autocracy that was arresting all national development. This last was more especially the case after the palace had finally dominated the Porte under Abdul Hamid. In the edicts of Hatti Humayun of 1856, and in the Hatti Sharif of 1839, there was still behind the

specious *Phrasenseligkeit* some real faith on the part of the
Porte in its own progressive possibilities. But under the
Asiatic autocracy of Abdul Hamid all professions of faith
in constitutionalism had become purely obstructive. When
the Constantinople conference endeavoured to prevent the
Russo-Turkish War by recommending devolution and local
government it was outbid and outmanœuvred by the imperial
constitution of 1876. No such counterstroke was thought
necessary for the elaborate reform scheme prepared in compliance with article 22 of the Treaty of Berlin for Macedonia
and Albania ; it was simply put in the pigeon-hole where
the constitution was already reposing. In 1896 inconvenient
attention having been drawn to Asia and to the Aegean by
Armenian massacres and Cretan insurrections, this attention
was distracted by a display of Macedonian ' reforms '.
Christians were to be admitted to the administration and to
the gendarmerie, while inspectors were to reform and report
everything. Needless to say, the Christians showed no
inclination to expose themselves uselessly either as ' mouavin '
or as gendarmes ; and the inspectors were merely so many
more Palace agents for the more thorough spoliation of
officials and peasants. By July, 1901, the ferment in Macedonia and fear of Europe produced another Palace scheme.
The Macedonian administration was divided between a commission at Constantinople and an Inspector-General at
Salonika, both under the personal control of Abdul Hamid.
Thus all pressure by the Powers, or strictly speaking by
Great Britain through the Powers, recommending remedies
for Byzantine over-centralization, was perverted by the Palace
into an aggravation of the evil.

The time was fast running out during which remedy by
peaceful intervention of the Powers would be possible. In
February 1903 Austria and Russia as ' mandatories ' ! of
Europe, or shall we say of England, recognized that action
was necessary ; but the action they took only made things
worse. The principle of the Palace reform was adopted, with

the difference that foreign assessors and gendarmes were
substituted for local Christians. This was sound in so far
as the foreign gendarme, being protected, could be efficient
to the extent that his powers and personality permitted. As
a matter of fact his jurisdiction was regulated generally by
the size of his boot-sole. It was worse than unsound in so
far as it permitted the introduction into Macedonia of
numerous Austrian and Russian officials. While the gendarmerie secteurs or districts were carefully drawn so as to
discourage any development into a partition on ethnographical lines, they were not so drawn or so distributed
between the Powers as to discourage local opinion from
seeing in them political designs of the Great Powers. Moreover, although the Austrian and Russian *condominium* was
confined to an advisory capacity, the exclusion of the rest of
Europe could not but be considered as ominous by observers
who had as many reasons for suspicion as had been given
to the Balkan States and to the parties in Macedonia. The
Christians saw an attack upon their future autonomy, or
upon their future annexation to the Balkan state of their
choice ; the Moslems saw an attack both on their social
supremacy and on their imperial sovereignty. Before even
the Austro-Russian reform policy of 1903 had been elaborated
and explained in the so-called Murzsteg programme of
October, there had been trouble, due quite as much to apprehension of Austria as to hatred of Turkey. It would not be
profitable, even if it were possible, to trace the cross-currents
of Macedonian politics so as to assign motive forces to all
the movements of this period ; but in the premature Bulgar
rising of Razlog and Monastir in 1902 and 1903—in the
Albanian rising in Kossovo—in the assassinations of Russian
consuls at Ipek and Monastir—in the Bulgar dynamite outrages in Salonica—in the calling to power in Sofia of the
Turkophil Petrov ministry—and in the rapid growth of
a Macedonian Moslem party, may be seen symptoms of
general dissatisfaction on the part of both Christians and

Moslems with the development of Austro-Russian control. It may be that the methods of the mandatory Powers were inspired by no ulterior motives ; but if so they showed an ignorance of the situation little to be expected from governments so deeply interested and so well informed.

So unsatisfactory did the situation become that the government of Great Britain, now free of its African troubles, insisted on reinforcing—or it might be more correct to say in replacing—the Austro-Russian intervention by one which included the other more liberal Powers. The addition of France, Italy, and Great Britain as intervening Powers infused •some real force into the reform movement and inspired some faith in its *bona fides*. It made possible a satisfactory settlement had there been still time left for the deliberate methods of the Concert; for while the change was in form merely the addition of British and French financial agents to those of Austria and Russia, in fact it meant business. The real significance of the fiscal separation thereby effected was shown by the Sultan's resistance. It required a naval demonstration in November 1905 and the occupation of the custom houses of Mitylene and Lemnos to force on him the acceptance of the new proposals. The British proposals were a real instalment of autonomy, and with drastic administration and perhaps a little further amplification would in time have accomplished their purpose ; but it may be suggested that no more force would have been required to compel the Sultan to establish a formal autonomy, such as would at once have secured permanent peace by putting Macedonia in the way of settling for itself the Macedonian question. But Great Britain was unable to carry Austria and Russia so far against German opposition, and perhaps could not have moved alone without risking worse dangers to European peace. Therefore during the three years that still remained before Macedonia took matters into its own hands, Great Britain did everything possible to force on a peaceful settlement by guaranteed autonomy, short of

imposing it by taking or threatening to take an independent
in:tiative. The reasons that prevented such an independent
British initiative do not concern us further than that they
must be held indirectly accountable for the Balkan wars.
No proposals for autonomy could succeed which did not
command the confidence of Bulgaria and of Macedonia :
none could command such confidence which did not offer
a sufficient guarantee not only against the despotism of the
Ottoman Government but also against the designs of the
Austrian Government; for no such guarantee could be given
except by an Anglo-Russian progressive policy in the Balkans.
As Great Britain could not assume so much responsibility
and Russian policy remained merely diplomatic with the
Austro-Russian agreement of 1897 for a basis, the last
opportunity passed.

Under these conditions the Balkan peoples, whether Greeks,
Bulgars, Serbs, or Albanians, had no wish that the Macedonian reform scheme should run its course, with the risk
that they would change King Log of Stamboul for King
Stork of Vienna. The Bulgars and Arnauts, the two fighting
nations of Macedonia, had already resisted by force of arms
any chance of reaction in the guise of reform. Their attempt
to keep the Austrian wolf from the door had only brought
him in as a sheep-dog. It was their other enemy, the
Ottoman wolf, that saved them by appearing in the guise
of a bell wether who needs no dog.

The transfer in 1906 to Salonica of the head-quarters of
the Committee of Union and Progress, which gave this
new Macedonian movement its central organization, its
political programme, and its popular name of 'Young
Turk', indicates clearly from whence came the impulse
that started the Turkish revolution. But for the opening
given it in organizing and directing the movement of the
Macedonian Moslem, the Committee would have remained
an insignificant conspiracy of exiles in Paris; and the 'Young
Turk' would have found no more important place in history

than have the Young Englanders. There was no possibility of the Committee making a start either in Constantinople or in Asia. The Constantinopolitan Levantine is not prepared to risk anything to reduce the centralization and corruption on which he lives, and the ignorant loyalty of the Asiatic Turk is proof against all reforming ideas. The driving force of the Turkish revolution was not, as is usually the case in revolutions, the ideas of an intellectual class instigating the lower classes to revolt for the rights of man— as, for instance, was the Russian revolution which immediately preceded it. It was rather such a revolt as can be paralleled in Spanish-American politics—the revolt of a progressive and prosperous province against the spoliations and humiliations to which it is subjected by a corrupt clique in the capital city.

It may seem wilfully paradoxical to call Macedonia a progressive and prosperous province, but all such descriptions are relative. The Moslem landowner of Serres and the Jew merchant of Salonica were, owing to their association with the ruling class, relatively prosperous when compared with other classes in Macedonia. They were also the most progressive class in the Empire, owing to their association with the Christian races round them. After a quarter-century of educational propaganda a Macedo-Bulgar peasant might still be far below the educational level of his free Bulgarian kinsman, and yet be a highly enlightening neighbour to a Moslem landlord. Just so that Moslem landlord when driven into Asia Minor as a mouhadjir (refugee) has had a highly improving effect on the agricultural methods of the Asiatic Moslem. As for the Salonica Jews, their native intellectual vitality and their connexion with the ruling cliques of Europe accounted for the high standard of political capacity and of practical ability that distinguished the movement.

But for one important difference this Moslem-Jew movement would none the less have remained what it was in

origin—a revolt of one more element in Macedonia against
annexation to Austria and the Hamidian autocracy—a movement not much more important than the immediately
preceding entry into the *mêlée* of the Kutzo-Vlach ' nationality '. This difference lay in the fact that the movement
was a Moslem movement : that Islam is in the Balkans
a bond, so that where one Moslem leads others will follow :
that the Macedonian garrison was Moslem, so that command of the garrison carried with it command of the Empire.
When the Moslem Macedonian committee had through
modern ideas as to Hamidian tyranny secured the more
intelligent and liberal elements of the army of occupation,
and through Moslem intolerance of the threatened Christian
supremacy had secured the more fanatical and reactionary
element, the movement was carried at once by its own
impetus from the status of a local Moslem rising to that
of an imperial military revolution. So swift was the transi-
tion that it is not strange that the connexion has largely
escaped foreign observation. Hamidianism and Byzantinism had brought it about that the whole political life
centred in the Palace, and that the whole strength of the
Government was concentrated not in the Turkish provinces
of Asia, where it would have been safe, but in the overgrown
garrisons of a disaffected province of Europe, politically
and strategically isolated from the Empire. The process
of transformation of a local reform into an imperial revolution, which Abdul Hamid had so often worked for his own
diplomatic ends with so much success, was now worked
democratically against him. But this time it was a reform
from inside, and a popular, not a paper, revolution.

The motive of the Moslem Macedonian movement appears
very clearly in the moment chosen for the outbreak. The
leaders preferred to risk a failure of a premature explosion
by advancing the date of it from the end of August to the
beginning of July 1908, rather than risk the greater danger
of the foreign Powers strengthening their hold on the

province. The meeting of King Edward with the Tsar at
Reval was interpreted, no doubt rightly, as portending an
Anglo-Russian agreement on the Macedonian question, and,
no doubt wrongly, as assuring British support for Russian
designs there. At the same time a fresh collision between
the Albanians and the Austrians in Old Serbia was, no
doubt erroneously, exaggerated into the excuse that Austria
was supposed to be looking for in order to regularize its
military and administrative hold on Old Serbia.

Every day's delay seemed dangerous, and early in July
1908 the coalition of the Ottoman Moslems and Jews
declared its Holy War against Europe. This democratic
war could be prepared with even greater secrecy, and declared
as even a greater surprise than the secret and surprising
coalition of the Balkan Christians four years later, for there
were no governments to conclude conventions or concert
a policy. The military operations were equally simple.
Bodies of Albanians took the field in Old Serbia, and detachments of troops under the leadership of Young Turks took
to the mountains in South Macedonia, both demanding the
constitution of 1876. By July 23 success was so far assured
that the constitution was proclaimed by Albanians at
Ferizovitch, and by Young Turks at the more important
Macedonian centres. The following day the Sultan formally
confirmed the proclamation.

The swift success of the revolution ended immediately
all chance of a peaceful settlement of the Macedonian question by provincial autonomy under European guarantee.
In trying to make the Empire reform Macedonia, Europe
had succeeded in making Macedonia reform the Empire.
The whole internal and external situation was transformed
at one stroke. The Concert, whose conservatism fortunately
never carries it to the point of opposing a democratic national
movement, once that movement has declared itself, at once
conformed to the change of circumstance. The whole
structure of European intervention, foreign officers, fiscal

advisers, &c., had the ground cut from under it, and disappeared without leaving a trace. It is open to question
whether it might not have been better for the Powers to
have persisted in their policy of control, so as to have retained
a means of pressure on the new régime and a *point d'appui*
from which they might resume their control if necessary.
But such persistence was not practicable; for those friendly
to the Young Turks were anxious to give them a free hand,
and those who feared them were anxious to give them
plenty of rope. The driving force that had kept the policy
of autonomy going came from the British House of Commons,
and of the two parties there, one welcomed in the Young
Turks a confirmation of a secular belief in the Ottoman
Empire and its integrity, the other welcomed a conversion
of the Empire to democracy.

Precautions and safeguards would, moreover, have been
out of place in the glow of enthusiasm which irradiated all
Macedonia in the summer of 1908. The millennium had come
and had chosen for its birthplace, of all places—Macedonia.
The subjects of Abdul Hamid had liberty, Moslem and Christian were to have equality, and all the Balkan races were
to live in fraternity. ' Henceforth,' announced Enver Bey,
the popular hero of the revolution, ' we are all brothers:
there are no longer Bulgars, Greeks, Roumans, Jews,
Mussulmans: under the same blue sky we are all equal,
we glory in being Ottoman.' When such a sentiment could
be received with general applause, it would have seemed
cynical to see in the last words of it a cloud that threatened
the blue sky, and to suggest that there is one glory of the
Bulgar, another glory of the Greek, and another glory of
the Turk. But who could doubt that the winter of their discontent was over, and the summer of 1908 made glorious
by the sun of the Young Turk, when the whole land was
full of signs and wonders? Every day brought fresh marvels
and fresh miracles. Righteousness and Peace have kissed
each other: the Greek archbishop and the president of

the Bulgar Committee have publicly embraced at Serres. The mighty are put down from their seat: the Young Turks have imprisoned a Moslem policeman for insulting a Christian at Drama. The lion has laid down with the lamb: Sandanski, the Bulgar partisan, has called on the Turkish pasha at Monastir. But above all, Abdul Hamid, the sower of tares, is bound, and Babylon is fallen. ' How has the oppressor ceased, the Golden City ceased. The whole earth is at rest, they break forth into singing.' Hearken to the voice of the coolest of Foreign Secretaries of the coldest of Frankish peoples : ' The Macedonian question and others of a similar character will entirely disappear.'

Who will say that these moments of expansion and enthusiasm, however fleeting and futile, had no value. The Macedonian millennium ended one century of waste and warfare, and it may have been the beginning of another. But in itself it has been one of the great spiritual achievements of humanity in our time. It came driving through the corruption and despair of Hamidianism like a breath of fresh air in a dungeon :

> An air of the morning, a breath
> From the springs of the East, from the gate
> Whence freedom issues, and fate,
> Sorrow, and triumph, and death.

CHAPTER IV

THE OTTOMAN REVOLUTION AND ITS WARS

§ 10. Ottoman Civil Wars.
§ 11. Balkan Racial Warfare.
§ 12. European Political Wars.

When like Heaven's Sun girt by the exhalation
Of its own glorious light, thou didst arise,
Chasing thy foes from nation unto nation
Like shadows : as if day had cloven the skies
At dreaming midnight o'er the western wave,
Men started, staggering with a glad surprise,
Under the lightnings of thine unfamiliar eyes.
Thou Heaven of earth! what spells could pall thee then
In ominous eclipse?—a thousand years
Bred from the slime of deep Oppression's fen,
Dyed all thy liquid light with blood and tears:

SHELLEY—*Ode to Liberty:*

§ 10. OTTOMAN CIVIL WARS

THE Ottoman Empire, as distinct from the Turkish nation, is an association of Asiatic peoples with common social standards and a coeval stage of civilization, of which association the Sultan is the symbol, and the Turkish army the sanction. For in this association the European provinces and peoples have no part : they are dependencies under military administration. The Empire in its prime might have been compared with the present British Empire, which is, in part, an association of Anglo-Saxon communities under an emperor-king secured by a British navy, and, in part, a military administration of Asiatic peoples. Moreover, the Ottoman Empire depended, as the British Empire to-day depends, on the continual adjustment of an equal balance between the progressive forces of nationalist autonomy and the conservative forces of imperial autocracy.

The fundamental institutions of the early Empire, embodying

and combining these forces, consisted in respect of Christians in the representation given to them through their religious authorities, in their recruitment for the imperial army and through conscription for the Janizaries, and in the power delegated to Christian functionaries through Court and civil employments. The Patriarch, the Janizary, and the Hospodar were imperial institutions which might conceivably have developed in conformity with modern conditions so as to provide the necessary equilibrium between local liberties and a central control. A steady development of the Christian millet might have prevented disruption from within by relieving the nationalism of Albanians and Bulgars from the necessity of becoming separatist; though it would not have retained Greeks, Slavs, or Roumanians within an imperial federation. A little more development of a system of universal national service, such as that of the janizaries, might have prevented disintegration from without by enlisting the more progressive peoples in support of the Empire, and thereby keeping its military efficiency abreast of the times. As it was, the failures of the various reforms and revolutions to arrest the decadence of the Empire seem all attributable to the impossibility of reconciling the nationalist and imperialist forces. As a result, in every case, war—religious war working on the Islamic fanaticism, or economic war working through Byzantine extortion—has perverted the revolution or the reform into an aggravation of the Asiatic autocracy, and has driven local liberty into maintaining itself by nationalism and separatism. Such revolutions and reforms have therefore ended only in disorganizing the imperial polity and disintegrating the imperial possessions.

There have been two striking instances of the working of war on Ottoman imperialism and Near Eastern nationality; the one, the revolution of Mahmoud II just one hundred years ago, the other the Young Turk revolution of the last five years. The revolution of Mahmoud II coincided with the outbreak of the war of Greek independence and an epoch of Near Eastern warfare. As a result, what might have been a peaceful infiltration of European institutions and ideas became a series of civil wars between the Young Turkey of the day, headed by the reforming Sultan, and the Old Turkey, with its primitive but practical imperial constitution based on the provincial power of the Beglerbeys and the military power of the Janizaries. The new wine burst the old bottles even as to-day the Young Turks burst into shreds the imperial institutions of yesterday. Nor did reform bring civil disruption only, for in spite of the training of Mahmoud's ' new model ' by officers of Napoleon and of Abdul Hamid's conscript millions by officers of Von Moltke, the result has been military disaster; and this because in neither case was the scheme of reform given time to establish itself before it was prematurely overworked by war. Defeat in war cannot do more than check the growth of a nation; but the growth of an empire is a far more delicate development and requires either a long period of peace or the impetus of a great national expansion in the imperial race. Neither the revolution of Mahmoud II nor that of the Young Turks could rely on any great national impetus; but a period of peace from the Great Powers and from the ' Great Idea ' did seem the just due of the makers of the Macedonian millennium.

The relationship of the Ottoman Empire with the neighbouring empires and with the Balkan nations remained still essentially one of war; for no real peace was possible between imperialist claimants to the succession in Constantinople with the economic predominance in the Near East and nationalist claimants to the succession in European Turkey with political predominance there. This relationship of war now appeared in a series of wars more or less special in their object and sporadic in their outbreak, but all interconnected with each other and introductory to the War of the Coalition.

In the previous chapter we have seen the Young Turk revolution result in the general acceptance of a new Ottoman constitutional State as an imperialist solution of the Macedonian question. We have now to trace the swift collapse of this imperialist settlement under the stress of national forces within the Empire, and under the shocks of imperial rivals without. The attempt to combine European and Asiatic communities, the former akin to neighbouring nations and the latter antipathetic to them, in a constitutional empire on a basis of proportionate parliamentary representation and equal civil right, was probably doomed to failure in any case; but it will be seen that it was the work of war that broke up the new imperial constitution at once into its national component elements.

The main difficulty in the New Empire was the difficulty of reconciling the new and the old : the new principles of liberty, equality, and fraternity with the old principle of Moslem and Rayah : the new constitutional régime with the 'good old rule' of Constantinople : the Young Turks with the Old Turks : the followers of Comte with the faithful of the Khalif : and the 'intelligentsia' with Islam. An almost equally vital weakness lay in the impossibility of getting Turks and Greeks to work representative institutions together; the former being a ruling caste of little or no capabilities in that direction, the latter a subject majority of exceptional political capacity. There were, however, two points in favour of success—the provincial origin of the movement in Macedonia and the predominance, among the original movers, of neutrals such as Armenians and Jews.

The Young Turk leaders at Salonica were well aware that the decadence of the Ottoman Empire was largely due to the precipitate pouring such new wine as theirs into the old bottles. But, on the other hand, they knew that the Ottoman Empire had all along existed only by exploiting the civilization, the capital, and the science of Europe, and that unless it could continue to do so, it must come to an end as an

Empire. The early Empire had lived for centuries on the exploitation of the accumulated resources of the Empire of the East and on the exhaustion of the resources of its subject European communities. The later Empire, between the reforms of Mahmoud and the reaction of Abdul Hamid, had maintained itself by exploiting the material resources of European science and wealth. Why should not this process now be extended to mental and moral resources? Why should not the example of Japan be followed? Why should not the Empire be endowed with European political life and an intellectual point of view, provided that Mahmoud's mistake of going too fast and Abdul Hamid's mistake of going too slow were both avoided?

The way in which they thought it might be done was by keeping Salonica as the centre of the new political and religious thought, and leaving Constantinople as the centre of the old faith. Constantinople would be the connecting link which would be educated and Europeanized from Salonica, only so far and so fast as the ancient privileges and prejudices could be peacefully extinguished and expropriated. Salonica should play the part of Petersburg in the regeneration of Russia by Peter the Great, not that of Marseilles in the French Revolution. The Young Turk imperialists, with their positivism, their belief in scientific and economic progress, and in the power of money and political organization, were indeed as alien to the Turkish nation as was Peter the Great. They knew this and hoped by acting from a distance and in discreet retirement, to remain the motive power and the guiding genius of an imperial renascence. In this way might a progressive and positivist temporal power, in the form of a constitutional Sultanate, be reconciled with a conservative and Moslem spiritual power in the form of the Khalifate.[1]

---

[1] 'La concentration du Sultanat et du Khalifat a été nécessaire jadis pour l'œuvre de conquête ; elle l'est aujourd'hui pour notre défense . . . actuellement la Turquie ne peut ni se séparer du Khalifat ni le séparer de son pouvoir temporal.'—Ahmed Riza, *La Crise d'Orient*, pp. 21, 24.

This might retain unprejudiced the ancient prestige of the Khalifate while adding to the Sultanate such new prestige as could be secured by a judicious admixture of constitutional institutions and forms. The Sultan would become a combination of a Pope and a Permanent Secretary for Foreign Affairs, while the country would continue to be administered by the Porte under supervision of the Committee's organizations. In this way also might such a crisis be avoided as might lay bare the two fatal dualisms of Old Turk and Young Turk, and of Turk and Greek.

The first difficulties were successfully overcome. The Committee were saved the ordeal of constitutional discussions by being able to revive simply the constitution in abeyance since 1876. Abdul Hamid, after being defeated in an ingenious intrigue to retain his autocracy by installing the Committee openly in the capital under his own presidency and his grand mastership of their masonic organization, accepted the rôle allotted to him with an amiable alacrity. The one essential for the execution of this programme was peace ; and, in the six years since the revolution Turkey has not been given six months' peace.

The first result of the revolution had been peace, even in Macedonia ; and the first impulse into war came, not from the Balkan nationality movement, but from the imperialism of a European Power. The revolution had been in June 1908, and, in October, Austria annexed Bosnia-Herzegovina, and Bulgaria declared its independence. For six months the Young Turk régime tried to maintain its credit with Islam and Imperialism by loud insistence on its rights ; but it was notoriously helpless before a diplomatic combination disposing of such military forces. In selling Turkey's imperial rights as was done in the Austro-Turk and Turco-Bulgar agreements (February to March 1909), they made the best bargain possible, but they stood convicted before the Empire of that very sale of imperial privileges for which they had attacked Abdul Hamid. They were, moreover,

held responsible for the vizier Kiamil's negotiations, of
a similar nature, as to the Bagdad and Adriatic railways.
This, together with the offence given by their irreligion, and
their loss of control over the Constantinople garrison, offered
their enemies an opportunity for overthrowing them. A party
of Islamic ultras, calling itself the Mohamedi or Volcan faction,
and disposing of unlimited funds and unbridled fanaticism,
had already appeared in the Chamber, and through hodjas
and softas had started an agitation among the populace and
garrison of the capital. On April 13, the counter-revolution
cleared Constantinople of the Committee and ended the
constitutional phase of the revolution. Islam had overthrown the ' intelligentsia ', and war had banished all peace.
The result of this coup was the Turkish civil war, short and
sharp in itself, but bringing in its train a whole series of
suppressed wars.

Abdul Hamid and the Byzantine powers of evil had
counted on dealing with the constitutionalists of 1908 as
easily as with those of a generation before. In the eyes of
these reactionaries, the constitutional movement had served
its purpose, as in 1878, when it had got rid of foreign interference ; it could now be got rid of in its turn. Frankish
ideas and ' framason ' associations were nothing new, and
would give little trouble once the troops were won back.
So probably argued the old diplomatist at Yildiz, making
the old diplomatic error of ignoring moral forces and treating
a problem in dynamics as a problem in statics. But the
inconvenient mess that Abdul Hamid counted on mopping
up and emptying down his Byzantine sink was the spring
tide of the Asiatic nationality movement, topping the dykes
that had kept it back for centuries. The westerly wave of
that tide, flowing into Asia through Japan, had swept away
the entrenchments in Manchuria of the great European
Land Power, had shaken all the European military occupations of Asia, and had already stirred the last remaining
Asiatic autocracy of Europe. The Young Turk movement

was an easterly tidal wave of the Asiatic nationality movement which was to strike the Ottoman autocracy with full force.

By the spring of 1909, Abdul Hamid, by free recourse to the ' moral' influences of Byzantinism and Islamism, had recovered command of the garrison at Constantinople. It speaks well for the vitality of the revolution that, for the most part, the officers remained proof against bribes or fanaticism. Had Abdul Hamid possessed such qualities of mind and body as would have allowed him to put himself at the head of his troops, Mahmoud Shevket, with his army from Salonica, would have had a more serious task than the railroad trip to Tchataldja and the skirmishes in the Pera suburbs. But the civil war, though short, was not bloodless. Many lives were lost on both sides before the Sultan's adherents surrendered ; and many more lives, including those of some American missionaries, were lost at Adana in Armenia in massacres instigated for obvious reasons by Old Turks, and hushed up by Young Turks, for equally obvious reasons. Thus the civil warfare accomplished itself with a merciful swiftness. Abdul Hamid was deposed and interned at Salonica, now become the loyal city of the Empire, and a Macedonian Committee reigned in his stead.

Abdul Hamid rose to power meanly, used it meanly, and fell meanly. He was, indeed, so mean a tyrant that it goes against the grain to say anything in his favour. But to give the devil his due, it may be said that he was an ingenious designer and could handle his tools. Whether diplomatizing in his audience-chamber or cabinet making in his workshop he had a cunning hand and a cool head that would cut humanity to waste like so much dead wood, and handle edge tools without ever cutting himself. The pathos of Abdul Hamid's personality is caused by its apparently embodying all the spiritual despair, all the moral decadence, all the physical degeneracy for which his régime stood. Over the whole spirit of the Hamidian Empire, over its barren reforms, and over its equally barren reactions, hangs this gloom of despair, this shadow of death.

> The kingdoms of Islam are crumbling,
> And round me a voice ever rings,
> That tells of the doom of my country,
> Shall I be the last of its kings ?

With the sweeping away of the cobwebs of Hamidianism and of the old spider himself by Mahmoud Shefket's revolutionary army, the whole atmosphere changed. In the ranks of the army with which the Young Turks retook Constantinople were Christians, Jews, and Moslems, all united by one common cause ; and the Macedonian millennium seemed once again revived. But the common cause that moved the army was destructive, not constructive. It implied a common resolution to suppress Hamidianism and Byzantinism in favour of progress and liberty; not a resolution to resign old national instincts in favour of new imperial institutions. Jew, Moslem, and Christian marched against the mediaeval despotism of Abdul Hamid in the ranks of the revolution, as later Bulgar, Greek, and Serb marched against the more modern despotism of the Committee in the ranks of the coalition. The first was the conflict of the ' intelligentsia ' with Islam, the second the conflict of nationalism with imperialism. In both cases the alliance held good only until its work was accomplished ; then the brothers in arms of the Macedonian millennium and of the Balkan Bond turned their swords against each other.

When, after a fortnight, the Young Turks returned to power, the evil effect of the international ' war ' with Austro-Bulgarian diplomacy and of the consequent internal war with Hamidian diplomacy were at once evident. The rift between Old and Young Turkey had been ruthlessly laid bare, and no further bridging of it was possible. The hand of the Young Turks had been forced and their unwritten constitution of checks and balances had been rendered unworkable. There was no choice but to take over complete control of the Sultanate and the Khalifate. The substitution of Mahmoud for Abdul Hamid implied that the Committee of Union and Progress was thenceforward the real executive, and not merely a consultative extra-constitutional caucus. The Committee still remained at Salonica ; and Old Turks, such as Kiamil, were still used as figureheads. But the constitutional and social rift between Old and Young Turkey had to be closed by the absolute ascendancy of a Young Turk junta, based, not on any representative system, but on the army and a secret association. An empire on this basis was far more effective for war than would have been the constitutional Empire ; but it no longer afforded a reconciliation of nationalist rivalries by means of representative government. War, as usual, had given the course of events a deflection leading to new wars.

The dualism of ancient and modern imperial authority in the Ottoman Empire had been exposed by Austria, the secular enemy of the past ; the dualism of nationality and imperialism was to be exposed by the Greeks, the enemy of the future. This latter dualism is omnipresent in Ottoman affairs, and there had always been two main policies of reform, the one represented by English, the other by French ideas. The first had for principle a provincial autonomy which might serve as a safeguard against separatism by affording a safety valve for nationalism : the second had for principle an administrative organization which should combat such centrifugal forces by giving the Empire economic and political solidarity. The British remedy for the decline of the Empire was the good Vali ; the French remedy was the good Vizier. In view of the greater success of English over French methods in ruling an empire, it is permissible to assume that the English were right ; all the more in view of the success of applications of the English system, as in Lebanon and Samos, and in the failures of the French system, as in the Roumelian laws of the vilayets.

The two systems were reproduced among the Young Turk reformers, even so early as their incubating period in Paris. The Committee of Decentralization and Separate Action in the Rue de Berlin, and the Committee of Order and Progress in the Rue Bonaparte, were afterwards represented by the Union Libérale (after 1909 the Entente Libérale) and by the Committee of Union and Progress. The Young Turks of the Union Libérale were mostly men of position, who, for that reason, perhaps, favoured decentralization of imperial power and delegation to provincial proconsuls who would secure a sufficiency of local liberty and be personally responsible to the Empire ; in other words, a restoration of the régime of the Beglerbeys destroyed by Mahmoud. The Young Turks of the Committee of Union and Progress were, on the other hand, imbued with the ideas of Comte, whose *Système de Philosophie positiviste* would find salvation in the *coup d'état* of Napoleon III and the Committee of Public Safety. Unlike their colleagues of the Union Libérale, these radicals of the Committee had a clear programme and a compact organization. Using the Jewish associations of Salonica and the masonic societies that permeated the Empire, they succeeded in creating an organization which numbered nearly half a million members with an annual income of as many pounds or perhaps more, with the army in its pay and the whole political power in its pocket. As against this combination, the liberals could bring the support of the more disaffected and detached provinces, Arabia, Albania, and Greek Macedonia.

There was one point, however, on which the Turkish leaders of both parties were agreed, and that was the necessity of keeping this division of policy from declaring itself in the Ottoman Parliament in such a way as to weaken the Empire. With this object in view, the liberal party of decentralization became members of the radical caucus before the first elections ; and these latter were arranged so as to give a preconcerted proportional representation to each community. But already the disintegrating force of nationalism, and especially of Greek nationalism, was at work. The arrangement was not observed and the liberal nationalists, mostly Greeks, secured more seats than was intended. Moreover, the perfunctory allegiance to the Committee of the Greek and Albanian deputies was thrown off as soon as Parliament met, and a liberal opposition appeared composed of nationalists, Greeks, and Albanians, which joined with the Arabs and the Old Turks of the Volcan faction. This open division contributed powerfully to creating the counterrevolution, and when the Committee returned to power, their next task after checking the imperialist reaction was to check the nationalist revolution by purging the Imperial Parliament. The Khalif had been made a loyal supporter of the Committee, now the Chamber was to be converted into a loyal partisan of it. But these reprisals, which deprived the different minorities of all constitutional means of pursuing their home-rule ambitions, only drove them into nationalism and separatism. After the civil war the relations of Turks to Arabs, Albanians, Greeks, and Bulgars changes with surprising suddenness from coalition in the cause of progress into civil war as to the method of it.

The Committee professed to be enforcing their arbitrary authority as a provisional measure only, until the safety of the Empire was secured; but they were now driven to abandoning the fiction of a *pax ottomanica* and to admitting the fact of an all-pervading warfare by proclaiming martial law. Coercion produced conspiracy, and a ' terror ' followed in due course, in which individual supporters of separatist propaganda were imprisoned or even assassinated, while disaffected districts were harried with fire and sword.

War, in the sense of actual fighting, had broken out first among the Turks themselves in the civil war between the Committee and the Khalifate. Similarly in the civil war between the imperialist Committee and the nationalist communities fighting first began with those nationalists who also had imperialist aims ; not, as might have been expected, with the nationalists who, like the Greeks, were out-and-out separatists. The Turks of the Khalifate were as good imperialists as the Turks of the Committee, and fought them only on a principle of imperial policy. The Arabs, as the chosen people of Islam, combined imperialist ambitions in Constantinople with autonomous ambitions in Arabia. Albanians could claim to have saved the Empire in Europe from foreign subversion during the evil days of Hamidian decadence, and to have brought about the revolution by their armed action, as at Ferisovitch : now they claimed openings for their great administrative abilities and a recognition of their provincial liberties. Next came the Macedo-Bulgars, who had no more than a federalist imperialism with which to temper their nationalist aspirations. Last came the Greeks, whose Great Idea aimed not only at detaching Greater Greece from the Ottoman Empire, but at displacing that Empire from its imperial capital in favour of Greek nationality.

Civil war broke out first in the Hauran, where 10,000 troops were employed in a pacifying campaign ; and was soon followed by war in the Yemen, in which the Arabs took Sanaa and occupied 30,000 Turkish troops (1910–11), until the outbreak of the Tripoli war against the giaour reunited Turk and Arab, intelligentsia and Islam, for a time.

Almost simultaneously came the parallel Albanian outbreak in European Turkey; which, owing to its being a Balkan affair, and under European observation, had a closer relation to subsequent events.

After the failure of the counter-revolution of April 1909, in which the Albanians had played a prominent part, the Committee proceeded to the pacification and disarmament of Albania ; but during the summer of 1909 only the less warlike lowlands were occupied, while Issa Boletinatz skirmished, not without success, on the highland borders. In April 1910, 15,000 Albanians at Prishtina delivered an ultimatum to the Committee, even as two years before they

had declared war on Abdul Hamid at Ferisovitch. Their
main complaints were against service in the Yemen, destruction of the towers, and the census. Put into general terms
this meant that the Albanians were fighting for their lives,
their liberties, and their lands. The reply of the Committee
was more uncompromising than any which the Sultan had
ever ventured to make ; and 50,000 men, regulars and
irregulars, under Torgut Pasha, invaded the mountains of
the Maltsori. There was severe fighting round Tuzi and
fearful devastation of the valley villages. The highlanders
were driven in thousands to take refuge with their old
enemies the Serbs and Montenegrins, until the latter pro-
tested against the burden of supporting those who had once
been the privileged bullies of Servia *irredenta*. It was not
until after two years of savage warfare that the growing
difficulties of the Committee with their Christian constituents
led to a truce being made with the Albanian Moslem ; the
terms of which, by granting the more essential demands of
the Maltsori mountaineers and exacting only a nominal
allegiance in return, amounted to a practical recognition of
the independence of Albania while in principle repudiating it.
After the fall of the Committee, these favours were extended
by the liberal ministry to all the Albanians. Consequently,
though the Albanians had the worst of the fighting and were
forced to suppress the provisional government they had established in the Mirdite country, they may fairly consider the
campaign of Torgut and his Kurds as their war of liberation :
even as the Greeks do that no less terrible campaign of
Ibrahim and his Egyptians in the Morea.

But, apart from its interest as the initiation of Albanian
independence, this campaign had an important effect on the
general Balkan situation. In the first place, the old Albanian
association with the Turks had been rudely broken, and
a temporary truce made in the old feud with the Serbs.
Thereby, for a time at any rate, one of the difficulties of any
joint action by Balkan nationalities in Macedonia had been

in great part removed. In the second place, the apparent success achieved by Torgut in pacifying Albania encouraged the Committee to allow him, on his return in the autumn of 1910, to try similar measures against the nationalists of Macedonia.

During the summer of 1909, nationalist activity had reappeared in Macedonia in the actions of various bands, more especially Bulgar. In November 1909 the Committee passed a provisional law for the pacification of Macedonia, of which the following provisions indicate the character : village authorities and the population of a locality were personally responsible for any action by bands in their neighbourhood (art. 14) : families with missing members might be imprisoned at discretion (art. 25) : membership in a band was punishable with death (art. 18) : concealment of arms or unsatisfactory replies were punishable with beating. The application of this ' law ' by Torgut resulted in some 12,000 prisoners, 5,000 killed and wounded, 2,000 refugees in Bulgaria, and as many more in the mountains.[1] What was even more serious for the nationalists was that the places of these Christian refugees were filled as fast as possible with Moslem refugees; and thus the Balkan States saw their resources exhausted by support of refugees at the same time that they saw their hopes in Macedonia diminishing with the diminishing number of their adherents there. The refugees accordingly were driven back whenever possible, while arms and assistance were refused them for political reasons. The reader can try to imagine for himself the horrors of their situation—none the less horrible that it was reproduced with the rôles reversed three years later. This policy of Moslem repopulation was indeed the measure most severely felt by Balkan nationalism. Previous blows had struck at national rights which, if lost, could be recovered, but this was a blow at the very root of national

[1] Vide report to the Chamber of M. Pavloff, a Macedonian deputy, and one time member of the Committee.

life—the land. The idea of repopulating Macedonia with the scattered Moslems of Europe, Bosniaks, Pomaks, Tartars, Turcomans, &c., was probably of Zionist origin and accounted for by the Jewish element on the Committee. But the attempt to apply it profoundly alarmed the Macedo-Bulgar and Serb. The Bulgar could remember the fearful results of previous experiments of the same character in 1876 with Circassians and Kurds, and saw himself evicted from the land from which he had been gradually ousting the Moslem overlord and which he hoped shortly to convert into free Bulgarian territory. The Greek in his turn had to suffer in Epirus from the introduction there of Albanian settlers.

So much for the provinces; but in the capital the nationalists were no better off. After the disillusionment of the winter 1908–9 and of the counter-revolution, the Committee not only decided to bring the new representative institutions under control, but also to begin to get rid of the old ecclesiastical privileges. This amounted to attacking the Christian minorities on both flanks, and the small hold that the constitutional guarantees had on public confidence is shown by the different result of these two attacks. The Committee were allowed to abolish the liberties of the Chamber, but failed in their attack on the liberties of the Churches; for the Churches had the support of the whole nationalist movement, whereas the Chamber had only that of the fast-dying federalist imperialism of the Bulgar and Serb nationalists. Accordingly, when an attempt was made by amendments to the Constitution to restrict the ecclesiastical authorities in the representation of their communities to strictly religious matters, and to deprive them of their control of education and civil affairs of their community,[1] the Young Turks met their first definite defeat. It had

---

[1] The amendments to arts. xi and xvi look harmless enough, but the policy inspiring them appears clearly from debates in the Chamber and the action subsequently taken.

already been made clear to the minorities that Ottoman representative institutions were merely a stalking horse for the absolutism of a positivist and militarist Young Turkish junta ; and the proposed Ottoman system of education with its compulsory Turkish[1] and separate religious instruction, seemed a no less obvious attempt to sweep away such guarantees as remained. For the last time, all the Christian communities in Turkey joined together to resist the attack, and even the Grand Rabbi dissociated his community from the Judaeo-Turk Committee. The Committee gave in (November 1909) and confirmed the ecclesiastical authorities in their civil functions. The defeat should have served as a warning against uniting the nationalist minorities and their corresponding nationalities against the Empire ; but it did not.

By the end of 1910 the Young Turks had roused to action all the nationalist movements of European Turkey, mesmerized for a moment by the Macedonian millennium, and had, for the first time in history, united them, even down to the Albanians, against the Empire. The policy of Moslem resettlement had alarmed the rural population : that of repression of the Christian schools and civil authorities had alarmed the townspeople : that of pacifying the provinces by fire and sword had made the peaceable peasant despair : that of controlling the capital by secret societies and assassination had made the federalist into a separatist.

Yet all this evil to humanity and to its own cause had been done by the Committee with the best intentions and the highest motives, in pursuit of the excellent principle that there could be no better régime for an Ottoman citizen than complete civil equality grounded on a general social

[1] The movement of the literary associations of the Yemi Kalemler and Yeni Hayat to modernize Turkish and make it an official language was an interesting but not very important enterprise. Turkish may have a future, but it is of no value as an imperial bond, and the imperialist movement was only burdened by taking it up. A Turkish national movement would, however, find a strong stimulus in cultivating this interesting tongue.

regeneration and guaranteed by representative political institutions. It is very instructive that the relentless philosophy and radical principles of the French imperialism inspiring the Committee led the Empire to swift disruption where the British imperialism of the Liberal Union would have left it to slow disintegration. Dying empires can be kept going by grafting growing peoples on a suitable stock : they can also be stimulated by severe pruning ; but they cannot be either forced or propagated to order. The Young Turks succeeded only in destroying confidence in their power to control events and to give every claimant his due. It was Frederick the Great who said that if he wanted to punish a province he would turn it over to be governed by philosophers ; but he did not look far enough ahead. The province would no doubt suffer considerably from the philosophers, but it would, as a result, free itself from Frederick the Great. The Young Turks meant well, and in the end they accomplished good; though not what was good in their own eyes.

It has been asserted already that there are only two ways of dealing imperially with nationalism—either concession (in the form of federation or devolution) or coercion ; and that the former will probably end in separation and the latter in savagery. The Young Turks had decided against the first alternative and were being rapidly driven into the second. The policy of coercion and resettlement begun in 1909 had by 1911 become that of the Israelite towards the Amalekite. But even the newest of brooms cannot make a clean sweep of its enemies nowadays ; and nothing short of a clean sweep will serve. The Koran or the Sword was a practical radical policy ; but the Constitution or the Kurbash was not. The Young Turk reformers were bound to fail even as fifty years before the Old Turk reformer Midhat, the author of that Constitution, had failed. Midhat had tried liberal institutions and radical repression against the Bulgars of the Danube, and found that while either by itself might be a sedative to disturbance, together they made a stimulant. But so forcefully did the Young Turks pursue their policy that in a few months they had transformed the Macedonian millennium into pandemonium.

§ 11. BALKAN RACIAL WARFARE

We have seen how the Young Turks, without originally intending war with either Arabs, Albanians, or Macedonians, were driven by the imminence of war in their Empire into a series of wars which united against them all the national and separatist forces it contained.

We have now to trace the effect of these internal wars on the foreign relations of the Empire to those independent Balkan nations which were connected with nationalist parties in the Empire. It will be seen that even as war forced itself on the imperial relationship of a Government based on a pacificist and positivist revolution, so it forced itself on the international relationship between the Ottoman and the Balkan Governments—relations which were, for various reasons, pacific though not pacificist.

The pacific element in relations of the Empire with Serbia and Bulgaria was especially marked at the time of the Turkish revolution; all the more that the traditional diplomatic reasons for good relationship were, during the few months of the Macedonian millennium, relieved for a short time from the demand for war of their kindred democracies in Old Serbia and Macedonia, still under Turkish misrule. The Macedo-Serbs and Macedo-Bulgars had accepted the solution of a constitutional Empire whole-heartedly; and their co-operation had not the effect of that of the more politically expert Greeks, who either instinctively or intentionally exposed at once the fatal fallacies in this imperialist solution of the Near Eastern Question. To the Serbs and Bulgars, the constitutional Empire might at best be accepted as a peaceful procedure for accomplishing their nationalist aims by a process of federation or devolution;

and, at worst, as a provisional pacification which would relieve the governments of the intolerable burden of the armed truce, and which would allow an economic development of European Turkey, all in their favour. For the Bulgar and Serb rural population only requires peace to swamp Moslem landlord and Greek trader with its pullulating prosperity.

The Ottoman Government on their side were, at first, no less well disposed, and their first Macedonian policy was on Hamidian lines, in encouraging Bulgars and Serbs at the expense of Greeks. A 'provisional law' provided that church and school buildings and properties should be assigned to that ecclesiastical authority for which the majority in the locality elected; whereas hitherto, the Bulgar exarchate and Serb bishoprics had been limited to localities where the whole population was of that persuasion—the Greek patriarchate taking the rest. This would have given to the exarchate two-thirds of Macedonia, and would have gone far to prevent the reappearance for some time of the Macedo-Bulgar agitation for annexation to Bulgaria. But the Greeks succeeded in getting a Russian veto imposed on this policy of the Young Turks—at the moment in difficulties with the counter-revolution. It was the first appearance of Russia as a factor for war; but thereafter, Russian interventions at critical moments are frequent, and are found to be more and more conducive to war as a Balkan war policy takes the place of the other policies at one time and another preferred by Petersburg.

The particular protégés of Russia, the Serbs, were more especially well disposed to the Young Turks. For the Serbs, the Austrian Empire is the enemy, not the Ottoman. The Serbs had found in the outlet by Salonica the only escape from the economic wars waged against them by Austria-Hungary, culminating in the veto placed on the Serbo-Bulgar commercial treaty of 1905 and the 'pig' war of 1906. The keeping open of this economic easement was of more immediate importance to Serbia than establishing, politically, its remote reversionary interest in the territory over which it passed. The Serb-Macedonian propaganda which had been revived (1905–8), had done some harm to Serbo-Bulgar relations, but little to those with Turkey; while the harrying of the Albanians by the Young Turks had had the hearty support of all Serbians. Serbia had even appealed for help to Turkey when Serbian aspirations for a national expansion and an outlet to the sea in Bosnia Herzegovina, were discomfited by the Austro-Bulgarian *coup* in 1908; and, during 1909, Serbia was planning a Balkan alliance against Austria. It was as a Serbian defiance of Austria that the famous formula—the Balkan peninsula for the Balkan peoples—was first proclaimed. When the pacification of Albania was extended to Macedonia in 1910, the Serbs suffered least, and their protests to the Ottoman Government were perfunctory—appealing only for a milder application of the objectionable legislation, not for its repeal. In the Ottoman Chamber the Serb deputies remained adherents of the Committee throughout. Serbia was diplomatically and democratically pro-Ottoman, and its conversion to action against that Empire by Russia was the principal contribution of imperialist diplomacy to wars that were in the main the work of democratic national forces.

The first result in Bulgar-Macedonia of the Turkish revolution had been the giving up of the guerrilla warfare and conspiracies of the ' Internal Organization'; and the second had been the growth of open political action in societies combined under the name of ' National Bulgar Organization', which, following the lines of the Committee of Union and Progress, was as well organized and as active. It had, moreover, in respect of the Bulgar constituents of the Empire, the same mission of moral development and constitutional defence that the Committee itself exercised on behalf of the Turks. At first the relations between the Bulgar and Turk

organizations were those of two allied political parties.
The agreement as to the seats to be allotted to Bulgars, and
that as to common action against the counter-revolution,
were both observed scrupulously and with mutual satisfaction. But by the end of 1909 the Committee, far from
being, as at first, a political caucus of the Macedo-Moslem,
had gone far on its way to becoming an executive council
of the Empire, and had begun suppressing the other nationalist organizations, of which the Bulgar Committee was
the chief. Accordingly, in November 1909 a ' provisional
law ' as to associations not only prohibited every nationalist
society, but even all political associations (art. 4) : the
Committee itself complying to the extent of professing
that it was an ' Ottoman Association for the propagation
of Commerce and Industry '. Of course, Bulgar political
activity was only driven underground, where it resumed
the subterranean operations and organization of the insurrectionary ' Internal Organization '. But another result was
that the political outlet of Macedo-Bulgar nationalism
was diverted from Constantinople to Sofia. There it began
again to work actively for war, while the relations between the
Macedo-Bulgar Committees in Macedonia and the Macedo-
Moslem Committee at Constantinople got steadily worse. The
disarmament of 1910 was directed chiefly against the Bulgars,
and powerfully aided their efforts at Sofia to make war.

The Bulgar Government was well aware that their interests
lay in peace, not in war, but above all they were bound to
have either one or the other definitely. The State had
been prepared for war since the troubles of 1903. It was
now maintaining a peace effective, proportionately to population, half as much again as that of France, and a slightly
larger proportionate annual charge for the army than that of
the wealthiest of European countries. Unless the new régime
in Turkey afforded some prospect of a permanent peace, it
seemed likely that the country would soon have to choose
between war and ruin.

The old imperial relationship of a vassal Bulgaria to a suzerain Turkey had always given very unsatisfactory results, and it was obvious that the relationship would become even more difficult with the drastic Young Turk than with the diplomatic Abdul Hamid, while it would be complicated by the Bulgar representation in the new constitutional Empire. With Bulgaria independent, a Turco-Bulgar alliance would become possible, at least so King Ferdinand, the director of Bulgarian diplomacy, seems to have argued; and though, like all diplomatists, he often underestimated moral forces, he very rarely miscalculated political factors. Bulgaria was now de facto sovereign and the equal of Turkey, having terminated the fiction of suzerainty which previously had falsified the relationship of the two peoples. That fiction of suzerainty had hampered Bulgaria in establishing with the Empire under Abdul Hamid those economic relations which were indispensable to its prosperity and development. By imposing impossible imperial responsibilities when there was no democratic relationship, it had aggravated the perpetual friction between Bulgaria and Turkey as to Macedonia, while weakening the position of Sofia in control of the Macedo-Bulgar agitation. Once definitely a separate State, Bulgaria might renounce the annexation of Macedonia in return for acquiring such economic relations with it as would secure its absorption in the end all the more surely for the temporary renunciation. But the situation was not enough under control for such long-range policy. Negotiations with Turkey were pushed forward and Sofia offered a compensation of £4,000,000 for Turkey's lost sovereign rights, asking in return for the final settlement of the six special arrangements signed in 1904, and ever since awaiting ratification. The most important of these, by linking up the Bulgar and Macedonian railways gave Bulgaria an outlet to Salonica and an economic penetration through Bulgar Macedonia. This was to be the basis of a Turco-Bulgar alliance, which

was at this time no less desired by the Young Turks than by
King Ferdinand. Delegates met, an agreement in principle
was arrived at, and half the Bulgarian reservists were
demobilized in earnest of the alliance. But the policy could
be carried no further. The Young Turks found that their
Islamic ultras, already planning the counter-revolution,
could not be induced to accept an agreement with Bulgaria
that looked like a surrender, unless it were helped through
by a rectification of frontier; and King Ferdinand had already
too much difficulty with his militarists and Macedonians to
go as far as that. The matter hung fire until Russia stepped
in (January 1909) and converted the Turco-Bulgar agreement into Russo-Bulgar and Russo-Turk arrangements, by
which Bulgaria, instead of Turkey, became liable to Russia
for the remaining annuities of the 1878 war indemnity:
a diplomatic device so ingenious that one can scarcely grudge
the credit given it at the time for being disinterested.

During 1909 all prospect of a Turco-Bulgar association
gradually disappeared under the stress of the democratic
forces on either side, and it was probably abandoned by
King Ferdinand after his visit to Constantinople in March
1910. The growing conviction that the Young Turk régime
was an impossible one for imperial and international purposes would have been confirmed by this visit; all the
more, perhaps, by the disposition shown to treat him still
as ' Vali of Eastern Roumelia ', and to give preferential
treatment to the King of Servia, whose visit succeeded his.

With the summer of 1910 came the ' pacification ' of Macedonia, and thereafter, though the policy of Bulgaria remains
pacific, it is no longer a constructive policy for dealing with
the Macedonian question, but merely a conservative marking
time. The advent of the turcophil Gueshoff ministry
(March 1911) secured for Bulgaria a provisional commercial
arrangement in return for a *pro forma* repression of the
bands, and some amenities passed with Constantinople.
But the political relations of Bulgaria with Turkey were

those of armed anticipation, and in Macedonia, Bulgars and Turks were at war already. Thirty thousand refugees burdened the country, and the Macedo-Bulgars and Bulgarian militarists could not be long prevented from forcing this suppressed war into open war.

But the outbreak was delayed by various forces which might conceivably have availed to give time for an attempt at another international solution of the Macedonian question, now that the imperial solution had clearly failed. Bulgaria was in close touch with Austria, who was pacific, and was bound to have regard to Russia; and Russia was not as yet ready for war. But the main guarantee for peace was that Greece and Bulgaria had not yet been forced into a truce in their traditional and racial feud.

The relations between Turks and Greeks were from the first the least promising for peace. In the first fraternizing phase of the Ottoman revolution, Turks and Greeks had, for the moment, forgotten their feud. The Greeks had been given the Ministry of Agriculture in the first constitutional Government, and, as a result of Turkish resentment at the Bulgar declaration of independence, Ottoman Greeks were in high favour. This artificial alliance was dissolved by the Cretan proclamation of union in October 1908, which, although disavowed by Athens, was followed in November by negotiations as to Crete on the part of King George in the European capitals. It was converted into a sharp antagonism by what was considered an even worse breach of faith in internal politics. The first Ottoman elections had been ' arranged ' by the Committee of Union and Progress, allotting a certain representation to each community, a precaution for which there was much to be said in the circumstances. But the Greeks either would not or could not make their community carry out the compact, and consequently the elections turned out even more favourable to Hellenism than if they had been contested. This obliged the Young Turks to resort to forcing results and falsifying returns. Thereupon arose clamorous complaints of unconstitutionalism from the Greeks, of a character very damaging to the new régime and very detrimental to any chance of overcoming its difficulties. As soon as the Ottoman Parliament met, the Greeks, followed by the Albanians, and by the Arabs in an independent group, formed a federalist opposition by associating themselves with the party of the Liberal Union, in opposition to the radical imperialist policy of the Committee. This liberal nationalist opposition by its policy of defining the issues and dividing parties was considered responsible by the Young Turks for the difficulties that followed—such as the fall of Kiamil in February 1909, and the loss of British sympathies, and also to some extent for the loss of Islamic sympathy, the counter-revolution, and the civil war in the April following. The Austrians, by seducing the Bulgars into joining them in humiliating the new régime, had made a combination of the intellectuals with Islam impossible ; and now the Greeks had led away Albanians and Arabs into a policy which made a co-operation of the various communities in a constitutional empire no less impossible. Therefore, argued the Young Turk, Greeks, Albanians, and Arabs can only be retained by coercion—that is to say, by reconquest ; and for this the Greeks are to blame.

The Young Turks, seeking for a spirited foreign policy with which to rehabilitate their régime, had decided that Greece was the enemy, and that the moment had come to give Hellenism such a check as that of 1898 ; which had given the Hamidian régime ten years more of power when apparently on its last legs. By the summer of 1909 anti-Greek feeling was running high in Constantinople and was fomented by the Government, which had now decided to work off on Athens the humiliation put upon it by Vienna. This was a task of no great difficulty, for Greece was vulnerable in two points, the position of the Greeks who were Ottoman subjects and the position of Crete which was under Ottoman suzerainty.

The weapon of economic war that had proved an effective

riposte against Austria was, when used against Greece, a deadly thrust; for the difficulty of dealing with the Cretan question had already reduced the Greek Government to the verge of revolution. When the Committee of Union and Progress began to imperil Cretan union and the boycotting labour-guilds of Kerim Agha began to imperil Greek commerce, the Greek Government found itself faced with a choice between submission which might mean revolution and defiance such as must involve defeat. As it was, the damage caused to Greece by the boycott carried out by the dockers and lighters guild was not costing the country much less than actual war. The Greeks are the sole shippers and traders of the Empire and the second in importance in the trade of the Levant. The effect on Turkey of a boycott against Greeks can be compared with the effect in America of the shipping embargo of President Jefferson; while the effect on Greece was worse than that of Napoleon's ' continental system ' on British trade. It meant ruin to the Greeks of the Empire and a heavy loss of revenue to Greece itself. Moreover, while Greek shipping business was thus harried, Greece was given to understand that there was no prospect of proceeding with the long-promised junction of the Greek railway system with that of continental Europe: a disappointment of political as well as of economic importance. Finally, Greece saw with dismay an exodus of Hellenes from the Ottoman islands and mainland, driven out by the boycott and by the obligation of military service that was now enforced upon them. Thus did the Young Turk strike with telling effect at the most vital and vulnerable points in the growth of Greater Greece— the common commercial interest of the Greek nation with its colonists in the Empire—and the control of the urban centres of the Empire exercised by those colonists.

The Young Turks were intentionally driving Greece to extremities by economic and diplomatic warfare in the hope of eventually giving it the *coup de grâce* in actual war; for

Turkey had learned how to turn against a minor European State the process of exhaustion by exasperation often used against the Empire by European Powers. Indeed the military revolution produced by Turkish foreign policy in Greece was very much the same in its origin as the military revolution of the Young Turks had been—Crete taking the place of Macedonia as the cause of revolution. Both revolutions were due to popular discontent at the failure of the Government to maintain the rights of the State against rival races and intrusive Powers ; and both were directed against the dynasty owing to the direct responsibility assumed by the sovereign for the national policy and its failures. But Greece is a far more highly developed democracy than Turkey, and the seizure of power by a committee of officers instead of, as in Turkey, providing immediately a simple but efficient executive for effecting the necessary reforms, only caused a temporary confusion and collapse. The Crown was discredited and the foreign relations of the State were thereby gravely prejudiced ; for it was left without any permanent and efficient authority for foreign transactions. The national forces were disorganized and the legislature became merely a bureau for registering the decrees of a military junta. Finally the army and the navy fell out and there was a naval mutiny only suppressed with loss of life. And yet so wonderful are the workings of revolution, that while apparently reducing Greece to impotence, the effect of this crisis was to provide the one factor which had hitherto been lacking to qualify the Hellenes to resume the lead in Balkan affairs.

Since the death of M. Tricoupis in 1896 there had been no dominating personality to give direction and driving power to Hellenism. Fifteen years of party faction and fifteen months of the military league had prepared Greek public opinion to accept a dictatorship. Fortunately for Greece, the emergency produced the man, and the personality and political power of the new ruler of Greece was such as gave that country a distinct advantage over the other Near

Eastern nations. For they, like Bulgaria, had entered the lists under the leadership of men owing their position to everyday politics; or, like Turkey, had adopted the more primitive emergency machinery of an absolutist committee. M. Venezelos came to Athens clear of any previous connexion with the crisis in politics there, but with the reputation of having alone been able to control affairs in the even more disturbed democracy of Crete. As a Greek of Greater Greece he had the advantage of standing for an independent policy and an imperial point of view, and he could claim a national mandate such as the party politics of Athens could never have offered. As Premier of Crete he was summoned to Athens in the first place by the military league as adviser, and, at the first opportunity (October 19, 1910), he was made Premier of Greece by the King.[1]

It is very creditable to Greek democratic capacity that, not only was the right man found immediately, but that he was as immediately given a free hand and full powers. More-over, there was in this no question of a faction in power imposing their nominee on the nation; for, on the new Premier's first appeal to the country, the Greek electorate voted *en masse* for him against all their previous party leaders. The new Premier's party came into power with 240 votes in a Chamber of 279 members.

It was in Crete that the Young Turks had found their best field of operations against Greece. Even as Austria had exploited the Macedonian revolution to rob Turkey of its rights over Bosnia-Herzegovina, with the result that the reformed régime had been reduced to extreme peril by an Islamic reaction and by the counter-revolution of 1910, so Turkey had now in turn exploited the Cretan situation. Events had favoured this Turkish policy. The foreign contingents had

[1] King George deserved considerable credit for this readiness to put in power an opponent who had more than once given his dynasty trouble. It was M. Venezelos who was responsible for Prince George leaving Crete when his remaining as High Commissioner was endangering the policy of union instead of advancing it.

left Crete in July 1909, and the islanders then hoisted the
Greek flag. The Turks had at once sent their fleet to Kar-
pathos, mobilized in Thessaly, and sent threatening notes to
Athens. The Powers intervened and lowered the Greek flag
(August 1909), which was at once followed by military
revolution in Athens. The Porte renewed its pressure on
the Powers and its provocations to Greeks and Cretans until
a naval revolt at the Piraeus in September seemed to put
Greece at its mercy. Public subscriptions were started for
an Ottoman fleet, and in August 1910 two cruisers, the
Torgut Reis and *Barbarossa*, arrived at Constantinople amid
pan-Islamic paeans. Never was Greece in greater extremity
than in 1910–11, only a few months before its greatest
expansion.

To Greece, as to the other Balkan States, foreign affairs
stand in the first place ; for the democratic government of
those Greeks who have been already enfranchized in the
Hellenic State is a matter of small concern compared with
the diplomatic guiding into the fold of those who still await
emancipation. In this task, Greek statesmanship is tested
more especially by its success in making the lost Hellenic
sheep struggling at the narrow entrance to the national fold
keep line ; for the stronger and the more clearly Greek, such
as Crete, must be made to wait until the weaker and less
clearly marked, such as Macedonia, have been safely penned.
Crete, with its determination to annex itself to Greece in
despite of the Powers and in defiance of the Porte, was at
this time a serious embarrassment to the nation. Crete was
playing the game of Turkey by driving Greece, all disorganized by disturbance, into a single-handed war with the
Turks. The Protecting Powers, who alone stood between
Crete and a Turkish reoccupation, were unfavourably affected
by the breakdown of Greece and by the bravado of the
Turks ; though not, it is to be hoped, by their bribes. Russia
had taken up the question of opening up the Straits to its
warships, for which the European situation was so favour-

able that Turkish opposition alone remained to be dealt
with. The Russian official press [1] now began to advocate
the permanent establishment of Crete as an autonomous
principality under the Sultan guaranteed by the Powers, and
the reoccupation of the island for that purpose by international troops. This would have been almost a breach of
faith after fourteen years of promise of union, the last as late
as a note of October 28, 1908. Paris influenced by Petersburg
and interested financially in Turkey, Berlin anxious to pro-
pitiate the Young Turks, and Rome for various reasons
supported the proposal; [2] but London stoutly insisted on
maintenance of the provisional status and the promise of
union. Next summer, 1911, came the Morocco crisis, which
the Young Turks endeavoured to exploit to their own
advantage by again pressing for a permanent settlement,
à propos of the expiration of the High Commissioner's term
in September. It is said that Great Britain was offered
a settlement of the Bagdad railway question in return for
its assent; [3] but, whatever the faults of British diplomacy,
such trafficking finds no place in it. In the summer of 1911
British diplomacy alone stood between Greece and an international intervention in the Cretan situation, such as would
have meant internal anarchy and probably an Ottoman
invasion. It was in this delicate diplomatic situation, when
the sailing of every transport of Turkish troops for the
Yemen was a cause of sleepless nights to Greek statesmen,
that the Cretan organized democracy kept on driving the
disorganized Greek democracy into war. The advent of
M. Venezelos brought a general restoration of order. The
King came out of his retirement at his country seat, the
Crown Prince was restored to his military position, the new
constitution was voted (June 1911), and 171 new laws were

[1] *Novoye Vremya*, June 1910, *passim*.
[2] *Journal des Débats*, June 29, 1911.
[3] Victor Berard, *La Mort de Stamboul*, p. 196. Compare the arrangement between Germany and Russia of November 1911 by which Germany
abandoned Persia in return for a Persian extension of the Bagdad line.

passed. Better still, the improvement of the status of Greece in foreign affairs, though less obvious, was no less important. Crete was at once got in hand, and it became clear that the new Premier of Greece had resigned the Cretan premiership in form only. Crete had nearly caused a Hellenic catastrophe by insisting on hoisting the Greek flag; now, it did its best to create one by insisting, with the support of the Athenian populace, in sending deputies to the Greek Chamber. The Powers who, in the interest of Greece, had been forced into the *opéra bouffe* business of hauling down the flag, now found themselves engaged in a sort of harlequinade, pursuing Cretan deputies about the Aegean, and shipping them back on cruisers to Crete until all had, more or less deviously and disguisedly, reached their destination at Athens. M. Venezelos supported the Powers by expelling the Cretans from the Chamber; and, finding that the public peace and his position were imperilled, at great public inconvenience adjourned Parliament. It became obvious that Greek affairs were in the hands of a personality who could control them; and one, moreover, with whom foreign States could contract with confidence. This was an asset to Greece of the greatest value; for, if the Cretan Premier had succeeded in compelling Crete to bide its time, he had only done so by imposing on Greece the Cretan policy of a Balkan Coalition. The Cretans had none of the mainland Greeks' inherited horror of the Bulgar, and only looked on the latter as an obstacle to union which might with advantage be changed into an instrument. Crete had had, for over twenty years, to see the union, indispensable to its economic existence, postponed in deference to Greek policy in Macedonia. It was obvious that Epirus, the Roumlouk, and Salonica, could only become Greek by an alliance either with Turks or with Bulgars. The former seemed safe but slow, the latter risky, and, if possible, more repugnant: the former had been the traditional policy, and had involved the recurrent sacrifice of Crete. It was such a sacrifice that

had caused the military revolution, and that in turn had caused
the succession of a Cretan to control the national policy.
That M. Venezelos would adopt a pro-Balkan policy was, therefore, a foregone conclusion to those who correctly appreciated
his position and rightly appraised his personal power.

But, even with M. Venezelos at the head of affairs, and
both Greek and Cretan democracies loyally supporting him,
it did not seem possible in 1911 that Greece could, for many
years, contemplate any aggressive action. The material
changes that were necessary contained labour for a decade :
the moral changes might have taken a century. The party
system had to be reformed, and political corruption remedied :
confidence in the dynasty restored : the army and navy
reorganized and redisciplined : in short, the whole national
policy had to be reconstituted and rehabilitated. But there
is nothing that succeeds like success ; and so much is this
so, that more growth may sometimes be made in the convalescence from collapse than would have been possible under
ordinary conditions—always provided that the nation is
young. One important factor in favour of rapid reconstruction was the international control of the Greek finances,
which had kept up the national credit through the crisis,
and had served as a source of cash supplies at critical moments.
A foreign debt administration had been imposed, owing to
insolvency : a foreign dictatorship had been brought about
by mutiny—and it was these two institutions that now
co-operated in creating the moral confidence which won
for Greece in a month more than half of the remaining unredeemed Hellenic inheritance. In such strange ways does
a nationality movement, like all moral movements, profit
by persecutions and fulfil itself in failures.

Under these conditions, a coalition of the Balkan Christians against the Balkan Moslem had become the democratic
force in the situation long before it became a diplomatic
fact. The alliance of Greeks, Bulgars, and Serbs against
Turks was one which for a time had all the democratic

driving-power of a 'nationality' movement. As we know, it was not a 'nationality' movement—nationality being a deeper-rooted matter than any association for a common cause, however closely connected with nationality that cause may be. But the close connexion of the Balkan coalition with nationalism, and the superficial resemblance of the nationalist rising in the Balkan Peninsula to the historical nationalist eruptions of the last centuries in the neighbouring Italian and Iberian peninsulas, misled much contemporary opinion into seeing a permanent constructive amalgamation where there was only a temporary association for a destructive purpose. Some of the more boldly democratic theorizers, accustomed to seek a popular principle in every political phenomenon, went so far as to infer an essential element of unity in the Balkans, and, by applying the principle of nationality to the whole peninsula, arrived at the logical solution of a Balkan Confederacy or even a Balkan Federal State. But it must be remembered that so far from there being any common national element between Greeks and Bulgars, these two nations could never have been brought together, even in a diplomatic alliance for a particular purpose, but for the temporary predominance of the Cretan policy and point of view at Athens, and of the Macedonian policy and point of view at Sofia. Even so it proved impossible to conclude a formal partition treaty, and the two nations joined in attacking the Turks under no delusions whatever as to their attitude towards each other. Europe, naturally enough, supposed that two nations fighting side by side in a common crusade and in a mutual undertaking, must have some common sympathies and mutual confidence. Consequently, Europe was shocked at the subsequent charges of breach of faith and treachery brought by either ally against the other. But between Greek and Bulgar there never could have been confidence, and once Turkey was defeated there was no common cause to betray.

§ 12. European Political Wars

The Young Turks, in their innocence of international affairs and in their youthful enthusiasm, had confidently assumed that the European Governments would welcome their advent; but it was obvious that the succession of young and untried rulers, combined with the new lease of life which they might give to the 'sick man', would be a strong temptation to foreign beneficiaries to try to realize their reversionary interests. If the revolution was to be the death struggle of the Empire, it was the interest of a State like Austria or Italy, which had claims on one of its provinces, that those claims should be realized *inter vivos* to escape the delay and expense of probate by the Concert in congress assembled. If, on the other hand, the Empire was on the point of convalescence, it was better to realize such claims before it was restored to strength, and succession to them was indefinitely postponed. The only ground for hesitation was the doubt as to whether the Empire was still a sick man or whether it was not already a strong man armed. Diplomatic opinion, always cynically disposed, decided for the former, and the first foreclosures were made even before the end of the Macedonian millennium.

The rival claimants among the Balkan principalities for the European territories of the Empire were Greece and Bulgaria: the rival claimants among the Great Powers were Russia and Austria: as a result of the Turkish revolution Austria induced Bulgaria to join in a diplomatic deal on the most approved lines of *Realpolitik*: a deal, be it noted, which was in disregard of all principles of democratic diplomacy, and which was to cost both Powers dear in a very few years. This Austro-Bulgarian aggression constituted the first of the ' predatory' Balkan wars, though a bloodless one, as well it might be ; for the objectives both of Austria and of Bulgaria were merely empty forms.

Bosnia-Herzegovina had been under Austrian administration since the Treaty of Berlin. The fierce fighting with which the Austrian occupation had been resisted had been smothered many years before under the weight of the imperial garrison ; but the racial and regional associations of the provinces with free Serbia and Montenegro had made the fiction of Ottoman sovereignty a useful pretext for denying the self-governing institutions which would infallibly become instruments of a Serb national movement. Now this pretext was no longer possible, for here was an Ottoman free press advocating the extension of the Ottoman franchise and of representative government to those provinces under Austrian military occupation. Obviously the only way out of the difficulty was to regularize the Austrian occupation, and give the provinces an autonomy such as would not impair the Austrian autocracy. This could not be done, unfortunately, without impairing the integrity of the Ottoman Empire at a critical moment in its development, and repudiating the Treaty of Berlin at a somewhat critical juncture for both European and Balkan peace. Even if the Turks of Salonica and Stamboul were too divided politically to fight for what was only an empty treaty right, the Serbs of Belgrade and Cettinje were not too politically divided to join in fighting for a territory so full of importance to the Serbian national movement. The Serbs would be supported by Russia, and Russia by the Sea Powers of the Triple Agreement—all signatories of the Treaty of Berlin and sympathizers with the constitutional reform in Turkey. These dangers were, no doubt, recognized, and the obstacles they opposed to a policy of adventure and aggression were dealt with by Vienna with much diplomatic success. The Bulgarian Government, whose dynastic dignity had been offended by the Young Turk, was promised Austro-German support if it similarly shook off the fiction of Ottoman suzerainty by declaring Bulgaria independent and a sovereign kingdom. The German Government, which had seen its economic interests in the Ottoman Empire menaced by the rise of the Young Turk nationalism and the recovery of British influence, was willing to support its ally Austria for European reasons, even to the risk of war. The predominating military force of Europe as well as that of the Prussia of the Balkans being thereby secured, Vienna summarily annexed Bosnia-Herzegovina on October 7, 1908. Prince Ferdinand, two days before, had proclaimed himself Tsar of an independent kingdom.

In spite of the apparently unsubstantial character of the booty, and the very substantial political predominance and military preparations of the aggressors, a general European war might well have resulted, and a popular *casus belli* would have turned the scale in favour of war ;[1] but, failing such cause, the democratic influences for peace just held good. The British and Russian peoples had both only just emerged from costly wars, and both were preoccupied with internal progressive movements : either people would have required a good deal of working up before they welcomed an aggressive war in the cause of Turks, young or old, or

[1] Such a war would have been much like that of the Crimea, both in its formal *casus belli*, its origin in a political rivalry, and its ephemeral results. The German Governments would have been fighting for Eastern expansion, the one in Turkey in Europe, the other in Turkey in Asia. Of the Slav Governments, Russia would have been fighting, as it had fought before, for expansion southwards : Serbia, for its national existence. The Serbs are the Russians' nearest kinsmen outside Russia, their dynasties are Russian protégés : in their territories lie all Russian expectations of penetration and exploitation of the Balkan Peninsula. Greece would not have missed so good an opportunity of challenging the Bulgarian claim to Macedonia and the Balkan hegemony. Italy would have found an opportunity of extending long-deferred ' national ' developments in *Italia irredenta*. Between France and Germany there is still a valley of dry bones in Alsace-Lorraine, that a breath would people with armed men. The protection of real reform in the Ottoman Empire, and of the principle of nationality in the Balkans, even at the cost of war, would have found some support from British democratic opinion; while, at that moment, all opinion influenced by diplomatic considerations would have welcomed the opportunity of breaking, once for all, in alliance with France and Russia, that Prussian menace in the North Sea which was then the main occupation, almost the obsession, of its foreign policy. [Since this note was written, further Austrian action against the Serbs has had the result here anticipated.]

Serbs, far or near. Moreover, the Russian people had not forgiven the British Government its alliance with Japan; and the British people had not forgiven the Russian Government its treatment of the Russian constitutional movement. Armageddon was averted for the moment, but the Austro-Bulgarian declaration of diplomatic war against the Empire caused a diplomatic war in Europe only less costly in military expenditure and loss of goodwill than a military war. The Triple Agreement accepted its diplomatic defeat and did not appeal from it to arms; and the peace imposed on them by the Triple Alliance was one which allowed the Triple Agreement no compensations even in concessions as to form. The British protests against the breach of decent respect for treaties, and the Italian proposal that at least decorum might be patched up by a conference, were alike ignored. Serbian national aspirations were cleverly appeased and diverted against Turkey by the withdrawal of Austrian garrisons from the Sanjak (the strategic strip separating Serbia from Montenegro), and compensated by some relaxation of the Austrian military control of the strategic strip that separates Montenegro from the sea. The Young Turk was fobbed off with a money payment and some promises.

On the face of it the Austro-Bulgarian diplomacy had been a success. It seemed as though at the cost of a mobilization Austria had got Bosnia-Herzegovina and Bulgaria had got sovereignty and independence; and that it had been asserted finally that the German, Magyar, Rouman, and Bulgar interest ruled the Balkans to the exclusion of the Serb, Greek, Turk, and Albanian interest—an appropriate revenge in Macedonia for rebuffs in Morocco. But none the less it was a blunder, not only in the general interests of Europe but in those of the accomplices. Bulgaria, in pursuit of a dynastic policy, had lost sight of the democratic principle of the Balkan Peninsula for the Balkan peoples. In order to acquire a sovereignty which added nothing to the practical independence already acquired, the Bulgarian Government had seriously prejudiced its position in the Peninsula. It had united against itself the Serbian and Montenegrin governments, hitherto divided by dynastic dissensions, and had removed the Austrian wedge from between them. The Turks and Greeks were angered: the Sea Powers of the Triple Agreement, signatories of the Treaty of Berlin, were affronted: the Land Power of the agreement, Russia, was dangerously annoyed. Even the *quid pro quo* conceded to Austria was a blunder in democratic diplomacy; for with Bosnia-Herzegovina and the Sanjak still under a joint Austro-Ottoman rule Bulgaria was in a better position. It was indeed poetic justice—though perhaps the penalty was excessive—that in retribution for crowning Ferdinand Tsar with the help of the predatory Power in the Peninsula and at the cost of the national movement of the Serbs, Bulgaria had to renounce the crowning of its own national movement with Macedonia. For, if in respect of Macedonia the Serbian Government betrayed the Bulgars in 1913, the Bulgarian Government had betrayed the Serbs five years before in respect of Bosnia and Herzegovina; even if we admit the Bulgarian claim that it was due to Bulgarian intercession with Austria that the Serbs did not come off worse in 1908. Thus do the peoples pay in the long run the penalty of a predatory and unprincipled foreign policy, however immediately profitable it may seem.

The price paid by the Austrian and German peoples for the share of their governments in this transaction lay mostly outside the Balkans. The nationality movements of these older and larger peoples are in a less sensitive stage, and so the price paid has not been so obvious and is not to be reckoned in loss of provinces or in dramatic defeats. But Austria-Hungary has paid none the less for the adventure in heavy mobilization and other military expenditure, in financial crises and stringencies, in commercial and industrial losses and liquidations, and in political difficulties with the Slav populations within and without the Empire.[1] Although

[1] These various indemnities levied by the force of circumstances on

an open war over the Austrian adventure was averted, relations with the Serbs now almost amount to a ' suppressed ' war ; and the cost of mobilization and of increased armaments would have paid for many wars of an earlier age. Thus the *coup de main* of Bulgaria and Austria must be counted as the first of the series of wars in the Near East with which we shall have to deal.

The next Balkan conflict, the Tripoli war, which broke out in October 1911, was separated from the Austro-Bulgar *coup* by three years and immediately preceded the War of the Coalition. While the Austrian *coup* gave the first definite impetus to the ' suppressed ' civil wars that followed the Macedonian millennium, the Italian campaign gave the final impulse that led from the civil warfare into the open War of the Coalition. Neither intervention was a cause of the War of the Coalition, but both contributed powerfully to its outbreak in 1912.

Italy had long held a reversionary interest in Tripoli, the last section of the African Mediterranean littoral still unoccupied by one of the great Sea Powers of the Triple Agreement. France, in occupying Tunisia, in which Italy had really more claim to an interest, had had to recognize this reversion. It had again been tacitly admitted in the agreement by which Great Britain left France a free hand in Morocco in return for a free hand in Egypt. As to the Land Powers, the allies of Italy in the Triple Alliance, they owed

Austria-Hungary for its policy of adventure proved to be but a small instalment of the total reckoning to be required of the Empire. The disaffection of the Slav provinces resulting from the annexation was met by a campaign of repression, which ended in a successful conspiracy against the life of the Archduke Ferdinand—the able, if arbitrary and adventurous, heir to the throne—to which his consort also fell a victim. The resentment of the Imperial Government was chiefly directed against Servia, who was openly accused of complicity ; and the reprisals undertaken against that State have involved the Empire in war with Russia, the patron of Serbia, and have plunged the whole of Europe into war. Austrian imperialism has, therefore, in fatal conjunction with Serb nationalism, made an explosive mixture, which has fired the whole European magazine.

Italy compensation for leaving her out of the Bosnia *coup*; and Turkish rule in Tripoli was of no value to Austria or Germany. Russia and the Balkan States would welcome anything which weakened the new régime in the Ottoman Empire; and indeed that Empire might be supposed to be willing to let Tripoli go as it had Bosnia.

The Austro-Bulgar aggression had not resulted in open war, for the aggression against Serb nationality was one which had been already fought out in the Bosnian insurrection, and the aggression against Turkey was against an imperial suzerainty, not against a national sovereignty. The Bosniaks had already fought out their war of independence against Austrian domination in the 'eighties, and the change from Austrian administration to Austrian annexation did not affect the national liberties of Bosnia and Herzegovina themselves. On the contrary, it somewhat improved their chances of getting self-government, of a sort. But a 'nationality' war, and a very barbarous war, resulted from the Italian aggression against the Empire, because it did violence to the racial, religious, and political feelings of a primitive but virile people. The Tripoli Arabs, like the Bosniak Serbs, were of a different race though of the same religion as the Turks, and, unlike the Bosniaks, had never been strong supporters of the Sultan— probably because the Ottoman administration in Tripoli had come to be much more centralized and Byzantinized than it ever was in Bosnia. The long sea route was, to a race of townsmen like the Ottoman officials, or of landsmen like the Turkish troops, a far greater barrier than any land journey. Except for supplying luxuries such as horses or slaves, and as a means of distracting the Sea Powers over frontier questions, Tripoli was of little value to the Turks. Indeed, had the Italian *coup* been coincident with the Austrian, the Empire would have yielded without a fight. But in 1908 Italy was distracted by the Messina earthquake; and moreover, being a young democracy, where public opinion has still a voice, it required time to work up the democracy to the point of supporting a diplomatic *coup* involving another African campaign. The Abyssinian adventure had left so deep an impression on Italy that the war party, consisting of the southern townsmen, especially in Sicily and Rome, and of clerical, financial, naval, and military interests, had no easy task in prevailing over the commercial, liberal, and labour interests of the better educated Lombards, Piedmontese, and Venetians. The King and the Premier, Giolitti, at last consented, unwillingly it is said; whereupon, following the approved predatory procedure, Rome decided to follow the example of Vienna and to outface Europe and the Empire with an accomplished fact. Accordingly, at the end of September 1911, Europe read one morning with much surprise and little sympathy that Italy had suddenly landed an army in Tripoli, which was annexed in November.

But if the Italian war party had expected as peaceful a settlement as that of Austria with Bosnia, it had forgotten that, a quarter-century before, Austria had had to crush Bosniak independence and Islamic feeling in a bloody war. The Arab Moslem, with the help of some Young Turk officers, among them Enver Bey—a host in himself—started a desert campaign against the Italians, which confined them and still confines them to the coast. A war with barbarians, however well conducted, or however highly civilized the troops may have been at the commencement, invariably degenerates into barbarities. The recent wars of the civilized powers in Africa have given melancholy proof of the rule that the methods of the war will be those of the more barbarous belligerent. Italy has had to pay for Tripoli in blood and treasure more than it can ever be worth.[1] The Italian Government has by a dubiously profitable investment prejudiced its international standing, nowadays as valuable to a State as national

[1] Italy has at last (January 1914) learnt the cost of the acquisition of Libya. It amounts to 957,000,000 francs, or £38,260,000, of which £2,000,000 goes to the Ottoman Public Debt, £31,440,000 is put down to the Ministry of War, and £4,840,000 to the Ministry of Marine. Besides this, about £860,000 is to be spent for civil purposes on railways and harbours.

standing is to a statesman. In return it can show no profit
as yet—not even military glory. For the Treaty of Lausanne
in October 1912, by which Turkey ceded Tripoli to Italy,
was due to the declaration of war in the Balkans and not
to the result of the obscure and indecisive skirmishes with
Turco-Arab forces in the desert nor to any naval demonstra-
tions of Italy in the Aegean.

The Tripoli campaign would have been a far more powerful
impetus to war in the Balkans but for the care taken by the
Italian Government to localize the disturbance it was creating—even at the cost of sacrificing still further Italian democratic feeling. Although Italians and Turks were at war,
this fact was not to profit the Balkan peoples: oppressed
Christians could look for no help from the ' crusade ' of
Rome against Roum. The policy of Italy towards the Balkans
was to be the same as that which had just denied all help
to the insurrection of the Maltsori Albanians. These were the
terms exacted by Austria for assent to the annexation of Tripoli;
and the naval operations against Turkish ports in Albania
and Epirus were abandoned on Austrian representations as
to their effect on the ' existing order ' in the Balkans. For
the Italian people, always generous in its sympathies towards
the nationalist hopes of its neighbours in the Balkan peninsula,
it might have been some consolation for the loss of many
grandsons of the Garibaldian generation in suppressing Arab
anarchy if their lives had helped, even indirectly, in the
emancipation of the Balkan peoples from the Turks. But they
had not even the satisfaction of feeling that they had contributed indirectly to the liberation of the neighbouring
peninsula. For the Tripoli campaign, while it cost the
Turks little or nothing, contributed considerably to the
growing strength of the Empire under the Young Turk
régime. By reconciling Turk and Arab in a Holy War in
Africa, the Tripoli campaign healed for a time the running
sore in Arabia which had for years drained the resources
of the Empire. Indeed, nothing but a joint campaign

against the Unbeliever could have stopped the Homeric war of Turk and Arab round the sacred walls of Islam.

An even more important and permanent effect of this war is seen in the result of the naval operations against the Aegean islands, which were intended to intimidate the Turks but had no other effect than to irritate the Greeks. The Italian occupation of Rhodes, Kos, and the |Dodekanesian archipelago did not weaken the Ottoman Empire, but it was an unprovoked attack on the legitimate aspirations of Greece. In June 1912, the Aegean islands proclaimed themselves an autonomous State, but this was, of course, ignored, and the only result of the Italian ¦occupation was to exclude these unfortunate little communities from emancipation by the Greek fleet in the following year. The tenure by Italy of these Greek islands as a security for the Turks not fomenting disorders among the Arabs is about as good a title as the tenure of Greek Cyprus by ¦Great Britain as a security for the Turks not fomenting disorders among the Armenians. The attack of Italy on the national aspirations of the Greeks contains factors making for future trouble ; although the political activities of the Greeks are such that they will probably regain their islands without having recourse to actual war.

The Italo-Turkish War brought no material contribution to the conjunction of political forces that was to cause the war of the Balkan Coalition. But, in the moral sphere of international relations, it was of great effect. It radically changed the moral situation in Eastern Europe by breaking the ice for the plunge into war, on the brink of which the Balkan Governments were shivering. The Concert might continue to preach peace, but two of the Triple Alliance that was controlling Balkan affairs had exploited that control to their own profit, and that by war.

There was still a third war incidental to the Turkish revolution, and contributing to the War of Coalition, the ' war ' waged in Eastern Europe by Petersburg against

Vienna. The Bosnia-Herzegovina ' war ' had been a diplomatic *coup d'état* : the Tripoli War an actual campaign : while the Russian intervention was a political combination conducted in the Balkan capitals, and perhaps the most dangerous to peace of the three. While preparations for it were made as early as 1909, it does not seem to have been adopted as the principal policy of Petersburg until perhaps as late as the winter of 1911–12 ; and, in the meantime, other more easily realizable objects had occupied Russian diplomacy.

Russian prestige had suffered severely from the Austrian *coup* in Bosnia with its seduction of Bulgaria and its coercion of Servia, respectively the prodigal son and the protégé of Petersburg. Russia was just resuming a Balkan policy after an enforced retirement under the stress of war in the Far East and of revolution at home (1905). The mainspring that moves the wheels within wheels of Russian diplomacy in the Balkans is the principle that war can be made both progressive and profitable—and that war in the peninsula was both in the interests of Russia and of its protégés in the Balkans. Except in combination with British internationalism, Russian interventions in the Balkans are factors for war. But the Young Turk revolution had, for a time, cut the ground from under Anglo-Russian association in Macedonia, and now the Bosnian *coup* spurred on Petersburg to a policy of independent initiative in search of compensation. The compensation chosen for various reasons was that of opening the Straits to Russian warships. With much trouble the necessary consent was secured after a fashion from Europe, and France proposed a conference for its realization. But the Young Turks would not negotiate with Petersburg on the subject— even when combined with a proposal for the restoration of Ottoman sovereignty in Crete under international guarantee ; and Great Britain, to whom the opening of the Straits, the denationalization of Crete, and the coercion of the Young

Turks were all alike distasteful, was clearly in favour of nothing being done. After this failure at *Realpolitik*, Russian Balkan policy seems to have been that of preparing for a Balkan war of some sort, while postponing it until more pressing problems elsewhere were out of the way. In the course of the next few years a series of international agreements simplified the position of Russia in Manchuria and Persia, the two other friction points of Russian imperial penetrations. It is difficult, even after the event, to get any clear idea of the purpose and proceedings of Russian diplomacy, further than that it has been going to and fro in the earth, and walking up and down in it ; for, even when it plays providence, it moves in a mysterious way. But the main features of the Balkan international situation of 1908–12 are clear enough to permit of a fairly accurate estimate of the part played by Petersburg.

In the nineteenth century the Ottoman Empire had been maintained in its military occupation of Europe because it chanced to hold a strategic point in the field of conflict between the imperialist expansions of British and Russian. In the twentieth it seemed at one time likely to be maintained by a similar conflict between Teutonic and Slav expansions. It was not until 1908, when the Austro-Russian self-denying ordinance in the Balkans had been broken in the spirit by the Austrian *coup* that the interests of the Great Powers in the Balkans were concentrated as elsewhere, into two groups—Triple Alliance and Triple Agreement. In this new conflict the reactionary *Realpolitik* of the Triple Alliance had scored heavily all along the line in Bosnia-Herzegovina and the Adriatic, Tripoli and the Aegean, Constantinople and Asia Minor. This aggressive action was bound sooner or later to force on the Triple Agreement a progressive policy, and a support of the principle of the Balkan Peninsula for the Balkan peoples. As to how this progressive principle was to be carried out, not only was there no Anglo-Russian agreement, but probably neither party had any definite policy. Both were still hesitating between the claims of Ottoman imperialism under the Young Turk and of Balkan nationalism as represented by Athens and Sofia. In the case of British foreign policy, this indecision appears in a determination to do nothing; which stood in good stead more than once to both imperialist and nationalist, especially to Turks and Greeks. In the case of Russian policy, the doubt is characteristically reproduced by an *en tout cas* sort of policy :—a policy that was to meet either alternative— whether a success of Balkan nationalism or of Ottoman imperialism : a policy with a double focus in the Pan-slavism of M. Hartwig at Belgrade, and in the Ottomanism of M. Tcharikoff at Constantinople. M. Hartwig began at once to work for a reconciliation and alliance between Servia and Bulgaria under Russian auspices : M. Tcharikoff laboured to secure the confidence of the Young Turks by support-ing them in their most imperialist ideals. The only two points in common to the two policies were that the immediate intention of both was a diplomatic restoration of Russian pre-eminence, and that, in the end, this would, in both cases, be consummated by war. But what sort of war was left for circumstances to decide when the time came, and that would most probably not be before the expiration of the Austro-Russian Agreement in February 1912. The terms of this agreement, originally concluded in 1897 and twice renewed, are not known ; but it seems evident that while it permitted the Bosnia *coup* and compensation for it in the Straits, it would not have permitted such a disturbance of the *status quo* as the Serbo-Bulgar Treaty under Russian patronage and providing for a war against Austria. But if the policy of Petersburg favoured a Balkan war, and did much to foment it, it was not prepared for a European war. For this reason Russian diplomacy worked hard to make peace between Italy and Turkey so as to remove that dangerous complication; and until February 1912 the whole force of Russian influence at Sofia was bent on keeping the

Bulgarians from going to war, while at Belgrade it was still occupied in working the Serbians up to it.

It seems likely that in view of the preference for peace of the Bulgarian and Serbian Governments, Russian influence was more important in sending Serbia to war with Turkey than in keeping back Bulgaria from it.

In October 1909 conversations began between Serbian and Bulgarian ministers. But nothing definite was decided on for two years. M. Milanovitch, the Premier, was of pacific temperament, and, personally, in favour of a pro-Turk policy. It is true that the radical party in Serbia, under the leadership of MM. Pashitch and Milanovitch, had for many years favoured the Bulgar alliance ; and that the advent of this party to power, and the lead taken by Serbia, under Russian instigation, in the *pourparlers*, was a prominent factor in the conclusion of the coalition. But this policy was anti-Austrian, not anti-Turk, as appears from the Treaty on which the coalition was based (vide Appendix), art. 2 of which was directed more against Austria than against Turkey. In other words, the motive of the Serbian Government in promoting a coalition was defensive against Austria, not offensive against Turkey ; and this was, no doubt, the original intention of the Russian promoters. But the course of events in Macedonia, and the great development of Balkan nationalism, with the growing difficulties of Ottoman imperialism, caused Petersburg to decide on a pro-Balkan policy, and to permit a war against Turkey. The political and philanthropic Panslavism which had been excited against Austria, had been turned against Turkey by the Young Turk persecutions. Matters had indeed come to such a pass in Macedonia that the democratic factor in the policy of any State having any popular opinion about Macedonia, as had Great Britain or Russia, had become militant ; while the diplomatic factor was disposed to be militarist and to promote an alliance between the Slav Balkan States, which, even if it produced war, would strengthen the Triple Agreement and the imperial prestige of the patron Power.

Thus, Russian ' diplomatic ' policy again came into line with such ' democratic ' opinion as could still find expression in Russia, which was, of course, strongly in favour of a war of emancipation for Macedonian Slavs ; and, also, renewed its relations with the persistent, if somewhat pusillanimous, pressure in favour of Macedonian reform that was still maintained by British diplomacy.

British policy had been completely *désorienté* by the Ottoman revolution ; for the revolution among its reconciliations had united the two opposing points of view which for a century had divided British public opinion on the Eastern Question. The Macedonian millennium consequently produced in British minds a wonderful muddle of the old formulae—as to integrity of the Ottoman Empire and the gentlemanly Turk, the oppressed Christian and the sanctity of wars of emancipation—with new theories of constitutional empire and Turkish regeneration. The constitutional and imperial element in the revolution so attracted British opinion that it would have allowed the Young Turk to Ottomanize and even to Moslemize Macedonia had he avoided gross offence in doing so. The first rumours of Macedonian atrocities got little attention, and even when they could no longer be ignored, little if any active democratic interest was developed. The democratic force that brought British policy into support of Balkan nationalism was very indirect and difficult to define, but it sufficed.

The Governments of the Triple Alliance, who still retained some control of the situation by means of their relations with Bulgaria, Roumania, and Turkey, were well aware that the main danger both to peace and to their predominance lay in the fact that Russia had been violently expelled by them in 1908 from her proper position in the Balkans ; and that there was also a danger of Bulgaria, in spite of the Austrian Alliance, being forced by the Young

Turk persecution of the Macedo-Bulgars into taking up arms on their behalf. The insurance of the Triple Alliance against these risks consisted in the diplomatic combination it arranged between Roumania and Turkey, which cut off Russia from the Peninsula and put Bulgaria between two fires. As a result of this policy, Roumania was announced in 1910 (with how much truth is uncertain) as having offered to Turkey military support in case of attack by Bulgaria; just as in 1897 an Austro-Roumanian alliance had been announced in order to deter Bulgaria from joining Greece, then at war with Turkey. The counter-stroke was effective, for even a Balkan Coalition supported by Russia would have been in a hopeless position against the Turco-Roumanian Alliance backed by Austria. However, even without this precaution, a Balkan Coalition seemed unlikely in 1910.

As the danger of war increased, further deterrents were tried by Vienna. From the occasion of the visit of the Grand Vizier to Vienna in the autumn onwards, Austria remonstrated continually against Turkish provocations, pointing out that Turkish policy, especially towards Greece, would produce a Balkan Coalition. The Austrian warnings were not without effect; but this effect was little more than a formal compliance with the wishes of the Triple Alliance. Turkish expressions of friendship were forthcoming. Mahmud Shevket, the Young Turk general, visited the Patriarch and Ahmud Riza made a Graecophil speech; but the commercial boycott and the Macedonian dragonnades were maintained.

When the last stage was reached in 1912 and the Balkan Coalition came to the ears of Vienna, a last effort was made for peace, and this time the Austrian pacificators had the full support of the Ottoman Government for what it was worth. The Committee had been driven from power and replaced by a more liberal party which was anxious to buy off the Balkan allies at the price of Macedonian autonomy. The Austrian and Ottoman Empires, the two reactionary forces that had so long blocked reform in Macedonia, then, when it was too late, competed in concessions. But proposals from such a quarter could carry little weight even though they were given a hasty approval by the Concert. The Russian Government, though necessarily giving them a formal approval as a mandatory of the Concert, probably did not intend to improve any remote chance there might be of Bulgaria accepting them; for Petersburg had not laboured at the Balkan Alliance in order to gain for Austria the credit of establishing Macedonian autonomy—a change accruing to the immediate benefit of the Triple Alliance and to the ultimate benefit of the Austrophil Bulgar. Russian interests required that the Austro-Bulgarian predominance in the Balkans, dating from 1908, should be terminated by the dramatic discomfiture of both Austrian and Bulgarian diplomacy, and should be replaced by a Russo-Servian predominance. Consequently, the fact that the declaration of war by Montenegro, the vassal of Russia, preceded by a few hours the presentation of the complete Austrian proposals for autonomy, may fairly be scored to the credit of Russian diplomacy.

The Austro-Turkish proposals for autonomy failed, first because they came too late, and secondly because they were Austro-Turkish and not Anglo-Russian. That is to say, these proposals for peace, although democratic in form, had no democratic force; because there was no democratic relationship between the Austrian, Turkish, and Balkan peoples to give public confidence and popular force to such a policy. This explains how it came about that the various governments of the Balkan States, though they were all in favour of an international solution of the question by Macedonian autonomy, none the less did not evidently consider Count Berchtold's peace proposals as justifying renewed resistance to war.

All parties and all publicists have joined in pouring scorn upon the Concert of Europe for failing in the responsibility they attribute to it of preserving peace. No small part of this scorn has filtered through on to Great Britain, whose efforts were almost entirely devoted to the useless but_thankless task of maintaining the Concert. It is the fate of such embryonic and esoteric institutions as the Concert of Europe—or the Court of arbitral Justice—or the Peace Conference, that far more is expected of them than they are capable of performing, or than it is desirable they should attempt. When armed Concerts and arbitral Courts do try to play the part of an omniscient and omnipotent Providence that they are so often blamed for not playing, freedom finds itself threatened by the reactionary troops of a 'Holy Alliance', or peace is menaced by the breach of some impossible obligation for compulsory arbitration. The business of a Concert is conservative and consolidating. It is far better for the march of progress that 'the steam-roller' should lag behind it than that it should get in front. Bearing this in mind and examining the action of the Concert in the crisis of August–September 1912, we shall be surprised, not by its dilatoriness and inefficiency, but by a promptitude and a perspicacity thanks to which the contending parties were offered at the last moment as good, or even better, terms than they could win by war. But the difficulty under which the Concert must always labour is that so much pressure from outside is necessary to start it that this same pressure will settle the cause before it can pronounce judgement—unless it gains time by imposing its mandamus and enforcing inaction. We have seen that while the Balkan coalition had made war almost inevitable, it had also made such an effect on the pacific and conservative elements of Europe and of the Ottoman Empire that by August the mere conclusion of the coalition had secured from Austria and Turkey proposals for a sort of autonomy and for a kind of European guarantee. Thereafter we find the mobilizations that followed at the end of September so stimulating the activities of the Concert that, in the short ten days before actual war, the two essential requirements for Macedonia were secured—a sufficient autonomy and a satisfactory ' guarantee '. It was at last a possible international settlement, but it came too late to maintain peace.

The efforts of the Concert met with no success, and were, indeed, simply ignored by the Balkan States.[1] Public opinion in Europe acquiesced in the Balkan refusal to accept European mediation at this stage and welcomed their appeal to arms. The final effort of the Concert to maintain peace by asserting that no territorial change would be permitted as a result of successful war, met with little approbation from public opinion at the time. This pronunciamento has since met with little respect from the Balkan States and much ridicule from the press. And yet this, too, was a well-considered step, and one, moreover, in the interests of those opponents of the Ottoman Empire in Europe who most attacked it. For the Concert, while preserving an appearance of impartiality, really insured Europe against a Turkish success. The success of the Allies, and the partition of Macedonia, in apparent defiance of the prohibition, does not prevent the prohibition from being sound policy. The business of such an international institution as the Concert is to insure against

---

[1] The conversations started by Count Berchtold in August had prepared the way, and the presence in England of the Russian Minister for Foreign Affairs facilitated proceedings. To save time, action was taken verbally through the Ambassadors at Constantinople. In reply to their representations, the Porte undertook to put in force the scheme for autonomy elaborated in 1880 by an International Commission. This scheme was discredited, both by intrinsic defects and by the treatment it had received, and, though there was no time to elaborate another, a brief concession of the main points at issue would have been a more effective appeal. As it was, when Vienna and Petersburg, after supplementing this proposal with a ' guarantee ', submitted it to the Balkan States, the only result was that Montenegro declared war before it could be formally delivered. The other Allies ignored it, and made their demands direct to the Ottoman Government. These demands, in essentials, were moderate enough, but by adding themselves to the Great Powers as ' guarantors ', the Balkan States made them sufficiently impossible of acceptance by even the ' Liberal ' Ottoman Ministry. The policy was the same as that of Montenegro, though the procedure was more guarded.

reaction and revolution. If the revolution justifies itself and the reaction is never realized, so much the better; in that case the Concert pays in loss of prestige, and that is a premium that costs no one anything. The Concert of Europe may review its proceedings with the calmness of Phocion, who, while admitting that the result of the fighting was happy, yet did not regret that he had counselled against fighting.

But enough of diplomacies and of foreign policies. It is the prevalent defect of works on foreign affairs to confine themselves to the reported proceedings and reputed policies of Governments personified, when the proceedings are often insignificant or else intentionally deceptive, and the policies are often either vacillating between two opposing factions or drifting under pressure of circumstances. The work of competitive diplomacy may, like war, sometimes directly facilitate or delay the movement of popular forces, though its principal effect is indirect and due to its success or failure in preventing war. But it is never creative, and very rarely constructive.

When the war came it was received by the European people, as represented in the public press, with unmixed satisfaction. The great democratic achievement of an alliance between the rival Christian heirs of the Old Turk quite put out of court any remains of democratic belief in the regeneration of the Empire by the Young Turk. The promise that the alliance offered of a permanent peace for Macedonia quite outweighed pacificist prejudice against open war. The swift success of the Allies was received with a chorus of approbation that soon degenerated into a competition in adulation. But the applause was not entirely a tribute to success : the European public would not have turned down their thumbs at any of the allies that had fallen before the Turks in this contest, as they did later when Bulgaria was beset and outnumbered. The Ottoman Empire could only have profited by victory in an increase of prestige to the party in power, not by an increase of territory. British public opinion had long come to agree with the opinion formed by an Englishman over two hundred years ago. ' Who doubts but the Grecian Christians, descendants of the ancient possessors of the country, may justly cast off the Turkish yoke which they have so long groaned under whenever they have an opportunity to do it ? '

CHAPTER V

THE WAR OF THE COALITION

§ 13. The Conventions.
§ 14. The Combatants.
§ 15. The Campaigns.

The hour is for harvest or fight
To clothe with raiment of red ;
O men sore stricken of hours,
Lo, this one, is it not ours
To glean, to gather, to smite ?
Let none make risk of his head
Within reach of the clean scythe sweep,
When the people that lay as the dead
Put in the sickles and reap.

SWINBURNE.

§ 13. THE CONVENTIONS

ENOUGH has been said to show that, if the writer's summing up of the situation is correct, a Balkan Coalition and a joint campaign against Turkey already existed *de facto*, and, by force of circumstances, as early as 1910. But the formal conclusion of the coalition compacts between the Balkan Governments took another two years; and then, close on their conclusion and as an immediate consequence, came the coalition campaign. It would be wrong to look on this campaign of conquest as a diplomatic *coup* and a preconceived policy of adventure; such as was, for instance, the Tripoli enterprise of Italy. Everything indicates that both the coalition itself and its campaign were separately forced on the Near Eastern Governments by a political force out of their control; a force which was, in the cases of Bulgaria and Greece, supplied by the democracy of an independent province—Macedonia in the case of Bulgaria and Crete in that of Greece—and which was supplied to Turkey by an all-powerful provincial organization, the Macedo-Moslem

Committee. Still waters run deep, and the undercurrent that was hurrying the Balkan people to war, ever faster as they came nearer to the final plunge, was obscured to the observer by diplomatic eddies and political backwaters. Even so late as the winter of 1910–11 the air was so full of official voices proclaiming peace, that only a man of the people with his ear very close to the ground could have heard ' ancestral voices prophesying war '.

The forces whose collision caused the War of the Coalition are to be found principally in Turkish and Bulgarian nationalism; and primarily not so much among the Turks and Bulgars proper as in a war party of which the nucleus is the Macedo-Moslem or the Macedo-Bulgar. The War of the Balkan Coalition is, as the writer has already endeavoured to show, an execution of the eternal justice of things—an execution, all the more violent for having been resisted—of a justice that will, in the end, be absolute; although there is little that is either eternal or just about the Treaty of Bucharest. But the work of war for Near Eastern nationalism is not yet complete, for in foreign affairs, as elsewhere, 'nicht jeden Wochenschluss macht Gott die Zeche.'

The chronicles of the Balkan wars supply plenty of texts for pointing the moral that war is a two-edged sword, and that the causes which take the sword perish by the sword; or, in more modern words, that war cuts both ways and does not pay. For we find that whereas the Macedo-Moslem and the Macedo-Bulgar forced on the war, and are therefore responsible for its outbreak, they have thereby benefited the Macedonian community but have destroyed their own cause. The direct result of the War of the Coalition was the emancipation of Macedonia from the Empire and the end to the supremacy there of the Macedo-Moslem. An indirect result of it was the annexation of Macedonia by Serbia and an end to the superior claim of the Macedo-Bulgar. Those who have lost most by the Wars of Coalition and Partition, and who have lost it in the bitterest way, are the Macedo-Moslem and the

Macedo-Bulgar. It will be shown now, that it was they who forced on a war of nationalism against imperialism; a war which, as already shown, might, but for them, have been avoided by an international settlement even so late as August 1912.

In the spring of 1912, while the Balkan States were concluding the coalition which should give the Balkan nations sufficient cohesion for their war against Young Turk imperialism, the Young Turk empire-builders were arranging the Ottoman elections so as to give themselves such control of the Empire as would permit them to go on with their war against Balkan nationalism. The elections were not even conducted on the lines consecrated by usage in young democracies, by which the party in power assigns such representation to its opponents and rivals as it thinks they will accept rather than appeal to force; for the Committee could not now afford to take any chances of another breach of the agreement by the Greeks. But the Greek-Albanian opposition had now turned their attention to the Macedonian garrison, and a new law, under the unexceptionable pretext of prohibiting officers from taking part in politics, was intended to prevent any political activity in the army in opposition to the centralizing policy of the Committee. The opposition met this attack by recourse to arms, the Albanians rose and inflicted sharp reverses on Turkish troops. Military mutinies broke out in Macedonia, while the navy was also in open insubordination. A Macedonian military organization called the League of Military Unity appeared, and, before it, the Committee's control of Constantinople collapsed (June 1912) as suddenly as did the Hamidian régime under similar circumstances four years before.

The Committee fell, like Abdul Hamid, because it had lost the support of the Macedonian garrison. The support of the packed Chamber counted for little, for as it represented nothing but the Committee it had no democratic force. The only really representative institution now left was the army, and the army had been alienated by the failure to prepare against the Italian raid, and by the wasting on civil war with Arab and Albanian Moslem the resources that might have been kept to quell the Christian Balkan States. Mahmoud Shevket, the Minister of War and the saviour of Young Turkey, was dismissed in deference to the demands of the military league mutineers at Monastir. A week later (July 10, 1912), Said Pasha, the Grand Vizier of the Committee, fell after a naval demonstration of the Italians outside the Dardanelles. A Ministry of Old Turks, with an average age of 65, came into office with the mission of making peace with the Italians, Albanians, and Macedonians. In this Ministry the Committee still had friends in the younger Mukhtar, son of the Vizier, and in Hilmi, and these relations were strong enough to prevent such reprisals as might have rendered the organization really powerless. The rôle of the Committee became that of an unconstitutional opposition—powerless to alter policy, but determined even at the cost of peace to prevent its realization.

The fall of the Committee was well deserved ; and had it been more complete it might have prevented the war. But their surrender to the constitution and to the federalist liberals was, like that of Abdul Hamid, only to gain time. He had relied on recovering power by civil war, and from the time of the fall of the Committee from power, they set about the recovery of their influence by forcing on a Balkan war. How far this was the result of conviction that war was in the imperial interest as the only way to prevent federation, and how far it was mere politics to bring the Committee back to power, it is difficult to say. What is more important is that, even after their fall, the Committee retained enough power to impose their policy on the Government, and thereby to make the Empire play into the hands of the Balkan coalition that were now ready for war.

By midsummer in 1912 even a real reversal by the Liberals of the centralizing and coercive policy of the Committee could scarcely have checked the impetus into war resulting from the conclusion of the Balkan Alliances—supposing such reversal could have been effected. But it could not ; for the Young Turks had still power enough in Macedonia to thwart the concessions of the Cabinet,[1] and, being relieved of responsibility, could devote their whole energy to forcing on the various wars within and without the Empire for which their martial minds were as fully prepared as their military machinery was not.[2] It is of course not so easy to bring home to them responsibility after their fall from power, when their bellicose activities had to express themselves in more or less subterranean proceedings instead of in public policy ; but a very little knowledge of the events in Macedonia during the summer of 1912 gives clear evidence of their machinations. Take, for instance, the events of August, the penultimate month of peace, when the fact of the Balkan Alliance was pretty generally known, and when the conservative forces in Europe with the help of such similar forces as remained in the Ottoman and Balkan Governments were straining every effort to find a pacific solution at the eleventh hour. In that month, when frontier incidents had already made a diplomatic crisis with Montenegro, the Ottoman Minister, a Young Turk, suddenly presented an ultimatum and left Cettinje—a provocation to formal war that was prevented from succeeding only by the Ottoman Government proving to be strong enough to repudiate their representative ; and by the fact that, if the mediaevally mobilizable

---

[1] ' The orders and directions issued from Constantinople, with the best intentions, are not obeyed in the provinces or on the frontiers. Here lies the real danger and the true cause of disturbances that may happen in the near future.'—*Near East*, Constantinople Correspondence, Sept. 14.

[2] An interview, reported in the *Near East*, with a leading Young Turk, in the winter of 1911–12, well expresses this policy and point of view : ' We can never really settle down to progress and reform until all these little neighbouring States have been thoroughly beaten and taught their inherent inferiority and their proper place. That we can only do by war. With an army of 800,000 at the minimum against a maximum of 450,000—how can we fail to win ? The Turk is a soldier, and does not require to be trained. He need only be armed, and of first-class weapons we have more than enough.'

Montenegro was then ready for war, the other Allies were not. The final *casus belli*—the Adrianople manœuvres—was supplied by another Young Turk plot also repudiated by the Government, but this time too late, because the Allies were ready. Nor was Young Turk activity confined to keeping up a supply, hot and hot, of *casus belli*. It also aimed at working up public opinion in the Balkan States to the boiling-over point. For while the statesmen of Bulgaria and Serbia were obviously struggling to restrain belligerent public opinion—the more bellicose in order to gain time to perfect their preparations, the more pacific in the hope of something preventing the war—a succession of provocations was supplied them from Macedonia such as might, and eventually did, force their hands. The supposed massacre of Serbs at Sienitza, the reported massacre of Montenegrins at Berane, and the provoked massacre of some hundreds of Bulgars at Kochana,[1] were in the circumstances likely to be as decisive as that formal declaration of war which the Macedo-Moslem militarists of the Committee no longer had power to send.[2] In vain did the official government of Old Turks do their best to end the Albanian and Italian wars and evade the Balkan war. The Old Turks were compelled to prolong their negotiations for peace with Italy so as to preserve an

[1] The Sienitza incident, first announced as a massacre of thousands of Serbs, reduced itself to the murder of one—but only after the required effect on public opinion had been produced. Whether the bomb-throwing at Kochana, which provoked the killing of Bulgar peasants there, was a Macedo-Bulgar incitement to massacre, or a Young Turk intrigue to excite war, matters little to the argument here, which only asserts that it was one or other. The difficulty of the pacific elements in the Bulgar Government, caused by the agitation over the Kochana incident, was increased by there having been another Bulgar massacre at Ishtib the year before, for which no satisfaction had been given by the Turkish Government. At Kochana there were 100 killed and over 200 wounded.

[2] The *Daily News* special commissioner reported July 10, 1912 : ' So far as my observation goes, the present condition of the province is worse than it was in 1908, when I saw the Murzsteg programme at work.' This is confirmed by two authorities, the first favourable to the Old Turk Government, the second to the Young Turk.—H. Woods, *Fortnightly*, April 1912 ; Pears, *Contemporary*, June 1912.

appearance of bellicose obstinacy such as their political position forced on them; while every concession of a liberal and decentralizing character to Albanians or Macedonians was used unscrupulously against them, being represented as trucklings to Austrian domination and treason to Moslem predominance. Moreover, although unable, or unwilling, to turn the Government out and take their place, the Committee kept it disorganized and distracted by constant ministerial changes due to their intrigues. The situation might be summed up by saying that the peace party in control at the capital were completely checkmated and counteracted by the war party in control at Salonica. As exponents of the belligerent policy of the Macedo-Moslem minority, and fully exploiting the advantage of being the only organized political party, the Committee could pursue their policy of action with greater effect out of office than when hampered by the responsibilities of the Imperial Government, and they used their power relentlessly and unremittingly for forcing the country into war. The Empire, as a whole, did not want to fight the Balkan States for the privileged supremacy of the Macedo-Moslem over the Albanian and the Macedonian. But the Macedo-Moslem intended to fight for that supremacy and to use the whole forces of the Empire in that fight.

So once again an organized and obstinate minority forced an unorganized and obedient majority to fight for the privileges of the minority: once again imperialism forced an Empire to fight against its true imperial interest; and once again ' nationalism ' won, and imperialism lost.[1]

On the Bulgar side there was no such clear dividing line

[1] It may seem bold to assert that the majority of the Empire were averse to war. No doubt once the war was started the appeal to racial and religious pride was not unavailing; but even so the old war spirit of the Anatolian Turk does not seem to have been effectively excited. The following observation of an Anatolian private is probably fairly representative : ' In the old days we fought for the Moslem, now we fight for the Memleket (country), but my Memleket is over there ', pointing across the Bosphorus.

between the peace party and the war party. There were the two different points of view, but at this late hour on the eve of war, public expression of differences of political opinion was avoided. None the less, it seems safe to assert that the Bulgar Government and the majority of the Bulgarians would have been willing to wait a few years longer for Macedonian autonomy by way of concession from Constantinople and by international guarantee, rather than pay the price of a war and a partition; but that the Macedo-Bulgars had decided that war must be forced on immediately. The Macedo-Bulgars were, moreover, in respect of Sofia, somewhat in the same position as the Macedo-Moslem war party in relation to Constantinople, or the Cretan war party in relation to Athens. They had no control of the Government, but had a strong influence in it owing to their control of events in Macedonia, the centre of public interest and the source of public opinion. Thus by the autumn of 1911 the Internal Organization is again found to be in control of Bulgar-Macedonia. From 1893 to 1908 it had been practically a revolutionary provisional Government of the Macedo-Bulgars, and now it had resumed its activities in Macedonia and Sofia. Whether such provocative events as the ' massacre ' of Ishtib, in the autumn of 1911, when the Balkan Alliance was in course of construction, or that of Kochana in August 1912, when war was in contemplation, were direct or indirect results of the Macedo-Bulgar activity, is unimportant. The Macedo-Bulgar party meant Bulgaria to go to war, and events had put it in their power to have their will. After the Sofia demonstration, organized by them, which followed the Kochana massacre in August, the Bulgarian Government found it necessary to inform the Macedo-Bulgar leaders that war was decided upon. How far this decision was forced on the Bulgarian Government it is difficult to say ; but it is known that even in the army there was a body of opinion averse to it.

War, when it came, was fought for causes that were already

won, between Governments that did not want to fight. Neither the Old Turks and liberal federalists, nor King Ferdinand and the Austrophil pro-Turk ministry of M. Gueshoff, wanted war; and as we have already seen, Macedonian autonomy was already secured by international intervention.

It is the dangerous peculiarity of a really democratic war that its immediate imminence is not indicated by friction in superficial diplomatic relations. The menace of an Anglo-Russian war of policy in the 'nineties of the last century, and that of an Anglo-German war of policy in the last ten years, were both so displayed in diplomatic relations, that pacific public opinion was sufficiently cautioned, and had time to assert itself and avert successfully the danger of war.[1] On the other hand, the preliminary procedure of the Balkan Alliance was a slow and subterranean one of conversations between premiers, correspondence between princes, and finally a series of secret conventions between the governments. Where princes and premiers feel assured of the approval of public opinion, they can assume vital responsibilities of peace and war on the strength of summary agreements between principals. It is only when diplomacy is out of touch with democracy that such transactions are voided as being internationally invalid or criticized as being constitutionally *ultra vires*. The negotiations being directed against the two Empires, Austrian and Ottoman, that hold the Balkans as between hammer and anvil, had to be conducted with a secrecy that excluded the use of the usual diplomatic channel. The coalition would probably, in any case, have become a diplomatic fact, but the concealment of its existence in its delicate infancy contributed to its success. It is especially interesting to note that while the comparatively easy task of bringing together Serbia and Bulgaria was

---

[1] The resemblance between the conditions preceding the Balkan wars of last year and the European wars of this year has proved to be closer than was supposed when this was written—and the danger has not been successfully averted.

discharged by the Russian representative at Belgrade, M. Hartwig—in the more difficult and delicate business of the first overtures between Greece and Bulgaria, recourse was had to the intermediary of a private British subject, Mr. Bourchier, *The Times* correspondent in the Balkans. It is as satisfactory as significant that the most democratic of the diplomatic designs that have changed the face of Europe should have been entrusted to the more democratic of the two professional forms of international representation.

The success with which the secret was kept and the swiftness with which the two Governments passed from their traditional feud to a transitory fellowship, can only be understood if it be recognized that the diplomatic conversations and conventions were merely ratifying a confederacy already concluded between Macedo-Bulgar and Cretan. Moreover, the suspension of hostilities between Greek and Bulgar in Macedonia which began in 1908 had become more marked with every year, until in 1911 they were already fighting side by side against the Moslem in the Macedonian guerrilla war that preceded the Balkan War of Coalition. The significant change in the Bulgarian Constitution in August 1911, which gave the king power to conclude secret treaties, roused no opposition in Bulgaria ; and the indications that M.˙Venezelos was using the extraordinary powers accorded him for internal reconstruction to bring about a revolution in foreign policy met with no objections in Greece.

It is not necessary to suppose that the Powers of the Triple Alliance had no idea of what was going on.[1] The

---

[1] Nor is it to be supposed that other Powers, less directly concerned, were not uninformed. We know that *The Times* was cognizant, and loyally kept the secret, even after continental papers had announced the alliance. The utterances of public men are subject to the same double responsibility. Even so late as September 20, ten days before mobilization, M. Pashitch, one of the two Serbian originators of the alliance, informed a deputation of merchants that ' the Government's intentions were peaceful '.

deficiencies of the mediaeval diplomacy that still obtains in the Balkans is not so much in the overlooking of diplomatic facts as in the underrating of democratic forces. The Russian Government, as we know, was fostering the Serbo-Bulgar Alliance, and, if it showed some underestimate of the Graeco-Bulgar relations by continuing, so late as 1911, to urge Greece and Bulgaria into closer ecclesiastical relations on Panorthodox lines, this only argues a miscalculation of the democratic forces that were driving them into the same camp rather than into the same church. When, in 1912, the coalition was taking its final diplomatic shape in military conventions, Austria showed a very accurate realization of what was happening, and a sound recognition of what should be done. Only, as usual, action was taken too late. For if, as we may suppose, Vienna was correctly informed of all that was passing at Belgrade between Serbia and Bulgaria, the Austro-Hungarian proposals to the Powers to guarantee Macedonian autonomy might well, a few months earlier, have been enough to postpone military action by Bulgaria, the pivot of the coalition. But, by August 1912, the decision for war had already been taken, and nothing short of military intervention could have stopped it.

The Balkan Coalition was, by the summer of 1912, fully constituted in a series of secret treaties, negotiated during the winter 1911–12 by secret correspondence and personal conferences between the premiers, in consultation with their sovereigns only.[1] The character of these treaties clearly shows the pace at which the Governments were being hurried into war. The first, the Serbo-Bulgar Treaty, is a political alliance, making provision for the future under various political contingencies, among which a war with

[1] According to *The Times* correspondent, Mr. Bourchier, the Serbo-Bulgar Treaty was arranged in a conference between MM. Milanovitch and Gueshoff in a railway carriage in October 1911 ; that between Bulgaria and Greece was agreed on at the meeting of King Ferdinand and the Greek Crown Prince, George, at the coming of age of Prince Boris in February 1912.

Turkey is only indirectly contemplated. In the succeeding agreements by which the coalition was constituted, the *casus foederis* becomes, more and more explicitly, a war with Turkey—as the forces at work hurry the Coalition Governments to that event. A war against Turkey was neither the purpose of the Serbo-Bulgar convention, nor was it even considered as a probable consequence of it by the Governments that concluded the treaty. The defensive form given to this treaty was not merely *pro forma*, whatever it may have been in the case of the Graeco-Bulgar convention, when that came to be signed some months later. The Serbo-Bulgar Treaty was intended to be kept secret from the two Empires against which it was directed : in the hope that the substance of it would not be a provocation, as it would have been if published; though the suspicion of it might have a good effect on Austrian and Ottoman policy.

The Serbo-Bulgar Treaty was signed, unlike the others, by both sovereigns : provision was made in it both for the realization of the Bulgar policy of Macedonian autonomy and for that of the Serb policy of Macedonian partition : it had the especial sanction of Russia in the formal acceptance by the Tsar of the arbitration of disputes, and it was concluded between the two Balkan States which had always been in closest relation to each other. Yet the treaty was torn up at the first tension. The fact was that the democratic sanction given to the coalition was good only for a joint campaign of Greek, Slav, and Bulgar armies against the Turkish garrisons : even as the democratic sanction given to the Macedonian millennium was good only for a joint campaign of European, Moslem, and Christian against an Asiatic Byzantinism. The campaign once carried out, the combination dissolved, and no paper obligation could hold it together.

The Serbo-Bulgar Treaty in March was followed by a Montenegro-Bulgar arrangement in April. Montenegro had been one of the first States to make overtures for an

alliance, which in the autumn of 1911 were responded to
favourably by Bulgaria and Greece, but put off by Servia
for political reasons. The hearty co-operation of Montenegro was, in any case, never in doubt; and indeed over-
precipitate action was doubtless considered a greater danger,
for a treaty of alliance between Montenegro and Serbia
was not signed until the outbreak of war in September 1912.

The most important treaty of all, the Graeco-Bulgar, is
also included in the appendix. It was not concluded until
May, and follows the main lines of the Serbo-Bulgar Treaty,
but without any provisions for the future, any military
conventions or any reference to Russian arbitration.

Another difference between the Serbo-Bulgar and the
Graeco-Bulgar Treaties, showing the swift change in the situation, is to be seen in the distinction that while the former
is really defensive in fact, the latter is so in form only
Thus, in the Graeco-Bulgar Treaty the obligation really
is to take the field together on any systematic violation by
Turkey of the treaty rights of either signatory or of the
law of nations, nominally it is only to make joint representation to Turkey as to violation. The whole existence of the
Empire in Europe being at this time a systematic violation
of treaty rights, and any joint representation being in the
then temper of the Young Turks tantamount to a challenge,
the elaborately ' defensive ' drafting could not conceal the
' offensive ' object of the agreement. But the manœuvre
served its purpose in mollifying the pacificist proclivities
of the European public : without in any way moderating
the policy of the Empire when, in due course, the agreements
came to its ears via Vienna. The short term, moreover,
for which this Treaty was concluded suggests that a more
rapid and effective procedure was already in view than mere
peaceful representations.

A chronicle of the months of May to September 1912 is
interesting and instructive to those who, like ourselves, have
knowledge of the event and of the forces at work. On the one

side there were the calculating conservative forces of the governments of the Balkan States and of Turkey, at first genuinely pacific and then merely procrastinating until the proper moment for declaring war should have come. On the other side was the headlong head-down pressure of public opinion inflamed by the incitements of the war party on either side and hurrying the governments into hostilities. It is difficult, and not very important, to fix the exact dates at which the war policy traversed its decisive developments ; but the following leading events show the period and the pace. The hurried conclusion in May of the Graeco-Bulgar agreement, followed by the no less hurried mission of the Bulgar Premier and Foreign Minister to Livadia, to secure Russian sanction for their policy, are evidence that by that time war was expected sooner or later, and rather sooner than later. In the same month, large purchases of horses in Hungary and Russia by the Serbs and Turks respectively indicate a beginning of the military preparations which thereafter continue unremittingly ; although these preparations were for the most part reported only in the case of Serbia— a result due to her exposed position. In June Serbia voted a special credit of twenty million francs for war purposes and another million for a secret purpose: Bulgaria began to press forward anxiously a large loan in Paris : and Turkey raised £10,000,000 from the Ottoman Bank, beginnings of the subsequent efforts to raise money at all costs before the war closed the supply. In July the French and Russian press began to announce the Balkan Alliance. In August a great public meeting in Sofia of delegates from all over Bulgaria, summoned in protest against the 'massacre' at Kochana, demanded autonomy or war ; and on August 26 the Sofia Government secretly decided on war in October— consulted the Allies—and obtained their assent. In August also came the intervention of Austria, and Count Berchtold visited Bucharest. In September a Turkish threat to hold grand manœuvres in the Adrianople district, though almost

immediately withdrawn, was used as a pretext for mobilization by Bulgaria and the Allies on September 30, and Turkey
followed suit on October 1. Montenegro anticipated the
autonomy proposals of the Powers by a few hours with
a declaration of war on October 8. On October 17 Turkey
ordered the Bulgar and Serb representatives to leave Constantinople, and the following day they, with their Greek
colleague, handed in a declaration of war. Until mobilization
was begun journalistic and diplomatic opinion continued
to discredit the probability of it. This was partly due to
an adherence to such generally accepted formulae as that
which prescribed the spring as the only possible season for
war in the Balkans. As a matter of fact, whatever may have
been the case long ago, under present conditions the autumn—
after the harvest is in, the autumn manœuvres over, and
the malaria ended—is the most convenient time for beginning
war with a well-clothed, well-supplied army; and to a practical
government like that of Bulgaria such considerations probably hastened the declaration. But it was deeper and
stronger forces than mere military considerations that forced
on the war.

If we try to get the War of the Coalition into historical
perspective, and contemplate it in relation to the course of
events preceding it rather than as an event by itself, we shall
find that this historical perspective will considerably alter the
respective prominence of the parts played in the war by the
three Allies. The War of the Coalition, considered as a war and
from a military point of view, is primarily a war for military
supremacy between the Bulgarian and Ottoman forces in
Thrace; secondarily a war between Europe and Asia for the
possession of Macedonia; and lastly a war for maritime
supremacy in the Aegean between a future Greek Empire
and an effete Ottoman Empire. Considered as a political
event and from a political point of view, the respective rôles
of the belligerents take a different order of importance, and
we find that the war between the Greeks and Turks is the

most interesting and pregnant in its results; while the wars of Serbs and Bulgars against Turks, of Bulgars against Greeks and Serbs, and of Roumanians and Turks against Bulgars, became merely ephemeral or eccentric events. The Wars of Partition have no doubt a place in history as a prelude to a European epoch as yet scarcely begun, but the War of Coalition closes an epoch which began a century ago. These wars show well that profit by war is not always proportionate to success in war, for the political consequences of these wars correspond rather to the requirements of historical movements than to the results of military action. It is indeed one of the disadvantages of realizing a national policy by means of a war that success in battle does not necessarily bring a satisfactory settlement to the victor. The very exhaustion caused by his efforts exposes him to being robbed of his conquests unless his title to them is a much stronger one than mere military conquest. Even conquest reinforced by treaty-right may not be enough. The strongest title of all is that which rests on the fullness of time and is enforced by a tide in the affairs of men, taken at the flood.

From the military point of view nearly the whole interest and importance of the war centres in the Thracian campaign; and the war was over when the main Bulgar army had driven the main Turkish army behind the lines of Tchataldja that defend Constantinople. Mere readers of the papers whose attention is exclusively engaged ·by bloody battles, big battalions, and brave deeds, will take this view; and they are accordingly shocked when the spoils do not go to the victors and brave men are cheated of their rewards. But those who have read the pages that precede may be prepared to take a larger view and consider the Balkan War of Coalition not so much as a war, or as a coalition, but rather as a campaign in the century-long warfare by which the Greeks are winning their way back to their maritime empire of the Aegean, lost five hundred years ago. From this larger point

of view the Bulgar Thracian campaign becomes a mere
gallant vanguard action in which force of circumstance and
the irony of fate brought this gallant race to fight in the
front line of its worst enemy. We have seen how the force
of circumstances drove the Bulgars from their democratic
pacific association with Turks and Albanians into a ' diplomatic ' alliance with their Greek rivals and their European
repressors ; and we shall see how their false position as vanguard in a Graeco-Turkish war brought them no better treatment than the services of soldiers of fortune usually receive.
The possible profit of the Bulgars from the campaign was,
like that of any foreign contingent, no more than their
military strength could enforce for them. When that was
exhausted by driving the Turks through Thrace and behind
Tchataldja, they were not so much better off by the conquest
of the empty Thracian uplands and its valley villages of
Turks and Greeks, but so much the worse off ; for while
their military prestige was increased by their successes, their
military power was reduced by their exertions and expenditures. From the larger point of view of political tactics, the
Bulgar advance through Thrace was only the covering operations of ' friendlies ' thrust forward to clear the way for the
real permanent advance of the Greeks through South Macedonia and the Aegean. If the Serbian ' friendlies ' have been
well paid for their support and the Bulgars ill paid, that is
on account of obvious reasons of Greek policy towards these
frontier tribes. If this is an' overstatement it may none the
less serve to counteract the undue attention that has been
given to the military point of view, which puts the Bulgar
operations first, the Serbs second, and the Greeks last.

There is nothing incompatible between the argument that
the Balkan War of Coalition was, in its ultimate object,
a campaign in the re-establishment of the Greek Empire,
and the argument that, in its direct origin, it was a fight
between the Macedo-Moslem and the Macedo-Bulgar. It
was the military power of the Macedo-Bulgar supported by

the Bulgarian army, and the Macedo-Moslem supported by
the Ottoman army, that blocked the Greek advance by land
to Constantinople. When these two obstacles cancelled each
other, that advance was at once realized and now represents
the main result of the war.

The first result of any ' reconstruction ' in the Balkans
had to be a liquidation of long-overdue liabilities to the
Greek movement—so long overdue that they would necessarily be a first charge on any proceeds. Claims such as those
of Greece to Crete, to southern Epirus, to the Roumlouk,
and to the Aegean islands had been filed long before those of
Bulgaria to South Macedonia or those of Serbia to the
Sanjak. This explains why the Greek movement stood to
win whatever had been the result of the Bulgar-Turk campaign. If the Turks had won and advanced to Sofia it is
the Bulgars who would have paid : the Greeks would, at the
worst, have escaped scot-free, as in 1897, but more probably
would have retained Epirus and the Roumlouk with Crete.
In the event of the Bulgars winning, as they did, the way
was cleared for the Greeks to advance to their ethnographical
frontier including Salonica and possibly Kavalla, without
injuring their prospects of acquiring Constantinople later.
The Bulgars are better fighters than the Greeks ; but their
true objective was not Constantinople but Salonica, and such
misdirection tells on the driving power of an army, however
victorious and virile. If it had been a Greek army that
came against the lines of Tchataldja in November it might
very likely have taken more than the disease and disaster-
stricken defence and the diplomatic dead-lines that kept out the
Bulgars to keep the Greeks out of the final goal of the Great
Idea. Similarly, if an adequate Bulgar force had been firmly
established in Salonica and Monastir, it would have taken
more force than all the surrounding Balkan States could
ha 'e developed, or than European civilization would have
permitted, to turn them out. It was a knowledge of this
that maintained the Bulgar contingent left in Salonica, and

that caused the desperate effort to throw a similar contingent
into Monastir which resulted in the War of Partition. As
it was, the fact that Serbia and Roumania enabled Greece
to realize its extremest claims in Macedonia, and that Turkey
saved Thrace from Bulgaria for the benefit of a future Greek
Empire, looks like mere Greek luck and Bulgar blunders.
But when the turn of events favours a cause this is in itself
evidence that a debt long overdue to that cause has been
liquidated. The ship of state that is carried on the full
force of the flood tide will be kept by it off the rocks, and
even if it touches will drive clear : the armed nation whose
strategy is sound will find tactical developments play into
its hands. It is highly unjust that the Greek nationality
movement should have made most out of the Balkan Wars
if we look only at the Greek military and naval contributions to these wars ; and in so far as a settlement is unjust
it is unstable. But if we consider the whole history of the
nationality movements in Greece and Bulgaria we will
find the present partition of Macedonia, even though it may
be in some respects provisional, is not disproportionate.
The Greek nationality movement has been in action four
times as many years as the Bulgars—the accumulated
sacrifices it has made are probably four times as great, and
yet even with the advantages gained in this last year, the
movement has probably quite four times as much work
before it as any other.

§ 14. The Combatants

In the history of nations the race is not always to the swift
nor the battle to the strong ; but time and opportunity come
to all men. The Bulgars have shown themselves in this last
quarter-century swifter than eagles in rising towards the
level of European civilization, and stronger than lions in
fighting its battles ; but in this year of war the time and the
opportunity were not theirs. The real importance of the

Bulgar-Turk campaign in Thrace is that it affords a criterion
of the stage reached in the respective regeneration of Greece,
Bulgaria, and Turkey.

The victory of the Bulgars over the Turks is generally
considered as that of a developing over a decaying nation.
This is, however, a half-truth, for the Turkish race is decaying
only in so far as it is still dominated by the decadence of the
capital. Such domination is now in decline; for the Young
Turks with all their faults are neither Byzantine nor Levantine. Thanks to the revolution of 1908 Turkey had become
rather a very crude European State than a very corrupt
Asiatic Empire. The war, therefore, must be regarded
primarily as a war between a State, Bulgaria, having thirty
years of undisturbed development, and a State, Turkey,
having only five years of troubled growth. That is to say,
Bulgaria could bring to the war a whole new generation of
education and enthusiasm. Turkey had still only the old
human lump with a dash of new leaven. This 'new model' of
regenerated Bulgars were supermen compared to the Turkish
mediaeval host of peasantry, commanded by a few fiery
spirits whose modern enthusiasms and education were neither
comprehensible nor congenial to the mass. The Turks were
a lump of sound dough, but still dough, leavened with a little
fire-water.

Bulgaria had reached the second stage in the manufacture
of a nation, where the materials have been worked into
a uniform and usable shape: a product that is as suitable
for war as for peace. With a later stage of manufacture will
come distinction of type, differentiation of class, development of artistic and literary expression and of a national
soul. Turkey was and is still in the first stage—a collection of
raw materials, of mediaeval machinery, of modern designs,
and of undeveloped motive-power. But so imposing was
this collection that those who reckon the forces of a State
by units of man-power or money-power confidently expected Turkey to win; and the stocks of the Balkan States

were more affected by the declaration of war than were those
of the Empire. But the professional in the art of war knows
that the forces of military superiority cannot be so simply
reckoned, and that there are other less easily calculable
mental and moral factors. The ten million of the Balkan
States were outnumbered almost two to one, and the
command of European capital enjoyed by the Empire was
still, curiously enough, probably double that of the Balkan
Governments ; but the following quotation from the British
authority on the art of war can be put in the first place as
an explanation of the Bulgar victories : ' Superior numbers
are an undoubted advantage ; but skill, better organization
and training, and, above all, a firmer determination in all
ranks to conquer at any cost, are the chief factors of success.'

On the Turkish side the campaign in Thrace shows that the
democratic vitality of the Young Turk régime had not had
time to permeate the vast mass of militant Turkey. While the
superficial improvements in material matters such as equipment were so striking as to excite great expectations, the
more radical reforms had not had time to do more than
deteriorate such energies and efficiencies as still survived
from the old system. A dose of reform too long deferred
may fail for a time because it finds the patient too far gone
or too old to assimilate it. Thanks to the effort of the new
régime the troops were better clothed, better armed, better
equipped, and in some respects better commanded. When
the new educated generation has grown up and the new
lessons have been learnt, the spade work of this generation
of Young Turks will bear fruit ; but the Anatolian and
Syrian peasants, born and bred under Hamidian conditions,
would probably have fought better under all the accustomed
anachronisms, *eskisi gibi*. As it was, the privates were, for
the most part, incapable of using their new magazine rifles,
as was shown by the heaps of unused cartridges, stripped
from the clips and thrown away, and by the inefficiency of
their fire at the ranges of modern war. The company officers

were for the most part quite incompetent to protect their commands against the new conditions of modern gun and rifle fire, even as demonstrated by Bulgar peasants. The commanding officers showed themselves incapable of manœuvring the masses of men over the vast distances of a modern battle ; and indispensable modern appliances such as field telephones and railways were not available or were not made use of. The commissariat organization showed itself unable even to supply the simple requirements of bread and water on a short double line of railway between two centres of supply such as Adrianople and Constantinople. The central war department showed that it could not secure itself against even the commonest forms of corruption in that most corrupt of trades—army contracts. The railways, by their spasmodic activities, merely disorganized the slow advance which is alone safe with a Turkish army. Commanders-in-chief picked up scraps of information as to their own troops from correspondents. Whole army corps were left without food for days.

The Japanese and the Bulgars show that newly emancipated races can learn to work European methods and mechanisms of war ; but the Turks, like the Chinese, have been later beginners, and, as beginners, have been beaten by more precocious pupils. Want of mobility has always been the defect of Turkish armies, and modern military mechanisms often aggravated the evil. Want of morale has not, so far, been a defect; but there is no doubt that the Young Turk policy of admitting Christians to the army—though necessary politically and probably justifiable militarily in the long run—was for the moment a grave disadvantage. The total proportion was kept so small as to seem unlikely to affect the morale—probably some 5 or 6 per cent.—and of these, the Armenians, estimated at some 8,000, are said to have fought well. But the racial solidarity of the Ottoman army was none the less injured; as the feudal system of it had been injured by Mahmoud's reorganization a century before with equally disastrous results. While the Macedonian campaign was more particularly affected by this innovation, desertions to the enemy were frequent in Thrace also, and distrust of the Christian disheartened the Moslem. Further injury to morale was caused by the difference between the two classes of officers, the old and the new, the ranker (*alläilie*) and the college cadet (*mekteblie*). The officers of the old fighting school had been got rid of in large numbers in 1909 owing to their dislike of the new régime, and thereby much good ' stiffening' had been lost; because the *alläilie*, though a poor commander, was a campaigner of the first rank. The regulars (*nizam*) had to a large extent become used to the college officers and had a sufficient supply of them. But the reserves (*redif*), which got the inferior college officers and not enough of them, had little confidence in the new men, and got on as best they could with a few ' rankers ' and the ' non-coms.' [1] Even the better class of college officers were rather products of a privileged caste than of professional competence—with the inevitable result that inspiriting individualities, such as Enver Bey and a score or so of kindred spirits, played a part that saved the situation to some extent, while it also made confusion worse confounded. The Turkish cavalry was dashingly led, as it always is in a caste-commanded army, and the Bulgar cavalry was insignificant, as it generally is in a democratic force ; but the American and English civil wars have shown that an undue prominence of cavalry action is not a symptom of a sound system or of ultimate success. The Turkish sabre could no more win in the end against the Bulgarian rifle than J. E. B. Stuart or Rupert of the Rhine against their opponents. Daredevilry and dash count for little against discipline and doggedness, and the daredevils had, as usual, their counterpart of ne'er-do-wells, who preferred Pera clubs to Tchataldja trenches. But in other and more important effects the propinquity of the capital had a disastrous effect

---

[1] One *redif* battalion which passed through Pera was observed to have only four officers.

on the Thracian campaign : a point worth noting in relation
to the theory that Constantinople is to be found at the bottom
of all Turkish disasters. It was the disturbing effect on
Turkish strategy of political considerations created by the
nearness of the capital to the seat of war that contributed
largely to the Turkish collapse.

The Turkish army, like any mediaeval machine of merit,
would work well if in a mediaeval milieu. It was crude
and clumsy, but fool-proof : it was slow and stupid, but
economy of energy was no object : it had no head, and
not much heart, but it had a heavy hand. In guerrilla war—
in a very slow advance *en masse* against inferior forces—or
in holding positions against superior forces, its faith in
itself and physical endurance made up for its deficiencies of
strategy, tactics, supply, transport, and all the modern
machinery of war.

The military capabilities of the Ottoman Government
under the new régime were not in essentials much in advance of those of Hamidian times. They still consisted in the
power of putting a body of troops in the field adequately
representing the raw military material of the country, within
a time adequately conformable to the conditions of East-
European war, and with an equipment more than adequate
in comparison with that of their enemies. But that was
all ; and we now know that this, which only a hundred
years ago was still pretty nearly the first and last of the
whole art of war, is to-day only the last and least of it. The
general strategic idea of the Turk of 1912 in Thrace, as of
the Turk of 1897 in Thessaly, was to accumulate a vastly
superior mass of men, and then to roll it slowly forward.
A Turkish army of to-day has little mobility, but once in
motion it can gain considerable momentum. The Greeks
in 1897 gave Edhem Pasha six weeks in which to get organized
and under way ; and, besides that, the problem of supply
was still further simplified for the Turks by a fertile country
and a feeble enemy. The demand made upon the Ottoman

organization in the Thessalian campaign was scarcely as heavy as that put on it by peace manœuvres, and under such conditions a Turkish army will advance as steadily and behave as well as it did in Thessaly. But a very little hustling, such as it got in Thrace, and it resolves itself into a mob incapable of effective action in its front, and capable of any excesses against a real or supposed enemy in its rear.

Much has been written and will be written about the strategy of the Thracian campaign, but it was simple enough in itself, though from a political point of view there was one curious complication in it. Each of the two combatants was animated by one leading impulse, by one chief national pride. That of the Turks was to vindicate their title to be the military ruling race of Eastern Europe—a claim all the more cherished that it was both the sanction of their political system and the symbol of the social superiority by which they had conquered Eastern Europe five centuries before. Confidence in the result of any future appeal to arms consoled the Turk Moslem for his daily discomfiture in every other walk of life. Consoled by this confidence, he could affect contempt for every evidence of frankish and rayah superiority in the competition of modern civilization. To the Turk, as to every military caste, war was the desirable political condition in which his own superiority would again be shown incontestably. In the world of the Turk free men war, and slaves work. His ' good old times ' was the age of ' the good old rule, the simple plan ', and it was in his power at any moment to bring back that golden age. The pride of the Young Turk was to sacrifice everything which makes life worth living to the Oriental—to shun delights of quiet enjoyment, of religious enthusiasm, or of sensual pleasure, and to live laborious days of political and military training, so that when the day of days broke, the Ottomans might be justified of their faith in the sword of Osman.

The Bulgars, on the other hand, had a more modern *morgue*, though one hardly less dangerous to the peace of a continental civilization based on a balance of competition and combination. It was the pride of the Bulgar to have forced his way by himself to the foremost place among the progressive forces in Eastern Europe. He had done everything for himself, and done it in record time. It had been done in the face of an opposition from the empires east, west, and north, such as would have relegated any other race to a century of obscurity. Only one thing he owed to others, and that was his original emancipation. He had out-diplomatized the diplomatic despots, whether Turkish or Russian ; but he had never defeated the former in fair fight, and he owed his freedom to the latter. Now it was to be his pride to pay off this mortgage on his moral independence by driving the Turk out of Europe, and by outdoing the Russian feat of arms which had freed him. He had already earned the applause of progressive Europe by defeating conservative Europe at its own game of intrigue : now he would earn its gratitude by defeating Asia at its own game of war. He would free, not only the unredeemed of his own race, but even the unredeemed of his Greek and Slav rivals.

Such was the pride that went before the Bulgar's fall, and such was the haughty spirit that went before the Turk's destruction. Both ambitions make a strong appeal to our sympathies, and it is strange that the arbitrament of war should, in both cases, have struck most directly and most heavily just at the main moral motives that sent both combatants to war. The Turks by military incapacity lost to the Bulgars their historic claim to military supremacy ; but on the whole improved their status in civilization as compared to other Balkan communities, if only by the fearful lapses of the Balkan peoples into barbarism under the strain of a state of war. The Bulgars, on the other hand, by political incapacity, lost the claim established by

a quarter-century of phenomenal independent development
to being the leading political power in the Balkans and the
most practical and progressive of peoples; and gained only
barren military honours, and no less barren sympathies.[1]

§ 15. The Campaigns

The point of honour and the pride of race affected the
fortunes of war differently in the two cases of Turks and
Bulgars. In the case of the Turk these moral forces took
effect by warping sound military strategy to a political
purpose. In the case of the Bulgar they did so by warping
sound political strategy to a military purpose.

In view of the relative efficiency of the two armies and
of the manifest impossibility of holding the whole political
frontier from Uskub to Kirk Kilisse, the sound military
strategy for the Turks was to act on the defensive at Uskub
and Adrianople, and fight the decisive actions of the war
in defensive positions well withdrawn into the interior,
and at an easy distance from their main bases of operations.
By doing this they could have retained a sufficient political
control of both Thrace and Macedonia; while concentrating
their own strength and attenuating that of the Allies with
the guarding of long lines of communications, the garrison-
ing of centres, the guaranteeing the safety of the capital from
stabs in the back, and so forth. The further the Allies had
to go before they could strike, the less force would they
strike with, and the better prepared the Turks would be
for them. But in view of the political position, a defensive
strategy could not even have been contemplated at Constantinople. A Government which has done its best to avert

---

[1] A philosopher who combines in paradox the points of view of the
day before yesterday with those of the day after to-morrow, writes:
' It is one of the deadly fallacies of Jingo politics that a nation is stronger
for despising other nations. As a matter of fact the strongest nations
are those, like Prussia or Japan, who began from very mean beginnings,
but who have not been too proud to learn everything from the foreigner.'—
G. K. Chesterton, *Heretics*, p. 165.

war, and is in power under sufferance of a bellicose opposition, is not in a position to allow an enemy to approach
the walls of its capital. An Imperial Government holding
a province against the forces of 'nationality' is not in
a position to allow armies embodying those forces to overrun
that province. So the Turks were morally compelled to
hold the political frontiers in their widest extent, that is to
say, the frontiers covering Uskub and Adrianople; for to hold
the Kavalla Dedeagatch isthmus, between the Bulgar mountain guerrilla and the Greek fleet in command of the sea,
was manifestly impossible, while the promontory of Old Serbia
and the Sanjak had to be abandoned also. Accordingly,
every man available was pushed up to the Kirk Kilisse
front, while the Macedonian main army spread itself out in
a dispersed offensive on the Serbian frontier, and a containing force went south into the Roumlouk to check the Greek
advance. The Turkish position in Thrace was, from a military
point of view, a strong one, for its right flank rested on the
difficult hill and forest country of the Istrandja-Balkan
along the Black Sea coast, and its left on the equally difficult
Despoto Dagh, with its fierce Moslem Pomaks; while its
centre was Adrianople, a fortress generally considered impregnable, and a fortified position at Kirk Kilisse, reputed
to be more formidable than it probably was. Both these
centres of the Turkish front were connected by rail with
the capital, which was at a convenient distance. From this
position, with a little more time, the Turkish army could
no doubt have accumulated a forward momentum against
which the Bulgar advantages of superior mobility and
modernity would have been, to a great extent, unavailing.

Time might have saved the situation for the Turks in Thrace,
but in Macedonia their prospect of success was far poorer.
Their 'central position' might have been an advantage under
very different conditions, but as it was it seems to have
been no more advantageous than that of a bag fox turned
out in the middle of the pack. It was clearly the right

tactics for the garrison of Macedonia to get to ground in the most convenient earths and to be dug out. This would keep in being both the Ottoman army and the Ottoman sovereignty long enough to allow of something turning up elsewhere. But it was fatal to divide a force of the character of the Turkish troops in conditions such as those of Macedonia into two field armies—a large one to take the offensive in the north, and a small one to defend the south against the Greeks—to waste men, material, and morale in rear-guard actions against the concentrated columns of an enemy in a superiority of as much as two to one in the north and a good deal more in the south, and then to risk everything on the result of a general action, such as Kumanovo, under-taken in the jaws of the Serbo-Bulgar concentration. It has been said that the Turkish force, using its interior lines, should have acted in turn against each column of the Allies, and defeated each in detail; but this would have required a more mobile and reliable force. It is probable that it was some vague general purpose of this sort that caused the Turks to risk a general action at Kumanovo against the least formidable of their opponents, the Serbs. The result of their defeat there and of the advance of Serbs from the north, combined with that of Bulgars and Serbs from the east, was to drive the remains of the Turkish main army across central Macedonia to Monastir. There the Turks, who had shaken off an incompetent commander and the less military and non-Moslem elements, collided with the Greek left flank, which was engaged in driving the small Turkish containing army through the mountains to Salonica. The Greeks had the worst of this, their most important encounter, which was also the only Turkish success of the whole war. The Turkish army, which seems to have fought better as its plight became more desperate, fought at Monastir one of the fiercest battles of the war against the pursuing Serbs. Driven out from there, it threw itself over the mountains into Epirus, and, alone of the Macedonian forces, found at last its proper tactics in digging itself in at Yanina, against a Greek investing army. Had Uskub, Monastir, or Salonica held out with Scutari and Adrianople, instead of Yanina, who knows but that the Turks might have recovered Macedonia as they did Thrace? But, as it was, the southern army surrendered at Salonica without attempting a defence, and even the defence of Yanina was not very prolonged. So the military operations in Macedonia left no such problems for the peacemakers as did those in Thrace, owing to the resistance of Adrianople. On the other hand, the very swiftness and completeness of the Allies' success in Macedonia imperilled their relations to each other; for the Serbians and Greeks were able to enter the second stage of digesting their conquered territory, while the whole Bulgar strength was still chewing what it had bitten off in Thrace.

The resistance of the garrison of Yanina to the Greeks, and the resistance of the garrison of Scutari to the Serbs, had more direct effect on the political results of the war than all the bloody battles and combats in the field. For it was the resistance of these garrisons that made it possible for Europe to establish an autonomous Albania. Similarly, if the Macedonian army had played its proper part in a prolonged defence of positions politically important, it might have achieved what was, politically, its best prospect of success—the establishment of Macedonian autonomy under the joint auspices of Europe and the Empire. The loss through this mistake was not confined to the Empire, but, in the end, fell also on Europe. By not making a longer defence of Macedonia, the Empire lost all chance of retaining any suzerain rights there, such as might have saved its imperial prestige. But the collapse of the defence was also the cause of the second war—the War of Partition—with all its future prejudice to peace. For a Bulgar-Serb siege of Uskub, and joint Graeco-Bulgar operations against Salonica would, most probably, either have resulted in a guaranteed autonomy of Macedonia or would, at least, have kept the alliance alive long enough to effect the partition arrangements it contemplated. To complicate further the situation caused by the complete collapse of the campaign in Macedonia, there came the military and political consequences of the prolongation of the siege in Thrace. The former prematurely raised the question of partition, the latter prevented a prompt and proper solution of it. Besides these main difficulties, every minor incident contributed to aggravate the strain on the alliance. Thus, Salonica surrendered to the Greeks who entered without firing a shot. This gave the Greeks a better title to that town than the Bulgar force which entered a few hours later from the north, after hard fighting. Moreover, it resulted in the Greeks giving terms to the Turks which were no disadvantage to Greek ambition but highly embarrassing to the Bulgar aspirations in Macedonia. In Monastir, on the other hand, the Serbs, after heavy losses in fighting, conquered the Turks without Bulgar assistance; thereby acquiring a title which treaty obligations would with difficulty invalidate.

It was no fault of the Bulgars that the course of events in the Thracian campaign could not be made to keep pace with that of the Macedonian campaign; but they were in a false position politically, which left them only a choice of evils—a risk of military disaster or a risk of political discomfiture. They knew that the true Bulgarian political objective was Macedonia, and not Thrace, and that every consideration of political prudence imposed the greatest economy of energy in Thrace. On the other hand, they knew that if the Turkish avalanche, that would accumulate in Thrace, once began to move on them, it would roll up or roll round all defence in which the whole aggressive activity of the nation was not engaged. A Bulgar defensive would be swamped, and thence, slowly but surely, the Turkish flood would submerge all Bulgaria.

The prudent political element, none the less, knowing

that Europe would not allow Bulgaria to be crushed by Turkey, were prepared to face the risk of a temporary devastation of their country, rather than take the risk of being for ever deprived of Macedonia by Greeks and Serbs. Europe would turn the Turks out of Eastern Roumelia as out of conquered Thessaly in 1897, but a Graeco-Serb partition of Bulgar-Macedonia would not be considered the concern of Europe. On the other hand, the military party knew that the Turks could only be decisively beaten in Thrace, and considered that a vigorous offensive there would not only defend Bulgarian soil from violation but would effect the conquest of Thrace and leave time and force enough to secure Macedonia afterwards. The policy first decided on appears to have been a compromise, and contemplated a division of the Bulgar force into three, one of which was to conquer and hold its share of Macedonia, another to do the best it could with an offensive defensive in Thrace, and a third in a central position which might act as a reserve or a reinforcement to whichever wing wanted it most. But in the end, as is always the case in war, military pressure overcame political prudence. Once war is in sight, the only possible policy is that which promises the best prospect of successful warfare, not that which offers the best chance of a successful peace. War cannot be kept in its place as a means to an end, but always becomes the end itself. Accordingly, we find that sound strategic reasons caused the Macedonian campaign to be subordinated entirely to the Thracian campaign. The Macedonian army became a reserve on which to draw for reinforcements to the Thracian army ; while the central reserve force was removed to the extreme left wing at the end of the Thracian frontier furthest from Macedonia, and was there used to effect a vigorous offensive against the Turkish right. Thus the Bulgar forces were redisposed as though the political objective had become the capture of Constantinople and not the capture of Salonica.

By this move an immediate military success was made safe,

and an ultimate political discomfiture was made sure. The Turkish right at Kirk Kilisse was crushed, and the Turkish front was hammered back into a collapsing concavity. The left held its own round Adrianople, and the right fought fiercely in the difficult country of the Istranja Balkan, while the centre was driven sagging southward over the open downs, with the momentum of its amorphous mass of men and material started rearward instead of forward. Every mile that it was driven increased its disorganization, and every hour added a pressure of hunger and hardship to that of the enemy. Then followed the five days' fighting known as the Battle of Lule Burgas, which was nothing more than the impact of the Bulgar influx on the sagging Turkish front at a spot in its retreat where the railway gave it a rallying point. The shock of this impact finally broke the defence, hit unexpectedly, and hustled out of all co-ordination. The Turkish host staggered back—a starving and stricken multitude—behind the shelter of the Tchataldja lines, with perhaps one quarter of its men still effective. The Bulgars, only less exhausted because excited by victory, toiled after in slow pursuit, vainly hoping to reap the fruits of victory in Thrace in time to gain a second harvest in Macedonia—where others were already reaping what they had sown. But, for such a forcing of the event, they were very ill provided and ill placed. Want of cavalry, and of railway, or even road communications, made pursuit ineffective—for starving Turks, without arms or formation, could drag themselves quicker through the mud homewards than could starving Bulgars invading a hostile country. Every mile that the Bulgar army advanced from the railway base at Yamboli was an added weakness. The railway through Thrace was blocked by Adrianople, the Black Sea route by Turkish cruisers. The desert downs and devastated Greek and Moslem villages of Thrace could not supply or shelter a regiment, much less an army: every loaf and cartridge must come to the front— every wounded man go to the rear, by buffalo transports over unmade tracks—buffalo transport making five or ten miles a day over a line of communications hundreds of miles long!

It was done somehow; but at an appalling loss of the principal national capital of an agricultural State—the peasant and the plough-ox. Great Britain could sacrifice men by the thousand and horses by the hundred thousand to the conquest of South Africa, yet no factory failed of labour, no field lay fallow; but the Bulgarian crusaders and their cattle sacrificed to the barren conquest of Thrace represented so much more difficulty and delay in the national tasks of making Bulgaria European and of making Macedonia Bulgarian. It was no doubt this consideration that made the Bulgars reluctant to pay the cost of storming Adrianople, and resolved to force peace by pressure on Constantinople. If so, it was a miscalculation; for you can coerce a despotism by threatening the capital but not a democracy; and what would have been effective action against Abdul Hamid was ineffective against Enver Bey. So it came about that when within a fortnight the Bulgar army had cleared Thrace and shut up what was left of the Turkish forces in Adrianople and Constantinople, the Bulgarian prospects of profiting by the war were less favourable than before fighting began; while the promise of a peace satisfactory to European progress was less good than if the Turks had been in Sofia. Such a parlous business is even a successful and salutary war in the cause of progress.

There have been no lack of Job's comforters to assure Bulgaria that the adversities which were to accumulate on it as a result of this war were due to this or that fault. A moderate indulgence of the instinct that misfortune must be deserved is both human and wholesome; and, if we knew more of Job's circumstances, we might perhaps, like his comforters, trace some of his calamities to spiritual pride and self-sufficiency. But those who have sought practical reasons for the dramatic discomfiture of Bulgaria have, for the most part, seen them in mere tactical mistakes made by Sofia;

either in not concluding peace more promptly with Turkey at this juncture, or on a later occasion in making war too precipitately on the Allies. It has been said that on reaching Tchataldja the Bulgarian army should have forced it at all costs, and should have dictated a peace at San Stefano ; and it has also been said that when the Turks first asked for an armistice peace should have been granted them, even at the cost of renouncing the annexation of Adrianople. Peace in Thrace at the first practicable opportunity and at any possible price was, it is true, the proper policy for Bulgaria ; but it was also the policy that Sofia pursued. If it was pursued in vain, it was only abandoned after both the suggested alternatives had been attempted. The attempt to force the lines of Tchataldja was far more serious than was generally realized abroad ; costing between ten and fifteen thousand men. The failure of it was complete enough to stop further attempts ; being only in part attributable to unfavourable circumstances of the occasion—such as fog—unexpected entrenchments, &c. On the other hand, a withdrawal from Thrace, which had already become ' New Bulgaria ', was as politically impossible as the raising of the siege of Adrianople would have been strategically suicidal. Bulgaria had the wolf by the ears and could neither kill it nor let it free. The whole defensive in Thrace represented national energy engaged on a wrong objective—a sacrifice which had either to be doubled by the conquest of Tchataldja and Adrianople, or to be thrown away by uncovering them. Moreover, neither Adrianople nor Tchataldja could be taken, except at so heavy a cost that no effective energies would be left for pursuing the true Bulgarian objective in Macedonia, or for keeping a reserve for imposing respect on Roumania.

Under the circumstances an armistice was in the interests of both parties and negotiations began outside Tchataldja on November 25, and were concluded in ten days. The Bulgars put on a bold front and demanded as a condition the surrender of Tchataldja and of the fortresses Adrianople, Scutari, and Yanina, now representing all that was left of the Turkish rule in Europe. The situation was much the same as that in 1829 when Diebitsch, under pressure of a Russian army in extreme difficulties, and with the assistance of foreign ambassadors in excessive despondency, bluffed and bullied that prototype of the Young Turk, Mahmoud II, into a disastrous peace : a peace which could only be imposed on an indignant Empire by a reign of terror in the capital of the most cold-blooded character.[1] If the Turks had given way, all would have been well ; for the armistice would have contained all the elements of a permanent peace, and the formal ratifications would not have caused the delays and difficulties that led to all the subsequent troubles. But while the Bulgars did their best to get a truce which would really be a treaty of peace, all they succeeded in getting was a truce which allowed their various enemies to prepare further war against themselves. They were forced to accept an armistice which merely maintained the respective forces in their positions. The Bulgar army before Tchataldja was enabled to remain there indefinitely through the opening of the Adrianople rail and the Black Sea route ; while a time limit was imposed on Turkish procrastination by refusing the Turks similar facilities for Adrianople, Yanina, and Scutari.

The negotiations that were opened in London on December 13 were thus entered into by Bulgaria with no better means of pressure than the limited period of resistance of the fortresses, especially Adrianople ; for the others were in any case lost to Turkey. Adrianople, and with it Thrace, was clearly the only matter still open to dispute as between the

[1] There are many grim accounts, by eyewitnesses, of the street executions that went on day and night, and the rows of the corpses of ' suspects ' laid out in the street, each with his head under his arm and his sentence pinned on his breast. The advantage of putting the autocracy into commission is that in such a crisis one politician, Nazim or Shefket, can die instead of a whole people.

Allies and Turkey on the mainland—so that Servia and Montenegro accepted the armistice readily enough. But Greece refused—in order to keep the Turks out of the Aegean, while Greek sovereignty was being established in the islands—and in order to keep the Bulgars out of Macedonia, while Greek sovereignty was being extended there. As the Greek fleet could strike no vital blow and the fortresses were good to hold out some considerable time, the armistice was all to the advantage of the Turks. It allowed the Turks themselves to rally and reinforce their troops behind Tcha-taldja; and it gave time for their friends to excite and exploit the various disruptive forces within the alliance and the disturbing forces without it that already showed signs of nullifying its achievements.

CHAPTER VI

THE CRISIS

§ 16. First London Conference and Turkish Militarism.
§ 17. European Complications and Balkan Militarism.
§ 18. Second London Conference and Greek Militarism.

A man of violence enticeth his neighbour
And leadeth him in a way that is not good.
He that is slow to anger is better than men of war,
And he that ruleth his spirit than he that taketh a city.
The lot is cast into the lap ;
But the whole disposing thereof is the Lord's.

Proverbs.

§ 16. First London Conference and Turkish Militarism

WE have now come to a crisis of the Eastern Question and to a climax of the Balkan nationality movements, comparable in character and importance to that reached at the Treaty of San Stefano after the Russo-Turkish War in 1878. The progressive purpose of the war, in either case, had been successfully accomplished by substituting the rule of a progressive and national democracy for that of a decadent and imperial absolutism. The knots of the political situation had all, it seemed, been cut by war, and nothing further appeared necessary for the re-establishment of peace and the resumption of progress than to give the special *fait accompli* the force of general law, and to make certain adjustments of detail. But we have seen how this responsibility for giving formal effect and final execution to the arbitrament of war was ruthlessly bargained away by the Powers at the Congress of Berlin. A similar responsibility was now to be as recklessly betrayed by the Balkan States themselves ; for, if the repudiation of the settlement at San Stefano through the jealousy of the British and Russian Governments prolonged the miseries of the Eastern Question for a quarter-century and caused the War of Coalition, the jealousy of the Greek and Bulgar Governments, in a similar situation, has had as disastrous an effect.

From the apex of achievement attained by the armistice of November, Balkan affairs slid swiftly into the abyss. From the point we have now reached onwards this review of events will be a dismal record of reaction and ruin. In November 1912 it seemed as though a war of the peoples had for once accomplished in little more than one week what the wisdom of public men had been unable to achieve in over one hundred years. But the most obvious characteristic of war is its waste, and not the least of its waste is the wasting of its own winnings. Let us sum up how matters stood at this climax before seeing what caused the turn for the worse, and to what deplorable disasters that turn eventually led.

When the Bulgars had driven the Turkish forces in Thrace behind the defences of Constantinople, they had accomplished the primary purpose of the coalition, that is to say, the forcible expulsion of the Ottoman Empire from Eastern Europe. The operations against the Turkish corps in Macedonia and in Albania were comparatively insignificant, and in the same subordinate relation to this main purpose was the overpowering of the Turkish contingents in the Aegean islands. The importance of the Macedonian and Albanian operations of the Allies concerned mainly the secondary purpose of the coalition—the peaceful partition of Macedonia. It is, however, to be noted that by the time the Thracian campaign had finished its first stage in November, it was clear that the course the Macedonian campaign was taking was such as might well make grave trouble between the allies if the difficulties involved in questions of partition were given time to develop. At this early date, and at any time until the resumption of the Thracian campaign, these difficulties could probably have been dealt with without serious risk of a war of partition. But, even in November, the prospect of trouble between Bulgaria and Serbia over central Macedonia was obvious enough to make Turkey determine to procrastinate as long as possible before making a definite peace. Another inducement to the Turks to keep issues open was the intervention of Vienna, which had mobilized considerable Austrian forces in protest against any Serbo-Montenegrin aggrandizement and possibly with a view to preventing it. Such Austrian action promised a very present help to Turkey, for it might even portend a war between the Austrian and Russian Empires, or, failing that, it must ensure an exclusion of the Serbs from Albania. This would divert the Serbs upon Macedonia, and inextricably complicate the situation there, because Serbia would require ' compensation ' in Bulgar-Macedonia for the loss of Albania, and an outlet to the Aegean in substitution for the outlet to the Adriatic. Besides this threatening development, the efforts of the Greek armies and of the Bulgar contingent to assert their competing claims to Salonica and South Macedonia were so straining relations between these two countries that, unless the tension was relieved, a rupture was bound to result. Thirdly, Bulgaria was already threatened with a new complication from the Roumanian side ; for Roumania, by now, had put forward a definite claim to ' compensation ' at Silistria and on the Dobrudja frontier. The principal strength of this Roumanian claim lay in the support it found in Berlin, where also was the patron of the Turk or, more strictly speaking, of the Turkish Army. The military overthrow of the Ottoman, who had been trained and armed by Germany—at the hands of the Bulgar, who had been trained and armed under French auspices—had been a shrewd blow to German military prestige in Europe. It had been as severe a blow to the German political position in the Empire itself, where Berlin had just begun to recover from its association with the Hamidian autocracy and to re-establish itself with the Young Turk. It was as desirable

in the eyes of Berlin and Vienna that the Turks should
retrieve their reputation and that Roumania should be
rewarded for its allegiance to the Triple Alliance, as that
Serbia, the thorn in the side of that Alliance, and Bulgaria,
the broken reed that had pierced its hand, should both be
humbled. The Turkish war party could accordingly feel
that in postponing peace with a view to renewing the war
it had the support of one of the two great armed camps
into which the European Concert might then at any
moment have resolved itself. It was these conditions that
inspired the Turkish war party—the Committee of Union
and Progress—to impose a policy of procrastination upon the
Turkish peace party—the Kiamil ministry. With so many
possibilities of Bulgaria being taken in flank or rear with a
knock-out blow, it was clearly worth while for the Turkish
war party to come up for another round and continue clinch-
ing and sparring for time rather than throw up the sponge.

On the other hand there were strong forces working for
peace. The first was that both Bulgarian policy and Bulgarian public opinion realized the need of a prompt peace,
and that while they were up the Tree of Dilemma in Thrace,
others were picking up the Apple of Discord in Macedonia.
This knowledge was unfortunately nullified by a slowness
and stiffness in bargaining, characteristic of a peasant State,
aggravated, perhaps, by consciousness of an unparalleled
achievement and of universal approbation. The farmer who
lives on the land cannot be expected to deal in it, or in
the fruits of his labour, in the large-handed, light-hearted
manner of the financier, to whom acres and wheat are merely
currency for exchange. In these negotiations the Bulgar
statesmen were like farmers at an auction of their fields,
or at a sale of cattle ; but the fields were their national
heritage, won with blood, and the cattle were their compatriots. Allowing for national feeling, which in the Bulgar
is all the more strong for being silent, we must recognize
that the Bulgar, in this hour of his success, showed both

modesty and moderation.[1] Those who criticize the Bulgar
plenipotentiaries for not being more conciliatory in the
winter of 1912–13 forget that the total renunciation of
Adrianople was impossible, and that this alone could have
secured a peace approved of by all parties in Turkey. A
withdrawal from Adrianople would not only have betrayed
the coalition, but would have been considered a betrayal
of Bulgaria. The surrender of Thrace and the restoration
of Turkish supremacy there would have been a sacrifice
such as a victorious nation in arms, however temperate,
could scarcely have accepted. Therefore it seemed that,
without military pressure such as Sofia single-handed could
not bring to bear on Constantinople, or without political
concessions such as it could not afford to make, peace in
Thrace was unattainable and another war in Macedonia
almost unavoidable. The question remains whether any
outside influence could have successfully supplemented
the Bulgar pressure for peace ; and in this connexion our
thoughts turn to that Anglo-Russian association which
has already been shown to be the most powerful influence
for progress in the Balkans. It will be remembered that
it was that association which was the main outside cause
of the War of Coalition ; it therefore seems probable that
it would have been that same association which would
provide the outside pressure now required to end that war
with a successful and permanent peace.

It was indeed as much in Russian interests as in British
that the War of Coalition should realize the results already
achieved, in a formal peace. Only with the formal recognition of such a peace, by the Balkan States and by Europe,
could Petersburg feel secured in the restoration of its

[1] *The Times* correspondent, an experienced and impartial friend of
Balkan peoples, thus describes the effect of the change in the situation
on the various national characters : ' The Bulgarians took their victories
with the same stoicism as their subsequent misfortunes ; in the hour
of triumph the stolid calm of Sofia contrasted curiously with the high-
flown exuberance of Belgrade, the gushing hysterics of Bukarest, and the
Pindaric magniloquence of Athens.'—*Times*, October 23, 1913.

Russian predominance in Eastern Europe, lost by the events
of the past decade. Only thereby could London feel secure
as to the peace of Europe, which it considered dependent on
the restoration to the Triple Agreement of its predominance
in Western Europe. Such a peace would enable Petersburg to appear as the dispenser of rewards—to the Serbs
for their constancy—to the Bulgars for their conversion—and
to the Roumanians for their conformity. Such a peace
would entitle London to claim that it had been seeking peace
through the two-power standard and ensuing it through
the Triple Agreement. Such a peace would have given the
Anglo-Russian association a claim on the confidence of the
British and Russian peoples such as would have considerably
changed its character; for the British people earnestly
desired the peace of the Balkans while the Russian people
no less earnestly desired their goodwill. While both points
of view, the 'diplomatic' and the 'democratic', are here
stated, it would seem that the motive power in Russian
policy was mainly 'diplomatic' in character, while the
British policy was rather of 'democratic' colour. The
British 'diplomatic' design of asserting the superiority and
solidarity of the Triple Agreement was in fact counterbalanced by the growing 'democratic' determination not to
strain relations with Germany further. The restraining factor
in the case of Petersburg was rather the 'diplomatic'
apprehension lest Berlin might again, as in 1908, support
Vienna in the Balkans, and thereby bring about a crisis and
a challenge of strength, in which Russia would stand alone.
There was no reason to suppose that London, when it came
to the point, would go as far in support of Russia in the
Balkans, as it had gone, two years before, in support of
France in Morocco. Therefore the Anglo-Russian association
could promote peace only by proceeding as a constituent of
the Concert and not as an armed camp. But procedure
through the Concert involved a renunciation of all independent intervention, though it did not preclude indirect

influences, and this so weakened and wasted Anglo-Russian pressure for peace as to make it much less likely to succeed in the limited time available.

The peace of Europe was more important than the peace of the Balkans. It may be that independent intervention by the British Government alone, in a naval demonstration for the enforcement of peace, would have been enough to prevent the renewal of the war ; seeing that, being obviously disinterested, it could scarcely cause any resentment, still less any risk of a European war which nobody wanted and by which nobody could win. But, as we have already seen, there was no sufficient force of public opinion to enable the British Government to take a strong line in stopping with a firm hand a war which had done its work. Nevertheless, the responsibility of London to further and facilitate peace was fully recognized, and everything was done, short of strong, independent action, to force on pacification through the Concert. Action by the Concert is, however, dilatory and negative ; and, moreover, the Concert was no longer the same influence, in regard to Balkan affairs, that it had been only two months before. The Concert, however remotely, is a representative institution ; and it had undergone in those two months somewhat the same change as a representative Chamber in which the Ministry has changed as a result of an extension of the franchise. It was Vienna that had been spokesman for the Concert in its last pronunciamento in August of 1912 as to the *status quo*. But it was London that now proclaimed the new policy of the European Concert, for London was spokesman for the Triple Agreement which had been 'put in office', so to say, by the Balkan Alliance. The British Premier on November 9 declared that ' the map of eastern Europe has to be recast . . . the victors will not be robbed of fruits that have cost them so dear '. London, in the previous summer, while still ' out of power ', had done its best to preserve peace by pressing forward the Austrian proposals of August ; but now it could pursue the restoration of peace in its own way, subject to securing Austrian approval of it. The disinterested and ' democratic ' character of London diplomacy was now recognized, both by the Balkan plenipotentiaries and by the European Powers, in the choice of London as the place for the peace negotiations and of the British Foreign Secretary as their presiding personality; while the claims of Paris, pressed by the French Minister for Foreign Affairs (a presidential candidate), were rejected. The respective influences of the three governments constituting the Triple Agreement are indeed appropriately represented by the character of the contribution made by their different capitals to the settlement of the Balkans. London justified its selection by imposing, after one failure, a peace which satisfied the ' democratic ' requirements of the situation. Paris afterwards took its proper place as the focus for financial readjustments. Petersburg was appropriately selected as the scene of the necessary ' diplomatic ' dispositions. If, in every case, these centres of civilization laboured in vain, the failure was not due to want of skill or bad machinery. In every case the work was done skilfully and swiftly.

The procedure provided by London for the peace negotiations was admirably adapted to the situation, in that it did away, as far as possible, with circumlocution and correspondence. Correspondence is desirable only when delay is an advantage and issues must be defined. But in this case delay was a danger, in view of the fresh difficulties arising; while such a definition of the issues as would accentuate the differences already existing within the Concert and between the Allies might be doubly disastrous. The situation was one requiring friendly conference, not formal correspondence; and accordingly two procedures were improvised, both of which were from the point of view of the protocolist unprecedented.[1] One procedure provided for a reference to

---

[1] The first procedure was, no doubt, an application of the lesson learnt by modern diplomacy, that terms of reference, cases and counter-cases, oral arguments, judicial arbitrations, obligatory awards, &c., can, under

the representatives of the two groups forming the Concert, with a view to joint recommendations on questions specially concerning the Great Powers. The other procedure provided for a conference between the plenipotentiaries of the Balkan States, with a view to a final decision of the questions specially concerning the belligerents.[1] Diplomacy is often abused for being stereotyped, and stupid in its methods ; but both those who criticized British policy in the Balkans for its conventionality, and those who commended it for its correctitude, have overlooked the new procedure it introduced in the conduct of foreign affairs—a practical precedent worth more than most proposals of unprofessional peacemakers.

The situation as regards the prospect of peace at this crisis may be summed up, so far as Bulgaria and Europe are concerned, as favouring the forces for concluding peace rather than those for continuing war. Moreover, when we come to consider the situation in Turkey, we find that, there also, the peace policy of London as ' mandatory ' of the Triple Agreement appears, at this time, to be predominant. For the Turkish reverses had resulted in the resignation of the liberal ministry of Mukhtar ; and this ministry, which, since the outbreak of war and the failure of its ' liberal ' policy, had come under the influence of the Committee, now

certain conditions, be dispensed with to advantage. A round table conference or expert inquiry, with no particular powers, can often bring about agreement where correspondence or more contentious discussion would only accentuate divergences. The second procedure is interesting as being an international recognition that the Balkan States are out of leading strings ; and as implying a realization that, in international as in domestic relations, moral atmosphere and appeal can often do more than authority with young people. The Balkan States have not made good use of their first opportunity for managing their own affairs. All the same, a settlement by Balkan delegates in London will probably always be worth more than a settlement by European delegates in the Balkans.

[1] If formal provision could also have been made for settlement of the impending issues between the Allies, it would have been better ; but London was not concerned with this issue, which, when it later became acute, was referred to Petersburg.

gave place to one of distinctly anti-committee tone, under the anglophil Kiamil Pasha.[1]

The Committee and the Young Turk radicals now constituted an opposition war party; while the more prudent patriotism of the Elder Statesmen, as we may call the Government of moderate liberals under Kiamil, were anxious for peace. Both parties were worthy of patriotic support. The Young Turks saw the future safety and progress of their country dependent on recovering, at any cost, the lost European possessions and the lost imperial prestige. This was a policy in which they were likely to receive, and did receive, sympathy and support from all centres of militarist and imperialist opinion, as well as from their own political organization. The Elder Statesmen were not so blinded by ' seeing red ' as to be unable to perceive that the Empire would be the better for concentration in Constantinople and Asia Minor ; that it should economize its energies on internal development and international independence, and not waste them in trying to restore a dominion in Europe which had become no more than a drain on its strength, a drag on its progress, and a draft on its financial and political independence. Everything depended on the power of the party in office to impose its pacific policy on the popular party.

The pacificists in Constantinople played their part with firmness and prudence. They disorganized the plans of the Committee by vigorous action against leading members of it, while depriving them as far as possible of grounds for opposing peace by putting forward proposals such as even the most extreme war party could scarcely have criticized

---

[1] That Kiamil was a noted anglophil is too important a fact to, be passed over. But, to avoid misunderstandings, one may observe that it is a characteristic of immature democracies for their leading men to become associated with those older communities where their political training was acquired, or whose political traditions they admire. This has been especially marked in Greece and Turkey, where political standards and traditions have, for different reasons, been slow of development. It is much less so in Bulgaria and Roumania, where development was rapid.

on the score of moderation.[1] The peacemakers in London were equally careful that no opening should be given to the Turkish war party; for while strengthening the hands of the Ottoman Government by a joint recommendation to make peace in the name of the Concert—a measure which ended the hopes of the war party that the Concert might collapse—they also dissuaded the delegates of the Allies in London from trying to force the Ottoman delegates to come to terms by presenting an ultimatum—a measure which would have enabled the Turkish war party to appeal to imperialist passions in Turkey. The joint recommendation of the Concert was that Adrianople should be ceded to the Allies, and that the Aegean Islands should be left to the disposition of the Concert. The Kiamil Ministry received the recommendation on January 17, decided on its acceptance and, in order to strengthen itself in the execution of this decision, summoned a ' Grand Council' of the principal religious, civil, and military dignitaries, which formally gave its approval on January 22. Peace on terms that were a good basis for a permanent settlement, and at a time when a fresh outbreak of war might still have been prevented, seemed to have been achieved successfully thanks to the mediation of London. But it is difficult to stop war otherwise than by forcible intervention from outside, or by the internal exhaustion of the belligerent forces. War is a state of possession by anti-social passions that must exhaust itself or be exorcised by stronger forces. Europe treated the Balkans as a Bedlam, and, by shutting up the patients together in the interests of society, aggravated their disorder. The war fanatics should perhaps have been separately treated with

[1] The first six sittings of the Peace Conference were spent in rejecting absurd Turkish proposals, and in discussing various Turkish points of procedure. On January 6, 1913, the Balkan delegates suspended the Conference at its tenth meeting, as the Ottoman delegates insisted on retaining the vilayet of Adrianople and the Asiatic islands. The Powers then intervened, and after some delay, due to the dilatoriness of one of them, presented a joint note on January 17.

the strait waistcoat and the cold douche that will be some day the recognized cure of war fever.

On the day following the decision of the General Council, the Committee effected a successful *coup d'état*, and assumed control of the government. The Porte was invaded by a small party, under the Committee leaders, Enver, Djemal, and Talaat Beys : all the leading personages of the Elder Statesmen were seized, and Mahmoud Shevket was made Grand Vizier. There was no resistance or disturbance, and the shooting of Nazim, Minister of War, by the conspirators, was an assassination which condemned the whole enterprise in the eyes of Europe, and which later cost the Committee in reprisal the life of its most valuable member, Mahmoud Shevket himself. Nazim Pasha was of value as a soldier and a statesman, and Mahmoud Shevket even more so, while neither could be spared in a young polity, badly in want of leaders enjoying the public confidence. But ' à la guerre comme à la guerre ', and in the eyes of the Young Turks, the Elder Statesmen were all guilty of a betrayal of their country, to say nothing of a breach of its constitution. It would be foolish to interpret the *coup d'état* of January 23 as a mere successful conspiracy for power, taking advantage of a public crisis for party purposes. The Committee could probably have put itself in power any time after its withdrawal from responsibility six months before, and the first result of the proclamation of peace and the loss of Adrianople would certainly have been the final downfall of the anti-Committee régime of the ' Elder Statesmen '. Indeed, the worst accusation that can be brought against the Committee is that they allowed the Elder Statesmen to come into power and negotiate for peace merely to gain time for a renewal of the war.[1] On the other hand, to resume power before peace was concluded, and accept

---

[1] This supposition is supported by the efforts of the Young Turks to prolong the negotiations, and by their postponement of the *coup d'état* until the last possible moment.

the responsibility for the disasters of political opponents, would have been idiotic from a party point of view. It seems indeed indisputable that the conspiracy, with all its ugly features, such as the political tampering by officers with troops at the front,[1] and the cowardly murder by officers of a commander-in-chief, the enemy being at the gates, can be ascribed to a purely patriotic inspiration and a perfectly sound military judgement. The young Turks were both politically and patriotically justified in holding that Thrace and Adrianople were not lost as long as Adrianople held out, and the foreign situation remained obscure. If the Empire, that is to say the army, was prepared to make further sacrifices to keep this territory, it was the duty of the Young Turk opposition to resume control if it could, so as to give such sacrifices every chance of success. If the situation has been here correctly summed up, history will in all probability decide that their policy was justifiable, and that in the stress of circumstances their procedure was excusable. Whatever may be the decision of historic opinion, the event itself, as usual in this ' Morality play ' of Balkan affairs, has already judged their enterprise with the most unexceptionable equity. Thus we find that, while their sound policy has been rewarded by the recovery of Adrianople and Thrace, yet this has been effected by force of circumstances and by no feat of arms ; while their unsoldierly proceedings have received their appropriate retribution in the entire loss, during the second Thracian campaign, of the Young Turk military prestige, which the first campaign had left uninjured. For after the fiasco of Enver Bey's Armada and the failure of the sortie from Tchataldja, there could be no doubt that the first campaign would

---

[1] In the middle of December, thousands of boxes of sweetmeats were sent up to Tchataldja, nominally as a patriotic gift. Each contained a leaflet to the effect that the army was being sold by Nazim and the Cabinet, and that those who wanted to save Adrianople must support the Young Turks.—*The Near East* Constantinople Correspondent, January 31, 1913.

not have ended differently had the Young Turks been in control.

One thing is certain, that the policy of the Young Turk party in renewing the war was the policy of the Young Turkish people, as expressed through the only representative institution in working order at the moment—the army. The wisest national policy—the policy of cutting losses and concentrating resources—was not the popular policy, though it was the policy that inexorable laws of circumstances had been forcing on Turkey for a century. The laws of national development have allotted Thrace to Europe and the Turks to Asia, yet war allowed these laws to be defied— for ' inter arma leges silent ', laws of nature as well as laws of nations. But such considerations were of little weight in the circumstances, and there could be no doubt that, owing to the passions roused by war, the *coup d'état* was a true expression of the only corporate opinion in the Empire capable of expressing itself. It was, at all events, immediately accepted as such abroad. The negotiations at once broke off in London, and hostilities were resumed.

It is an absorbing, if academic, occupation, endeavouring to estimate whether the change of Government at Constantinople so altered conditions for the worse—that is to say, so diverted the course of events into war—that no foreign intervention would have saved the situation. Before criticizing the Concert, and more especially the British mandatories and moving spirits of the Concert in the London Conference, for not preventing it from breaking up, we must consider the great difficulties of the crisis, and the fact that no warning of it was given, and that a course of action, imperilling, perhaps, the peace of Europe, would have had to be decided upon within a few hours.

In the first place, it would have been very difficult for the Triple Agreement to carry the Triple Alliance with it in an assumption by the Concert of the pacification and partition of eastern Europe. The relations between the

Triple Agreement and the Triple Alliance, in respect of the War of Coalition, were somewhat those of a constitutional Government to a constitutional Opposition in respect of a Government measure. So long as the Opposition was treated in conformity with custom and comity, it would not obstruct unduly nor declare war. But, on the other hand, it could scarcely be counted on to co-operate in the peaceful passage of measures which realized the policy and would redound to the profit of those in power. Therefore, if the Triple Agreement was to undertake a settlement of the Eastern Question, it would have to rely on its own forces to impose it on the countries concerned. Moreover, unless this execution proceeded with perfect smoothness against the open opposition of those minor Powers, such as Turkey, which it prejudiced materially, and against the veiled opposition of the Great Powers, which it prejudiced morally, the Concert would have collapsed as the coalition did, with even more disastrous results. It would have been a poor service to humanity if, in trying to avoid the frying-pan of a war between the Balkan Allies, the civilized world had been thrown into the fire of a war between the European Alliances. Everything, therefore, would have depended on this most difficult undertaking—namely, the settlement of the Eastern Question by Europe—being smoothly carried through; and it must be remembered that the European powers had quarrelled and quibbled over this question for more than a century, and had, at last, handed it over to the Balkan States to do their best with.

This brings us to the second difficulty, which is the question whether the Balkan States themselves would have welcomed the settlement being again taken out of their hands, and would have heartily supported the proposals of the Triple Agreement, supposing, as may be very possible, that the Young Turk Government would have welcomed an intervention which would have saved their face and stopped the war, and would have yielded to such pressure as the

Triple Agreement could safely apply without over-straining the Concert. Such pressure would have been a naval demonstration in the Marmora, combined, perhaps, with a Russian military demonstration in Asia Minor. Even so, the risk of the course of events getting beyond control would have been great. Warships cannot be sent into mined and hostile waters without danger of incidents irritating to public opinion : military occupation of alien territory cannot be effected without political consequences. Even when peace had been imposed on Turkey, the task would have been only half accomplished, as this would have involved responsibility for the partition of Thrace, the Aegean, and Macedonia. Could the partition proposals of the Triple Agreement have been imposed on the Allies without a hitch ?

Supposing again, in view of Bulgar desire for peace, and the easy accessibility of Serbia or Montenegro to Russian pressure, and of Greece to Anglo-French pressure, that this too had been accomplished. Would the Triple Alliance have accepted the situation, and would it have contented itself with constitutional discussion of the settlement in the Concert, loyally renouncing the more effective means of opposition to it in privately supporting the demands of Turkey, Roumania, or Greece against it ?

Finally, for reasons which will be clear later, if they are not so already, the initiative and the impetus of such intervention would both have had to be supplied from London. Now, while the vital principle of the British position in eastern Europe and Asia is the relationship between the British national democracy and the democratic nationality movements of the Balkans and Asia, that principle has to be subordinated, because of imperial and international complications, to the maintenance of good British diplomatic relationship with Islamic and Teutonic polities. In concrete terms, this means that, for the nonce, British foreign policy must consider Indian and German susceptibilities, even when this involves a renunciation of good work in the cause of peace and progress. For it is a disadvantage of undemocratic empires and diplomatic ententes that they increase the difficulties of a democratic diplomacy. The difficulties therefore attending intervention were such, it will be admitted, as might well give pause even to a British statesman who would have had the support of all political forces in his own country and would not have been suspected by any of the political factors abroad. It was a situation where a fool would have rushed in most fatally and an angel would certainly fear to tread. It is well for British prestige and the peace of the world that, anyhow, the former calamity was avoided.

§ 17. European Complications and Balkan Militarism

We have seen how the Balkan belligerents failed to come to terms in the Conference of London, and the War of Coalition entered its second phase—a phase during which the great catastrophe of the War of Partition was to become inevitable. We have also considered the reasons which induced the Concert to let the war go on, and to face almost certain war between the Allies, rather than a risk of war between the Triple Agreement and the Triple Alliance. Those conducting the operations of the Concert in London considered their first responsibility was to insure the success of the negotiations between the Powers in the conferences of ambassadors. In this a very complete success was achieved, though the questions dividing the Powers were arranged at the cost of aggravating the differences between the Balkan States.

We shall now see how the failure to terminate in due time the ' primary ' and ' progressive ' War of the Coalition caused that war to degenerate and develop into a series of ' secondary ' and ' suppressed ' wars between the Balkan States and the neighbouring Powers. We shall then have to notice how these in turn combined to create secondary 'open' wars between the Balkan States themselves. Such were the bloodless Bulgar-Roumanian war in the Dobrud-scha; the bloody second campaign in Thrace between Bulgars and Turks; and, most brutal of all, the Macedonian war of the Greeks and Serbs against the Bulgars. Later on we shall find that these again have caused or contributed to tertiary wars, such as the struggle still proceeding of Albanians against Serbs; of Macedo-Bulgars against Greeks and Serbs; and of Thracian Bulgars against Moslem Pomaks. Thus does even a progressive war, like some horrible disease, reinfect and reproduce itself, unless it be drastically dealt with on reaching the crisis of its primary stage. While all these wars, whether bloody and atrocious 'open' wars or 'suppressed' wars of mere military mobilization and diplomatic negotiations, have a clear common origin in, and a clear common connexion with, the course of the primary war, yet their relations to each other and the way in which they reinfect each other are most complicated and confused.

In order to get an idea of the danger to the peace of Europe from the outbreak of open war, and of the difficulties between the Balkan Allies and the Triple Alliance that caused that danger, we must consider the effect of the Allies' campaigns in Thrace and Macedonia on the neighbouring Great Powers of the Triple Alliance. We have already noticed the eastward economic advance of those Powers—that of Austria through the Sanjak, Old Serbia, and Salonica; that of Italy into the Aegean Islands; that of Germany through Roumania and Constantinople. These lines of advance were now blocked by the Balkan Alliance and by the impending partition—irretrievably blocked in the case of Austria, the most important of them.

The main danger to European peace lay in the difficulty of Viennese policy adapting itself to the new situation imposed on it by the despised Balkan Governments and the much dreaded Panslavism. It is very much to the credit of the Austrian Government that it did accept the situation, subject to an amendment—the establishment of Albanian autonomy. It is doubly to the credit of the Austrian Government that this amendment was, in itself, a signal service to the progress and peace of Europe, and this even though it undoubtedly contributed to the War of Partition. This achievement of the pacific influences in that Government, among which that of the Emperor Francis Joseph is the most prominent, is all the more striking, seeing that events in Austro-Serbian relations give ample evidence of a strong Austrian war party. In the Austrian Empire there is, as has been pointed out, a dualism between the Hungarian and Slav elements, the former being ever prepared to fight to prevent any extension of Slav power in the Balkans. There is also a dualism in the Government, and even, it is said, at Court, between the radical *Realpolitik* that inspired the *coup* of 1908, and the conservative pacificism that fortunately kept control in 1913.

It was, as we have seen, against Austrian military adventure and ambitions in Macedonia that the Serbo-Bulgar alliance was directed, quite as much as against Turkey ; and Austro-Serbian relations, prior to the war, gave no indication that Serbia would be permitted to annex any even of Old Serbia, to say nothing of Albania or of the Sanjak. The relations of Budapest to the Serbs within the Empire, and of Vienna to those without it, were very strained. The suspension of the constitution in Croatia, and of the Serb ecclesiastical privileges in Hungary, had perhaps no very direct relation to the Balkan situation. But the filling of the frontier with troops, the fortification of islands in the Danube, and the prevention, in every possible way, of Serbian military preparations, seemed evidence that the militarists were in control. Fortunately, where no great force of public opinion can be excited, the step from military preparation to actual war is difficult to take ; and, in the absence of any popular demand for war, the pacificism of the venerable emperor proved a sufficient protection to the peace. None the less, few would have anticipated that Vienna would have accepted such an aggrandizement of Serbia as the campaign in Macedonia made a *fait accompli*; and some have sought to explain Austrian renunciation of Macedonia by reluctance to allow of an Italian compensation in Albania, such as would have been claimed by Rome under a secret agreement dating from 1887. Whether such an agreement existed or not, the Austrian insistence on an independent Albania was no doubt inspired rather by ' diplomatic ' jealousy of Italy and Russia than by any ' democratic ' belief in the principle of Albanian nationality.

The Austro-Serbian difficulty in respect of Albania began from the turning-point in the Macedonian campaign, the battle of Kumanovo, where, on October 23 and 24, something over a hundred thousand Serbians defeated half that number of Turks. Owing to defective Serbian tactics the fighting was much harder than it need have been, but this, in itself, made the eventual defeat of the Turks all the more complete. It became evident at once that the Turkish command of Macedonia was at an end, and that strategic dispositions might safely be guided by political rather than military considerations. Macedonia was won, and from the vantage point of southern Macedonia the long-sought Serbian outlet to the sea seemed open on either hand. The only barrier between Serbia and the Adriatic was now the ' political ' frontier of Montenegro, a Serb State, and the mountains and clansmen of Albania, the hereditary enemies of the Serbs. The road to the Aegean, on the other hand, was barred by the partition provisions of the treaty with Bulgaria. The Albanian outlet was accordingly chosen, for while a Serbian advance to the Adriatic was bound to cause objection by Austria and would perhaps even lead to an Austrian occupation of Belgrade, yet, in such a case, the Balkan Alliance ensured military succour from Bulgaria, and the Triple Entente might be counted on for moral support. But before the Balkan Alliance could change front against its western opponent Austria, it had to finish with its eastern opponent Turkey. Clearly the proper policy for Serbia was to give no time for the establishment of diplomatic dead-lines by the Concert; but with one hand to occupy Albania, and with the other to free the Bulgar and Montenegrin forces as soon as possible by giving a *coup de grâce* to the Thracian and Albanian campaigns. This was accordingly done. Some 40,000 Serbians were hurried off by train to press the siege of Adrianople, and about the same number were sent by forced marches through the Albanian highlands to the Adriatic; while siege guns and other assistance were sent round in Greek vessels to reinforce the Montenegrins, who were making no headway against the citadel of Scutari. The remaining Serbian forces in Macedonia drove Djavid's Turks back upon the Greek advance. The Greeks, who were bent on their political objective—Salonica—failed to co-operate by encircling Djavid, who, after a desperate defensive action at Monastir, passed out of the Serbian field of action to establish another centre of resistance at Janina. None the less, by the time the armistice was signed on December 2, not only was the whole Sanjak and all Old Serbia, Macedonia as far south as the Kuprulu line, Perlepe, and Monastir in Serbian occupation; but North Albania was so also, with Elbassan, Durazzo, and San Juan de Medua, while a Serbian-Montenegrin force was pressing Scutari. Vienna was faced with the *fait accompli* of a Serbian aggrandizement such as exceeded its worst apprehensions, and which had developed at such a pace that formal protest or, still less, effective preventives, were not feasible.

Nor was the other Adriatic power, Italy, any better suited by the Serbian advance into North Albania, which was accompanied by a Greek advance into South Albania. Nothing but the last dying ember of Turkish resistance at Scutari and Janina and the first feeble embryo of Albanian nationality in the provisional government at Avlona still stood in the way of a Serbo-Greek partition. In this situation, under the conditions of, say, fifty years ago, there is little doubt that Austria would have taken military action against Serbia with the co-operation of Italy against Greece, and Albania would have been partitioned between the two great Powers. Those who doubt that there has been any ethical improvement in international relations will do well to examine this case of Albania, by which the liberties of a weak nation were secured by the operation of the custom of Europe on the lawlessness of military powers. It is curious to see how the riddle was solved, and how out of the eater came forth meat, and out of the strong, sweetness. In vain did the Viennese militarists conspire to stir up a war fever by improvised incidents such as the ' Prochaska affair '.[1] In vain did Roman diplomatists try to bring about some combination by which the diplomatic dilemma might be avoided. The solution was to be found neither in arms nor in diplomacy, but in the principles of European solidarity and Albanian nationality—the one as represented by the conference of ambassadors in London, the other by the convention of notables at Avlona. On October 5 a Provisional Government was proclaimed at Avlona, and on December 20 Albanian autonomy was adopted in London. The crisis had found its solution, thanks to the force of European opinion and the opportunity given to it in London of expressing itself in practical politics.

Of course much was still left to be done by the Concert. After the North Albanian frontier had been defined, Serbia and Montenegro had to be forced to respect it. In the case of

---

[1] M. Prochaska, Austrian consul at Prizrend, had associated himself with Albanian opposition to the Serbian occupation. The Serbian Government, having complained of him and other consuls, and the Austrian Government having failed to get into communication with him, stories were spread of his having been maltreated, and, later, that he and others had been murdered. The report of a Commission of Inquiry, which showed these tales to be tendentious inventions, confirmed Austrian public opinion in its opposition to a policy of adventure.

Servia this caused two bloody secondary wars—and in the case of Montenegro required a ' suppressed ' war in a naval demonstration by the fleet of Europe against the mountain State. The southern frontier was not defined until the following year, and the difficulties with the diplomatic Greeks took longer in settling.

The preoccupation of the Greeks in establishing themselves in southern Macedonia and Salonica, the comparative unimportance to them of southern Albania, and the prolongation of Turkish resistance in Epirus, all combined to make the Italo-Greek conflict over the Adriatic littoral less acute and to postpone it to a later stage. The Concert under the presidency of the British Foreign Secretary eventually succeeded in securing for the new Albania the fertile lands and civilized population of South Albania necessary to Albanian development but assigned to Greece in the projected partition with Serbia, and in buying off Greece with the islands. But the exclusion of Greece from South Albania prejudiced Graeco-Bulgar relations in Macedonia as much as the expulsion of Serbia from North Albania prejudiced Serbo-Bulgar relations. For Greece was determined, if possible, to have a contiguous frontier with Serbia, and the substitution of a joint frontier in Macedonia for that planned in Albania served as an additional inducement to Greece to support Serbian pretensions to Monastir and to keep the Bulgars to East Macedonia.

Expulsion from North Albania and exclusion from the Adriatic was a far heavier blow to Serbia than was the loss of Koritsa to Greece. Italy had in the Aegean Islands, occupied in the Tripoli war, an easily available compensation for Greece, just as Austria had in the Dalmatian coast strip very suitable compensation for the Slav States ; but neither power showed any inclination to make such concessions as would render the evacuation of Albania easy to the Balkan Allies. It is indeed to be feared that Albanian independence recommended itself in some quarters less as an expression of Balkan nationality than as an expedient for breaking up the Balkan Coalition. Serbia, repulsed from the Adriatic, would probably be embroiled with Bulgaria; for it was obviously imposing an excessive strain on the treaty obligations of the Serbian Government to require it to surrender Albania to Austria and Macedonia to Bulgaria. If this were effected, Bulgaria would, with Serbian help, have added Thrace to the territories partitioned under the treaty; while Servia would have been robbed of her supplementary conquest by Austria, without being able to receive or even to claim the Bulgarian aid against Austria for which the treaty provided. Thus did Viennese diplomacy astutely achieve its object of breaking up the Balkan Coalition without breaking up the European Concert.

In yet another quarter we find the expansive energies of the Balkan Coalition checked and turned inward upon themselves by the Powers. The Bulgars were given to understand that they would not be permitted to occupy either Constantinople or any point on the Sea of Marmora, for the same reasons of Russian diplomacy that deprecated the occupation by Greece of the islands commanding the Straits. We have here a concession by pro-Balkan Petersburg to pro-Ottoman Berlin that cost as little as the concession of Albanian independence by London to Vienna. Russia was as unwilling that the Bosphorus and the Dardanelles should come under the control of Bulgaria and Greece as was England that Albania should be partitioned between Greece and Serbia. But the effect on Macedonia was somewhat the same, for Bulgarian and Greek ambitions were thrown back from Constantinople on Salonica and Kavalla, perhaps with some sort of assurance from Petersburg that compliance in Thrace would be compensated in Macedonia. Again, there was still another region in which the Great Powers either out of design or indifference increased the tension between the Balkan States and contributed to causing the War of Partition, that most unnecessary and disgraceful of conflicts. Bulgaria, turned back upon Mace-

donia from the Marmora, was at the same time put under
pressure from the Danube. The ensuing ' suppressed ' war
between Roumania and Bulgaria takes its place between such
diplomatic suppressed wars as that of Austria with Serbia,
and such open democratic wars as that between Bulgaria and
Serbia. This is consonant with the international position
of Roumania, which is according to circumstances and choice
either a dependent European State or a dominant Balkan
State. For while its policy and geographical position render
it dependent as a European secondary State both on Austria
and Russia, its progress and population render it dominant
in the Peninsula in case of bad relations between the Balkan
States. The policy of Roumania towards the coalition began
by being European and ended by being Balkan; and though
self-seeking was not on the whole dishonest. For no concealment was made of the fact that Roumania would have
to be reckoned with in the settlement ; and as there could
be no question of the Macedonian Vlachs securing any
territorial recognition, there was no particular reason why
Roumania should join in fighting the Turks. But, on the
other hand, as Roumania had not joined the Allies, Roumanian
claims for an accession of territory seemed to be without
moral force. Nor was there any obvious geographical or
ethnological claim for such an aggrandizement. Roumania
irredenta is under Austrian or Russian rule: there is also a
district of Serbia largely populated with Roumanians, though it
is not important enough to justify Roumania in overstepping
so obvious a national frontier as the Danube. Moreover, if
the Dobrudscha frontier with Bulgaria is geographically
weak, yet Roumania in this region had no ethnological
claim, as its border territories already included districts
of Bulgarian population. It was here none the less that
the accession of territory was claimed, probably because
Russian sanction could be obtained for an extension at the
expense of Bulgaria, though not for one at the expense of
Serbia.

It need not be made a reproach to Roumania that in putting forward this claim at the crucial moment when peace was in the balance it combined with the intervention of the Powers of the Triple Alliance in turning the scale in favour of the war. Roumania has been called the gendarme of Europe; but in the Balkans gendarmes often prefer profiting by disorders to preventing them. Accordingly, no sooner was Bulgaria engaged with Turkey than Roumania put forward a claim to compensation in view of the prospective aggrandizement of Bulgaria. This claim, though put forward as compensation for prospective Bulgarian expansion, was really an exploitation of prospective Bulgarian exhaustion, as is shown by the fact that the claim did not diminish, but augmented as the Bulgarian shares of the spoils and the Bulgarian powers of resistance decreased. War is a policy quite as much as a procedure, and sometimes the profits of the policy can be secured without paying the full cost of the war procedure by belligerents sufficiently progressive and prudent to confine themselves to an aggressive neutrality. Roumania is the most progressive of the Balkan States, and the Roumanian rôle in the Balkan crisis has been conspicuous for its prudence. Both the Austrian and Roumanian policies of aggressive neutrality in relation to the Balkan war were inspired by the precept that when thieves fall out honest men come by what is not their own; but, nevertheless, there is an impression that the procedure of Roumania might serve as a precedent for a European Power in a European war. There is no doubt that such policy is often advocated by a large, though perhaps decreasing majority of those concerned with European relations. It is a policy which seems politically sound and morally satisfactory only when expressed in the formulae familiar to all students of foreign affairs—a precaution which Bucharest somewhat naïvely ignored until its policy had already come in for severe criticism. ' The simple plan that he shall take who has the power and he shall keep who can ' is paraphrased in diplomatic jargon somewhat as follows : the ' balance of power ' in the Balkans being threatened by the ' preponderance ' and ' prestige ' of Bulgaria, the ' strategic strength ' of Roumania was to be increased by a ' rectification of frontier ' as compensation from Bulgaria. Now whether such formulae do or do not represent facts in western Europe, they most certainly misrepresent them in eastern Europe, as will later be shown ; and there is no reason to suppose that Roumanian statesmen were really much influenced by such calculations in deciding on self-interested intervention. Whether such intervention was in the ultimate interest of Roumania is a question which will be considered when the ultimate results of its action are summed up. For the present we have only to consider the course of the ' suppressed ' War of Partition declared by Roumania against Bulgaria. The Roumanian demand for Silistria and a strip of Bulgar territory along the Dobrudscha frontier amounted to a declaration of war, as is shown by the fact that it was a demand very difficult to deal with otherwise than by war. The Roumanians had no case against Bulgaria either in international law or in international equity. They had, on the other hand, such cause of complaint against Europe and the *status quo* of the Treaty of Berlin that they can scarcely be blamed for having had recourse to any remedy. The remedy they chose, that of ' suppressed ' war, was effective for their purpose since it threw upon the Triple Agreement as the patrons of the Allies the obligation of satisfying Roumanian aspirations. It is accordingly interesting to find the Russian and British governments, the authors of the original injustice to Roumania at Berlin when Bessarabia was taken away in return for the Bulgar Dobrudscha, now compelled to carry this injustice farther by compensating Roumania with another strip of the Dobrudscha. The transaction was given such propriety as forms of procedure can afford. The Roumano-Bulgar dispute was referred, at the instance of London, to the ' arbitration ' of the ambassadors at Petersburg.

' Mediation ' would have been the proper term, for there were
no rights to arbitrate, but only a state of war to terminate.
The so-called arbitral award was, in fact, a diplomatic
deal negotiated between the ambassadors in Petersburg of
the Triple Alliance on behalf of Bulgaria and those of the
Triple Agreement on behalf of Roumania. The foregone
conclusion of the mediation was a compromise arrived at
towards the end of March which gave Roumania Silistria
and a ' strategic frontier ' including a strip of the Bulgarian
Dobrudscha. The new ' international ' frontier from Silistria
to Cape Shabla was accepted by both parties under the
pressure of Petersburg. It was arrived at by the same
procedure—a conference of ambassadors—and on the same
principles—a compromise of ambitions—as the ' international ' Enos-Midia line in Thrace, which London had already
proposed on behalf of the Powers and which was later to be
imposed on Bulgaria and Turkey. Indeed the course of events
is almost the same in this Bulgar-Roumanian ' suppressed '
war as in the Bulgar-Turkish open war, an important point
of resemblance being that the Roumanian intervention was
not really the cold-blooded, calculated despoiling of a neighbour in difficulties, but a ' forward ' policy forced on the
Government by a militarist opposition and by the army.
The international compromise of Shabla-Silistria no more
satisfied the Roumanian war-party than that of Enos-Midia
satisfied the Young Turks ; it was a pacification, not a peace.
The compensation was not considered satisfactory by
Bucharest, which, in accepting it, let it be understood it
would get more if any opportunity offered. The War of
Partition gave the opening, and Roumania, like Turkey,
violated the international frontier at the first favourable
opportunity, renewed the war with an invasion of Bulgaria,
and finally made another peace under the auspices this time
of the Triple Alliance. Meantime the Roumanian claim, and
the support given it in Russia, had two direct effects on the
situation, both unfavourable to a pacific solution. One was

the resignation of the Russophil and pacific Bulgar premier, M. Gueshoff, the other was the encouragement of the militarist party in Turkey.

The reorganization of resistance by the Committee of Union and Progress in the winter of 1912–13, after the break-up of the first Conference of London, was an astounding feat, comparable to that of the Committee of Public Safety in the French Revolution. The Turkish Committee of the twentieth century showed no less activity than did the French in the eighteenth century, as well in military as in civil administration, and if they had less time at their disposal than the French Committee, they had more command of men and money. Therefore, if they organized no victory, it is perhaps legitimate to infer that they did not deserve to; and if they have produced no Napoleon and not even a Carnot, it is perhaps evidence that there is in Turkey no matrix of military material, which under the fierce heat of revolution could be made to create a gem of military genius. It is indeed difficult to explain from a purely practical point of view why the Young Turks failed; for although they had been forced to resume the war before they were quite ready, they made a spirited tactical beginning, and the strategic position was all in their favour.

The Bulgars had now no choice but to devote their remaining energies to Adrianople, for the Macedonian and Roumanian situations were becoming so critical as to call imperatively for a conclusion of the Thracian campaign. But in order to operate against Adrianople they had to maintain their main army in its advanced position before Tchataldja. There it had a fresh Turkish army impregnably entrenched in its front, with another entrenched in its rear at Adrianople, and a third hardly less strongly entrenched in the Gallipoli peninsula in its rear flank; it had for its communications two hundred miles of bullock transport exposed to attack both from the Black Sea and from the Sea of Marmora, both these seas being available for the transport of Turkish troops. A Bulgar *coup de main* against Tchataldja or Bulair had been proved to be no less hopeless than those already attempted against Adrianople. Moreover, Adrianople was clearly able to hold out long enough to give the Tchataldja and Gallipoli armies time to make the Bulgar position in Thrace untenable, provided only that the Turks could take the offensive effectively. Fortunately for the Bulgars it was soon clear that the Turks could not; for a mainly naval offensive against the rear of the Bulgar containing force at Tchataldja by way of the Black Sea was repulsed with the loss of a Turkish ironclad, and a flotilla of transports under Enver Bey that made a similar attempt on the rear of the Bulgar containing army by way of the Marmora was also repulsed with heavy loss. The only result of these offensive Turkish operations was to correct the defects in the disposition of the Bulgar forces. The Bulgar line was withdrawn out of easy striking distance from Tchataldja and Bulair, and thereby covered its exposed flanks, while it blocked even more securely the Turkish road to the relief of Adrianople. The converging in Thrace of the two bridges between Asia and Europe, that by Gallipoli and that by Constantinople, enabled the Bulgar inferior force to use its position in central Thrace to contain superior forces advancing from Asia. The Turkish force could not strike effectively at any distance from its bases behind Tchataldja and Bulair, because neither the machinery nor the morale left to it was enough for an aggressive advance against opposition. The offensive in Thrace had passed to the Turks, but they could make no effective use of it. The second Thracian campaign consists only of the reduction of Adrianople and the vain attempts of the Turks to push back the Bulgar covering force and relieve it.

Thrace was no longer the arena in which success would decide political issues over the whole field of war. The war in Thrace had passed through the primary phase in which war is the only means of finding the line of least

resistance between contending natural forces, and had
entered the secondary phase when war is only a means of
forcing on some political purpose of a more or less national
character.

The ' secondary ' war of the Young Turks in Thrace
was, like the Roumanian secondary war, dependent for its
success as much on the European political situation as on
any military action in Thrace. Military action was postponed by the Young Turks until it was seen whether the
Bulgar-Roumanian or the Serbo-Albanian ' secondary ' wars
would not produce a collapse of the Concert. But when it
became clearer that the Concert was strong enough to
maintain the peace of Europe, and to make a good beginning
at restoring peace in the Balkans, further postponement of
action in Thrace became inadvisable, all the more that the
Bulgars were pressing home an assault on Adrianople. On
March 25 a force advanced from Tchataldja against the
Bulgar positions, and was repulsed with heavy loss. It
seems to have been relatively small in numbers, not more
than 50,000, and unsuitable in other respects for such an
offensive. The fighting was severe, as testified by the admitted
loss of one-quarter of the Turkish strength. The counter-
stroke failed to relieve pressure on Constantinople, and the
day following Adrianople surrendered. The Turks immediately invited the mediation of the Powers, and on March 31
they received the conditions of such mediation. These
were, the Enos-Midia line in Thrace and the cession of the
Aegean islands to the Powers for disposition—the same
terms as had been accepted by Kiamil in January. Thus,
the only result of the secondary war in Thrace had been to
force the Bulgarian army to take Adrianople at heavy cost,
and to permit the Greek fleet to complete the seizure of
the Aegean islands at very little cost. It may be said that
the renewal of the war was only a stage in a preconceived
policy which did eventually lead to the recovery of Thrace.
But the proceedings of the Ottoman Government cannot

be reconciled with any programme of this sort, or with any policy other than that of a characteristic procrastination. Thus, if the Ottoman Government had been acting with appreciation of the fact that the moment had come to release the Bulgar force from Thrace, with the best chance of their creating a ' secondary ' war in Macedonia, they would have come to a direct agreement with Bulgaria as soon as possible. Such an agreement, moreover, would have allowed Bulgaria to divert its forces into Macedonia, while leaving it open to Turkey to advance in their rear when circumstances permitted. The course the Ottoman Government did take, in calling in the Powers, was such as gave the best opportunity for allowing a peaceful arrangement between Greece and Bulgaria, and a permanent arrangement between themselves and Bulgaria.

§ 18. SECOND LONDON CONFERENCE AND GREEK MILITARISM

War is a fever in the social system. The first London Conference of Balkan plenipotentiaries marked a crisis in the disease which ended in a relapse, thanks to the Young Turk war party. The second London Conference represented a rally, which was decided in the same way by the Greek war party. It may be objected that there is evidence that in the first case Bulgar diplomatic obstinacy, and in the second case Bulgar military aggression, were the real reasons why the Conference of plenipotentiaries in London failed to establish a general peace. But in assigning responsibility for the resumption of hostilities it is necessary to go below the acts of Governments to the forces that produced them. Thus we have seen that Bulgaria had got itself into a strategic and political position in which its Government could at no time bring about such a peace as the nation would accept. Turkey might have brought about a permanent peace at the time of the first Conference, but with the second Conference, owing to the fall of the fortresses, Turkey was no more a controlling factor. Servia was still a secondary factor, and moreover was neutralized by Austria. Greece alone was really in command of the situation.

It has already been stated that the real force of the Balkan war was an over-deferred expansion of the Greek nationality movement. This theory seems to be supported by the curious way in which the other competitive forces now begin to cancel themselves out or collapse. By the date of the second Conference, the ground had been cleared for the Greeks by the exhaustion of their rivals.

The Ottoman Empire was at an end of its easily realizable resources in men and money. Bulgaria, its principal opponent among the Allies, was even worse off. Like Turkey, an agricultural state, the loss of every peasant and of every plough-ox was even more serious to Bulgaria; because the peasant of a prosperous and progressive State, such as Bulgaria, has a higher actual and a far higher potential value as a semi-manufactured article, capable of further working up, than has such raw material as the Anatolian peasant. A Bulgar peasant is of more value than the proletariat soldier of a developed society such as ours, the latter being often a social. surplus product. The drain on the working capital of the Bulgarian agricultural industry imposed by the bloody battles of Thrace and those two hundred miles of ox-wagon and mud-road communications was such as no people can long support. Already one-tenth of the male population had been killed or crippled, and perhaps one-fifth of the farm animals destroyed. As for business, the moratorium was absolute, the whole energy of the country being absorbed in the war. Indeed the organization of the whole State for the one purpose seems to have been admirable, and all measures were taken to ease the strain as far as possible. Thus, the large body of prisoners were distributed so as to help the women in field work; relief was freely given to the destitute, and even the insurance premiums of the men at the front were paid for them. Such providence will no doubt result in a recovery that will be as surprising as all the other feats of this people—who can accomplish the extraordinary by being merely in everything extra ordinary. But there is a limit even to the most effective and economic exertion, and Bulgaria by March 1912, the time Adrianople fell, was exhausted. Money could still have been got, but only at a price so exorbitant as to be prohibitive to any but a far more improvident Government. Men there were still, but they were men that had fought to a finish in a crusade, and could scarcely be expected to engage with zest in a war of conquest. To sum up, the Bulgars and Turks had cancelled each other out by wearing each other down. There remained the Serbs and Albanians.

In the case of the Albanians and Serbs, there was no question of exhaustion. The Serbs had entered the war with a reserve of ready money available, and their losses in Macedonia, though heavy, had not been such as to cripple their power, compensated as they were by the impulse given to them by the conquest of Macedonia and the cleaning from the slate of the long list of national disasters from Kossovo to Slivnitza. But the Albanians had suffered scarcely at all, for those that had enlisted on the Turkish side had evidently done so merely as a precaution, and once the tide turned against the Turk they had withdrawn to their hills. They would have fought for the Turks as long as Turkish rule had any prospect of surviving, but, as soon as it was clearly dead, they reserved their energies for their old race enemies, the Serbs. But for the intervention of Europe in their favour, they would have engaged all the spare energies of the Serbs in a struggle for North Albania and Old Serbia. As it was, the Serbs, thrown back from the Adriatic and Scutari, turned their eyes towards the Aegean and Salonica. But there was nothing in this diversion to render inevitable a war with Bulgaria for Monastir, as has often been suggested. Serbia would have

been far better suited with an autonomous Monastir and
Salonica than with a Monastir annexed to Bulgaria and
a Salonica annexed to Greece. Serbian relations with
Bulgaria were good. They had fought side by side in Macedonia, they were to fight side by side in Thrace. The Serbian
Government, under M. Pashitch, was a strong one, capable
at this date of restraining its army. There were the clearest
treaty obligations providing for the case of autonomy or
of partition. The exclusion and the expulsion of the Albanians
from Old Serbia and North Macedonia promised occupation
to the army for many years. On the whole, the Serbs and
Albanians could have been expected to cancel each other
out at least during the spring of 1913, provided things had
been left to themselves.

But things were not left to themselves. There remained
the expansive force and national ambitions of the Greeks;
the former in no way exhausted, the latter violently
excited by easy conquest, and with nothing to check them
but the prudence of such pacific influences as the Government still retained. Money was still ample, if not abundant;
for the expenses of the war had been paid so far from reserves,
and foreign credit had not yet been called on. The naval
war had merely consisted of blockading an almost passive
Turkish fleet in the Dardanelles, and the one naval action
forced by the Young Turks had only proved the incontestable superiority of the Greek navy. The land campaign
in the Roumlouk had been of the kind that leaves the
superior and successful force stronger at the end than at
the beginning. For the Greeks had encountered no more
resistance than was enough to stimulate the troops, and no
more hardship than was enough to toughen them, as
they pressed victoriously forward into a country that welcomed them as deliverers. Although the Greek Government
were the least ready for war of the Allies, and the army
that they were able to put into the field at the beginning
of the campaign has probably been much overestimated,
there is no doubt that they outnumbered the Turkish

containing force by at least two to one. The quality of the Turkish containing force is said to have been very inferior; and this is confirmed by its swift expulsion from the difficult passes of the frontier and by its no less swift surrender at Salonica. The reverses the Greeks sustained in their collision with the battered and broken main force under Djavid, and the resistance these troops later opposed to them when hunted down and surrounded in comparatively open country in Epirus, show that the Greeks would never have reached Salonica at all, had not the back of the Turkish resistance in Macedonia and Thrace been broken by Serbs and Bulgars. As it was, they not only reached Salonica, but reached it stronger than they started; and much stronger than any troops which the Bulgars could spare from fighting the battles of the Allies in Thrace in order to maintain their formal claim to Salonica. It is true that the failure of the Greeks to contain Djavid at Monastir and the stand his forces made at Janina somewhat delayed and distracted their Macedonian operations, but Janina fell on March 6, and the whole Greek forces were thereafter set free to deal with Macedonia. This was three weeks before the fall of Adrianople liberated any of the Bulgar forces, and three months before the signature of the Treaty of London allowed the Bulgars to change front and divert their main force to making good their rights in Macedonia. The three months of free action which were thus secured by Greek diplomacy for the Greek armed forces were well used by the latter in extending and establishing the Greek occupation by informal warfare with the Bulgar contingents, as will be described later. But these three months were not the only achievements of Greek diplomacy in asserting the command of events which the force of events brought to Greek policy. The Greek position as against Bulgaria was made almost inexpugnable by understandings with Serbia and Roumania. Bulgaria could only attack Greece on the narrowest of fronts, and that remote from any Greek vital centre; while such Bulgarian attack would have to be carried on with no less than three other enemies operating within easy striking distance of Sofia. When we add to this that Greece could count on the neutrality of all the Powers of the Triple Agreement as well as on that of the most powerful partner of the Triple Alliance, Germany—it will be admitted that seldom has a minor State found itself so completely in control of a European crisis. It may, perhaps, be hoped that such power may seldom again fall to a minor State which has so heavy a claim against the past, and so much ability to enforce it at all costs to the future.[1]

It has been asserted with some confidence that in April 1913 Greece alone was capable of bringing about a pacific settlement such as would have prevented the subsequent secondary wars and the unsatisfactory settlement of Bucharest. Some appreciation of this responsibility may perhaps be recognized in the private overtures made to Sofia by the statesmanlike Venezelos. But the Greek government failed, unfortunately, in the difficult task of curbing the ambitions of its own war party while conciliating those of its allies. It is as a contributory cause to this failure that the writer is disposed to consider the disastrous assassination of the prudent and pacific King George of Greece, at the very turning-point of the crisis in March, as a calamity comparable to the overthrow of the prudent and pacific Kiamil at the previous crisis in January. Kiamil might have saved Turkey from the secondary war in Thrace and the onus of remaining a Balkan State ; King George might have saved Greece from the secondary war in Macedonia and the odium which for a time made ' Balkan State ' a term

[1] Such power, within a few months of writing this, fell into the hands of a minor State with disastrous consequences. Serbia, supported by Russia, and consequently by the Western Sea-Powers, in its nationalist expansion at the expense of Austria, has given a signal instance of the danger to a diplomatic structure, such as the balance of power, arising from a democratic stress such as a nationality movement. A static equilibrium, however imposing, must in the end be overthrown by a dynamic force, however insignificant. Serbia has thrown all Europe into war because the basis of European peace was artificial.

of opprobrium.[1] The murder of King George by a Greek degenerate was followed by the murders *en masse* that were a feature of the War of Partition.

It is still doubtful, and perhaps may remain so, whether the Macedonian War of Partition was a preconceived political Greek design to exploit the situation, so as to exclude Bulgaria from Salonica and Monastir and from as much more of Macedonia as might be possible, or whether it merely developed from the determination of the army to act according to the ' simple plan ' that guides armies and their commanders. The political situation was, however, so obvious that any private in the Greek army was capable of grasping the basis of the arrangement with Serbia—that, Bulgaria having been used to break the power of Turkey, Serbia should be used to break the power of Bulgaria. Bulgaria might be paid with Moslem Thrace, Serbia with Bulgar Macedonia. In this way the Greeks would not only partition off Macedonia as it pleased them, but would establish such bad relations between the other Balkan States as would give them the predominant position in the Balkans.

By the beginning of March the Greek militarists seem to have assured themselves of Serbian support sufficiently to make a forward policy in Macedonia safe in view of the preoccupation of Bulgaria with Adrianople. The efforts of the Greek forces in Macedonia were accordingly devoted to occupying as much territory north and east of Salonica as possible. On March 14 the attempt to encircle the Bulgar contingent in Salonica brought about the first serious collision between the Bulgars and Greeks at Nigrita; which was followed by others as the Greeks isolated the Bulgar detach-

---

[1] There is, indeed, much that is comparable between the last scene in the public careers of the Vizier and of the King. Their pacific part was the result in both cases of a long life of hard practical experience of the internal requirements and international relations of their respective countries. For Kiamil was over 80 years old, and King George, though not an old man, was in the fiftieth year of his reign. Both were, moreover, disposed to the Anglo-Russian point of view for personal reasons, while, curiously enough, both were succeeded by a militarist régime with German proclivities.

ments and pushed their outposts as far as Leftera in the neighbourhood of Kavalla. After the death of King George on March 18, it may be assumed that this party of action was in control of the Greek forces of Macedonia, and was pressing its militarist and monopolist policy on the more prudent and pacific government of M. Venezelos. The last efforts which that statesman was able to make to prevent a war of partition appear in the offers made by him to Bulgaria in the course of the next two months, that the Greek claims to Salonica should be recognized in return for a renunciation by Greece of all claim to the Greek port of Kavalla and the valuable hinterland. The negotiations opened by M. Venezelos for a peaceable partition on the basis of Greece receiving Salonica and Bulgaria Kavalla, and those initiated by M. Pashitch for a revision of the Treaty to increase the Serbian share, met with no response from Sofia. There is, however, some question as to what these offers amounted to in respect of what most concerned Bulgaria—the possession of Monastir ; for these overtures which began early in March were kept strictly secret so as not to weaken the joint front still opposed to the Turks. No doubt the Bulgars would have been wise to accept these offers—and to us, with a knowledge of the event and of the strength of the Greek position, it seems a grave error that they did not. But the Bulgarian government were politically no longer strong enough and not as yet militarily weak enough to renounce Salonica ; even if thereby they could have saved Monastir from Serbia— which seems very improbable. They preferred to consider the Greek overtures, like the Serbian, as being merely diplomatic devices, and the real policy of both their allies as being expressed in the efforts of their forces to extend and establish their occupation of the disputed territories. It is possible, however, that had the Bulgars been less distrustful, M. Venezelos and M. Pashitch might have saved the Alliance by making good their expressed readiness to refer the position to mediation, and by thus restraining, with outside help, their respective militarist factions. But this is very doubtful ;

and we shall probably be safe in assuming that from the
death of King George Greek militarists daily drew the policy
of their country away from the Balkan Alliance and the
Triple Agreement, towards the more congenial *Realpolitik* of
separatism and the Triple Alliance.

Henceforward we find Greek policy profiting by the
unexhausted condition of the Greek forces to pursue a policy
of territorial expansion at the cost of Bulgaria in the south
of the Peninsula; just as in the north we find Roumania
coming forward to profit in the same manner and the same
quarter. Greece had entered the Balkan Alliance for obvious
reasons; Roumania, for equally obvious reasons, had kept
out of it—but by April 1913 their policy had become very
much on a par.

So much for the action of the Greeks in Macedonia: now as
to their action in London where the diplomatic fight was to
be fought out. Janina fell on March 6; Adrianople on
March 26; Scutari did not fall until April 23. The decision
of the Powers as to Scutari and as to an independent Albania
had deprived the operations there of any direct effect on
the conclusion of peace; but the consequential coercion of
Montenegro was indirectly detrimental by diverting the
energies of the Powers to a side issue at a very crucial moment.
This, combined with the protraction of the pourparlers between
the Powers and the Allies, caused a considerable delay, and
it was not until the second week in May that the plenipotentiaries again arrived in London. The time had not
been wasted, however, by the London peacemakers, who
showed, moreover, that they had learnt the lesson of the
failure of the first Conference, and did not intend to risk
another relapse into war by leaving the Balkan delegates so
entirely to themselves. The delegates found that they had
only been convoked in order to approve the terms of peace
already drafted for them—terms representing the decision
of Europe as arrived at by the representatives of the Great
Powers in the Ambassadors' Conference.

This procedure was welcomed by the principal belligerents,

Bulgaria and Turkey, whose delegates it was understood were ready to sign without delay. But the Greeks and Serbians were for obvious reasons not so well suited by this arrangement. Greece did not want the second Conference to make peace until they were finally established in Macedonia and Albania, just as they did not want peace at the first Conference until they were established in Epirus and the Aegean. The Greek delegates accordingly began a campaign of procrastination which prolonged the proceedings until the end of the month. The treaty was eventually signed on May 30 under pressure from the British Government, the Secretary of State having curtly informed the delegates that they must sign the draft treaty or leave London.

The terms of the Treaty of London afforded a sound basis for a permanent settlement. The Ottoman Empire was restricted to a strategic frontier—the Enos-Midia line—which secured them in their capital and in the command of the Straits. Of the remaining Ottoman territory, Albania, the Aegean Islands, and Mount Athos were taken *en dépôt* by the Powers, and financial questions such as that of the indemnity claimed by the Allies and of the liability for the Ottoman debt claimed by Turkey were to be reserved for a special International Commission to meet at Paris. These terms, had they been imposed diplomatically on the Allies in December, might have resulted in peace and averted the War of Partition. But by the end of May matters had gone too far between the Allies for any peaceful solution that was not imposed on them by armed force. No doubt a provision might have been inserted in the Treaty of London for the partition or autonomy of Macedonia without carrying intervention much further in principle than the mediation of the Concert as to the frontier in Thrace. But such a provision would probably merely have ended in the Treaty being repudiated even sooner than it actually was ; for if the Concert proved unable to impose the Thracian settlement on Turkey it would probably have failed even more swiftly and

surely in imposing a Macedonian settlement on the Allies.
Moreover, such a Macedonian settlement, with a procedure
in case of disputes, had already been provided in the Serbo-
Bulgar treaty under Russian auspices, and the Concert had
consequently no jurisdiction. This difficulty might perhaps
have been overcome by taking Salonica and the disputed
hinterland *en dépôt* until an agreement as to its partition
was arrived at by arbitration or otherwise—under menace
of making it an autonomous Free City failing such an agreement. Moreover such intervention could have been made
effective, at least as regards Salonica itself, by a naval
demonstration: it would have been acceptable in the Balkans
to all but the more militarist factions: it would have
avoided all the Serbo-Bulgar disputes as to the partition
clauses of the treaty by bringing into force the alternative
casus foederis of Macedonian autonomy; and it might have
recommended itself to Vienna, whose refusal to co-operate
in effecting a Macedonian settlement was the chief cause of
the failure of the Concert in this respect. But it is easy to
make such suggestions with full after-knowledge of the subsequent developments and with little information as to contemporary difficulties. All that can be said with certainty
is that there was a strong contemporary impression that an
opportunity was missed and that this seems likely to become
the judgement of history. Indeed it is a melancholy probability that but for the success of the Powers in making
a partial peace for Bulgaria with Turkey and Roumania
there would have been no war made by Bulgaria against
Greece and Serbia. For even Bulgars swollen with success
would not have attacked Greece and Serbia unless they had
supposed they were safe from Turkey and Roumania.

It is curious that even as force of a nationality movement
compelled the diplomatic militarism of Vienna to become
an instrument in the pacific creation of the Albanian nation,
even so the same force compelled the democratic pacificism
of London to become an instrument in the militarist campaign
for a Greater Greece.

CHAPTER VII

THE MACEDONIAN PARTITION

§ 19. Rights and Wrongs.
§ 20. Pacifications and Partitions.
§ 21. Excesses and Exterminations.

'This field is mine, he says, by right,
If you poach here there'll be a fight
It 's mine—'
    'It ain't—'
        'You put—'
           'You liar—'
'This is my field.'
     'This is my wire.'
'I'm ruler here.'
    'You ain't.'
      'I am.'
'I'll fight you for it.'
      'Right, by damn.' . . .
[*They fight.*]
You've knocked me out, you didn't beat me;
Look out the next time that you meet me,
There'll be no friend to watch the clock for you
And no convenient thumb to crock for you.
And I'll take care with much delight,
You'll get what you'd a got to-night.
      MASEFIELD, *The Everlasting Mercy.*

§ 19. RIGHTS AND WRONGS

THOSE who have read the preceding chapters will already be able to assign the various Wars of Partition to their various causes, and they will have recognized that these causes had direct connexion with those of the War of Coalition. The Wars of Partition were conflicts between national interests which broke out more or less violently as wars, owing to war having been made the prevailing relationship in the Balkans; for if progress be forced to have recourse to war, as it had been in the Balkans, then when the main progressive impetus has been exhausted minor particularist interests will try to realize themselves by the same rough and ready procedure. The War of Coalition was caused by a general progressive impetus towards accomplishment of certain arrears in the European nationality movement; the Wars of Partition were caused by particularist interests of a nationalist or imperialist character. The difference in the proportion of progressive leaven in the two wars is marked by a deterioration of moral tone in the conduct of the Wars of Partition; and this applies, it should be observed, not only to the relations between Balkan peoples with the result of ' atrocities ', but also to those relations with the European Powers with the result of such ' attentats contre les bonnes mœurs' as breaches of treaty and repudiation of awards.

When the Balkan Coalition broke up, the European Concert very nearly broke down. Thus we have seen how the relationship of the European Powers to the Balkans was represented by the proceedings of the Concert, under the predominance of the Anglo-Russian Agreement and under the presidency of the British Secretary of State; and we have seen how this concerted and collective action of Europe made peace between Bulgaria and Turkey in Thrace, and between Bulgaria and Roumania on the Danube in the Treaty of London and the Award of Petersburg, while also successfully settling the Albanian question and the Aegean Islands question. We have also seen that the Concert had not enough corporate strength to stand the strain of imposing a settlement of the Macedonian question. We shall now see how separatist and self-interested elements in European diplomacy exploited the Macedonian imbroglio and encouraged a War of Partition whereby the Thracian and Danubian settlements were also thrown back into the melting-pot.

It would be easy and not altogether erroneous to divide the relations of Europe to the Balkans into pacific and progressive as distinct from militarist and reactionary, and to place in the former category the collective and concerted

action of the Conference of Ambassadors in London, and in
the latter the separatist and secret action of some of the
diplomatic missions in Balkan capitals; in which case we
should have to ascribe policy and procedure represented by
the first category to the Triple Agreement and that of the
second to the Triple Alliance. It would be easy to compare
the language of the Tsar's telegram prohibiting a war of
partition with the language of Count Tischa, the Hungarian
premier, in favour of the right of the Balkan States to go
to war with one another; and to deduce therefrom that the
Triple Alliance made the War of Partition against the efforts
of the Triple Agreement. It is true that the Tsar's telegram
found as cordial a reception in London as the Austro-
Hungarian pronouncement found in Berlin. But probably
the importance of such *obiter dicta* has been much exaggerated, and a classification of the two groups into pacificist
and polemist, democratic and diplomatic, progressive and
conservative, would, like all classifications, become very misleading if used as a basis for conclusions. All the same, if
a ' democratic ' as distinct from a ' diplomatic ' point of
view be adopted it will be found that the influence of London
falls to one end of the scale, that of Vienna to the other.
From such a point of view the Powers will range themselves
in order of progressive and pacific influence as London,
Petersburg, Paris, Rome, Berlin, and Vienna. But the
order of the intermediate four Powers is not constant; and at
one time Berlin will take the second place and Petersburg
drop to the fifth, accordingly as some ' diplomatic ' interest
or ' democratic ' influence gets for the moment the upper
hand. With London, however, the motive seems to be
almost consistently ' democratic ', even when the method is
most ' diplomatic ', as in the somewhat cynical repudiation
of the Bulgar reliance on the Thracian settlement ; whereas
with Vienna it seems to have been almost consistently
' diplomatic ', even when, as in the Albanian settlement, its
results were most pacific and progressive. Further, it is to

be remarked that so long as the Balkan Alliance was maintained, the relationship between the Balkan States and Europe was pacific. For it was maintained on the one side by the Coalition, under the leadership of statesmen such as MM. Venezelos, Gueshoff, and Pashitch, and on the other by the Concert centred in the conference of ambassadors in London. These corporate bodies—inchoate and embryonic as they were—represented in their relationship respectively the common interests and collective opinion of the European continent and of the Balkan peninsula as distinct from the particularist and separatist self-interests of imperialist or nationalist factions. But as the Balkan Alliance weakened, we find chauvinist policies and militarist parties in the Balkans coming individually into touch with those of the powers whose interests coincided momentarily with theirs ; while the sound collective ' democratic ' relationship of the Coalition with the Concert becomes thereby undermined by all manner of ' diplomatic ' relations. Diplomatic intrigues between Petersburg and Belgrade or between Sofia and Vienna, the financial interests of Paris, the imperial interests of London, the economic interests of Berlin, and dynastic connexions in all directions, all combine to complicate the situation. The one clue that guides us through the confusion of wars of partition and conflicts of ' penetration ' that precedes the Treaty of Bucharest is, as has been pointed out, the *Realpolitik* of Athens.

There is indeed no real difference, when we eliminate all political and diplomatic superfluities and come down to essential forces and actual facts, between the moral forces and military facts governing the Greek advance against the Ottoman forces, through the Roumlouk on Salonica, and the advance against the Bulgarian forces through Macedonia to Kavalla. In both cases it was the irresistible advance of a national force against contingents detached for a political reason from a national force engaged in a life and death struggle elsewhere. The engagements against the Turks were on a somewhat larger scale, but the fighting was less severe. The fighting against the Turks was moreover in districts of Greek population, and was therefore free from the odious features of the warfare with the Bulgars.

It has already been pointed out that the ' democratic ' or popular relationship between nations is only pacific when a certain stage of common culture and community of interests has been reached; and that when it has not reached that stage, international difficulties can sometimes be solved only by war. It is possible that this is the case in regard to the Graeco-Bulgar rivalry for the mixed districts of Macedonia ; and that the atrocious warfare by which the population has within a few months been roughly redistributed on either side of a Graeco-Bulgar dead-line is a crude operation necessary to the future peace of Graeco-Bulgar relations. It may be said that without such an operation by war it would have been very difficult to draw a line, and that the process of division in the end would have been as painful though more prolonged. But the permanence of the present settlement must depend on the perfection with which the process of extermination and expulsion has been accomplished, and even modern methods in such matters will take time in Hellenizing districts so thoroughly Bulgar as the valleys round Serres.

The difficulty in dividing Greeks and Bulgars in Macedonia lay, as has already been pointed out, in the Greeks holding the littoral and ports right along to Thrace, while the Bulgars held the hinterland right across to Epirus. An ethnological frontier was therefore economically impossible and some other basis had to be found. The main ethnological feature of the situation was that Salonica and its commerce were preponderatingly Jewish—a fact which favoured an international rather than a national solution in the establishment of the town as a free port or as the capital of a small autonomous province. But this solution could only have been imposed on a recalcitrant Greece by the Concert, which, as we have

seen, was not in a position to take action with regard to
Macedonia. When we come to political claims we find the
Greek ' geographic ' claim to Salonica as an access to the
undoubted Greek populations of the Chalcidic peninsula
could be countered by a similar Bulgar claim for access
through it to the Bulgar populations of Monastir. As a commercial port and an outlet, Salonica was of little importance
to either compared with its importance to Servia; and if, as
a commercial outlet, it would be more used by Bulgaria, as
a commercial centre it would be more used by Greeks. In
the absence of any treaty provisions, the most obvious basis
for partition was that of actual military occupation, and the
behaviour of both parties showed from the first that they
recognized that possession would be nine points of the law.
The War of Partition was inevitable unless the Concert intervened, from the moment when the Bulgars detached the
force which had been co-operating with the Serbs and sent
it on a political mission to counter the Greek occupation of
Salonica. The Bulgar claim to Salonica by right of capture
was asserted by the force under General Todoroff, who entered
it only an hour or two behind the Greeks. The General
formally claimed it for his Sovereign, and King Ferdinand
subsequently visited it, so that the Bulgar title in this
respect was very nearly as good as that of the Greeks. If
the Greeks could claim that the garrison had surrendered
to them, the Bulgars might retort that the Greeks would not
have been there but for the Bulgar operations in Thrace
and the Serb operations in Macedonia. If the Greeks contended that in abandoning the Greek littoral from Kavalla
to Enos to the Bulgars they were treating their ally
generously, the Bulgars might reply that the concession of
such isolated and insignificant Greek settlements was far
outweighed by the economic disadvantage of converting
Salonica, the natural commercial outlet of the southern Slavs,
into a Greek military outpost.

If the Bulgars could claim Macedonia by right of an

' intensive' cultivation there of Bulgar nationality during the last quarter-century, the Greeks could claim that the historic civilization of Macedonia, in so far as it survived, was Greek. Greeks and Bulgars always had fought for Macedonia : as soon as Asiatic control was removed they began again; and unless European control prevent them they will go on.

The Wars of Partition may be said to have begun from the date when the Greek and Bulgar troops first came into contact at Salonica, and from the day when almost simultaneously the Serb armies occupied Monastir, and established themselves in territory allotted to their ally by the Treaty of Alliance. Thereafter, while supporting the Bulgars in Thrace, the Greeks and Serbs continued to fortify themselves in the disputed regions of Macedonia in anticipation of a Bulgar attack as soon as the Thracian and Danubian situation released the Bulgar troops. Hostilities began with the aggression of the Greeks at Nigrita on March 5 and with the fortification by the Serbs of their positions on the Ovtche-polye and at Monastir. The Serbs already held all they wanted; but the Greeks pressed their line on northward, dislodging the scattered Bulgar detachments, with the result, during the spring, of further ' incidents ', or, in other words, engagements at Pravishta, Leftera, Panghaion, and Anghista.

The dispute between Serbia and Bulgaria, although certain features caused it to bulk larger in the eyes of western Europe, was much less essential and inevitable than the Graeco-Bulgar struggle. Both in respect of the forces that made it and the form it took, the Serbo-Bulgar war is of less interest and importance. Thus, the mixed population of the regions in dispute between Serbia and Bulgaria is not a mixture of two distinct and hostile types, like Greek and Bulgar, but a middle type of Macedonian Slav, which only of late years, and rather artificially, has acquired a Bulgar rather than a Serb character. Thus also, the districts in dispute were not essential to either nation, and, as possessions held against resentful rivals, would be more a burden than a blessing. It is difficult to say whether Monastir would be harder to hold as a Bulgar salient thrust between a hostile Greece and Serbia, or as a Serbian salient thrust between a hostile Bulgaria and Albania. The possession of central Macedonia was rather a matter of national honour to either State—to Bulgaria who had given it its own national culture and character in spite of a quarter-century of Ottoman oppression, and to Serbia who had freed it from that oppression. In this respect, the Bulgar title seems as much stronger in international principle as the Serbian armed occupation made theirs the stronger in international precedent. As far as international law is concerned in such a matter— which is not very far—the Bulgar position was almost unassailable. The Treaty of Alliance, concluded only a short year before, had been calculated for, and did in every respect cover, the issue. Art. 2 of the secret treaty, which had been concluded with every formality and signed by the sovereigns themselves, recognized as Bulgarian all regions south of a line drawn from the junction of the Old Serbian, Bulgarian, and Turkish frontiers, to Lake Ochrida, and reserved for the arbitration of the Tsar the question of the ownership of certain specified districts north of the line. The treaty was too explicit to be garbled and too formal and fresh to be repudiated; moreover M. Pashitch, the premier, had been one of the parties to it. Nothing could free the Serbs from this obligation but revision by the Bulgars or rupture by war. When it was found that Bulgaria would not revise, the efforts of Serbia to escape from the obligations of the treaty were very unedifying, and still more so were the efforts to avoid the odium of a breach of treaty by confusing the issues and even by corrupting the text. The Serbian contentions that annexation of Thrace by Bulgaria and the augmentation of the Serbian contingents there had so altered the conditions as to nullify the contract, were worth nothing in international law and of very little weight in equity, for both matters were quite outside the scope of the contract. The Serbian claim for a contiguous frontier with Greece and compensation for Albania and Thrace was a political advantage which had been resigned for value under the treaty. The fact that Serbia was in occupation of territory assigned to Bulgaria was the very situation for which the treaty had presumably been concluded. M. Pashitch seems to have done his best to escape from the dilemma of having pledged the honour of his country and of the Crown to an obligation which an all-powerful army would not allow him to execute; but, unfortunately, he was dealing with a nation, Bulgaria, the strength of whose foreign policy lies in the punctilious fulfilment of its national obligations, and the weakness of whose diplomacy is its rigid exaction of a similar scrupulosity in its neighbours. It was very characteristic of the Bulgarian Government that it should have relied on Turkey, Roumania, and Serbia to respect contracts which had become very disadvantageous to them and had lost all but a moral sanction, while it fought with Greece. To the Bulgarian mind the Serbian demand for the revision of the treaty was like a business man asking his partner to revise the deed on which a successful business was based, because the partner had made a larger fortune in another concern. To the Serbian mind, the Bulgar intransigence was like an elder brother refusing to increase the younger's share when their joint inheritance had turned out unexpectedly large. The Bulgars considered the proceedings of the Serbs an injustice; the Serbs considered the policy of the Bulgars an injury. We have seen the same insoluble problem in the relations of Saxon and Celt, insoluble because expressed in different moral terms. While recognizing that our Saxon point of view puts us on the side of the Bulgar, and deploring the efforts of journalistic critics and Job's comforters to justify the misfortunes of the Bulgar nation by maligning the Bulgar character, yet we must not overlook the fact that to the Slav point of view the Serb case may recommend itself more strongly than to us.

Certainly the rôle of the Slav Power in respect of this Serbo-Bulgar dispute is best seen in the light of this explanation. The treaty had been settled under Russian auspices : its sanction was Russian arbitration : its signatories were in this matter practically Russian agents : its subsistence was the only security against a bloody war between Slavs and semi-Slavs. Russian diplomacy was no doubt in a difficult position, but one which was still under complete control; and a satisfactory solution was possible if the disputants could have been given confidence in the arbitral authority. It proved, however, to be beyond the powers of Russian diplomacy to convince Bulgarians as to the disinterestedness of Russian intervention and to persuade them to renounce their treaty rights. As has already been made clear, Bulgaria is not a protégé of Russia in the sense that Serbia is; and while Bulgaria, by acceding to the Alliance, had acquired merit at Petersburg to the extent that it had been given a free hand against Turkey, it nevertheless feared that Petersburg would not scruple to aggrandize Serbia at the expense of Bulgaria. It would obviously be a diplomatic ' score ' if Petersburg could reward Serbian allegiance and retain Roumanian adherence at the expense of Bulgaria ; and whether this did or did not affect the attitude of Russia in respect of the reference to arbitration and might or might not have affected its award, the knowledge of it could not but make Serbia more exacting and Bulgaria more suspicious. About the same time that the Petersburg award had amputated a corner of northern Bulgaria for the benefit of Roumania, Sofia seems to have ascertained or assumed that Petersburg intended to undertake arbitration between Serbia and Bulgaria in the sense desired by the former—that is to say, arbitration upon the treaty and not under the treaty. This of course meant tearing up the treaty and repartitioning Macedonia in a manner less favourable to Bulgaria.

Sofia was the more angered in that it had supposed—as has since been asserted on the good authority of the *Times* correspondent—that as a reward for abandoning another attack on Tchataldja after the fall of Adrianople, Russia had undertaken to maintain the treaty; but such understandings as to conditional undertakings are a common cause of misunderstandings in diplomacy. In any case, about the time that peace was being signed in London, and the Concert, but for the Russian prerogative of arbitration, might have been imposing a solution or at least a suspension of the Macedonian imbroglio, Russia proposed to Bulgaria the renunciation of the whole ' contested zone ', as well as that of the districts of Kratavo, Kuprulu, and Krushevo on the Bulgar side of the line. Not only was this a serious addition to the Bulgar districts already ceded to Serbia under the treaty, but it left so narrow a promontory of Bulgar territory between the Serbian frontier and the line of Greek settlement as to make an impossible economic and strategic frontier. Bulgaria is undoubtedly better off now without the Bulgars of Monastir than if they had been retained under such conditions.

§ 20. Pacifications and Partitions

The crisis came simultaneously with the conclusion of peace with Turkey and the signature of the Treaty of London on June 1—when the Greeks and Serbs concluded an alliance on May 29, with which Roumania was associated. Nothing stopped the immediate outbreak of war but the unreadiness of Bulgaria, whose armies were still in Thrace. On the other hand, nothing could preserve peace but general demobilization and a delegation of plenipotentiaries to confer at some neutral centre. Great Britain urged demobilization, and Russia arranged a meeting of the Premiers for May 29; but both demobilization and the departure of the Premiers for Petersburg were delayed day after day. Serbia proposed demobilization to Bulgaria, which, as Serbian troops were entrenched in the disputed territories, was fairly safe, and Bulgaria assented on condition that the territories in question were jointly occupied. Bulgaria pressed arbitration on Serbia, and Serbia consented, provided that the whole question were arbitrated *de novo*, and that by Russia. This was also fairly safe in view of the Russian award in favour of Serbia being considered a foregone conclusion. Petersburg endeavoured to reconcile Bulgaria to accepting arbitration of the whole Treaty by indications of inclination to the Bulgarian cause, but Sofia was either incredulous or uncompromising. This failing, Petersburg attempted to force matters, as had been done in London in the peace negotiations at the second Conference, by the publication of a peremptory telegram addressed by the Tsar on June 8 in duplicate to the Sovereigns of Bulgaria and Serbia, giving them good advice as to observance of their treaty obligations and acceptance of Russian arbitration, and a stern admonition as to the consequences of going to war.[1] Excellent as was the motive and manner of

---

[1] Telegram of the Tsar of Russia to the Kings of Serbia and Bulgaria, June 8, 1913.

'The news of a proposed interview between the Premiers of the four allied States at Salonica previous to their meeting at Petersburg, had given me the greatest pleasure. This intention seemed to indicate a desire on the part of the Balkan States to come to an agreement and to consolidate the alliance which has hitherto given such brilliant results. It is therefore with regret that I learn that this decision has not been carried out, and that the Balkan States appear to be preparing for a fratricidal war which would tarnish the glory that they have acquired in common.

'In this grave situation I make a direct appeal to Your Majesty, as is required by the rights and responsibilities of my position. For it is to the decision of Russia that the peoples of Serbia and Bulgaria have, by the terms of their alliance, referred all disputes as to the applications of the provisions of that treaty and the conventions relating to it. I therefore call upon Your Majesty to remain faithful to the obligations assumed under the Treaty, and to submit to Russia the settlement of the present dispute between Serbia and Bulgaria.

'Considering the function of arbitrator not as a privilege, but as a

this missive, it was interpreted as implying a support of the Serbian position; while any pacifying effect which this assumption of almost suzerain authority over the Balkan sovereigns might have had was immediately combated by a pronouncement of Count Tisza, the Hungarian Premier. This statesman, with the authority of Vienna and the approval of Berlin, asserted that the Balkan States had a perfect right to make war,[1] which was interpreted as assuring Austrian support to Bulgaria in driving Serbia out of the claims that had been jumped. Europe, therefore, received without surprise the reply of King Ferdinand to the Tsar, which rather by its tone than its actual terms showed that the Russian pronouncement had not removed all danger of war. The Serbian reply was not published, probably from fear of its effect on relations between Russia and Serbia, but it is generally understood to have been as unsatisfactory.

Once more it was proved, at the cost of war, that Russian and Austrian diplomacy was too intimately and imperialistically interested in Balkan affairs for those Governments to arbitrate successfully between Balkan democracies. Their intervention had merely defined the issues and redoubled the pressures by adding to them the weight of the two Empires. Moreover, both pronunciamentos certainly increased the difficulty of the position of MM. Gueshoff and Pashitch, the two premiers, whose authority was the best guarantee for peace— they being both among the founders of the Balkan Coalition. M. Gueshoff's resignation on the date of the Tsar's telegram,

regrettable obligation which I cannot avoid, I feel that I must warn Your Majesty that a war between the allies would not be a matter of indifference to me. I wish it to be clearly understood that the State which begins this war will be held responsible therefor in the eyes of the Slav cause; and that I shall consider myself in no way bound as to the attitude that Russia will adopt in respect of the possible results of so criminal a struggle.'

[1] The wording used by Count Tisza was : ' The Balkan States can decide for war; we shall, of course, regret that, but the decision is within their right.'

was accompanied by that of his collaborator, M. Pashitch. M. Gueshoff was succeeded by Dr. Daneff, whose rigid assertion of Bulgar rights as delegate in the London Conference augured ill for his success in a situation where concession and conciliation were especially required.   M. Pashitch resumed office; but something of the same change had apparently taken place in the Serbian Premiership, for his first act was to make a declaration in the Chamber as to the Serbian case, which, from its character, greatly exacerbated relations and stultified a meeting between the two premiers, from which much had been hoped.   Pronunciamentos were made by the Serbian Crown Prince, and proposals in the Serbian Chamber for declaring the annexation of the disputed districts followed; while Bulgaria said little, but busied itself with transferring troops from Thrace to Macedonia. It was clear that in both countries the war party was getting the upper hand.   The quarrel now became open, and was pursued in the press of Europe with a clamour on the part of Serbs and Greeks, which inspired suspicion as to the strength of their cause.   In comparison the impressive silence of the Bulgars contributed not a little to the general opinion that they would deal with their diplomatic difficulties as effectively as they had hitherto done.

The difficulties that faced Bulgaria were formidable, and the Graeco-Serb alliance directed against Bulgaria, with which Roumania was to be associated should hostilities break out, seemed to render successful military operations impossible.   On the other hand, their prospects at arbitration were, for the moment, not unpromising, and seemed likely to improve as international opinion hardened in their favour.   It was, therefore, with a shock of surprise that Europe learnt on June 29 that Bulgaria had taken the aggressive, and ordered a general advance of its forces against the Serb positions.   What had happened is still obscure in its details, though obvious enough in its general developments.

The accession to power of the Russophil premier, Dr. Daneff, had caused a most dangerous strain to be thrown on the relations between the Government and the command of the army, which remained in the hands of the Austrophil General Savoff; for these relations in Bulgaria, as in the other Balkan States, were already strained to breaking-point. Whether King Ferdinand, like King Constantine, in any way threw his weight on the side of the militarists and against his premier is not certain : in any case, he did not, like King George, risk his popularity by making himself an influence for peace. The Government, under Dr. Daneff, was absorbed in diplomatic manœuvres for position in the very critical stage of the negotiations with Petersburg for a pacific partition, and believed itself to have secured a settle-ment favourable to Bulgaria. The army, under General Savoff, found itself at last launched upon its true objective in Macedonia, and faced there by the fortifications erected by intrusive Serbs in the heart of Bulgar Macedonia. The military party in command had no faith in Russian favours, but believed that the avowed Viennese policy would suffice to neutralize any Russian reprisals and secure the Bulgar army a fair field and no favour for a short time. No more was required, for the commander-in-chief was convinced he could drive the Serbs from their entrenched positions on the Ovtchepolye with the Fourth Army and hold Veles, and with the Second Army drive back the Greeks and take Ghevgheli, while leaving the other three army corps in reserve for eventualities.[1] The political calculation seems to have

[1] The following telegrams from General Savoff have been published and generally accepted as authentic :

Headquarters, Sofia.
Cypher. Most urgent. 8 p.m. 15/27 June.
To the General Commanding Fourth Army at Radovitza.

In order that our not replying to the attacks of the Serbs may not affect the morale of our forces, and in order that the enemy may not be thereby encouraged, I order you to attack the enemy with the utmost vigour along the whole line, without developing your full strength and without engaging in a prolonged action. You should endeavour to establish

been that the Serbs could be driven behind the treaty frontier before any diplomatic complications could develop : that Bulgaria could then either go to Petersburg for absolution, or face it out; and that, once the Serbs settled, Greece would give little trouble either diplomatically or militarily. It was a typical militarist diplomacy, in which everything was subordinated to a success in the field, and everything depended on a *coup de main* coming off. It did not come off, because of a military miscalculation in over-estimating the driving power left to the Bulgar attack and in under-estimating the defensive strength of the Serbs.

yourself strongly at Krivolak on the right bank of the Bragalnitza, on hill 350, at Bogoslav on hill 550, at Sahad (Ovtchepolye), and in the neighbourhood of Dobreno.

Open fire preferably at nightfall, and under cover of night effect a vigorous attack along the whole front. This operation should be carried out to-morrow evening the 16 June.

SAVOFF.

Headquarters, Sofia.
Cypher. Most urgent. 3.15 p.m. 17/29 June.
To the Generals Commanding.

In a previous Order I have instructed the Fourth Army to advance and the Second Army to concentrate for an attack on Salonica, after completing its operations against Tcayezi.

Generals commanding will remember that our operations against Greeks and Serbs are being carried on, without a formal declaration of war, for the following reasons :

1. To raise the *morale* of our troops, and to show them that our ex-allies are our enemies.

2. To compel Russian diplomacy, by danger of a declaration of war, to make a speedy settlement.

3. To force our allies to take a more conciliatory attitude under pressure.

4. To occupy forcibly the territories claimed by us and held by them, until foreign intervention stops further military action, which action must therefore be prompt, as intervention may come at any moment.

The Fourth Army will, at all costs, occupy Veles, which it is of great political importance to capture

The Second Army, as soon as it is concentrated, will, if the operations of the Fourth Army permit, advance against Salonica. For this it will be reinforced by two or three brigades.

If the railway line Krivolak-Ghevgheli is occupied, it must be held in strength and by entrenchments. This will assure us both banks of the Vardar.

SAVOFF

This militarist policy was not only diplomatically unsafe, but the military position of the Bulgars was strategically unsound. Not only the Bulgar forces operating against the Greeks on a front facing south from the Takhino Gol on the Struma to the Vardar, but also the forces operating against the Serbs on a front facing west from Kochana to Ghevghelyi, were supplied by the roundabout railway via Seres and Adrianople, and were cut off from Bulgaria and from each other by difficult ranges. Moreover, the Second Bulgar Army under General Ivanoff was probably never more than 60,000 strong, i. e. four divisions, and was depleted by one division sent against the Serbs even before the Greek pressure developed. This force was spread over a long line, and it seems doubtful whether the Bulgars either at Kilkish or Doiran were able to bring a third of the number of the Greek forces into action. This was insufficient to hold a line of such political and strategic importance as that of the Doiran-Drama railway, against at least 120,000 victorious Greeks. The Serbs, moreover, had had eight months in which to fortify themselves, and considered the country as already theirs. If their position was legally weak, morally and materially a Serbian force entrenched on the Ovtchepolye could scarcely find itself in circumstances better calculated to bring out its fighting qualities. Besides, since the Macedonian campaign, the Serbs, like the Greeks, had recuperated their energies, and had been working themselves up for a fight with the Bulgars.

The Bulgars, on the other hand, had just been hurried from a campaign which had drained their strength, and were now asked to renew their efforts against an entirely new objective, and in a fight which possibly their more deliberate disposition could not work itself up to welcome as the Greek and Serb temperament could. This war shows a marked loss of tone in the Bulgars, which found expression in a reluctance to remain under arms, attributed partly to such material distractions as the requirements of the harvest. The harvest was, however, only a pretext; for the men knew that the women could get it in, as, in fact, they did. But as has always been experienced in the case of armies in which the non-military temperament preponderates—as in the Boer forces or the citizen armies of the United States—such forces are formidable in exact proportion as their moral convictions or political passions are engaged. It is one of the most valuable of the compensating conditions which preserve the world from another Napoleonic deluge—until political and moral degeneration again calls for it.

Moreover, in this relatively ineffective condition the Bulgar Army was asked to do too much. Political conditions had dictated a surprise assault without artillery preparation, and the Serbs were not surprised. The Bulgar army in Macedonia was like a prizefighter who has 'lost his punch', and the blow intended to knock out the Serbian army only staggered it. Meantime, the contingent, some 1,300 strong, politically occupying Salonica, was, of course, sacrificed: the officers mostly escaped in time, while the troops capitulated after a hopeless resistance and heavy loss. This was strategically insignificant though politically important; but a more serious matter was that after severe fighting the containing force under Ivanoff detached to hold the Greek main forces away from the strategic base at Doiran found itself too weak to do so.[1] The Greeks took Doiran on July 5, and began driving the Bulgars through the passes of the Belashitza, as they had driven the Turks through the Olympus; profiting in both cases by the main forces of their enemy being occupied with the Serbs. Defeat had changed the Bulgar's *coup de main* into a campaign, but their defeats had also corrected the defects in their original strategic dispositions. The Greeks were left to run their heads against the

---

[1] The severity of this fighting, compared with that of the War of Coalition, is shown by the figures of Greek and Serb losses in both campaigns, given on pp. 308, 311, especially by the disproportionately heavy loss of officers and the very few prisoners.

Rhodope, and between July 20 and 25 got into difficulties at Raslog, which might have ended in disaster for them. Meantime, pressure was maintained against the Serb positions in Macedonia sufficient to hold the main Serb forces there, while General Racho Petroff began to invade Serbia north of the mountains, so as to cut their exposed communications, and manœuvre them out of their strong positions in Macedonia. It seems quite possible that, if left to itself, the campaign would have ended in favour of the Bulgars. But it was not so left. The Bulgars had taken the sword—and they were to perish by the sword, though not by the sword that had been drawn in their face.

The *coup de main* in Macedonia was probably the result of a *coup de tête* at Sofia on the part of the headquarters staff there, and it seems quite possible that the Bulgar civil Government did from the very outbreak of hostilities do its best to stop them. But their efforts probably only made things worse for Bulgaria in the end.[1] Greece and

[1] The following is the account given by M. Daneff (published in the *Temps*, December 9, 1913) of the position and policy of his Government :

'. . . I was on the point of leaving for Petersburg, as M. Pashitch had just declared to the Russian minister, M. de Hartwig, that he would accept arbitration by the Tsar. It was then, the morning of June 30, that without the knowledge of the Bulgar Government, the Second and Fourth Armies—that is, two out of the five—attacked the Greeks and Serbs. This was a complete surprise to the Government, which had had nothing to say in the matter—in the first place because it was at that moment asking for Russian arbitration, which it had good reason to believe would be favourable to it—in the next place because it would be stultifying itself to alienate Russia—and finally because such an attack was most dangerous, as we were exposed both to Roumania and Turkey and short of war material. Such an attack was never contemplated by this Government, and war never was declared against Greece and Serbia. There is merely the fact of the attack by the Second and Fourth Armies on the morning of June 30. Who was responsible for this event will in due course be ascertained.

' On the following day, July 1, the Government ordered General Savoff to stop hostilities, and notified the Belgrade Cabinet that this had been done, requesting that firing be stopped on the Serbian side. The Government also approached Petersburg through the Russian minister. General Savoff stopped firing in obedience to his orders, whereby a regiment was lost, as the Serbs continued firing.

Serbia had welcomed war, and the initial fighting being in their favour, as well as diplomatic developments, they had no intention of making peace easily; for even if they were defeated, Roumanian intervention, of which they had already assured themselves, would have saved them from suffering therefrom.

Russian public opinion had been irritated by the tone in which that Austro-flirt, King Ferdinand, had replied to the Tsar's telegram ; it was incensed by the contumacious defiance of its warning by the Austrophil Commander-in-Chief General Savoff. Russian diplomacy seized the opportunity of teaching Bulgaria a sharp lesson, an opportunity which would not only restore Russian predominance in the peninsula, but would also reduce Bulgarian pre-eminence there— a result no less desired by Russian diplomacy. Orders were immediately telegraphed by Petersburg to Sofia to stop hostilities, and presumably also to Bucharest that Roumania was free under the arrangement recently concluded with Greece [1] to take action. It was in vain that Sofia, alive to the danger, definitely renounced all attempts to retrieve its fortunes in the field, recalled Savoff and

---

[1] Telegram from M. Venezelos to M. Take Jonescu, June 13, 1913. [Translated extract.]   (Roumanian green book.)
' The present moment is a critical one for the future of the Balkan peninsula, and Roumania cannot remain indifferent to the risk of a war between the allies or the possible results of such a war. . . .
' By an understanding with Greece and Servia, Roumania can make certain of the result of a war with Bulgaria, and can co-operate thereby in terminating once for all avowed ambitions for hegemony, establishing in its own interest complete equilibrium between Bulgaria, Servia, and Greece. Moreover, this is a rare opportunity for Roumania to acquire a far more radical rectification of frontier from Bulgaria, for in taking part in such a war it would not, as things are, come into collision with [word omitted, presumably " Russia "].'
The reply, June 15, 1913.
' [M. Take Jonescu] is in entire agreement with M. Venezelos, and the object of a Roumanian mobilization will be to impose peace on Bulgaria, and maintain the balance of power in the peninsula. . . . This mobilization has been postponed in consequence of the Tsar's telegram, but will be carried out if Bulgaria does not keep quiet.'

Petroff, and immobilized its armies in the face of active Greek and Serb counter attacks. It was too late, and the fresh outbreak of war spread with the usual speed of the epidemic that has got a firm footing and a fresh field.

By July 3 Roumania mobilized, and in order to facilitate Roumanian co-operation Athens and Belgrade declared war formally on July 5 and 6, while the Greek and Serb armies pressed their offensive on the Bulgar forces now immobilized in a helpless defensive. On July 10, Roumania, without further warning, withdrew its Minister and crossed the frontier. In vain Sofia demonstrated its passivity by announcing that the Roumanian invasion would not be opposed: this did not help diplomatically, while it showed such a condition of collapse that it brought down another thunderbolt from the clouds. On July 12, a Turkish army issued from Tchataldja and broke through the paper frontier of Enos-Midia, sweeping up the Bulgar garrisons. The Roumanian and Ottoman war dogs had been unleashed, and Anglo-Russian diplomacy could scarcely have brought them to heel again, even if it had really wanted to, without an open intervention dangerous to European peace.

The Bulgar armies being paralysed by the surrender of the Government, the Roumanians pressed forward without opposition towards Sofia, the Serbs pushed their way over their frontier, burning villages, the Greeks bore hard on the small forces still holding the Rhodope passes, and the Turks reoccupied Thrace, re-entered Adrianople, and invaded Eastern Roumelia. Dr. Daneff, after a last vain appeal to Russia,[1] resigned on July 17; and the first act of his successor, M. Radoslavoff, after forming his Government on July 20, was to concede all Roumanian territorial demands, and try to open direct negotiations with Greece and Serbia at Nish. But the quondam allies meant to press their advantage to the utmost, and did their best either to drive the Bulgars

[1] Vide the *Temps* of December 4, 1913, for the text of M. Daneff's dispatch to Petersburg of July 14.

from their defensive and enter Sofia, or to provoke them to an offensive which would put them to further diplomatic disadvantage. It was, no doubt, with the latter object that Serbia bombarded Widin three days after an armistice had been signed at the instance of Roumania. But the object of the latter State, which had gained as much Bulgar territory as it wanted, was now to increase Roumanian prestige by dictating a peace to the belligerents at Bucharest; and Roumania accordingly vetoed the ambition of Greeks and Serbs to dictate peace at Sofia. At Bucharest, Roumania could pose as a European power imposing peace : at Sofia it would be evident that Roumania was on an equal political and moral footing with Greece, Servia, and even Turkey. This it was that saved Bulgaria from further humiliation. A conference met at Bucharest on July 28, and peace was signed on August 10, a peace which left Bulgaria despoiled and disarmed. Bulgaria that had driven the Turkish Empire from European soil was left without a share in that soil but a barren and barbarous district of mountain and marsh, without an army to secure what remained to it, and without even the good name which might otherwise have disposed Europe to keep the Turks out of Thrace in compliance with their obligations. It was not the least of the Greek successes that the Bulgars were, owing to telegraphic isolation, incapable of effective defence in the atrocity campaign waged against them.

Never in all modern history has a nation undergone such a reverse of fortune : never has the danger of modern warfare as a political procedure been more sensationally exhibited. The lightning changes and landslide momentum that events may acquire when impelled by the passions of massed populations and enforced by the machinery of modern warfare, should give pause to the most adventurous. Once an international situation is in the state of liquidation represented by war, no engagements however sacred, no insurances however sound, can be relied on to save defeat

from becoming disaster. No doubt Bulgarians would have
found much disappointment in the results of their Government's policy of a settlement by arbitration at Petersburg;
but they would not have had to face such disaster as was bound
to be the result of the militarist reliance on a trial by battle
and on Vienna. For it was the fatal weakness of such a war
that the Bulgarian position could not be made war proof at
all points. Thus Bulgar military activities against Greece
and Serbia depended on Roumania and Turkey remaining
passive. For this passivity, Bulgaria relied on the award
of Petersburg and the Treaty of London being maintained
against the ambitions of its two neighbours. This showed,
not as their friends have asserted, an admirable belief in
international good faith, but rather the amateurish folly of
trying to combine two incompatible processes—exploiting
the dynamic forces of war on the frontier while counting on
the static forces of peace elsewhere.

No alliances and settlements can be relied on in a general
condition of war, unless they have the sanction of some force
superior to the self-interested motives for breaking them.
Bulgaria had, in this very War of Partition in which it had
engaged, two excellent examples of a territorial settlement
repudiated because it had become the interest of the stronger
party to do so. It would, of course, have been the wisest
course for the Bulgar Government not to risk the army
getting out of hand by bringing them into contact with the
Greeks and Serbs ; but, once the mischief was done and war
started, it would perhaps have been wiser to go through
with it. The Bulgars have been so much criticized elsewhere
for not making peace soon enough on other occasions that
it seems unfair to cavil at their having made it too soon
at this crisis. From the point of view of present economic
profit and loss no doubt a continuance of this war and
a siege of Sofia would not have been worth a peace territorially more advantageous than that of Bucharest. But it
is probable that had the war continued till the Concert was

forced to intervene, English and Russian opinion would have responded to the appeal of dramatic adversity and dogged determination and would have insisted on the Treaty of London being maintained, and a reasonable frontier in Macedonia. Even as it was, all the Powers except Berlin were in favour of Kavalla being assigned to Bulgaria, while Petersburg went some way towards expelling the Turks from Adrianople, and did check their advance at the Maritsa; Vienna also made reserves as to Kochana. Moreover, Vienna and Rome, for diplomatic reasons, would have favoured a check to Serbian and Greek expansion. But, as it was, Russian democratic opinion was little moved and English not at all; whereby all sorts of 'diplomatic' secondary considerations told against Bulgaria. Among these were French financial interests in Turkey and Greece, German dynastic interests in Greece and economic interests in Turkey, British 'diplomatic' sympathies with Turkey and anxieties as to Moslem opinion combined with 'democratic' disgust at the atrocities of which the Bulgars were accused by Greeks. The negotiations among the Powers for compelling the Greeks to renounce Kavalla were checked by the opposition of France and Germany, and were dropped as soon as it became clear that Bulgaria would yield Kavalla without further procrastination. Bulgarian resistance, both military and diplomatic, was indeed utterly broken, and peace at any price was their first object. Thus the Bulgars again missed an opportunity of getting better terms by a little playing to the European gallery—a little pleading to the European Governments *in forma pauperis*. But that is not the Bulgar way. While he can get anything for himself there is no man so stubborn and stalwart as the Bulgar, but what he finds he cannot get for himself he will not or cannot get through others.

The Treaty was signed on August 10 and ratified on August 25. The gist of the settlement was that Bulgaria, having called the tune, now had to pay the piper. Roumania annexed Bulgar soil up to the Turtukai-Baltchik Line—the

fullest extension of its extreme demands; and thus set the
example of repudiating a national bargain and revolting against
an international settlement—that of the Petersburg award.
The Powers, by permitting this without even a protest, undoubtedly encouraged the subsequent similar recalcitrance by
Turkey. Of course the Bulgar-Serbian Treaty was ignored,
and Greece and Serbia partitioned Macedonia between them,
leaving Bulgaria some territory in the mountains east of the
Vardar, and a strip of mountain and marsh on the Aegean
littoral. Bulgaria was compelled to demobilize by a military
agreement between the three other States enforcing the
Treaty; and the united diplomacy of the three States was then
directed to preventing a revision of its terms in favour of
Bulgaria by Europe. This revision was at first pressed by
Vienna and might have recommended itself in Petersburg, but
failing of any support from Berlin or Paris was incontinently
dropped. Revision by Europe having been abandoned, there
only remained the question of European recognition and the
terms on which it should .be conceded. The *locus standi* of
the Concert in regard to such recognition was their responsibility under the Treaty of Berlin in respect of the Territories
concerned. But the trials of Bulgaria were not yet over. It
had been forced to renounce its share in the conquests in
Macedonia; it was now to be forced to resign its conquests
in Thrace. These were held in virtue of its new title under
the Treaty of London; and Bulgaria accordingly appealed
to the Powers in general and to London in particular for
maintenance of that Treaty and for expulsion of the Turks
from Adrianople. But there was no response and no remedy.
Demobilized and disarmed by its Balkan neighbours, discredited with the Triple Agreement, and discarded by the
Triple Alliance, Bulgaria was left to make such terms as it
best could at Constantinople. Yet the Enos-Midia line in
the Treaty of London, though in form a clause in a convention between the Balkan States and Turkey, was in fact a
delimitation imposed by London in the name of Europe and

entrusted for demarcation to an international Commission. There was certainly some moral obligation for its maintenance by the Triple Agreement, or at all events by Great Britain. There was talk of financial pressure by France and of diplomatic pressure by Russia, but the only possible effective action, naval pressure by Great Britain, was not seriously considered. British statesmen gave Turkey solemn warnings, but the militarist junta in control of the Empire was not sensitive to such moral pressure. By the end of August M. Radoslavoff had given up hope of European intervention and sent General Savoff to Constantinople to make the best terms he could. An effort was made to retain Kirk Kilisse and the Maritza frontier, but the Turks imposed their own line, which left of Bulgar Thrace only a small wedge on the Black Sea coast and the western corner containing Dedeagatch, Ortakeui and the Pomak Rhodope, which latter had declared its autonomy as against Bulgaria. The Treaty of Constantinople was signed on September 29, and Bulgaria then reoccupied Western Thrace. A satisfactory settlement in other respects was reached with Turkey at the cost of abandoning the Bulgar claim for maintenance of 90,000 prisoners of war for nearly six months.

Macedonia and Thrace having been thus partitioned and pacified for better or worse, there remained the Aegean and Albania. The Macedonian partition had been left to the Balkan States altogether, the Great Powers relegating for the time being their somewhat obsolete obligations under the Treaty of Berlin. The Thracian partition had been left to Bulgaria and Turkey after a repudiation of any European moral responsibility under the Treaty of London. But the disposal of (*soin de statuer sur*) the Aegean islands had been specifically reserved to the Powers by Article V of the Treaty of London, and was moreover a matter clearly incapable of pacific settlement by direct negotiation between Greece and Turkey. Still more was Albania a matter for European rather than Balkan settlement. But even relieved of these two crucial questions, Greece and Turkey could come to terms only by a free use of other forms of European mediation. Thus various pecuniary questions such as the indemnity to Greek shipping, the maintenance of Turkish prisoners, the Imperial domains, &c., were left to the Hague Tribunal. The question of the railways with that of the proportion of the Ottoman Debt to be taken over, was left to the Paris Commission. Even so, the negotiations might have been broken off but for the good offices of Roumania in the person of M. Jonescu, who put pressure on Constantinople. The extreme difficulty the two nations had in coming to terms, as compared with the relative ease with which Bulgaria and Turkey agreed after far more exacerbating experiences, is a clear indication of the real line of cleavage in the Balkan wars. Bulgars and Turks may fight again—for there is unfortunately still a *res in lite* at Adrianople ; but Greeks and Turks must fight again, and very nearly did so within a few months of the signature of the Treaty of Peace. The closing scenes of the war, no less than its causes, show that the real race war was between Greeks and Turks.

It was the partition of the Aegean by the Powers under British guidance that almost caused another Graeco-Ottoman war. Greece held the Aegean islands and South Albania, both *en dépôt* with the Concert under the Treaty of London, and claimed also the Dodekanese, which under the Treaty of Lausanne was *en dépôt* with Italy ; for it was as undeniable that Rhodes and the smaller islands could have been occupied by Greece but for Italy's detention of them, as it was incontrovertible that they were inhabited by Greeks. On the other hand, geographically, the larger Greek islands, such as Mitylene, Chios, Samos, Kos, and Rhodes, were undoubtedly integral parts of Asia Minor, and strategically Lemnos and Tenedos were indispensable to the control of the Dardanelles. Vienna and Rome were pressing for the evacuation of South Albania by Greece before the end of the year under pain of war ; Constantinople was prepared to fight for the Greek islands; while Greece presumed on the diplomatic inability of the Powers, the naval incapacity of the Porte, and the nine points of possession. The solution suggested by London was that Greece should evacuate South Albania in return for being established in the Aegean islands; that Turkey should renounce the latter in return for the reversion of the Dodekanese, when evacuated by Italy, and for the retention of the strategic islands of Lemnos and Tenedos; and that Italy should return the Dodekanese to Turkish suzerainty in consideration for the transfer of South Albania by Greece to the Albanian principality. The proposal was both equitable and practical, and its defects did not prevent its affording a basis for a settlement. An inherent defect was that Italy had apparently no intention of retroceding the Dodekanese, and has not yet done so; and it was ill-conceived to transfer the larger islands with a stipulation that Greece should not fortify them. They remained, thereby, exposed to a sudden descent from the mainland—a strategic trouble to both Turks and Greeks. The partition of the Aegean has none the less proved to be so far a pacification; for the subsequent friction between the Greeks and Turks was due to attempts to redistribute population in accordance with the political partition rather than to redelimitate the partition.

The Albanian partition by the Powers has, however, taken longer in reaching the stage of pacification.

It is indeed worth noting, as evidence of the difficulty of dealing with Near Eastern nationality questions, that the settlements have been immediately satisfactory in inverse proportion both to their apparent fairness and probable duration. Settlements were reached as to Macedonia and Thrace almost immediately, and brought instant pacification; but both were unfair and unstable. That in the Aegean was delayed longer but will endure longer. That in Albania has been followed by civil wars imperilling its maintenance, but is undoubtedly the soundest and most satisfactory of the three.

The Ambassadors' Conference in London had decided on the establishment of an autonomous Albania under an International Commission of Control, and at the end of September this Government was set up, on the withdrawal of the administration by naval contingents. The frontier had been settled as early as March, Albania having to surrender Gheg centres such as Djakova and Prizrend to Serbia in return for recovering Scutari from Montenegro. The trading off of Arnauts was unavoidable, but it was no less unacceptable to the Gheg clans, who have as little respect for, as realization of, the difficulties of diplomacy. The delimitation of the southern frontier by international commission could not be begun before October, and was only completed in December on the basis of a compromise proposed in London. In November Prince William of Wied had been proposed to the provisional government at Avlona and accepted as sovereign of Albania; and by the end of the year the Albanian settlement seemed complete. But the little State was not to have so peaceful a genesis. Already in September Arnauts and Serbs had come into collision in the north, with the result that the Arnaut districts on both sides of the frontier were laid waste with all the horrors of Balkan warfare, and the Serb forces only evacuated Albania under menace of war from Vienna. The next trouble was an insurrection against the Prince and the Provincial Government on the part of the Moslem clans, probably encouraged by Young Turkish agents. The outbreak was met by the deportation of Essad Pasha, the defender of Scutari and pretender to the throne; but this strong step was followed by the flight of the Prince to an Italian warship in a panic following a defeat of the Dutch *gendarmerie*. The catholic Gheg clans failed to relieve the pressure on the capital Durazzo, which remained in a continuous state of siege. Finally in the south the Greeks and Hellenized Tosks set up an autonomous government of Epirus, which the Dutch troops, with such assistance as could be got from Albanian levies, found too strong to overthrow. An agreement was accordingly come to at Corfu guaranteeing certain rights to the Hellenized districts in return for their renouncing the unification with Greece which they desired. The difficulty in the south is indeed just the reverse of that in the north. There Gheg clansmen have been for diplomatic reasons subjected to their hereditary foes the Serbs. In the south Greek townsmen have for economic reason been subjected to their hereditary foes the Arnauts. Albania cannot be made to include the Ghegs of Prizrend, the historic capital of Old Serbia ; it cannot afford to exclude the Greeks of Koritza, the economic and intellectual centre of Albania. Meantime the small State is a prey to intrigues both Balkan and European. Serbs, Greeks, and Turks foster the various insurrections, the Prince is besieged in his capital and rules only over his own entourage, the Provisional Government is without resources, the Dutch contingent has left in disgust, the country is a prey to pillage and persecution.[1] Yet, as will be shown later, Albanian nationality is none the less a fact and should not be doubted because its only civil expression at present is by warfare.

§ 21. Excesses and Exterminations

'The Balkan War began as a war of liberation, became rapidly a war of annexation, and has ended, if all the charges are true, in being a war of extermination.' Thus did the British Foreign Secretary sum up the moral issue of these wars. We have now examined the genesis of the wars of liberation, and also that of the wars of annexation, and it only remains to inquire into the causes of the wars of extermination that unhappily are still being waged between the Balkan races. It is not the intention to examine the evidence of such mutual extermination, still less to reproduce stories of excesses by troops. It is unnecessary and undesirable for the present purpose to examine and pronounce upon

[1] As a result of the European War Prince William has abdicated and Essad Pasha has recovered control of Albanian affairs.

such charges in detail, because general social and political conditions both before and after the wars render such relapses not only indisputable but inevitable. Moreover, this thankless task has already been undertaken by especially competent persons, who have presented their conclusions in a special report to the Carnegie Peace Foundation.

One of the general principles in support of which evidence is here sought in the events of the Balkan Wars, is that the retribution exacted from those who cause war is exactly proportioned to the responsibility. Applying this to the question of excesses by the Balkan armies, we shall find that the worst sufferers are those Macedo-Moslems and Macedo-Bulgars who were rightly or wrongly the instigators of the wars. But this is, of course, only a remote relation between cause and effect, and in no way reduces such moral responsibility as there may be for military excesses. The historian of the future in dealing with this war of murder and malice will probably divide the responsibility under three different heads of offending. The original responsibility attaches to the parties who started a race war in Macedonia, which, under the best conditions, could not be carried on without wholesale crimes of this character. This responsibility must probably be equally divided between Serbs and Bulgars, and rather more to the latter. For though the Greek forces were more active in creating the situation that led to war, the Greek Government seems to have made proposals such as properly might have prevented it but for Bulgar intransigence. Under the next head falls the responsibility for deliberately using troops as a means of political pressure on undesirable races in the territories occupied, either by harrying them generally, or by sensational cruelties, such as would scare them into emigration. Without any inquiry into facts, it seems safe to divide this responsibility mainly between Serbs and Greeks, for the obvious reason that these States were occupying the whole of Macedonia, except the small corner round Kavalla retained by the Bulgars until the opening of the War of Partition. They also were in a position to use their occupying forces for such political purposes, whereas the Bulgars were not, for they could only afford to maintain small contingents sufficient to assert their title. Moreover, under this head Serbia is probably rather more guilty than Greece. The use of the Greek army against Bulgar non-combatants seems to have been risked under cover of accusations of similar abuses directed against the Bulgars at a time when the latter could not defend themselves: but they did so with effect later, and brought sufficient publicity to bear on Greek action to bring it within bounds; whereas Serbian action against the Albanians has never been checked by any efficient publicity. So long as the armies of occupation remained, nothing could be heard of atrocities; and whatever, if any, were the sufferings of the Bulgars and Arnauts under Greek or Serb rule, or of the Greeks in the small Bulgar corner, they had to be borne in silence. But when the Greek army drove the Bulgars out of the country they had been occupying, they of course acquired material for convicting or calumniating their predecessors. This brings us to the third head, the responsibility of exploiting an ' atrocity ' campaign for the purpose of affecting European opinion; and this responsibility, as our newspapers will give us ample evidence, must be ascribed mainly to Greece, whose lead was followed by Serbia. Bulgaria could not, indeed, be heard at all even in defence, because her communications were cut at the time chosen by Greece for the opening of the campaign. When Bulgaria could make itself heard, its defence was characteristically terse and to the point. It consisted of the publication of the contents of a Greek army mail bag, containing letters which showed that, whether the alleged acts of the Bulgars were done by Bulgar regulars, irregulars, or Moslems disguised as Bulgars, those of the Greeks were under orders. The ingenuity of the press campaign against Bulgaria, which in ordinary diplomatic affairs would be enough to discredit the possibility of its being a preconceived plan, need not prevent its having been so calculated in this case. Greek diplomacy was in complete control of the situation, and the campaign is characteristically clever in conception. The whole Greek ' atrocity' attack, in which the new King was given a leading part, is exposed to the suspicion of having been organized in order, in the first place, to divert attention from the intention of the Greeks to clear the Bulgar population out of such further territories as they might occupy; and in the second place in order that in the partition then proceeding at Bucharest the Bulgars might lose any European ' democratic' sympathy that might remain to them after their mistakes or that might have been restored to them by their misfortunes.

The question of the relative blame of each of these heads of offence and the respective share of each party will depend on the point of view taken in such matters. In the opinion of the author, the last indictment—that of exploiting an ' atrocity' campaign—is the most criminal, if proved. For, if the war of partition was a political crime, and if the persecution of alien populations was worse as being a social crime, the ' atrocity campaign' was worst of all, for it was a spiritual crime against the best instincts of humanity. Finally, before leaving this, the saddest scene in a sordid tragedy, it is worth noting, that whatever the complicity and culpability of the Bulgars may have been in regard to the making of the War of Partition, and starting the political persecution, both offences were fully taken into account and amply purged by the settlement at Bucharest. Moreover, it seems likely that either they were calumniated in this ' atrocity' campaign, or that they have since been converted; for their relations with the refractory Moslem population of the part of Thrace assigned to them seem to be as satisfactory as the relations of the Serbs with the Macedo-Albanians or the Greeks with Macedo-Bulgars are unsatisfactory. As for the Serbs and Greeks, if they were to blame, their penalty, no doubt, lies in the future. The form that it may possibly take will be dealt with when the political results of that settlement come to be considered. But so far, it seems likely that the law will be justified under each of the heads of offending given above—and that as political crime has found a political penalty, so social crime will find a social penalty, and spiritual crime a spiritual punishment.

So much for the question of military excesses during the actual campaign. But there remains the graver matter of political extermination of aliens in the new conquests.

The word 'extermination' in its etymology exactly expresses the political proceeding with which we are here dealing—expulsion of human beings out of a determined region. Such 'extermination' is as logical a political consequence of the Balkan wars as the excesses with which we have just dealt were a logical social consequence. A Balkan nationality declares open war and succeeds in extending its political frontier; it then continues a suppressed and social war in order to establish that frontier by making it racial as well as political. It 'exterminates' other nationalities within the new frontier until the line is co-terminous with its own nationality. The lesson has been well learnt in the Balkans as to the danger of a political frontier which overlaps other nationalities. Therefore, the less natural and national the new frontier is, the more vigorous and violent will be the process of extermination; the less civilized the exterminating government, the more savage will be the methods followed; and the more akin the annexed aliens, the less will their nationality be annihilated and the more must it be assimilated. It follows also that, assimilation being a more difficult and lengthy process than annihilation, the troubles between races that are closely akin, such as Serbs and Bulgars, will be longer of settlement than those between races entirely alien, such as Greeks and Bulgars. In the former case the exterminating process is one rather of slow education, in the latter rather one of rapid expulsion.

Taking these various extermination campaigns in order, the first place must be given to Roumania as being the most civilized and not the least effective in its procedure. In the newly annexed district of the Dobrudscha, with a population of about 300,000, more than a third are Bulgars, about a third are Turks, and only one-fortieth are Roumanians. The political institutions had been, as everywhere in Bulgaria, thoroughly democratic and entirely without racial or religious discrimination. Even better evidence of their liberality is found in the large proportion of Moslems, who seem to thrive on the liberty and equality of Bulgar institutions even more than as a privileged class in Bosnia. But the institutions given to the province by Roumania exclude the whole population, even from the restricted franchises of the rest of the country; and not only constitutional, but even all municipal institutions have been suspended or subjected to official control. The 200 Bulgarian schools have been suppressed, all endowments confiscated, all churches, even, closed or compelled to use the Roumanian language. Still worse, the title of Bulgars to their lands has been put in question by a legal chicanery. This latter policy clearly exceeds the limits of education and aims at extermination— it is not Roumanizing the Bulgar but Roumanizing his land. So much for extermination of nationalism by war in the conquests of a comparatively civilized State.

Next let us consider the policy of Greece in the large alien areas annexed in Macedonia. Here there could never have been any hope of assimilation, for nothing would ever make a Bulgar into a Greek or allow a Bulgar to live under Greek rule as Greeks can under Bulgarian institutions. This racial incompatibility was so well recognized that undoubtedly deliberate advantage was taken of the licence of war to lessen any difficulty in dealing with subject Bulgars after the settlement. Of the Bulgar population of Macedonia swept before them by the Greek forces or stampeded by the stories (many no doubt fictitious), of the excesses that threatened them if they stayed—few, if any, returned. The estimates of the number of emigrants vary from 50,000 to 100,000 Bulgars alone, without counting perhaps twice as many Moslems. For although the Moslem population were neither so seriously menaced nor so severely mauled, yet the emigration has, as usual, in their case been almost *en masse*. So that the proportion of the original Bulgar and Moslem population now left must be small, and there can be little need of special political action for its further extermination. That can indeed be safely left to the social action of the Greek immigrants.

Serbia is in a somewhat similar position as regards the hereditary enemy—the Arnaut of Old Serbia, who has been ' exterminated ' very thoroughly. But the Serbian relation both to the pure Bulgarian of New Serbia and to the Bulgarized Macedonian is somewhat different. Of the former many can possibly be Serbified as early as the second generation, as is shown by the Serbified Bulgars of the Pirot district. Of the latter most can probably be Serbified even sooner, supposing the process be undisturbed. The policy therefore is to expel the more national and irreconcilable elements, such as schoolmasters, priests, ex-soldiers, &c., and subject the remainder to forcible Serbification. The procedure amounts to a suspension of all political and many civil rights.

Thus the Constitution for Serbian Macedonia decreed in December 1913 is based on the Serbian Constitution of 1903, but there are many omissions, depriving the inhabitants of the New Serbian territories of liberties and privileges which the 1903 Constitution confers. For instance, the Constitution for New Serbia does not abolish the penalty of death for political offenders. It does not accord a free press without censorship. It does not grant complete liberty to hold public meetings. It does not permit self-government, nor does it give the right to elect deputies for the national Skupschtina. It does not authorize the administration of an oath in judicial trials, nor does it provide for trial by jury in courts of law, nor guarantee the stability of judges. It will be seen from the above that in the New Serbian territories police authority and supervision are supreme.

Coming to Bulgaria, we find that in the first impetus of military action measures were taken against the Moslemized Bulgars of the Rhodope—the Pomaks—which might to the suspicious suggest a policy of precautionary extermination. A large percentage of the male Pomak population was expatriated and interned at Adrianople, where far too large a proportion died of disease and hardship. The explanation that the Pomak population might take advantage of war conditions to attack their Bulgar neighbours as they have done on previous occasions, as at Batak at the time of the historic ' Bulgarian massacres ', is no better excuse than that proffered by the Serbs in regard to their treatment of the Arnauts. But it would seem that this was really in part a military measure and in part a police prevention, for nothing in the subsequent treatment of the Pomaks suggests a policy of expatriation or even of coercive Bulgarization. In the same way any excesses committed by the Bulgar troops seem accountable by spontaneous relapses into barbarism or specific revenge—and there is not the same suspicion of their being inspired or even instigated by a policy of extermination. Such a policy is not appropriate to the Bulgar disposition, which shows its oriental origin in the peculiar capacity for associating with other races without assimilating or being assimilated. Bulgar nationalism, strange as it may seem to say so of these Prussians of the Balkans, is far less essentially warlike than is Greek. The Bulgar nation is a political entity in which other races can and do participate on an equal footing with the inheritors of Bulgar nationality. The Greek nation is a racial entity embracing all manner of political allegiances but in which no alien race can subsist without assimilation. There is no need, therefore, to doubt the reports [1] that the Bulgar treatment of the Moslems and Greeks in Western Thrace is comparatively beyond criticism so far as the former are concerned, and relatively creditable as respects the latter. This is all the more noticeable, seeing that this territory was for long in the possession of the Greeks and Turks, and when taken over by the Bulgars was largely in the hands of a provisional government sworn to resist them.

It will be asked what limits can be seen or what bounds can be set up so that this Balkan policy of extermination may not too deeply disgrace a nominally Christian civilization. Besides such internal restraining influences as can be relied on to act as a check more or less and sooner or later, there are two external checks. One is fear of hostile action by the compatriots of the persecuted race, the other fear of European public opinion. Neither are strong checks, for owing to the conditions of the Macedonian and Albanian settlements, the Bulgar and Arnaut races which are suffering most are both left practically without remedy. There is no treaty between the protecting and the persecuting governments providing for the rights of the former's minority in the latter's territories, and, if there were, there is no means of enforcing it in the present military exhaustion of Bulgaria and Albania. This is not so in the case of Greece, and there the menace of a naval warfare in which the Greeks would have had a great advantage stopped the war of extermination against Thracian and Anatolian Greeks and secured some guarantees for their safety. So also Roumania has been strong enough

---

[1] 'So much has been said of the hatred between Turks and Bulgars, and of the solemn league and covenant whereby the Moslems of Western Thrace swore to resist Bulgarian rule to the last, that it is pleasant to be able to assure readers of *The Near East*, on the authority of one of the leading figures in the present Ottoman Government, that the situation of the Moslems of Western Thrace is, considering all things, decidedly satisfactory ; that Murad Bey, the new Bulgarian Governor of Gumuljina, a distant relative of Talaat Bey, is becoming popular among the Moslems of the annexed districts, and that the relations between the Bulgar officials, be they Moslem or Christian, and the Turks are steadily improving.'— Constantinople Correspondent : *The Near East*.

to protect the Macedonian Kutso-Vlach; and Greece has secured by a ' suppressed' war sufficient guarantees for the Hellenized minority of South Albania. But for the Bulgar and the Moslem of Macedonia there is no help other than in an appeal to the Treaty of Berlin—whose provisions were framed under very different circumstances—and to the Great Powers whose pressure under existing conditions cannot be effectively exercised. It is indeed a very complete turn in the wheel of fortune that Turkish and Albanian Moslems should be appealing against Slavs and Greeks to Great Britain as a Moslem Power, in virtue of the provisions designed by Great Britain as a Christian Power to protect the Slavs and Greeks against the Moslems.[1]

But the only means of pressure—suspension of recognition of the Bucharest settlement—is not a very effective leverage, and it is unlikely that Europe in general or England in particular will be able to spare any more active intervention in Balkan affairs for some time to come. Indeed all such remedial intervention by European civilization is dependent on that civilization itself retaining the freedom of action and the force of authority which peace alone can provide. The preoccupation of Europe with preparations for war leaves but small hope that the Balkan wars of extermination will be ended by European action or authority.[2]

---

[1] In reply to representations addressed by the All-India Moslem League to the Foreign Secretary upon the protection of the civil and religious freedom of Balkan minorities, Sir Eyre Crowe wrote on December 1 stating that the provisions of the Treaty of Berlin are in no way abrogated by the territorial changes in the Near East, and remain as binding as they have been hitherto as regards all territories covered by those articles at the time when the treaty was signed. He adds : ' His Majesty's Government will, however, consult with the other Powers as to the policy of reaffirming in some way the provisions of the Treaty of Berlin for the protection of the religious and other liberties of minorities in the territories referred to, when the question of giving formal recognition by the Powers to the recent territorial changes in the Balkan peninsula is raised.'

[2] Since writing the above, the European nations have become too busy exterminating each other to care about ' exterminations ' in the Balkans.

The protest of the Turks against Greek persecution is somewhat weakened by their having followed a very similar policy in regard to Thrace. Thrace was, of course, reconquered after only a short occupation by Bulgaria, but the opportunity offered by war was taken in order to carry out the nationalist policy of the Young Turk very drastically. Nationalism by war had been the policy in Macedonia which had forced on the War of the Coalition against Turkey. The application of the same policy to Thrace and Anatolia now very nearly caused another war with Greece, of which the issue would have been sufficiently doubtful to make the Ottoman Government willing to face it. It was of course obvious that the conversion, so far as Europe was concerned, of the Ottoman Empire into a Turkish nation made it indispensable that the Greek and Bulgar character of the remaining Turkish territories in Europe should be modified as far as possible. Turkey could never in future consider itself secured in Thrace and on the Straits while the interior was shared with Bulgars and the littoral wholly in the hands of Greeks. So the Bulgar villagers left after the campaign were still further reduced by the simple process of driving them over the frontier. The expulsion of the Greeks and their substitution by Moslem refugees from Macedonia was far more difficult. The Greeks were commercial, the Moslems agricultural; the Greeks townsmen, the Moslems landowners. But a few ' atrocities ' of the old Turkish type were sufficient to start an exodus not only from Thrace and the Gallipoli peninsula but also from the Anatolian littoral, such as threatened shortly to depopulate *Magna Graecia*. The fact that the Aegean islands were now in Greek occupation and were within easy reach, that the troops were returning full of resentment against the Christian, and that Moslem mouhadjirs from Macedonia were starving among the Greek villages, all facilitated the extermination process. As the scene in this case was the coast instead of remote mountains, and the sufferers were Greeks instead of silent Moslem Bulgars, there was no lack of evidence.[1] By the month of June a Greek estimate put the refugees from Thrace at about 100,000, and half as many more from Anatolia. The Turks, relying on the naval superiority secured them by the prospective delivery of two Dreadnoughts just completing in the Tyne and at Barrow, evidently intended to ' exterminate ' the Greeks from Thrace and the Anatolian littoral ; whereby, should the islands become, as was inevitable, *têtes de pont* for Greek propaganda on the mainland, a wall of European Moslems might be interposed between this new Greek frontier and the Greek communities of the interior. Greece as a result of the war was in far too belligerent a mood to brook such a blow to the 'great idea' ; and Turkey, too unfit and unwilling for another campaign, might have been tempted to fight by the exposed strategic and political condition of the great islands, as soon as ever the Dreadnoughts were delivered. Peace was secured and the Turkish policy of extermination stopped by one of the boldest strokes of democratic diplomacy that history records. President Wilson restored the balance of power in the Aegean at one stroke by recommending the United States Government to sell two fairly effective battleships to Greece. The advantage which Turkey was exploiting thus abolished, an agreement was rapidly reached by Athens and Constantinople. The policy of the United States President, both in its inspiration and method, should cause some searchings of heart to those who reflect what might have been the history of the Balkan Wars had the democracies of Western Europe been represented by such elevated inspiration and by such effective intervention.

[1] Thus as a result of a few outrages and an atmosphere of panic, 5,000 Greeks in a body took boat from Tchesme to the island of Chios, and 6,000 from Aivali to Mitylene. Their places were at once filled by Arnaut and Turkish Moslems from New Serbia.

CHAPTER VIII

PRESENT CONDITIONS

§ 22. Economic Results.
§ 23. Political Results.
§ 24. Moral Results.

Allons ! through struggles and wars.
The goal that was named cannot be countermanded.
Have the past struggles succeeded ?
What has succeeded—yourself—your nation—nature ?
Now understand me well:—it is provided in the essence
Of things that from any fruition of success shall come forth
Something to make a greater struggle necessary.

WALT WHITMAN.

§ 22. ECONOMIC RESULTS

THE results of war may be considered from three points of view : the economic, the political, and the moral.

The results of a war between western powers would be most conspicuously economic, and would chiefly consist in immense losses of capital, credit, good will, and such less tangible forms of property ; while the corresponding gains would be insignificant, and would probably, for the most part, be scored by neutrals. The gains by conquest would be relatively of small importance and restricted to overseas possessions ; for annexation of territory and administration of alien races in Western Europe is not worth the onus of international armaments, and the odium of international antipathies, entailed by such coercions of nationalism. The annexation of Alsace was as bad business for the Germans as the administration of Ireland is for the English. It would pay Great Britain to give Ireland self-government, even at the very remote risk of this leading to Irish independence ; and it would pay Germany to do the same for Alsace or Schleswig, even at the risk of autonomy leading to annexation by France or Denmark.[1] But the same would not be true of nations in a Near-Eastern stage of development; and it would not pay Serbia or Turkey to give self-government to Macedonia or Thrace at the risk of annexation eventually by Bulgaria or Greece. The fact is that the same process has taken place in western Europe in regard to national domain and international power as has taken place there in regard to private landed property and the political power it comports. A century ago in England, land was the basis of political power, and social position was proportionate to the extent of an estate; but to-day, land as the qualification for power has been displaced by capital in a form more convenient for the economic conditions of the age. In the same way, modern States take their position in the world by their capital resources and the proportion they invest in armaments; while the extent of their territories or the numbers of their population are only ruling factors in time of war. France has more power to make its national will felt in time of peace than has Russia; even as London has as yet more than New York. For while the land is still ultimately the source of all national life even in the western urban civilizations, yet in these civilizations the accumulated energies of previous generations in different forms of capital is so great that rural land is comparatively unimportant. But in the Balkans, circumstances are still what they were in Europe when land connoted power and property. Land in the Balkans is still the only basis for national development: the main source of national culture: the chief school of national character.

Augmentations of territory are therefore still of primary

---

[1] It did not seem probable when this was written that this familiar argument against annexation would be put to the proof. We shall now know within a few months how the profit-and-loss account of a general European war stands, and what the total cost is to each Power for its respective share of the responsibility in causing the war. It seems probable, even at this early stage, that the cost will be in accordance with the culpability.

importance to Balkan States ; while facilities for commerce
and industry, such as access to the sea and economic associations with neighbouring States, are, for the present, of
secondary importance. This peculiarity of primitive conditions must be constantly borne in mind in examining
Balkan affairs from a pacificist point of view. For, whereas
the economic association with foreign communities which
supplies the principal means of livelihood to western nations
can be assured only by peace, the territorial acquisitions
which are equally essential to the growth of a Balkan nation
can be secured only by war. A pacificist inquiry into a
western war would probably result in a balance sheet in
which—after placing to credit such direct profits as war
indemnities, revenues of new territories, the control of new
resources, and such negative advantages as damages to
rivals and monopolization of markets, and after entering to
debit loss of labour, of business, and of good will—an immense
deficit would be shown. But the same inquiry into Balkan
warfare might, quite possibly, show a profit, and would
probably do so if the territorial acquisitions were considerable and were estimated at their local value, which is, of
course, political rather than economic. In regard to the
present wars, the author is of opinion that the War of Coalition could have been made to show an economic profit to
each of the Allies in spite of the heavy cost of life and of
war material, even leaving all political gains out of the
account, in view of the great accession of territory. It does
not follow that a war which is politically justified will also
justify itself economically ; though the same conditions of
a long-overdue development which cause a war of liberation
are also likely to cause a war of annexation. But when
we come to the War of Partition we find that if the cost
of opening up Turkey in Europe to western democratic
development was not excessive, undoubtedly the cost of
distributing the shares between the partners was so. The
cost of the War of Coalition, considered as the purchase price

of a new property for western exploitation, was perhaps not such as would over-capitalize the enterprise; but the cost of the War of Partition, considered as expenses of flotation, has made the acquisition a very questionable investment.

In examining the results of the Balkan Wars, we find that the War of Partition has been as disproportionately costly for the Balkan States as it seems likely to be for Europe as a whole. It might have been expected that—given armies on a war footing and a condition of war—the prolongation of war conditions for a few months would have been cheap compared with the cost of preparing for and launching the previous war. But, upon inquiry, it appears that the War of Coalition was, economically speaking, just about the limit which the States engaged could manage on their accumulated cash and credit. The War of Partition, including therein the cost of maintaining the Greek and Serbian armies fully mobilized after the cessation of Turkish resistance in their spheres of operation, represents a burden disproportionately heavy, because in the first place it exceeds the credit and capacity of the States concerned, and in the second place it exceeds any immediate return from the territories annexed. Thus, at New Year 1912–13 we find Balkan funds less prejudiced by the war situation than those of western Powers; but they have come down heavily by New Year 1913–14. So, also, before the War of Partition it seemed most probable that, in spite of the increased debt resulting from the War of Coalition, Greece and Serbia might, as a result of the war, expect to get rid of the foreign financial control of that part of their revenues assigned to the service of the foreign debt. But now there is no question of this : the tendency is more likely to be towards making it a condition of further loans that the International Commissions be given some control over military expenditure, so that their savings may not again be used for making war. Again, before the War of Partition the Allies had countered the attempt of Europe to make them liable for a share in the Ottoman Debt by preferring a claim for a war indemnity calculated, if capitalized, to cancel such liability. But the War of Partition put an end to their counterclaim, while bringing them to such financial straits that they will probably all, like Serbia, be forced to accept whatever liability for the Ottoman Debt Paris may impose as a condition of financing their loans. Finally, the War of Partition has indefinitely postponed the good prospect which the Balkan Alliance enjoyed, of interesting British, and even American, capital, in its development. The War of Partition has handed them over tied and bound by the chain of their necessities to the closest ring of capitalists in the world. The control exercised by the Paris Bourse subjects borrowing from Paris to greater sacrifices of national fiscal and political independence than would borrowing in an open market.[1]

When we examine economic regions other than finance, we find the same disproportionate damage done by the War of Partition. Cost of living was not much affected during the winter of 1912–13, but the prolongation of the war through the following summer sent up prices in a way that shows that the second war seriously affected the domestic economy of the belligerents.[2] Again, during the War of Coalition, though fighting was severe, it was a war between armies, not between populations ; except, to a small extent, between Bulgars and Turks in Thrace, and, to a still less extent, between Greeks and Turks in Epirus. Moslem villages were, it is true, ruined, and an exodus of Moslem refugees implied a serious temporary loss to the Allies, and imposed a serious temporary expense on Turkey. But the War of Partition in Macedonia was a

[1] It may be remembered as evidence of this control, that at one time the Greek loan stood first for issue, but was put down to third place, because, it was said, of King Constantine's pro-Prussian pronouncements in September 1913. Also that an inopportune loan to Turkey by the Perrier Bank was stopped and the bank fined £30,000 for a technical breach of regulations.

[2] Bread rose 25 per cent. and fuel 50 per cent. in the Slav countries. In Greece, an attempt was made by the Government to regulate prices.

war of deliberate devastation and depopulation—a policy which, however explicable politically, is an economic extravagance for which the victor will pay as heavily as the vanquished.

These general considerations as to the cost of the war need no support from figures. Indeed, figures for the most part can only be estimated where direct losses are concerned, and no more than inferred in regard to indirect losses. They are, moreover, apt to be misleading. For example, there is no fixed standard of value, losses of men are more costly to Bulgaria than to Turkey, while money is cheaper to Turkey than it is to Bulgaria. Again, if we compare the proportion of the existing debt per head of population, we shall see that Bulgaria, with the same charge per head as in the United States, is in a position to bear the burden of several wars such as the present without bringing its burden of debt up to that of the other Balkan States.[1]

The direct losses of men, money, and materials cannot be given with any certainty ; and a satisfactory separation of war expenditure from peace expenditure is in most cases impossible. But when it comes to estimating the indirect cost of these wars—the respective value of men where humanity is cheap, and money where money is dear, still more of material bought in part payment of foreign loans— it seems certain that those officially responsible can have very little real knowledge of what the war has cost : an ignorance that expresses itself differently in each country. Some idea can be obtained, but it must be conveyed rather by facts than by figures, or, where figures are used, they must be considered as estimates rather than as statistics. The more important economic facts of the war are to be found in matters which lie outside of the range of figures and on the borders of politics ; perhaps because these Near Eastern

---

[1] The proportion of debt per head of population in 1912 was : Bulgaria, £6 ; Serbia, £10 10s. ; Greece, £13. The calculation cannot be made conveniently in the case of Turkey.

States are not yet at a stage of development where economics can be separated from politics.[1]

[1] (a) TERRITORIAL CHANGES (FIGURES IN SQ. KILOMETRES)

	Before the War.	After the War.	Result.
Turkey in Europe . .	169,300	26,100	− 143,200
Serbia	48,303	87,303	+ 39,000 [a]
Montenegro . . .	5,100	9,080	+ 3,980 [a]
Bulgaria	96,345	114,100	+ 26,100 − 8,340 [b]
Greece	64,457	123,343	+ 42,700 [c] + 5,600 [d] + 8,618 [e] 61,386 [g] + 4,468 [f]
Albania			28,000
Total Turkish territory in Europe and Asia partitioned			145,380
Roumania	131,350	139,690	8,340 [h]

[a] An increase of about four-fifths in both cases.
[b] Less Dobrudscha cession a net increase of 17,760, or of less than one-fifth.
[c] Continent.   [d] Islands.   [e] Crete.   [f] Samos.
[g] An increase of almost double.   [h] An increase of one-sixteenth.

The Dodekanese at present administered by Italy for Turkey is not included in the above ; the following are the principal islands :

	Area. Sq. miles.	Population.
Rhodes	565	30,000
Nikaria	103	13,000
Stampalia	50	1,500
Karpathos	150	9,000
Kos	110	10,000

The Dardanelles islands retained by Turkey are :

Lemnos	175	30,000
Imbros	98	9,100

(b) RESULTS IN POPULATION

I. Turkey in Asia (omitting autonomous areas) :

Asia Minor	10,500,000 [i]	
Armenia and Kurdistan . . .	2,500,000	
Mesopotamia	2,000,000	
Syria (without the Lebanon) . .	3,500,000	
Arabia	1,000,000	
		19,500,000

Turkey in Europe (as reduced by the war) :

Constantinople and Tchataldja . . .	1,250,000	
Adrianople, Turkish Thrace, and Turkish islands	750,000	
		2,000,000

Total estimated present population of empire . 22,500,000

[i] These figures are estimates based on fiscal statistics.

II. Turkish territories partitioned as a result of the war. Population estimated from Turkish and Balkan statistics :

Bulgar Thrace .	250,000	Vilayet of Yanina .	525,000
Vilayet of Salonica .	1,100,000	„ Crete . .	325,000
„ Monastir .	850,000	„ Archipelago	360,000
„ Kossovo .	1,025,000	„ Samos .	5,000
„ Scutari .	300,000		4,750,000[a]

[a] A decrease of about one-sixth in the total population of Turkey and of about two-thirds in the population of Turkey in Europe.

III. Estimated distribution among Balkan States of population of ceded Turkish territories :

	Additional population.	Anterior population (plus estimated increase since last census).	Present population.	Proportion of increase.
1. Greece :				
Continent . .	1,300,000			An increase of two-thirds.
Crete . . .	325,000			
	375,000			
Islands . . .				
	2,000,000	2,750,000	4,750,000	
2. Serbia . . .	1,175,000	3,000,000	4,175,000 }	An increase of three-sevenths in both cases.
3. Montenegro . .	120,000	280,000	400,000 }	
4. Bulgaria :				
Thrace . . .	250,000			
Macedonia . .	325,000			
	575,000			
Dobrudscha (ceded to Roumania) . .	350,000	4,500,000	4,750,000	An increase of one-twentieth.
Net Bulgar gain .	225,000			
5. Albania . . .	820,000			
6. Turkey, emigration from ceded territories	60,000			
7. Roumania . . .	350,000	7,250,000	7,600,000	An increase of one-twentieth.
8. Italy, Dodekanese .	60,000			

The net result therefore seems to be that the population of Turkey in Europe is decreased by two-thirds and of Greece increased by the same amount ; while those of Serbia and of Montenegro are both increased by three-sevenths ; and those of Roumania and Bulgaria are both increased by one-twentieth, and that of Italy by 60,000.

Note.—The above figures must be considered as estimates, not as statistical data. The estimates of journalists and publicists do not differ greatly in respect of the total additions to the Greek and Servian populations, but are very discrepant as to Bulgaria and Albania.

But the economic effects of the war can now be estimated in regard to such factors as transfer of land and population, changes in debt and revenue, with sufficient accuracy to suggest the result of these economic changes on the natural developments of the States concerned. Whether the economic effects of these wars will be to check, or to hasten, that development is the main question that concerns us here.

The economic effect of increases of territory which doubled the size of Greece, Serbia, and Montenegro, are best grasped as a whole by a glance at the map—figures of square mileage are of little help. As regards population, the appended estimates show that Turkey has lost about one-sixth of the total tax-paying population and two-thirds of its European population, while Greece has gained by two-thirds, Servia and Montenegro have each increased their population by a little less than a half, while Roumania and Bulgaria have increased theirs by one-twentieth; the general result being that the total populations of Greece, of Bulgaria, and of Serbia with Montenegro are about equalized at 4,750,000, the same figure as that of the population lost to Turkey. The estimate as to the effect of the war on debt is interesting,[1] as illustrating how the financial consequences of war have little relation to the political results. Thus the effect of the war, both for Turkey, the heaviest loser, and Greece, the greatest gainer, has been to increase the annual debt charge from about a quarter of the annual revenue to about a third ; although the contributing conditions in each case are very dissimilar. The effect of the war on net revenue seems to be approximately and for the present, that Greece receives a net increase of revenue of about one-third, Serbia neither gains nor loses, while Bulgaria is worse off by about one-fifth of its annual revenue, and Turkey by about one-third.[2]

For notes [1] and [2] see facing page.

¹ (c) EFFECT OF WAR ON DEBT

Turkey.

Before the War.	Debt (March 1912.)	Charge.	Revenue.	Pro-portion.
	£T.	£T.	£T.	
Funded	132,182,264	6,099,603	30,374,119	23% (about)
Floating	15,000,000 (about)	1,000,000 (about)		
After the War.				
Probable loans	28,000,000	1,750,000		
Probable liabilities	22,000,000	1,750,000		
Less proportion of debt transferred		1,000,000		
		9,500,000 (about)	25,000,000 (about)	38% (about)

Greece.

Before the War.	Debt (Dec. 1912).	Charge.	Revenue.	Pro-portion.
	£	£	£	
External	32,493,360	1,342,832	5,764,744	22%
Internal	6,409,032			
After the War.				
Probable loan	12,000,000	700,000		
Probable liabilities	6,000,000	300,000		
Probable share of Turkish debt		600,000		
		3,000,000 (about)	8,500,000 (about)	35% (about)

² (d) ECONOMIC EFFECT OF WARS ON REVENUE AND EXPENDITURE

Territory.	Annual Revenues. £	Net results.	Annual Charges.	£	Net results.
1. Greece :					
acquired by the War of Coalition a { Janina vil.	400,000				
Monastir	100,000	+2,200,000	Funded debt charges c		700,000
Archipelago b	200,000				
Salonica	1,500,000				
and by the War of Partition { Salonica	500,000	+550,000	Funded debt charges	50,000	850,000
Thrace, &c.	50,000		Floating debt charges	200,000	
			Share of Ottoman Debt	600,000	
		+2,750,000			−1,550,000
					+2,750,000
			Annual profit to Greece of		1,200,000

For notes a b c see p 303.

Territory.		Annual Revenues. £	Net results.	Annual Charges.	£	Net results.
2. Serbia:						
acquired by the War of Coalition	Kossovo	700,000 } +900,000		Funded debt charges[d] .	.	500,000
	Monastir	200,000	+1,200,000	Funded debt charges .	250,000 } −1,150,000	
and by the War of Partition	Kossovo	100,000 } +300,000		Floating debt charges .	100,000	+1,200,000
	Monastir	200,000		Share of Ottoman Debt .	300,000	
				Annual profit to Servia of . . .		50,000
3. Bulgaria:						
acquired by War of Coalition	Macedonia	950,000 } +2,200,000		Funded debt charges .	800,000	1,200,000
	Thrace .	1,250,000	+350,000	Floating debt charges .	400,000 } −1,850,000	650,000
lost by War of Partition	Macedonia	−850,000 } −1,850,000		Floating debt charges .	550,000	+350,000
	Thrace .	−1,000,000		Share of Ottoman Debt .	500,000	
				Annual loss to Bulgaria of . . .		−1,500,000
4. Montenegro *acquired*		.	50,000			
5. Albania:						
	Scutari vil.	150,000 }				
	Elsewhere	50,000	200,000			
6. Turkey:						
lost by War of Coalition	Roumelia	−5,500,000[e] } −6,750,000		Funded debt charges .	1,750,000 } 3,250,000	3,250,000
	Debt adm.	−1,250,000	−4,750,000[g]	Floating debt charges .	1,500,000	
	Thrace .	1,000,000[f]		Floating debt charges .		250,000
acquired by War of Partition	Debt assignable to Balkan States .	1,000,000 } +2,000,000				
				Annual loss to Turkey . . .		−8,250,000
						−3,500,000
						−4,750,000
						−8,250,000

If we now examine the effects of the war on each belligerent in turn, it will be evident from a glance at the table that Greece shows the best balance-sheet, taken all round. Whether these figures are at all accurate or not, their general result is confirmed by an examination of the facts in the case of each country concerned.

Thus, the profit to Greece is inestimably increased by the fact that the land acquired by that kingdom is almost all fertile, accessible, and inhabited by a well-developed and well-disposed peasantry. This is a most valuable consideration to a State of which, hitherto, only a fifth has been cultivable, and which has had to maintain itself largely on foreign foodstuffs. Moreover, the removal or reduction of this disadvantage cannot fail to have good results on emigration and exchange, two difficulties which have bulked large in Greek economics. Epirus is a province which nothing but maladministration of malice prepense has kept from becoming highly productive and progressive; while both there and in the Roumluk, the Greek, Vlach, and South Albanian population comprise three of the most progressive types of the Balkans, all amenable to Greek administration. The Roumluk, it is true, contains much barren mountain,

a The division of cost between the two wars is on the basis that the War of Coalition ended for Greece and Serbia altogether with the first London Conference, and for Bulgaria with the second.

b The division between Greece and Bulgaria after the War of Coalition is taken as that offered by M. Venezelos of Salonica to Greece and Kavalla to Bulgaria. The revenues of Greece are likely to be larger than the sum stated as they are drawn to a large extent from customs, and the Turkish duties are much lower than the Greek.

c The funded debt charges are those likely to be required for the service of the proposed loans; the balance of direct cost of the wars remaining as ' floating debt '.

d A considerable part of the expense of the War of Coalition to Greece and Serbia was paid out of reserves.

e This corresponds roughly to the revenues of Roumelia and the Archipelago as given on p. 322, note 1 (c).

f Thrace has been so wasted by war that these revenues will be halved for several years.

g This does not convey a very correct impression as to the result of the war to Turkey. The loss of Roumelia was really a gain.

and many Bulgar settlements likely to prove intractable; but the latter will, no doubt, be given small chance of making trouble, and will have been already, like the Bulgar populations of the Kavalla hinterland, largely replaced by emigrants from Greece. In Salonica and Kavalla, with their fertile valleys, the Greeks have gained two most promising ports, the pick of the spoils. The population of Kavalla is Greek, and the Jewish element in Salonica is not one likely to give trouble, though it will probably not maintain its position under Greek rule as it did under Turkish. It is true that both ports will suffer from being cut off by customs frontiers from their local demand and supply, but they will more than gain correspondingly by new connexions and through traffic. Moreover, Serbian Macedonia must be as good, and probably a better, customer for Salonica, even across a frontier, than ever was Turkish Macedonia. Greek Macedonia and the Greek littoral is highly fertile; the arables of the Lower Vardar and the tobacco plantations of Kavalla, of which the Greeks have got three-fourths, are at present the most profitable regions of what was once Turkey in Europe. While there are at present many Bulgars and Turks in this region, the Greeks have had a unique opportunity of getting rid of them during the last year, and seem to have fully availed themselves of it, and it will now be well within the power of the Greek Government to advance the line of Greek settlement to the political frontier. When we add to these continental acquisitions the large industrial and commercial islands of the Aegean, of which Chios, Mitylene, and Samos are as promising communities as are to be found anywhere, and when we include Crete, the prize of the Aegean—it will be seen that the new kingdom of Greece, so far as augmentation of territory and population goes, closes the war with a considerable credit entry. But territorial extension is not all the gain. For hitherto, the economic development of Greece has been considerably hampered by the isolated and practically insular position forced on it by the interposition of an Asiatic Empire between its railway system and that of Europe. But Greece has now not only secured Salonica, the European railhead for Smyrna, but can substitute the Piraeus for Brindisi as the railhead for Egypt and the Canal traffic. Brindisi has been unable to draw any permanent profit for Italy out of the through traffic, but the superior interest of the Greek port and its neighbourhood and the enterprise of the people will use such a through route to restore the Greek peninsula to its old position as the bridge between East and West. Passing on to less easily estimated items, it will perhaps be permissible to reckon off any increased burden of armaments which the new frontiers may impose, against the decrease in political friction, both internal and international, afforded by the elimination of a moribund neighbour, and the extinction of the irredentist movements of Crete, Epirus, and Samos.

In a word, this war has raised Greece from the minor Principality it has been in the nineteenth century to the secondary Power it will become during the twentieth, with a good prospect at the end of it of becoming a Great Power by accumulation of capital and the acquisition of Constantinople. This profit is one which cannot be computed in terms of money, and can only be discounted by moral considerations such as those which will be dealt with later. In view of this result, it would be misleading to attach much importance to such calculations of economic profit and loss as that in the preceding table. Greece has bought back the greater part of its lost patrimony as a bargain at a bankrupt sale, and has paid part of the price out of the accumulated profits from the portions of its heritage previously acquired. Had Greece been contented with a little less of Macedonia, the bargain would, no doubt, have been far better, for it then, probably, would not have been necessary to keep the fiscal freedom of the country in pledge. There was money available to begin the war, and enough would have been obtainable from internal loans to carry it through. The cash balance on which Greece went to war was largely the result of the international control which has existed in Greece since 1898, and the continuance of this control is the price which Greece has paid for the War of Partition. Its abolition was fully expected as a result of the War of Coalition, but such liberation is now, in the present state of the finances, impossible. Perhaps the most serious item to be entered to the debit side of the war will be the disturbance to Greek industry and trade. In this respect Greece is in a very inferior position to the agricultural and, socially simple Slav and Bulgar States. A third of the Greek revenues is derived from the customs, which will necessarily reflect the result of disturbance to business and dislocation of trade. For a time the artificial demands of war conditions will no doubt keep up receipts—for instance, the shipping industry has made large profits out of army transport—but after the present expansion there must inevitably be a period of loss and liquidation before Greek national economy can recover a healthy activity and profit by the new territories. It is impossible to guess as yet what this reaction will represent in the annual revenues of the State, still less what its cost to the nation will be. The sharper it is, the shorter it will be; and the increased civil and military expenditure already planned will not make the burden of it any easier to bear.

Passing from large considerations of national economy and coming to the financial conditions, the following would seem roughly to represent the budget of the war. Allowing £2,500,000 as the outside annual revenue obtainable for some time from the new continental territories, and £225,000 as the outside obtainable for some time from the islands, we find that the gross gain to the Greek revenues will increase them by as much as one-half. But nothing like this increase will be realized for some time, and the greater part of the new income will, for long, be required for development of the new territories; even though the greater part of the new continental possessions and all the islands have escaped from the war without damage. It was twenty years before the fertile plain of Thessaly stopped being an expense to the national revenues.

On the debit side of the account must be entered the sum for the cost of the war against Turkey and Bulgaria. The cost of the loss of life and waste of material is difficult to estimate, but it may be taken that the gain by spoil of war is not so complete a set-off to the latter as it has been claimed to be. An estimate of the cost of the war and a statement of the spoil taken will be found below.[1] The list of killed and wounded given below is, if anything, an overestimate, and compares favourably with the losses of

---

[1] COST OF WAR TO THE GREEKS

[The following estimates may be of interest as being the figures submitted by the Greek Government to the Paris Commission, and originally not intended for publication, for the purpose of supporting a claim for a war indemnity and of discounting the liability to a share in the Ottoman Debt in respect of the territories annexed. This may explain how they came to be larger than other estimates published elsewhere. They refer only to the War of Coalition.]

1. **Army :**

	Mill. frcs.
Maintenance of 215,000 men at 2 frcs. a day and 51,651 at 2·50 frcs., clothing at 92·50, and equipment at 42·80	160·768
War expenses :	
Artillery	18·19
Infantry (65 mill. cartridges)	12·37
Cavalry	·92
Engineers	9·36
Ambulance	6·31
Rail transport	36·0
Requisitions (45,064 animals, 6,081 carts)	30·37
Remounts	3·89
Hospitals	4·24
Miscellaneous	7·0
	318·529

X 2

the other belligerents.[1] The total cost of the wars cannot amount to much less than £16,000,000, and may be much more. This is a sum equal to about half the existing debt, and a quarter of this amount will be paid out of previous surpluses and economies.

		Mill. frcs.
2. Naval :		
Extra expenditure (fuel, war pay, war reserves, &c.)		26·59
Extra ammunition		4·67
Wear of guns		4·76
Vessels requisitioned (some 85 as cruisers and transports)		17·72
Damage to vessels		20·22
Miscellaneous		1·36
		75·342
3. Pensions to wounded		54·0
4. Prisoners' maintenance		20·0
5. Refugees' maintenance		2·0
		469·87 =mill. £18·8

This would make the total cost of the Turkish war alone over eighteen millions sterling, half as much again as the usual estimate.

(a) GREEK LOSSES

	Killed or Died.		Wounded or Sick.	
	Officers.	Soldiers.	Officers.	Soldiers.
War of Coalition (nine months)	138	5,031	189	23,313
War of Partition (one month) .	166	2,397	429	18,878
Total	304	7,428	618	42,191

(b) SPOIL OF WAR TAKEN BY THE GREEKS

(From a statement published in *Messager d'Athènes*, Dec. 31, 1913.)

Taken from the Turks : guns, 325 ; caissons and tumbrils, 425 ; quick-firers, 81 ; rifles, 100,000 ; shells, 46,867 ; cartridges, 34,657,000 ; armoured automobile ; 2 bridge trains ; 2 wireless equipments ; 2 aeroplanes and large quantities of war material, clothing, and provisions.

Taken from the Bulgars : guns, 84 ; caissons and tumbrils, 215 ; quick-firers, 9 ; magazine rifles, 7,900 ; mausers in large number ; shells, 7,910 ; cartridges, 1,200,000 ; 2 automobiles ; 1 aeroplane ; railway rolling stock, field hospitals, the *train de luxe* of the Sultan, clothing, cash, and large quantities of provisions valued at about £800,000.

[1] The war was financed thus :

		Mill. frcs.
1. Balance of 1910 loan		73·53
2. Surpluses of 1910–11		19·31
3. Economies on expenditure of 1912–13 and various .		30·0
4. Treasury Bills (National Bank) . . .		10·0
5. Treasury Bills, National Bank and Paris (Dec. 1912)		40·0
6. Treasury Bills, National Bank (April, 1913) . .		50·0
7. Treasury Bills, National Bank (May, 1913) . .		40·0
		262·85 =mill. £11

The Greek Government, then, is expected to become a borrower, in the end, of about £25,000,000, to pay for the war and to provide for the development and defence of the new territories. But this burden is by no means beyond what the country can bear without checking the pace of its economic development. Not only will the doubling of territory and population give a great impetus to trade and industry; but a notable improvement had been already proceeding in the national economy before the outbreak of war, which seems to be due to conditions such as are not likely to be permanently affected by war disturbances and war losses.

After the national bankruptcy of 1893, recovery was very slow, and was retarded by the disastrous war of 1898. The first, sign of recovery came with the reduction of the rate of exchange about 1903—a relief in every financial and economic activity which was due partly to the growing importance of the remittances from emigrants to the United States. Prices fell and commercial and industrial activity increased, until in 1909 the rate of exchange reached par, where it thereafter remained—with the result that there was for the first time in Greek history no budgetary deficit. Since then there have been surpluses.

Thus the economic effects of the war in respect of Greece may be summed up as possibly temporarily embarrassing to national finances, but of epoch-making effect on the era of economic expansion on which the country had already embarked previous to the war.

Passing to Serbia, we find that this State has about doubled her territory and increased her population by almost half as a result of the two wars. While not so fortunate as Greece in regard to the fertility of the new lands and the amenability of the population, Serbia has not much to complain of. The only irreconcilable elements are the Albanians; and, like Greece, Serbia has had an opportunity such as conditions of modern civilization seldom offer of driving the

Arnauts out of the fertile Slav lands which they had been gradually absorbing under the Ottoman régime. In regard to the Slav Macedonians, it is possible that the relentless campaign of serbification now proceeding will, in a generation, eliminate their Bulgar proclivities, and that they will become peaceable and productive citizens. The Greeks and Kutso-Vlachs will probably live contentedly under Serbian rule, for their liberal treatment is assured by political considerations, and their loyalty by their fear of Albanians and Bulgars. Therefore, in spite of the Serbian title to central Macedonia being purely political, it is quite possible that that province may settle down to economic development; and such Arnauts and Bulgars as remain will probably not, for the present, retard that development by disturbance; for the success of any conspiracy must depend on the co-operation of their countrymen in Albania and Bulgaria, and they will not be ready for conflict in the next few years.

The importance to Serbia of this accession of territory lies in the fact that disadvantages of position have hitherto prevented the country from acquiring a real economic independence—a condition which has, of course, restricted its political independence and retarded unduly its national development. It is only during the last decade that Serbia has succeeded to any extent in opening fresh outlets for trade so as to become at all independent of economic pressure from Austria. Even to-day, so-called sanitary restrictions on the export of Serbian live-stock or produce through Hungary can at any moment give a crippling blow to Serbian national economy. Serbia has now an outlet through Greek Salonica more commercially available and politically reliable than it afforded when Turkish. It has also acquired a possibly realizable outlet through Montenegro to the Adriatic, and another more easily available but less safe, through the new Albania. While Serbia is still an inland State and as long as the present European system endures must remain to some extent economically dependent on Vienna and consequently politically dependent on Petersburg—it has, as a result of the war, acquired new internal resources and new external relations which should enable it to enter a new epoch of independent economic and political development. Compared with the advantages of this long step towards an independence of its two patrons which Serbia has gained by the war, the disadvantages, to be debited to the war, of a continuance of its dependence on the financial control of a European Commission is a small evil, if an evil at all. For the influence of the commission is a wholesome one, and, as has already been pointed out, it is due to its action that Serbia has been able to finance this war so successfully. Continued dependence on the Paris money market is a more serious disadvantage which has already been noticed.

Complete economic independence of the Serbian nation is a condition precedent to any progress in the extension of Serbian nationality to the neighbouring Serb peoples now under Teutonic or Magyar domination. Therefore the accession of territory to Serbia on the east from an economic point of view furthers the national development of Serbia towards the west in Croatia, Slavonia, and Bosnia-Herzegovina. But, as will be shown later, this economic advantage is only a small set-off against the disadvantage of Bulgar resentment and the danger of Austrian repression.

The price in blood and treasure paid by Serbia for these advantages seems exorbitant when considered by itself, and excessive even when compared with the considerable gains.[1] Serbia, like Greece, was fortunate in having a good supply of money in the country at the outbreak of war ; and more fortunate in that the population is mainly agricultural and

[1] Serbian losses are officially given as :

	Killed.	Died of Wounds.	Died of Disease.	Disabled.
War of Coalition . . .	5,000	1,000	7,000	18,000
War of Partition . . .	8,000	1,500	9,000	30,000

Total dead, 31,500 ; disabled, 48,000.

profited by the excellent harvest. In so far as Serbians are mercantile they deal in foodstuffs, especially meat, for which prices are at present unusually high. Even when tension between Vienna and Belgrade was at its highest, Berlin did not venture to close the German market to Serbian meat. Moreover, Russian patronage is not only represented by the acquisition of Monastir and central Macedonia, but is probably responsible for the greater facilities which Serbia has enjoyed in the Paris money market. All these favouring conditions have combined to bring Serbia through the war with less financial strain and economic exhaustion even than Greece.

The account of the war may be worked out summarily as follows, in so far as the factors permit of being estimated, and in so far as any figures are obtainable.

Putting the total actual cost of the Serbian share in the War of Coalition at £11,000,000 [1] and in the War of Partition at £4,000,000, the total £15,000,000 will probably cover the outlay. Of this about £2,000,000 has been paid out of surpluses and economies, and Serbia, with the help of the Petersburg patronage, was given precedence of the other Balkan States in obtaining a war loan. This concession was, however, obtained by Serbia only at the cost of accepting the principle of liability for a share in the Turkish Debt.

So far as economics can be separated from politics in Serbia, the war account seems likely in the long run to show a profit |; but the War of Partition has left Serbia in so precarious

---

[1] For the purposes of the Paris Commission the Serbian Government estimated the total cost of the Turkish War at about £23,000,000. The estimate included the following items :

	Mill. frcs.
Ammunition and usage	25·43
Requisition of beasts and carts	4·1
Horses and mules	4·5
Railway transport	2·9
Maintenance of prisoners	16
Repatriation of Turkish refugees	2
Losses of Serbian subjects	2
Relief	5
Rebuilding of ruined villages	20

a position politically that it is difficult to say what is the real value of assets that look large on paper.

Vae victis in a Balkan war; and when we come to the war account of Bulgaria, we pass from the winnings of the victors to the woes of the vanquished. At the end of the War of Coalition, however, Bulgaria could have shown an account no less favourable than that of Serbia. With the whole of Thrace and with eastern Macedonia up to the Vardar and the Struma, Bulgaria would have obtained two districts (that of the silk industries of Adrianople and that of the tobacco industry round Kavalla) which are of the first value and fertility, being populated by Greeks, Turks, and Bulgars in about equal proportions. With the Turks the Bulgars get on well, and the Greeks would have accepted Bulgar civil government though they would have been a restless element. But these two districts were united by a third, consisting of impassable mountain ranges and a marshy coast—the former inhabited by the intractable Bulgar-Moslem Pomaks, the latter almost uninhabitable. It is this strip to which the Bulgar share has now been reduced. It is indeed a poor remnant; for with the exception of the Greek district of Xanthi, representing a quarter of the tobacco lands resigned by the victorious Greeks at one end, and the Moslem district of Gumuldjina, with its fraction of the silk industry, renounced by the victorious Turks at the other, the Bulgar acquisition represents perhaps the least desirable district in the whole peninsula—a most unpromising province of mountain, marsh, and Moslems. As an access to the sea its natural difficulties and disadvantages will tax heavily even so capable a race as its new owners. No doubt engineers can take a railway over or through even such triple barriers as those of the Despoto Dagh and of the Rhodope, and can make deep-water ports out of shallow bays such as those of Karagatch and Dedeagatch; but the Bulgar estimate for a line from the Maritza valley between Philippopolis and Seimenli by way of Haskovo Mastanlu

and Gumuldjina to Port Lagos is one million sterling and
three years for construction—which is probably an underestimate.   But before even this small sum is raised and
Bulgaria finally decides to develop commercially its present
unattractive Aegean littoral, a turn in the political wheel
may decide Sofia to risk trying to recover the natural outlet
by the Mesta and Kavalla.   Meantime, the Pomaks, whose
resistance was broken by severe handling during the early
campaign against the Turks, will, under the tolerant self-
government allowed them at present, become a factor of
future importance in the fighting strength of Bulgaria; though
economically their value will long remain insignificant.

The transfer to Bulgaria of the small triangle of Bulgar
hill country on the Black Sea coast is of little economic
importance.   It will, however, improve economic relations
between Bulgaria and Turkey by reducing the political
friction due to Bulgar population being left under Turkish
rule.   It makes, however, but a poor set-off against the broad
belt ceded to Roumania in the north, including the important
town of Silistria and a mixed population, largely Bulgar.
On the whole, from the point of view of immediate economic
advantage, the territorial changes resulting from the war
would seem for the present to have taken from Bulgaria
with one hand as much as they have given with the other.

When we come to consider the charges with which the
war has burdened Bulgaria, we find a debit total as enormous
as the credit total is insignificant.   The one redeeming
feature is the clearness and candour with which the situation
is put before the country by the Government, and the
courage and competence with which both country and
Government are facing their obligations.   The direct outlay
of the War of Coalition estimated on the same basis as in the
case of Greece and Servia must be put at about £20,000,000,[1]

---

[1] The following estimates are based on the official figures for the War
of Coalition submitted to the Paris Commission.   The same discount
must be made as in the case of the Greek data.

to which another £8,000,000 must be added for the War of Partition. Before the war the funded debt was about £25,000,000 and the floating debt £2,250,000 ; so that the direct cost of the war will more than double the funded debt, and the indirect cost may well eventually treble it. Of this new debt, the heaviest item is the requisitions, divided among some half-million families and totalling about £12,000,000, and these will be dealt with by a 6 per cent. internal loan. Another £16,000,000 had to be raised as soon as possible abroad by a foreign loan and in this the prospects of Bulgaria were poorer than any other Balkan State, or even than Turkey, all of them more favoured by Paris for political reasons. Bulgaria could only count for immediate

		Mill. frcs.
1.	Maintenance of 620,567 men at 1·40 frc. per diem . .	221·0
2.	Maintenance of 216,731 animals at 2·20 frcs. per diem .	121·0
3.	Clothing at 100 frcs.	62·0
4.	Equipment at 60 frcs.	37·0
5.	Artillery, 50 per cent. deterioration and ammunition .	63·0
6.	Infantry	60·0
7.	Cavalry, 75 per cent. deterioration	41·5
8.	Engineers, 75 per cent. deterioration	18·0
9.	Medical, 75 per cent. deterioration	12·0
10.	Transport, reckoned at ordinary receipts of railways for 8½ months	16·8
11.	Requisitions, 30 per cent. of 50,000 waggons and 50 per cent. of 216,731 beasts	58·6
12.	Remounts, total loss	14·8
13.	Hospitals	33·7
14.	Miscellaneous . . . . (or nearly £29,000,000, which with other items is made up to a total of nearly £31,000,000)	2·0
15.	Pensions £20 yearly for 20 years to families of 29,711 privates = 14,855,500 yearly, or at 5 per cent. a capital sum of	372,919,199
16.	Pensions £120 yearly for 20 years to families of 313 officers = 939,000 yearly or a capital charge of . . .	23,571,501
17.	Pensions £12 yearly for 30 years to families of disabled, say 10 per cent. of killed = 2,600,400 yearly or a capital charge of	75,379,953

471,860,653
or nearly £19,000,000

This makes a total cost of the War of Coalition to Bulgaria of no less than £50,000,000, and on the same scale and making the necessary omissions for the second war, this would be raised to about £65,000,000, without allowing for the damage due to the various invasions. The total losses over the war may well amount to £75,000,000, a vast burthen on so small a State.

relief in the financial support of Vienna, itself emerging from
a severe financial tension; but at the time of the Treaty
of Bucharest, in the crisis in the fate of Bulgaria when
ruin seemed imminent, Vienna could supply only £1,250,000
drawn from as many as ten banks. Bulgaria had been at
a disadvantage financially even before the war, as it began
war without a cash balance such as Greece and Serbia had,
and with the proceeds of the sale of Treasury bills to France
and Russia for £2,750,000 and £1,000,000 respectively. All
the same, Bulgarian credit has been maintained, and not only
have all obligations to foreign creditors been met punctually
in spite of pessimistic prognostications, but the Bulgar
moratorium was ended at the appointed time without prolongation as in the case of Greece and Serbia. Were the
market for Balkan loans more general—that is to say, were
London and New York interested as well as Paris—the
Bulgarian loan would probably rank first rather than last.
As it is, overtures to America having failed, the Bulgar loan
will probably be taken up in Berlin.[1]

Even the large totals mentioned above cannot represent
more than a small proportion of the indirect loss to Bulgaria
from these wars. For Bulgaria was fighting with its full
national force from beginning to end, and finally suffered
invasion from no less than four different quarters. It would
be impossible to estimate the losses caused by Greeks and
Serbs on the southern and western frontiers, and by Roumanians and Turks in the north and east. The economic
effect of the Bulgar war losses in any community less capable
of remedying them would be appalling. The death or disablement of one-twentieth of the male population, and those
in the prime of life, with the destruction of a fifth of the
plant of the principal national industry—the carts and cattle

---

[1] A Bulgar loan of £20,000,000 was promised by Germany in return for
concessions as to the construction of the Haskovo railway and port with
other considerations. But it is doubtful now whether Germany will be
able to carry out the contract.

used for agriculture—would cripple for a time any community; even allowing for replacement by female labour, by Macedonian refugees, and during the war itself by prisoners. The pensions resulting from such losses, allowing £20 a year for privates and £100 for officers, would alone make an annual charge of over £500,000, though the providence of the Government in paying insurance premiums in foreign companies on behalf of its soldiers may relieve the nation of some of this burden. On the other hand, the amount allowed in the footnote for pensions by no means represents the loss to an agricultural country of between fifty and sixty thousand labourers, and the loss to a young civilization of four to five hundred educated men.

On the other hand, there are compensating circumstances which will make the recovery of Bulgaria in all probability sensationally rapid. The loss of male life is of less importance to a country which with Serbia heads the list for excess of male over female population. As the normal increase of population is 30,000 per annum, it is reckoned that in twenty years the present ratio of the sexes will be restored. Moreover, in a few years' time the 100,000 Macedonian refugees which at present burden the country's resources, about half of them being in receipt of relief, will have been assimilated and will have become productive. In the second place, the social conditions in Bulgaria are such as to minimize the after-effect of the shock to the system. The manufactures of Bulgaria employ only some 8,000 hands, even the agricultural industry is on a small and simple scale, for not one-half per cent. of the proprietors own more than 50 acres. The harvest of 1912 having been got in, the whole male population could without difficulty devote itself to the business of making war. The harvest of 1913 was saved successfully in spite of the claims of war on labour, thanks to a very favourable season. There has been a considerable rise in prices in Bulgaria, which is chiefly owing to the loss of transport both rail and road, and to the scarcity of money, not to any permanent loss of productive power. The Bulgar peasant will in future have to bear a heavier burden of taxation, but even so it will not be anywhere near the load which retards the development of some rural populations and drives them into emigration. Bulgaria will still be more lightly burdened in this respect than her neighbours. The most serious item of European war—business disturbance and social shock—have not affected Bulgaria appreciably, for though the country has emerged economically from the condition of High Albania where war is the normal industry of the men, and agriculture of the women, it is not yet so far from that condition that it cannot restore it for a time without permanent damage. Thirdly, although the cost of the wars has been far heavier than in Greece and Serbia, a larger proportion of it will probably be borne directly by the present generation—the payment of requisitions out of foreign loans, as has been done in Serbia, is a form of finance which has considerable disadvantages. Finally, and first of all in importance, Bulgar nationalism is in its most vital stage—just beginning to develop a national culture and not yet severed from the soil.

> Fortunatus et ille deos qui novit agrestes.
> Illum non populi fasces, non purpura regum
> Flexit, et infidos agitans discordia fratres,
> Aut coniurato descendens Dacus ab Histro.

For the sake of completeness, the economic effects of the participation by Roumania in the War of Partition must be briefly examined. The speculative risks of an investment in war, even when it seems a ' soft thing ', are well exemplified in this case. Roumania had, it seemed, merely to march an army into Bulgaria, dictate to Sofia how much Bulgarian territory it would annex, and march out again. This was satisfactorily accomplished, but the victorious troops brought away cholera with them, which kept them mobilized for several months. In consequence the country was involved in a cost in life and money of about as much as the cost of a contested campaign. Deaths from cholera in the army alone numbered 1,500, and in the civil population were over 3,000, and the war expenditure amounted after all to over £8,000,000, a sum not so very far short of what the glories and gains of the War of Coalition cost to Serbia. These costs have been covered by a 4½ per cent. gold loan for £9,900,000, floated successfully in England, Germany, Holland, Belgium, and Roumania. It will be observed that Roumania has successfully freed herself from the financial bondage of Paris. The territory annexed from Bulgaria consists of 8,000 square kilometres, and contains an important town, Silistria, with a very mixed but amenable population of over 300,000, so that the new revenues should be able to meet the extra debt charge, and leave to profit any further economic resources that may be developed—less any further political reactions that may result from the annexation.

There remains only Montenegro, a State in which the economics of peace hardly come into consideration. The Ambassadors' Conference decided that Montenegro should receive a war loan in reward for compliance with its decisions as to Scutari, but the amount has not yet been fixed.

In examining the economic effects of the war on the Ottoman Empire, we find we have to deal with two questions—what was the economic effect of the Ottoman Government pressing on the War of Coalition, and, secondly, what was the effect of its participating in the War of Partition. These two enterprises must be kept distinct, as in respect of the Turks the two wars were differentiated in a way which they were not in regard to the Allies. The Greeks were really pursuing the same enterprise without change of front, and almost without a check, from the time they crossed the Turkish frontier until they came up against the Bulgar frontier; while the Bulgars changed front and charged into the War of Partition as an immediate and almost inevitable sequel of their original challenge to Turkey.

But, with the Turks, the two advances from the capital, one in August 1912, the other a year later, were distinct undertakings, each of which must be judged on its own economic merits. The first was an altogether unsuccessful attempt to maintain Turkish rule over Roumelia, the second was a successful attempt to restore it over Thrace. The general opinion is that the losses that had to be cut in the War of Coalition were economically disastrous to the Empire, and that they have only been retrieved, to some extent, by the profits picked up in the War of Partition. If, however, it can be shown that Adrianople with the larger part of Thrace was not worth a military promenade in the summer of 1914, it will follow that the policy of the Young Turks when they renewed war in the spring was a mistake, and that the provocations by which they united the Balkans against them in war was the greatest mistake of all. Estimating the items of the war account for the Empire is, in some respects, harder, in others easier, than in the case of the Allies. It is harder to establish the items of direct cost, such as loss of human and animal life, because such figures as are obtainable are only guesses, even if they are from official sources. It is easier, on the other hand, to estimate the economic results of territorial changes in the case of the Turks, because, as regards the European provinces, they can be considered as losing no more than they were receiving in revenue, and gaining all that they were spending on the defence. The economic value of Thrace to the Turks is represented by its revenues and by any surplus of them that may remain for imperial purposes; the economic value of it to the Bulgars lies in its resources and the potential national developments they may contain. The restoration to Turkish imperial rule of lands available for the national development of such a progressive State as Bulgaria means a loss to the economy of Europe. It is the same case of conflict between right of exclusion and right of expropriation that makes land tenure a perennial source of international and internal contention. Owing to the far greater value of this accommodation land for Bulgaria than it could have for Turkey, Bulgaria could, economically speaking, allow an outlay for the acquisition of it through war, far greater than Turkey could properly afford for its retention.[1] Hence, the recovery of Thrace by Turkey means a state of unstable economic equilibrium, which will probably, sooner or later, end in the recapture of it by Bulgaria through war. War, in such a case as this, may be compared, economically, to the compulsory powers for expropriation without which no new enterprise could establish itself against the resistance of vested interests and *vis inertiae.*

But apart from the question whether Turkey can retain Thrace and Adrianople, was it under present conditions a profitable investment, so to say, to resume possession of this province as soon as the political position permitted ?

First of all, taking the last available information for a normal time of peace before the revolution, we find that under the supervision of the International Commission, the local budget of the European vilayets showed a total deficit of nearly half a million.[2] Again, looking at the total receipts and expenditures, we find that the receipts for the whole of Roumelia, including the Archipelago, are only 14 per cent.

---

[1] The population of the vilayet of Adrianople is 69 to the square mile, that of the adjacent Bulgar province of Eastern Roumelia with Philippopolis is 140, or just double. When we come to compare Old Bulgaria with Macedonia, the difference is even greater. The fertile vilayet of Kossovo has 82, the mountainous province of Kustendil 249, or more than treble.

[2] BUDGET OF THE THREE ROUMELIAN PROVINCES IN 1324 (1908), WHICH WAS THE LAST BUDGET OF THE INTERNATIONAL COMMISSION.

	£T.
Local receipts (excluding revenues ceded to the Debt Administration and Customs)	1,900,000
Customs	500,000
Total	2,400,000
Local civil expenditure	1,340,000
Balance available for local military expenses	1,060,000
Total of local military expenses	1,488,000
Deficit	428,000

of the total revenue,[1] whereas the expenditure on Roumelia is at least 26 per cent. of the total.

Next, considering the matter from the point of view of profit and loss in the human resources of the Turkish nation, the total population lost to the Empire by the Treaty of London was about five millions. But of these, at most half a million could have been considered as possessed of any spirit of Ottoman nationality, and of this half-million probably a quarter-million would have emigrated to Anatolia— the remaining quarter-million were after all for the most part

[1] The following figures have been taken from the official bulletin for the financial year 1909–10 (1325), before disturbances were serious :

	£T Revenue.	Percentage Total Revenue.	Percentage Total Revenue, less that collected centrally.
Asiatic vilayets . . .	14,703,910	56·03	65·18
Vilayet Constantinople with Tchataldja . . .	2,695,110	10·27	11·95
Vilayet Adrianople . . .	1,123,735	4·28	4·98
	18,522,655	70·58	82·01
European vilayets . . .	3,672,273	13·99	16·28
Tripoli and Benghasi . .	362,833	1·38	1·61
Central Administration . .	3,686,708	14·05	
	26,244,579	100·0	100·0

(b) The following are the separate revenues from the European vilayets, calculated on a different basis, and including customs mostly under Salonica :

£T.

Adrianople 1,227,237
Salonica 2,026,894
Monastir 655,010
Kossovo 804,351
Janina 407,545
Archipelago 250,000

5,371,137

(c) The following show the revenues collected by the Debt Administration in the vilayets of Roumelia and the Archipelago :

£T.

For service of the Debt and Railway guarantees . 1,200,000
For the Ottoman Government 80,000

1,280,000

not Turks—moreover, many of them were in the Gumuldjina corner of Thrace, which under no conditions could be recovered from the Bulgars. Consequently, in all probability the recovery of every Ottoman national in Adrianople vilayet has cost Turkish nationality the life of at least one Anatolian Turk, and the retention of him will cause the life of another to be expended either in battle or in barracks. Whereas, had the Roumelian Turk been left to emigrate to Anatolia, where there is plenty of room, he and his two Anatolian guards would have represented a threefold gain. The problem of Turkish national prosperity will never be solved until it is remembered that the Empire on either side of the Straits is an equation with the factors on the western side all *minus*, and becoming *plus* only when transferred to the eastern side. When this has been done, Turkey will become a living nation : until it is done, it will remain a dying Empire.

No doubt, if Thrace, instead of being an annexe of the Ottoman Empire, could ever really be assimilated to the Turkish nation by ' extermination' of alien elements, it would be worth running at a loss for many years. But history has shown that Turkey in Europe can never become European Turkey, and that the Moslems in Europe, being Moslemized Europeans for the most part, can be better administered, and even more readily assimilated, by European nations than by an Ottoman Government; while the true Turks that cannot abide European ways emigrate into Anatolia, where their superior culture raises the general level of agriculture and civilization.[1] In short, by losing territory in Europe, the Turkish nation concentrates its national forces, and, if anything, gains in the process.[2]

[1] It will be sufficient to note the present prosperous condition of the ' Mouhadjirs' who emigrated to Anatolia during the latter part of last century from Roumelia, and of the ' Moraites' who settled in Adalia from Coron and Modon after the Greek emancipation, and contrast it with the disappearance of the Circassian and Moslem colonies transported from Asia to Europe.

[2] This doctrine of ' concentration' is none the less true for having been preached to the Turks as consolation for cessions of territory for

As things are, the Empire will continue to spend almost as much to retain Thrace and to recover Macedonia as it did to retain Macedonia. Whereas, bounded on the west by an international and inviolable frontier, such as the Treaty of London would have furnished had it been left to become the public law of Europe, Turkey might have finally turned its face to the East, where its national development and national destiny alone lie. There might then have been an end of the folly of conscripting Turkish peasantry by the thousand, and thereby checking their development and crushing them with taxation, merely in order that the anti-Ottoman non-Moslem populations of Europe may pay the interest on foreign loans through the international debt administration at Stamboul instead of through that at Athens or Belgrade. By such folly does war work against the true interests of nationalism.

It may be objected that an empire that can develop so much energy for the defence of its frontiers cannot after all be utterly decadent economically. The explanation is that the forces and resources it is exploiting for its imperial purpose are the vital energies and economies of the young nations it contains, and more especially of the Turkish nation. This becomes very clear if, after examining the effects of the bloodless participation in the War of Partition, and of the unpunished breach of the Treaty of London, we go a step further back and inquire into the economic effects of the great effort made by Turkey in renewing the War of Coalition, and breaking up the first London Conference. This effort, engineered by the Committee of Union and Progress, took Europe by surprise as much as did that more famous exploit of the Committee of Public Safety a century before. The provinces of the Ottoman Empire always seem to be depopulated, and its finances depleted without prospect of recovery; and it is not the first time that it has con-

about a century. It is especial anathema to the Imperialist Young Turk of European extraction.

founded all calculations by the innumerable Asiatic hosts that it can still put in the field and the inexhaustible European credit that it can still command to put them there. The former can be explained by the fact that the whole area of Anatolia, Armenia, Syria, North Arabia, and Mesopotamia can still be drawn on for the defence of the Empire in the name of Islam. So irresistible still is the appeal to militant Islam that the willingness of these Asiatics to have their lives wasted in war is subject to no such checks as restrict the use of civilized armies, and such as we find beginning to work in Bulgaria in the War of Partition. So inexhaustible is the supply of men that still can be commanded by the Empire, and so unquestioning is their militarism, that it is well, perhaps, that the factor of money becomes annually more important. The imperial command of credit can only be explained by the access that the Empire has already had for a century to the accumulated capital of Western civilization, first in France, then in Great Britain, now in Germany—perhaps some day in America. The more backward that imperial administration remains, and the lower that civilization is in consequence among the Moslem majority of the population, the more ready will the latter be to take arms in the imperial cause and against their own national interests. Similarly the more bankrupt the imperial finances become, the more ready are the moneylenders and armament firms of Europe to bolster its credit so as to save their bad money by sending the good money of the public after it. It is often easier for a bankrupt to raise money for extravagance than it is for a business man to get it for a sound enterprise. But in these Balkan wars the Empire came very near exhausting the supplies of Asiatic fanatics and of European financiers.

It has been said that the War of Partition cost the winners, Greece and Serbia, disproportionately dear, and prevented them from recovering their full financial independence, which they might have done as a result of the War of Coalition by itself. The same is even more true of Turkey, for the Empire had even earlier exhausted its easily available reserves of men and money, and had begun to exploit resources vital to its development and independence. This 'exhaustion' point was passed when the Young Turks broke up the First Conference of London in December 1912 and resumed the war; whereas, with the Allies, even in the case of Bulgaria,[1] it may be put six months later, at the Second Conference of London in May 1913.

The conditions under which war was resumed by Turkey in the New Year of 1913 are interesting in themselves as showing how primitive societies can continue to make war under conditions that would have imposed a peace of exhaustion on more civilized societies. As civilization advances the exhaustion point in war is more easily reached; and in dealing with wars between primitive peoples the mistake is often made of expecting exhaustion to take effect as it would in a war between communities of elaborate economic development. In Turkey the exhaustion point of expenditure of male population and money can be put some time in the first months of 1913.[2]

[1] The Bulgarian Government in December announced that it could, with the resources then available, continue the war for six months.

[2] Dividing the War of Coalition into the two phases of (a) the great field operations in Thrace and Macedonia, and (b) the secondary siege operations of Tchataldja with Gallipoli, Adrianople, Janina, and Scutari, we find that in the first phase the whole Turkish line of defence, men and material, had been practically annihilated as a fighting factor, and two-thirds of it destroyed as an economic factor. The entire destruction as a fighting force in the field of the two eastern and western armies of Thrace, and of the two northern and southern armies of Macedonia, the temporary loss of some 200,000 prisoners, and the total loss by death or disablement, mostly from disease and desertion, of as many more, would have exhausted the fighting energies of most European States. But in the few weeks' armistice, during the Conference of London, the army of Tchataldja was raised from the leavings of the Thracian armies and fresh Asiatic levies to a strength of some 150,000, while the army of Gallipoli, another new Asiatic force of over 50,000 men, was entrenched on the other bridge-head leading from Asia. Within two months the two lost armies of Thrace had thus been reconstructed and re-equipped. Though the men were drawn from remoter and less warlike races, such as

A peace in December, which would have avoided raising the second line, with its drain on those elements of the Turkish population which could least be spared—or, failing that, a peace in May, which would have spared many thousands of lives by sending back both prisoners and effectives to the fields three months sooner—such peace would have been an economic gain to the Empire, for which the subsequent recovery of Adrianople can be no adequate equivalent. It may indeed be asserted with some confidence that the effort to put the army of Tchataldja into the field and to keep it there for two months exhausted the Empire—first, of all available Anatolian peasants, for the proportion of less valuable Syrian and Arab conscripts increased with each reinforcement; secondly, of all farm animals as far south as Smyrna, for when the army advanced to Adrianople in July 1913 it had to use camels; thirdly, of all available credit, for the interest on the Treasury bills issued in 1912 at rates up to 10 per cent. was not forthcoming in March, and there would have been no repudiation if more money could have been raised—fourthly, of all realizable assets, for, as will be seen later, everything that could be converted into cash had been pawned, from building sites in the Capital to the domains of the Sultan in Mesopotamia.

When we come to estimate the cost of the whole war to Turkey, we find ourselves in some difficulty as to what to assign to war in a State which has been of late administered in times of peace with as much concentration on military expenditure as if it had been at war. Thus, there has been a deficit of some £3,000,000 to £5,000,000 in an average revenue of about £27,500,000 since the revolution and the publication of the Budget. This deficit is fairly accountable to preparations for war; because the provision made

Syrians, Arabs, or Kurds, or from the less efficient ranks of the Turks, and though there was not quite so much modern machinery of equipment, yet this second line was almost as efficient as the first, and was far more effectively used.

for the army would be quite disproportionate for a force on a purely peace footing.[1] The deficit for the financial year ending March 1, 1914, approaches £11,000,000, in spite of a special war tax and war subscriptions which have brought in some, £17,500,000, and economies on ordinary outgoings.

As to the future, there seems little prospect of budgetary equilibrium, even though the war taxes have been prolonged for ten years, and even though the Powers have consented to allow the Empire to draw on the only revenue resource it has left by raising the import duty from 11 per cent. to 14 per cent. Thus, on top of a burden of funded and floating debt which already exceeded the economic strength of the country, and which represents almost entirely unproductive expenditure, between January 1, 1912, and September 1913, the Ottoman Government piled borrowings at ruinous rates to a total of at least £20,000,000, and probably nearer £25,000,000 —the equivalent of about a year's revenue, or an increase of the total debt by one-fifth. To this must be added £1,000,000 for arrears of interest at rates varying from 6 per cent. to 9 per cent.—another £4,000,000 for arrears of salaries, perhaps £12,000,000 for requisitions—and £3,000,000 still due on war materials. This altogether makes a floating war-debt of some £40,000,000 to £50,000,000, of which half at least had to be consolidated as soon as circumstances allowed.[2]

---

[1] In the Turkish Budget for 1910–11, the war estimates, including gendarmerie, were over £8,500,000, out of a total estimated expenditure of about £33,000,000, that is more than a quarter—and a larger proportion than even in France or Germany.

[2] The following statement represents the floating debt ascribable to the war, so far as it can be ascertained :

		£T.	
National Bank of Turkey	Feb. 14, 1912	1,650,000	Plus arrears of interest at 9 per cent. from March 13, 1913.
Ottoman Bank	May 2, 1912	1,540,000	Plus arrears of interest at 9 per cent.
	June 24, 1912	1,295,013	from April 16, 1913;
Tobacco monopoly	May 30, 1912	200,000	Plus arrears of interest at 9 per cent. from April 16, 1913.

It was not until April 1914 that Turkey succeeded in getting a loan of £32,000,000 from Paris—itself in severe financial embarrassment, caused largely by its heavy Balkan commitments. For this accommodation the Turkish nation have had to pay very heavily in railway and harbour concessions, and the security has cut deep into the independence of its Anatolian homeland,[1] while the extra taxation required to

		£T.	
Ottoman Bank and Deutsche Bank	April 29, 1912	300,000	Plus arrears of interest at 7 per cent. from April 16, 1913.
Deutsche Bank .	Aug. 26, 1912	33,000	
Treasury Bonds .	Feb. 1, 1912	5,500,000	
	Nov. 11, 1912	3,000,008	Plus interest at 7 per cent.
Lighthouse Administration	April 15, 1913	500,000	Plus interest at 7 per cent.
Tobacco monopoly .	Aug. 4, 1913	1,500,000	Plus interest at 6¼ per cent.
Administration of the Debt	May 22, 1913	200,000	
	June 17, 1913	200,000	
	July 10, 1913	100,000	Plus interest at 6 per cent.
	July 21, 1913	114,000	
	Aug. 2, 1913	500,000	
	Sept. 1, 1913	219,718	
Ottoman Bank	Aug 27, 1913	775,000	
Perrier Loan (for £4,000,000 nominal)	Dec. 15, 1913	2,000,000	
		22,624,739	

The loans obtained from the Tobacco Monopoly and the Lighthouse Administration should perhaps rather be classed as a sale of concessions, as the price paid for these advances was a continuation of the foreign monopolies, on terms very disadvantageous to Turkey. It is curious that the money with which Turkey was enabled to recover Thrace, in defiance of the decision of Europe, was obtained from two semi-European institutions, the Tobacco Monopoly and the Lighthouse Administration. This was, of course, merely a matter of business, as these enterprises took advantage of the urgent need of the Empire for ready money for their own advantage, and what the Empire did with the money was no responsibility of theirs. Whether the same may be said of the advances from the Administration of the Public Debt is a question.

[1] The loan negotiations covered the whole diplomatic field between France and Turkey. The status of French subjects in Turkey was regulated to the annihilation of Turkish ambitions of abrogating the privileged status of foreigners. In return, Paris agreed to a 4 per cent. increase of customs duties, and a tariff instead of *ad valorem* rates, as well as to various monopolies, to which London, Vienna, and Rome had already assented. Turkey further conceded to France the concession of the ports of Jaffa, Haifa, and Tripoli in Syria, and of Ineboli and Eregli on the

meet the charges is such as must cripple the productive power of a population already overtaxed.[1] If the Ottoman Government could have abandoned military adventure[2] to ' concentrate itself ' on the economic and political development of Asia Minor, the world would probably have been surprised at the sudden start that the new Turkish nation would have made in economic development when the latter was no longer retarded by political distractions. There are many symptoms indicating that the communities of the Empire are emerging from the stage of semi-civilization in which they have stagnated for centuries. Practical proof of this is found in the steady increase in revenue of late years in spite of incessant disturbances.[3] This improvement

Black Sea, as well as 1,250 miles of railway construction in Syria (Rayak-Ramleh) and in Anatolia (Samsun-Sivas-Erzindjan, Kharput-Angora, Van-Bitlis, and Boli-Havza). Moreover, the French abandoned the Bagdad Railway to the Germans by surrendering the £1,400,000 Bagdad stock held by French banks in return for rights in the 1910 loan to Turkey.

[1] ' Provisional ' fiscal legislation in force had, roughly speaking, doubled the rate of stamp duties, increased the land tax by one-half, the sheep and cattle tax with the income tax by one quarter, added a new succession duty of 10 per cent., and doubled the deductions from salaries for pensions, while reducing military pay.

[2] The first recovery of Ottoman credit after the establishment of peace was exploited in order to purchase the two Brazilian Dreadnoughts for £3,000,000 sterling. The prospect of the naval preponderance promised by the early delivery of these two vessels nearly brought about another war with Greece. This was prevented by the acquisition by Greece of two American battleships, and the Turkish Dreadnoughts have now, in consequence of the outbreak of war between Great Britain and Germany, presumably been commandeered by the former.

[3] The Ottoman revenues have, of late years, shown a steady increase, as is shown by the following figures, and this increase is expected by good authorities to continue after the war. ' I have no hesitation in affirming that the check in the steady improvement of the economic condition of the country for a number of years past is only temporary, and that in spite of the war and the financial straits of the Turkish Government there is every reason to believe that with peace assured the revenues will continue to show a steady increase.'—Sir A. Block, Report of Council of Ottoman Debt for the year 1913.

1908–9	£T25,176,793
1909–10	26,986,406
1910–11	28,239,366
1911–12	30,374,119

has been coincident with, and confirmed by, the real reforms in administration effected by the revolution. Since 1908 there has been, in spite of the disorganization and demoralization caused by civil and foreign war, a reform amounting to a re-establishment of principles of economy, efficiency, and energy in Ottoman administration. These two forces of Anatolian recovery and administrative reform would have sufficed to give the Turkish nation a good start ; but whether they can keep the Ottoman Empire going on militarist lines is doubtful. Even Young Turkish enthusiasm cannot keep an efficient administration with salaries unpaid, or an effective army with supplies in arrears. The Empire cannot be run on its present lines without further borrowings, and there will be no readiness in Paris or elsewhere to grant a loan unless some better security for peace be offered than at present exists.

Even as the Young Turks, by their centralizing imperialism, have brought self-government and separation within reach of the Albanians on the west of the Empire, and within sight of the Armenians on the east, even so by the extravagance of their militarism they may impose peace on the Empire by bringing its economic resources under control of foreign pacific interests. This control has already advanced considerably since the war, and has entered the phase of a partition between the Powers of the economic exploitation of the Empire.

The Young Turks adopted their policy of imperial regeneration by war with their eyes on Japan ; but they would do well now to turn them rather on Persia. A modern State must be a nation before it can become an Empire ; and the Young Turks, in order to retain or recover foreign dependencies, are engaged in pawning their national financial independence and economic integrity. Those advisers of Turkey who see in foreign financial and administrative control some guarantee against further dismemberment of the Empire by national movements are counsellors of ruin. No such foreign control ever checked a national movement. The foreign financial control of Macedonia, Crete, and Egypt was the beginning of the end of Ottoman rule there; and foreign control of Armenia or Syria will have the same result.

With the effect of war on the economic relations of western Europe with the Ottoman Empire, we come to a region where economics and politics are inextricably interwoven. Before even the wars of partition had resulted in territorial settlements as to Turkey in Europe between the Empire and the Balkan States, the Great Powers had already engaged in economic settlements between themselves and with the Ottoman Government involving the economic and political future of Turkey in Asia.

It does not come within the scope of this inquiry to trace the course of these economic wars of partition for Asia Minor. At one time Great Britain, France, and Russia were sole competitors—as they once were for Turkey in Europe. But of late Germany has taken the more prominent place. In order of value of financial and industrial investments France, Germany, and Great Britain now rank in ratio of 3 : 2 : 1.[1] Great Britain, however, still leads commercially, and this should give that Power an additional inclination against economic partition by means of railway and other developments financed out of the Customs. Russia also desires the maintenance of the economic *status quo* in Asia Minor for political reasons, because it cannot take its part in an economic partition for want of money power, and hopes for a military partition on the old basis of man power. There-

---

[1] According to itemized estimates published in the *Gazette Financière* of Constantinople the capital at present invested in the Empire by the three Powers in the funds, railways, and government concessions is represented by the following totals, in millions of francs :

	Funds.	Railways.	Concessions.	Total.
France	1,676	451	191	2,320
Germany . . .	902	336	42	1,465
Great Britain . . .	648	114	116	879

fore, in Asia Minor there is, in this respect, an Anglo-Russian interest for maintenance of the economic *status quo* which might have postponed the step towards economic partition, but for the recklessness with which the Young Turks have pawned themselves to France and pledged themselves to Germany.

For years before the Balkan wars both London and Petersburg had resigned themselves to German economic control of Asia Minor. Petersburg had already, as early as 1910, come to terms with Germany over its main enterprise, the Bagdad railway, and Paris and London had for various reasons now to do the same. A series of settlements have been, or are being, concluded, centring round this main enterprise of Germany.

Thus there has been a Franco-Turkish agreement, combined with Franco-Russian and Franco-German arrangements, by which, in return for a loan and for leave to raise the customs dues, Turkey assigns to France important railway and harbour concessions in Asia Minor and Syria, and agrees to a French arrangement with Germany for a delimitation of economic spheres in Asia Minor, and also agrees to a French arrangement with Russia to develop part of the northern sphere reserved for many years to that Power. The reason for this last deal is that Russia, having realized that development of its reserved region could no longer be postponed, has drawn France into it and across the main line of German economic expansion. A Russo-Turkish arrangement is also under negotiation by which Russia, in return for assent to an increase of the Customs— astutely reserved until all the other Powers had agreed— demands a representation on the Ottoman Debt administration, supervision of Armenian administration, and other advantages of a political character. Great Britain, who pays the piper in the customs, has only called a very small tune down in the Persian Gulf. An Anglo-Turkish agreement defines British and Ottoman political interests in that region; and an Anglo-German agreement determines British and

German economic interests there, especially as to the Bagdad railway. There only remains an Anglo-Italian agreement as to railway concessions in south-west Asia Minor in the neighbourhood of Adalia such as will permit Italy to evacuate the Dodekanese. We have, therefore, in these agreements, two main lines of politico-economic development, both antecedent in origin to the Balkan wars, but both greatly accelerated by their result. One is the gradual subordination of Turkish nationality to European—and principally German —economic enterprise : the other is the effort of the Triple Agreement to encircle and neutralize the German economic sphere by joining up their competitive spheres and heading it off from further expansion eastward. Thus we find the Bagdad railway as the main line of the great German economic expansion eastward, with Franco-Russian railway schemes cutting across it near its western end, and Anglo-Russian railway projects in Persia blocking its eastern end. The question which the Balkan wars have brought within sight is whether the Bagdad railway and the economic development it imports will assure to Germany such control of Asia Minor as was secured over Manchuria by the Russian railway ; or whether this economic control will be so countered and crossed by national ' democratic ' movements and international ' diplomatic ' moves that it will lead to no more than did the similar economic control over the Balkan Peninsula secured a half-century ago by Austria in the construction of the Oriental Railway to Constantinople. Austria has had to allow Anglo-Russian support of Balkan nationality movements to expel Austrian economic penetration finally from the Balkan Peninsula in this recent War of Coalition. Will Germany be in a similar situation in Asia Minor, say a century hence, and be suffering similar expulsion before an Armenian-Turkish-Arab Coalition ? [1]

[1] The sudden development of a European War of Coalition against Germany and Austria renders it less likely that Germany will be able to realize its schemes of economic expansion in Asia Minor. But the

For the present the immediate result of the Balkan Wars in Asia Minor seems to be a substitution of Western imperialism for that of Constantinople, effected in the guise of economic enterprises. Such economic enterprises bring with them political ' penetrations ', and they in turn may result in a partition among the Western Powers. But we have seen that the same process did not have this result in the Balkan Peninsula ; and Turks, Armenians, Circassians, Arabs, and Persians have as strong a national character and as marked a national culture as Bulgars, Roumanians, Serbs, Albanians, and Greeks. It is as easy nowadays to draw up partition schemes for Asia Minor as it was to plan the partition of the Balkan Peninsula a century ago ; but it is asserted here on the strength of political and historical analogy, that the Balkan Wars have accelerated extension eastward of the nationality movement, and have brought nearer, not a substitution of exploitation by western capital for exploitation by Constantinople, but rather a substitution of Asiatic nationalities for a declining Asiatic Empire. It is possible, therefore, that a remote result of these Balkan Wars, and of their subsidiary settlements, may be Wars of Coalition and Partition in Asia Minor a century hence. For even as the interventions of European Powers in Balkan affairs have changed the peaceful progress of nationality movements in the Balkans into periodic wars of liberation, so may the similar foreign interventions act in Asia Minor on similar national movements there. The work of war on Near-Eastern nationalism is likely to be much the same on both sides of the Dardanelles.

Passing to the economic results of the Balkan wars on Europe we find them to be of two kinds—the reactions on the external relations of European capital and enterprise with the Balkan peninsula and Asia Minor—and, secondly, the reactions on the internal conditions of European finance and industry.

foundations of German economic predominance there have been too firmly established to be ruined by anything short of a very complete collapse of Germany's position in Europe.

It is reactions of the former kind which we have seen at work at Bucharest and again in Asia Minor with somewhat sinister significance. It was the eagerness of capitalists and concessionaires in the great lending Powers to exploit the situation created by the war that confused and falsified the lines on which the belligerents might otherwise have worked out a more permanent peace. It was the ' diplomatic ' interventions of imperialist interests, either military or monetary, that displaced or diverted the ' democratic ' influences that were directing the course of events into an equitable equilibrium. The cost of these interventions has in some cases equalled that of war, and their economic and political effects have been no less striking than if war had been declared. To choose two only as examples : it was Austrian military opposition that drove Serbia out of Scutari and into Monastir, and it was French monetary support that brought Turkey back into Thrace. The economic effect on the Austrian Empire of the mobilization required for this purpose was more disastrous than the effect of active participation in the wars on any of the Allies. The Austrian budget estimated the cost of this mobilization at £16,500,000, or about what it cost Greece to double its territory and population, while the loss to the national economy of the financial crisis through which Vienna passed as a consequence of this intervention can only be guessed at. The list of bankruptcies alone shows that a war scare and a financial stringency may be more economically expensive to a modern capital than a six months' campaign, ending with an invasion, to such a primitive community as Bulgaria. Then taking the case of France, we find the Balkan commitments of Paris contributing to a financial crisis there which is none the less severe for having been successfully survived, but which by the time it is liquidated will probably have caused as heavy a drain on French thrift as a campaign in Morocco.

But the losses which these wars have imposed on Europe are not limited to those due to deliberate interventions. It is not so long ago that two nations could make war on each other with very little disturbance of their economic system, and with no disadvantage at all to those of neighbouring States. Indeed, it was then possible for third parties to profit by the preoccupation of rivals at war with one another. Third parties have even fomented wars between competitors for overseas territory or commerce and profited thereby. But nowadays, when nations go to war, it becomes the one concern of the Powers ruling the world to localize the war politically and economically as far as possible, so as to limit the loss with which they are threatened by the disturbance. A disturbance of the equilibrium established in all the various conditions of the European political and economic system has become so serious that the economic interests of the world are opposed on the whole to war and repress its outbreak or restrict its operations whenever possible. None the less, when minor States go to war, it is still almost as difficult to prevent them causing direct disturbance to the working of the main lines of commerce, or the wants of the main centres of population, as it is to impose on them respect for the rules of civilized warfare. Take, for instance, disturbance to neutral shipping and food supply, which one would suppose should be easily secured from disturbance by a war in the Balkan peninsula. But the war involved naval operations which closed the Dardanelles, thereby causing heavy losses for detention and demurrage of shipping and a dislocation of the trade of two main staples for the supply of Western civilization—grain and oil. It is difficult to indicate and impossible to estimate the loss caused to Europe by war conditions in the Levant ; for who could even guess at the cost of having the British bank rate raised from 4 to 5 per cent., as it was at the outbreak of war in October, or of having capital and gold tied up for months in unremunerative reserves, as it has been on the Continent ?[1]

[1] The Balkan War decided the Bank of England to raise its rate from 4 per cent. to 5 per cent. on October 17. (Annual Report, Messrs. Montagu & Co.)

The political effects of war can now be localized in most cases, because the conflict of armies and the conquest of provinces is becoming a less important process in national development than competition between capitalists and the consolidation of national credit. But the economic effects of war cannot be confined to the belligerents, and isolated, because it is now no more possible to charge the total cost of any war on the communities responsible than it is possible to charge any particular locality of a civilized community with the total cost of a particular local disturbance. Any levy made with this object is nowadays shifted and distributed at once by economic laws whose workings are not under political control, until the economic effect of the tax may well become the opposite to its political purpose. Thus the loss by war wastage is distributed over Europe by the borrowings of the belligerent Governments, which withdraw so much of the accumulated capital of Europe from productive investment elsewhere. These war borrowings have more than one evil connected with them. They make it possible to feed a war fever which otherwise would have burnt itself out by local economic exhaustion; and, owing to the close connexion between international money-lending and armament merchants, a proportion of the proceeds of the loan must generally be taken in the products of the latter. It is, on an international scale, the old profit of the Jew who made the spendthrift, ruined by costly luxuries, take more wine or pictures as part proceeds of the advance for which he was pawning his patrimony. But occasionally such transactions are a bad business, not only for the victim but also for the usurer; and they can scarcely ever be beneficial to the community. In the case of the Balkan wars financiers were hard hit by the prolongation of hostilities; and the enormous unproductive war expenditure of the year 1913, to which the Balkan wars were the most considerable contributor, made a load of undigested debt which will long lie heavy on the activities and energies of the European economic system. It is at least a slight advantage, that until this load is liquidated, militarist borrowers and armament brokers must be somewhat hampered in their operations in the Balkan Peninsula.

The amount of material and mental capital now invested in the manufacture and marketing of armaments makes this interest one of the most powerful political influences in the world. Though the business is even more international in character than most of the great industries of the world, unlike them it depends for its profits, like any other insurance business, on the prospect of warlike disturbance and not on the promise of peaceful development. Therefore, unlike other industries, it is found in international relations associating with the militarist faction and always ready to use its very considerable control of parties and of the press in order to exploit the alarmist and chauvinist possibilities of any new political development.

It does not indeed seem probable that without the alarmist agitation fomented by armament interests and militarist influences the political changes in the Balkan peninsula would have caused the general augmentation of armaments in Europe that followed the Balkan wars. The political changes were doubtless important, but they were enormously exaggerated. The Balkan alliance was presented to the German public as a pan-orthodox confederacy throwing the whole united weight of the Balkan States on the Slav side in the presumably impending Teuto-Slav race war. The extension of Austro-German economic predominance in Roumania and in the Ottoman Empire was presented to the Russian public as a walling-off of Russia from the rest of the civilized world. Though the Balkan alliance collapsed, and Roumania was detached from its German allegiance, the impression remained. When the war finally ended, both Germans and Russians were supplied with pretexts and subjected to pressure so that an increase of armaments might be secured. It seems to the author that the competitive increases of the Russian and German forces, followed by that of the French, were quite as much an economic consequence of the business enterprise of the armament interests as a political consequence of any change in the balance of power, or a moral consequence of any increase in public apprehension of aggression.

§ 23. POLITICAL RESULTS
(a) In the Balkans

The political results of wars can be divided into those which are democratic and those which are diplomatic in character—those which affect national development, and those which affect international interdependence. The former are the more important and enduring, but the latter are generally the more immediate and sensational. No more important or enduring consequences of any war could be found than the closing of a chapter in the history of the European nationality movement and the opening of the chapter of the same movement in Asia. Compared with this, the immediate diplomatic consequences of the war to the equilibrium of balanced armaments on which European peace depends are significant, but for the present not sensational.[1] The political results of the Balkan wars will therefore be considered first of all in relation to their internal effect on the democracies of the Balkans, and then in relation to the national movement in the Balkans as a whole. Thereafter the results of the wars on the European diplomatic situation will be more briefly dealt with.

The most notable political result of these wars in respect of the development of the nationality movement has been the formal recognition of Arnaut nationality in an Albanian State. This has been the consequence of a happy combination of democratic and diplomatic forces; though the diplomatic origins of the new nation are so obvious that perhaps they have bulked too large in public opinion.

[1] They have since become sensational enough.

It is true that considerations of Balkan balance of power largely influenced Vienna and Rome in combining for the creation of Albania. In both capitals the authorities on naval and military strategy would not hear of Serbia coming down to the Adriatic or of Greece coming up to it. In both capitals the experts in diplomatic combinations were pleased with the idea of inserting between Greece and Serbia a State hostile to both and friendly to Bulgaria and Turkey. While London, for both diplomatic and democratic reasons, was ready to support an Albanian policy, so as to combine the conferring of a favour on the Triple Alliance with a confession of faith in the principle of nationality. But, all the same, the real driving force in the creation of this new nation was 'democratic', and derived from the *de facto* independence of Albania. While the creation of Albania was the only political result of the Balkan wars which seems to be unquestionably satisfactory both on abstract principles and in the practical application given to them, yet, curiously enough, the Concert has been more criticized and ridiculed for it than for its undoubted failures in Thrace, the Dobrudscha and Macedonia. Yet such criticisms are not only unjust but unjustifiable ; for, in establishing formally the independence of Albania, the Balkan wars and the ambassadors' conference created nothing ; while they did, by recognizing a fact, prevent a century of warfare and waste. For if the independence of Albania was a fact, it was none the less one that was much obscured ; and the principle of Albanian nationality would have taken years in securing any form of political recognition but for the prompt acceptance and practical application of it by the Concert.

While Albania had a large measure of real independence, it lacked many of the recognized signs and symbols of Balkan nationality. Thus religion had played a large part in the national movement of other Balkan peoples, but the Albanians had Islamized to an extent which left them without the religious rallying cry. This islamization was really, however, no evidence of subordination to, or submergence in, the Ottoman Empire, but the contrary. The Albanian clan Islamized because the chief had done so, and in order to keep the clan community intact : the chief Islamized in order to keep his lands and position : whereas, in the more fertile and accessible regions of Macedonia, the feudal chiefs were replaced by Turks, their feudal vassals reduced to rayahs, and all independence suppressed. Therefore, when a Macedonian Bulgar or Serb Islamized into a Pomak or Bosniak he became an Ottoman, and the most fanatical supporter of the Oriental despotism without retaining his national character and consciousness—as did the Albanian. Spiritually there was little difference between Albanian Mohammedanism and Catholicism, while even ceremonially the two had much in common. Moreover, in the Bektashi sect, the Albanian had gone further towards adopting a peculiar national faith than any other Near Eastern, or indeed European, people. Much the same thing is observable in the political relations of Albania to the Empire. More fortunate in this respect than Greece, Albania was able to combine a sufficient measure of local autonomy with a very satisfactory share in the imperial authority. Having no racial affinities or political associations with enemies of the Empire as had the other Balkan races, there was no danger in leaving a nucleus of Albanian independence in the mountain valleys or in giving Albanians considerable power at Constantinople. Therefore it came about that in the eye of international law Albania, with its primitive but very pregnant social and political institutions, was considered as integral a part of the Ottoman Empire as Thrace ; whereas, in common knowledge, one-third of the country was as independent of the Turks as Montenegro.[1] As a matter of international fact Albania was more independent than Bulgaria or Serbia, though a fiction of international law

[1] In ten of the thirty kazas no taxes were paid to the Empire, and no Turkish official would have ventured there otherwise than by invitation.

denied it all existence as a ' moral person ' for want of recognition by Europe or the Empire. Yet Albanian indepen- dence was far less shaken by the abduction of Prenk Bib Doda than was Bulgarian by that of Alexander, and the Arnaut could not, like the Serb, be coerced by the withdrawal of plenipotentiaries or by an embargo on pigs. Diplo- matically speaking, at the beginning of this century Servia had a sovereign existence both externally and internally, Bulgaria internally only, and Albania not at all. But, democratically speaking, in degree of real freedom the order would be Albania, Bulgaria, Serbia. Moreover, though not expressly recognized, this independence had been tacitly admitted by diplomacy over and over again—as by Russia, for instance, in the partition planned at San Stefano, and by England in dropping the cession of Epirus to Greece proposed at Berlin. In all subsequent schemes of reform and re- distribution we find a dead line drawn round Albania, and the country left out of the scheme—and what better admis- sion of independence could there be ? The Albanians had no formal international status, nor even any formal internal autonomy, because so long as the Empire endured they needed neither.

Coming now to the more essential qualifications of nation- ality, we find that Albania is of a stock coeval and con- genital with the Greek and Latin, and therefore associates well with either, without being assimilated by them ; as may be seen by the survival for centuries of the Albanian colonies in Calabria and Attica. It is a stock with striking physical and mental characteristics, and a list of celebrated Albanians is surprising both in quantity and quality, as well as for the wide field in which distinction has been won. In all ages Albanians have forced their way to the front in the affairs of the world, more particularly in adminis- tration and the allied arts. The language has literary qualities and is of great interest to the learned. The national type and character is as striking, both in its good and its bad qualities, as the national territory; while a State of nearly a million homogeneous inhabitants should be able to hold its own and even something more.

All the same, it would have gone hard with Albanian nationality had not the imperialism of Western Powers found much the same interest in its preservation as the Eastern Empire had had. For Albania, once partitioned between Serbia and Greece, could only have reconstituted itself after whole centuries of repression and whole series of revolts.

It has been said that Albanians can associate with Italians and Greeks. The result of this is that the commerce of the country has been mostly Italian, while its culture has been very largely Greek, especially in the south. Greek peaceful penetration had indeed so prepared a partition that the annexation to Greece of southern Albania would not at first have been resisted by the peaceful Tosk population. Southern Albania is to-day Greek, much as Roumania was a century ago; and a century hence will no doubt be as little Greek as Roumania is to-day. But the Albanian cannot associate with the Slav; and the fierce Gheg tribes for centuries waged a war of extermination and expulsion against Montenegrins and Serbs, in the course of which much of the fertile valleys of the Sanjak of Novi-Bazar and of the plains of Kossovo and Monastir were acquired by the Albanian. The result of the fall of the Ottoman overlord was a War of Partition in which the Serb drove back the Albanian as ruthlessly as the Greek drove back the Bulgar, and took and garrisoned the principal coast-towns until expelled by the Concert. It took a joint naval demonstration to get the Montenegrins out of Scutari and an Austrian ultimatum to get the Serbs out of Durazzo, but it was done. Later, the Greeks were bought out of southern Albania by the British proposal to give them the Aegean islands as soon as they had gone; but the Greek element in the population of South Albania will no doubt give trouble until the Albanian state is definitely established. With the Serbs the Albanians can now probably deal themselves; indeed, their first act as an independent state was to re-invade their old territories in the Sanjak which had been assigned to Serbia, but only to incur a punishment which sent 80,000 refugees into the barren mountains. The whole situation has been throughout one which called for very considerable determination and diplomacy, and those who have acted on behalf of the Concert deserve very great credit therefor. There will still be a difficult period during which internal factions and foreign interventions will distract the new principality, and during which it will require some foreign financial and administrative assistance; but there seems now to be no fear of a final failure.[1] A suitable prince has been found who as a Protestant, in the prime of life and of fine presence, may overcome the preference for a native ruler. The present social and political conditions under which the power is shared between semi-civilized clan-chiefs and a German sovereign is much the same as that of Greece when Otho of Bavaria first landed there.[2] But Albania starts with this advantage over Greece, that it is not burdened with a disproportionate *patria irredenta*; for its present frontier corresponds closely enough to the ethnographical extent of the nation. Economically its existence is not so satisfactorily secured; for the hill tribes of the north are deprived of the fertile foothills almost indispensable to their existence. With increased civilization, emigration will, no doubt, relieve this difficulty, and the industrial development of the southern Tosks will afford the northern Ghegs employment and will thereby bring a new solidarity to the nation. The country, though deficient in ports, has plenty of natural resources—coal near Koritsa, petroleum, copper, and sulphur elsewhere—and with the exceptional ability that has been shown to abound in the

---

[1] This was written before the recent risings in northern Albania against the government of Prince William and the overrunning of Albania by Greeks and Serbs, but there seems to be no reason to modify the passage.

[2] The reign of Prince William of Wied, deprived of the indispensable support of Europe prematurely.

Albanian stock, will not be long in making up arrears of industrial development. Albania is the only case in which the Balkan wars have created a nation—or, more correctly, have obtained international recognition for a national entity. The political results of the war on the nations already existing have, however, been no less significant though less sensational.

The political effects of the war on the internal constitution of the countries concerned are very different in the case of each Near-Eastern nation. In all of them the personal position of the sovereign is of far greater importance than in western states and less simplified societies ; and this position has in every case been profoundly affected. Thus, the personal power of the political King Ferdinand has been much weakened, while in Greece that of the military King Constantine has been greatly strengthened. That of the citizen king of Serbia has been improved, that of the feudal king of Montenegro has been impaired. These gains and losses in reputation correspond with the results of the war in each case, rather than with the real responsibility of each sovereign for the respective gain or loss by war. Thus King Ferdinand, whose position has suffered most, could have claimed considerable credit for the conquests of the War of the Coalition, owing to the part his diplomacy had taken in the negotiation of the alliance ; while it seems pretty clear that he was in no way personally responsible for the War of Partition and its calamities. King Constantine, on the other hand, who has gained most in reputation, had no hand in the alliance and took a prominent part in the War of Partition. King Nicholas of Montenegro played a far more conspicuous part than King Peter of Serbia, and this, with his picturesque personality and position, might have recommended him, one would suppose, to a people still in the patriarchal relation to their sovereign. But King Peter has kept Bulgarian Monastir, while King Nicholas has had to surrender Albanian Scutari.[1] ' Conquering kings

[1] This unexpected result of a military crisis, in strengthening the

their titles take from the foes they captive make '—including the titles to popularity, the most important of all to these democratic sovereigns of the Balkans. The association of a democratic king with the militarist ambitions of a class is as great a danger to a modern monarchy as too close an association with the religious authority of a caste was to the old autocratic monarchy. For there are two chances of such association weakening the institution to one of its being thereby strengthened. The one chance is successful war, the two are unsuccessful war and no war at all.

When we look to the political results of the war among the Serbs we find an even more striking transformation in progress. Thus the territorial juxtaposition of Serbia and Montenegro is leading rapidly to a joining-up of their military and political forces. A federation of the two states would indeed be beneficial to themselves, and would serve as a nucleus for a future South Slav federation; but it is not a factor making for peace in the future relations of the South Slavs with the South Teutons, or the Magyars. Nor is it likely to realize itself without resistance from the Bulgar and Albanian races in the name of the Balkan balance of power. The Serbian domination over Arnauts and Bulgars in its new territories is not of a character calculated to make peace easy to the Bulgarian and Albanian Governments; and the stimulus given to Panserb propaganda in the Slav provinces of the Austrian Empire cannot fail to involve the Serbian kingdom in trouble with its powerful neighbour. The Balkan wars have converted the Serbian state from a peasant community to the political nucleus of a South Slav Confederacy. The change in international status and internal standpoint is scarcely less than in the case of

Serbian dynasty and weakening the Montenegrin, is partly attributable to the Montenegrin monarch having to take the responsibility for unpopular policies that were forced on that people, whereas the more modern constitution of Serbia safeguards the sovereign. Something also must be attributed to the greater success of the Serbian Crown Prince in the field, in comparison with his *confrère* of Montenegro.

Albania, and is pregnant with diplomatic considerations which will be dealt with in their turn.

The result of the war on Bulgarian internal politics has been that a so-called socialist party has risen from the ruins of the old party system, shattered by the failure of both the austrophil and the russophil party policies. It is difficult as yet to determine what this imports. Certainly not the form of politics and economics that ' socialism ' would imply in an industrial and urban population. Probably it means that a new party is required to carry on a national policy even more marked in its detachment and nationalism than that of the older parties—a development which may eventually tend towards republicanism. Bulgaria has had a very severe lesson of the evils of a ' diplomatic ' foreign policy, and in reacting towards a more ' democratic ' direction of foreign affairs it may make the position of the only Bulgarian diplomatist impossible. In any case Bulgarian internal politics and foreign policy will be dominated for many years by a determination to recover, if not Monastir, at least Central Macedonia. The Macedonian refugees will, for a generation at least, insist on no opportunity being lost in respect of this object, and the party divisions will continue to correspond to the form of foreign support by which it is expected to attain this. But the necessary support will no longer be sought in Russia and Austria, but rather in combinations within the peninsula. Bulgarian parties, instead of looking to the Russian Empire, will look to the Serbian nation: instead of to the Austrian Empire, to the Roumanian nation: instead of to the Ottoman Empire, to the Turkish nation.

One result of the war has been that there are now hardly any Bulgar districts left in the Ottoman territories, and the consequence of this is that the Bulgar Exarchate at Constantinople has no longer any *raison d'être*. With the transfer of the Bulgar Exarchate from Constantinople to Sofia, the last imperial Ottoman institution with which Bulgaria is concerned has come to an end. All military supremacy of Turkey ended at Lule Burgas: all remaining ties of political suzerainty were snapped when Bulgaria asserted its full sovereignty in 1908: all economic sovereignty of Turkey in Bulgaria disappeared a quarter-century before. The relations between the two countries were already on a basis of liberty; and now equality has been attained—with the consequence that a real fraternity has for the first time become possible. Turco-Bulgar relations are no longer falsified by any relics of Turkish imperialism. Bulgars and Turks are now two nations associated in joint resistance to an imminent imperialism of Greece. There is now a true democratic relationship between Bulgars and Turks which has become an important factor in the diplomatic situation.

Turkish national ideals suffered as heavily as a result of the War of Coalition as did Bulgarian from the Wars of Partition. In Adrianople the Ottoman Empire had lost the sacred city of Old Turkey, a shrine of its glorious past; in Salonica had been lost the sacred city of Young Turkey, the birthplace of future glories. Crete, the latest and most prized of all the Ottoman conquests, had been finally lost, as had Tripoli, the last link with African Islam. The Greek frontier had been carried into the Asiatic islands of the Aegean within sight of the homeland of the Turks. Constantinople itself was imperilled. Then had come the turn in the tide with the Wars of Partition. Adrianople had been recovered, and Bulgaria none the less converted from an antagonist into an ally. The Ottoman armies again had the road to Macedonia opened to them for the recovery of Salonica. The Ottoman navy had only to defeat the Greek fleet to recover the Asiatic islands, or even Crete.

The loss of Salonica and of the Greek islands is indeed a far greater blow to the Ottoman political organism than has generally been realized. The Islamized Jews and Europeanized Turks of Salonica and Macedonia were the founders and stalwarts of the Young Turk party which will for long impose their imperialist and militarist programme on the Government. The Greeks and Albanians were the founders of the Liberal Union, and in conjunction with an Arab group with a federalist and moderate programme constituted the Opposition. The Armenians and Slavs supported the Young Turks. This arrangement of political parties, which declared itself at the first election in 1908 and subsisted more or less thereafter, represented adequately enough the two main divisions of public opinion in the Empire. There were indeed only two ways of saving the Empire : forcible centralization, or a diplomatic federation. The Young Turk party in power tried the former and failed; and now the whole basis and balance of parliamentary representation has been transformed. The Young Turks have lost forty seats in Europe, but on the other hand their opponents, the Greeks and Albanians, have almost disappeared, and the liberal or federalist Opposition will in future be taken up by Armenians and Arabs. The Young Turks being absolutely in authority have not as yet allowed these possibly separatist sections a representation corresponding to their new importance ; but they will gain it in time. Meanwhile the Europeanized Turks and Islamized Jews cannot indefinitely maintain their position now that their country of origin has been lost, and as a mere Constantinopolitan party their position will be much weaker.

At present, however, the Young Turkish militarists have an unquestioned control of policy ; and will direct the whole growing strength of the Turkish nation westward against the growing strength of the Greek empire. But fortunately the exhaustion of the exchequer and the entire change of the strategic conditions caused by the loss of Macedonia and the Asiatic islands have imposed a fairly long period of preparation and recuperation before a war can be undertaken. Turkey will not be ready any sooner than Bulgaria, all the more that the former has to become a naval power and recover its supremacy, if it can, on the sea. The political result of the Balkan wars on the Ottoman Empire has consequently been to confirm it in its imperialist policy, and to impose on it the burden of naval as well as military armament.[1] It will be interesting to watch the effect of the new territories on the political life of Greece. The most notable result so far is a restoration, perhaps even a reinforcement, of the authority of the Crown. It is almost as though the advance made towards a restoration of the Greek Empire externally had brought about a corresponding advance towards imperialism in internal affairs. The dynasty had not been strong since the unfortunate Thessalian campaign forced on it in 1897; and by the events preceding the war the position and powers of the Crown, never thoroughly consolidated, were seriously compromised. The present sovereign, as Crown Prince, was deprived of his military command of the Greek forces in the Greek mutiny; and the monarchy was, in the opinion of many, only saved by M. Venezelos. It is therefore very curious to find that the success of the latter's foreign policy has accrued to the credit of the Crown, as figurehead of the military faction, while the premier has had to accept the responsibility of the few inevitable but

---

[1] Thus a British naval mission has been engaged to counteract that employed by Greece; the dockyards have been turned over to a British firm, so that lack of experience and equipment in maintaining material efficiency may not again handicap the Turkish navy; and the bankrupt State has begun competing with Greece in purchasing warships. In the naval war of last year, the object of the Ottoman navy was to maintain itself as a fleet in being so as to prevent Greek command of the seas from affecting the land campaign by a blow at the capital; and as Turkish ships if damaged could not be repaired, and the Greek ships were on the whole more efficient, it could only keep itself in being by refusing general action. The raid of the Hamidieh revealed how vulnerable the Greek State is to a naval offensive, a fact which the successful war in Thessaly in 1898 had caused the Turkish political strategists to overlook until the Cretan question created a rather spasmodic effort for strengthening the navy. But in a Turco-Greek war in the immediate future, the rôle of the navy will be far more important and far easier. With Bulgaria as a neutral instead of an antagonist threatening communications, an invasion of Macedonia from Thrace, even without command of the sea, becomes a much easier task strategically than holding it against invasion under the conditions previous to the war.

unpopular concessions. The conquests may result in further strengthening the Crown ; for these distant and undeveloped communities may weaken Greek democracy as a political organism while increasing opportunities for a benevolent despotism. The measures already planned to consolidate and centralize the life of the new and larger Greece—such as exaltation of the executive at the expense of the legislature, ornamentation of the capital, adulation of the army—are all symptoms of a new imperialism. It will not be long before Greece replaces Italy as the last promotion from the ranks of democratic nations to that of the imperialist powers.

In respect of the effect on the Roumanian polity of its participation in the Balkan wars, an interesting indication may be noted in support of the argument that those who make war pay for it. Roumania is one of the least democratically governed of European States, and it was the Roumanian upper class that threw the force of the country into a political war in which no popular cause was at stake and which was contrary to the true line of expansion of the Roumanian people. Although the direct result was profitable to, and not unpopular with, the Roumanian nation, it seems likely that an indirect result will be the revision of the Roumanian constitution and a reduction of the power of the governing class. It is curious that successful war should have the effect in Roumania of liberalizing institutions while in Greece it has shown a tendency to imperialize them. The reason is perhaps that in Roumania the war was promoted by the ruling class, while in Greece the war was a war of the people. This gives the apparent paradox that a war of liberation is not favourable to liberal institutions ; while a diplomatic war is often fatal to despotic power—a paradox explained in a previous chapter and exemplified in the history of the French and German Empires.[1]

[1] It will be possible to test this theory shortly on the larger theatre of a European war. If the British Empire is fighting a war of liberation against imperialism and militarism, then it may expect as a result that

The map of the Balkan peninsula shows that the wars have effected surprising changes in the distribution of territory. Greece, Serbia, and Montenegro have all been about doubled in size; Bulgaria has lost in the north as much habitable and cultivable land as has been gained in the south. When we come to examine the resulting political rearrangements we find the change to be even more startling. The old cleavage between east and west, between the Balkan nations and the Ottoman Empire, is gone, and has given place to a new cleavage between the Near-Eastern nations, including Turkey as one of them. The main difference is caused by the fact that Turkey has lost Macedonia as an appanage, but gained Bulgaria as an ally, and that the new line does not run, as did the old one, entirely inland, but is half of it in the Aegean. It is in Bulgaria and Turkey that the forces making for a Balkan disturbance are to be found. It is the still unappeased nationalism of Bulgaria and the still unabandoned imperialism of Turkey that menace the equilibrium of the Balkans. On the other hand, it is the disorders of Albania and the diversion of Panserb forces from expansion into the Ottoman Empire to expansion into the Austrian Empire that menace the equilibrium of Europe.

As a result of the treaty of alliance and of the War of the Coalition, Bulgaria had extended its frontier to the full limit of its ethnographical expansion with the exception of the Bulgar district of Pirot, which had always been Serbian, and some Bulgar districts south of Uskub; indeed, about Adrianople and Kavalla, the Bulgar ethnological limit was considerably exceeded. As a result of the War of Partition and the Treaty of Bucharest, Bulgaria was deprived of its conquests and driven far within its ethnological frontier. In so far as this proceeding was one of *raison d'état* and not

its political institutions will become more imperialist and militarist; while if the German Empire is fighting a war of aggression, then it may expect that its constitution will, as a result, be made more liberal and pacific. The converse is, of course, true in either case.

merely of *Realpolitik*—in so far, that is to say, as it was
a considered policy and not merely a course imposed on the
Governments of Greece, Serbia, and Roumania by their war
parties—it found its inspiration and sought its justification
in a doctrine of a Balkan balance of power which the aggrandizement of Bulgaria had disturbed. The result has been an
excellent example of the danger of basing such calculations
on purely material factors such as territory and population,
and ignoring moral forces such as national consciousness and
international comity. Greece and Serbia, in order to strengthen
themselves by annexing a quarter-million Bulgars, have
weakened themselves by antagonizing five million. A big
Bulgaria expanded territorially to its full ethnological extent,
and something over, and occupied in the economic development of its new territories, would have been no menace
to Greece and Serbia. On the contrary, such a Bulgaria
would have had every reason to encourage and support
Greek ambitions on the Asiatic littoral or in Constantinople,
and Serbian ambitions in Croatia and Slavonia—ambitions
which would permit Bulgaria to devote its whole energies
to economic activities. Bulgaria would, in such case, have
had nothing to gain by offensive alliances with the Austrian
or Ottoman Empires. Therefore it has come about that,
although the big Bulgaria has been reduced, while Serbia
and Greece have been reinforced until the three are approximately equal in size and population, yet the Balkan balance
of power has not thereby been restored, but has, on the
contrary, been rendered utterly unstable. The democratic
driving force for change that has been excited by partitioning Bulgarian Macedonia between Serbia and Greece is
a dynamic force far stronger than the static strength of the
new settlement. Not until that settlement has been consolidated by the passage of at least a quarter-century, and
confirmed by the passive acceptance of at least one Macedonian generation, will it be able of itself to resist the pressure
from Bulgaria. Until then Balkan international equilibrium

is democratically unstable, and can only be maintained by diplomatic props and ties.

The political effect of the War of the Coalition by itself might not have been a perfect balance of power between the Balkan nations as power is reckoned in terms of acres and populations, but would have been what is far more important, and that is a stable equilibrium—a balance of power in terms of national expansions and popular forces. Bulgaria in the centre would have been in a condition of rest and able to support the surrounding States in their expansions outwards—Serbia to the west, Greece to the east, Roumania to the north, and Turkey to the south. The Near-Eastern nations would then have had a good prospect of continuing their proper national development whenever circumstances weakened the resisting power of the great empires surrounding them. They would then have been in a fair way to form a coalition for the common defence and development of all Near-Eastern nationalities— a policy such as seems to promise the best prospect of growth to groups of nations encircled by encroaching empires.

But the War of Partition has left a situation by no means so simple in its main lines or susceptible of so satisfactory a treatment. The Peninsula is now divided by lines of friction between the Balkan nations, due not only to pressure where the partition has been inequitable, but also to pressure caused by the penetrations from the empires outside. As the Balkan nations still have to make front inward against each other, not only cannot they advance outward against the empires, but the latter can push them from behind on to each other's bayonets. Going from west to east, the first of these friction frontiers is that between Albania and Serbia, with Austria behind Albania, and Russia behind Serbia. The next runs between Serbia and Bulgaria, the latter habing Austrian support; and the next between Bulgaria and Roumania, the latter having Russia behind it. Between Greece and Bulgaria, between Greece

and Turkey, and between Greece and Albania, there is
a strong line of friction, the short march with Serbia being
the only Greek frontier that is not in friction. Thus, the
new territories of Serbia in Macedonia are pinched between
Albanian and Bulgarian pressure, and those of Greece
between Turkish and Bulgarian pressure—no good condition for their pacific development. In these conditions
the only democratic security for peace lies in the temporary
prostration of Bulgaria and Turkey, the two discontented
democracies; and the only diplomatic security lies in the
temporary predominance of Slavonic over Teutonic influences
at Bucharest, which causes Roumania to hold Bulgaria in
check.

The settlement of Bucharest was imposed against the
teachings of equity, of ethnography, and of experience in
professed pursuance of a Balkan balance of power. The
balance diplomatically arrived at was no balance when
democratically analysed, because it took account of figures
of population and acreage only, and took no account of forces
of public sentiment and national development. The settlement rested in fact on no popular basis at all, but on a political
arrangement between the Governments that profited by it—
Roumania, Serbia, and Greece. The preponderance of this
triple agreement of victors was enough to impose peace on
a broken Bulgaria and a bankrupt Turkey, but it was
a pacification by force, not a peace on any permanent foundation. Not only were Bulgaria and Turkey diverted from
their true line of peaceful development—Bulgaria in Macedonia and Turkey in Asia Minor—but Roumania, Greece,
and Serbia themselves by their greed for immediate gains
seriously compromised their national destinies.

Never, indeed, can there have been such a striking example
of the danger to the true nationalist interest of the Government being carried away by public passions excited with
war. The four nations concerned, Bulgaria, Turkey, Serbia,
and Greece, all have high destinies and vast developments

clear and open before them. In every single case war has not only made them blind to their true national objective, but has made them block the obvious path to it. We have seen how the Bulgar militarists exhausted the national fighting energies in Thrace and then stultified the national diplomacy at Petersburg; thereby deferring, if they have not destroyed, the Bulgarian destinies in Macedonia. We have seen how the Young Turks have mortgaged their economic and political future as an adolescent nation, in order to retain or recover by war moribund imperial appanages and suzerainties. We have seen how the Serbian militarists, in order to retain a province in repudiation of a treaty, have diverted the energies of their nation to the assimilation of an impoverished district with a hostile population in the south, thereby gravely imperilling the prospect of association with the wide provinces and wealthy peoples which await the advance of the Serbian people northward. We have seen how Greece, by allowing the army to force the Greek frontier too far and too fast towards the national goal—the Greek imperial city—has really raised against itself insuperable barriers to further progress; for Greece is now barred from Constantinople by the concentration of the whole Bulgar force against the Greek conquest of Macedonia, and concentration of the whole Turkish force against Greek command of the Aegean. We have seen how Roumania detached itself from the Triple Alliance, and the attainment of its national aims in Bessarabia, in order to plunder Bulgaria, and so set up an enemy in the rear of any advance northward.

The net political result of the Balkan wars and the Treaty of Bucharest, so far as the Balkans themselves are concerned, is that they have left an aftermath of wars of ' extermination ' and the seeds of future wars of annexation.

Let us not be too pessimistic, however. War is not a good way of getting things done, and it often wastes as much as it wins; but it can at least be depended on to get rid of the accumulations of dry rot and rubbish which choke the life out of political organisms. These wars have cleared away the ruins of the Ottoman Empire in Europe, and will clean up the rotting mass of misery they covered. They have given liberty and nationality to the great majority of a servile population; and, where they have failed to do so, if the evil prove insupportable and otherwise irremediable it will be fought out between free peoples. The old warfare of European rayah against Asiatic recruit, of the serfdom of one civilization against the soldiery of another, is for ever over and done with. With such a benefit to humanity as a practical result of the wars, there is no need to fear that brave men have died in vain. As to the future, while further war, at present, seems probable, every year gained without an outbreak is so much to the good: so much healing over of raw wounds—so much healthy absorption of national energies in peaceful activity—so much control of policy recovered by constitutional authority and pacific public opinion. A pacific readjustment of existing inequities is not impossible. For Greece and Serbia may have to concede such frontiers in Macedonia and the Aegean as would conciliate Bulgaria and Turkey owing to some change in the European situation; [1] or the present militarism of Bulgaria and Turkey may be mitigated by the accession to power of Bulgar Socialists or Ottoman Liberals ; or Roumania, as the *gendarmes* of Europe, may continue to keep order until time has brought redress or at least resignation.

> Time's glory is to calm contending kings,
> To unmask falsehood and bring truth to light,
> To stamp the seal of time on agèd things,
> To wake the morn and sentinel the night,
> To wrong the wronger till he render right.

---

[1] A resettlement of frontiers by agreement between the Balkan States or as an appendix to a general European resettlement has been raised from a possibility to a probability by the outbreak of the European War.

(b) In Europe.

The main political results of the Balkan wars are seen in the transformation of the map of the Near East and in the transference of the border line between European and Asiatic civilization from the Balkan Peninsula to Asia Minor. This has been expressed by some writers in the assertion that the Balkan wars have ended the ' Eastern Question '; by others in arguing that they have really revived it. The truth is, perhaps, that in so far as the Eastern Question was a social question of supremacy between eastern and western civilization, the Balkan wars have ended it by establishing Western political principles and social points of view, not only in Roumelia but also in Anatolia. But in so far as the Eastern Question was a political question of balance of power, the Balkan wars have reopened it by transposing the terms from those of a balance between European empires to those of a balance between Balkan nations. These wars have themselves neither created nor converted anything; for it is not in the power of war to do more than hasten or delay what would in any case have happened. But while war brings no permanent solution of any situation, it is a powerful solvent; and these wars have effected in a few months political processes which would otherwise have taken years.

The Eastern Question, or, more correctly, the Near-Eastern Question, can be analysed broadly into three historic chapters, corresponding to three geographical areas. The first chapter to be completed, with its corresponding area, constitutes the Mediterranean Question—the struggle first between east and west, and then between western Powers for control of the great east and west sea route. The second can conveniently be called the Metropolitan Question, and includes the competition for Constantinople and for control of the great commercial routes there. There is another chapter closely connected with this second question but belonging to another volume—the volume of the history of the Asiatic continent and of the twentieth century in Asia; for it is an indirect consequence of the Balkan wars that the volume of the Asiatic national movement has had its first chapter begun. The third chapter, and that with which European politics and Balkan wars are more directly concerned, is known to us as the Macedonian Question, and includes the struggle for the land routes east and west and north and south that cross in Macedonia.

Dealing first with the Mediterranean Question and the political effect of these wars on the position of the European powers there, we find in the first place that the development in the Near-Eastern nationality movement due to war has somewhat changed the character of that position. For the position of Europe in the Mediterranean is peculiar in this respect, that the tenure, say of Great Britain in Egypt, or of France in Algiers, is imperial and based on sea power; but their title is international and held as mandatories of civilization—as wardens of the marches between East and West. Consequently the development of the Near-Eastern nations by these wars has deprived the Western empires of much of their national mandate in the Mediterranean. A strong empire is required to supply the deficiencies of a weak empire ; but it can have no useful function in supplying the deficiencies of a nation, however weak. For example, if the Turks were content to be a strong nation instead of a weak empire, they could to-morrow get rid of the international yoke, even as Crete has done. The nineteenth century in the Mediterranean is the history of the subversion and substitution of eastern by western imperialism under a mandate from such international interests as those of commerce and capital. The twentieth century in the Mediterranean will, as a result in part of the Balkan wars, be the history of the subversion and substitution of western imperialism by eastern nationalism, the latter having a mandate from national culture and constitutional liberties. The Balkan wars need not be debited with having thereby brought nearer future wars between the Mediterranean nations and the western empires; for the mild and modernized imperialism of the western democracies, England and France, with sea power as its only weapon, is both morally and materially incapable of resisting by war a well-developed and determined national movement. Materially incapable, because the sea power on which their imperialism is based cannot suppress such a movement in view of the fact that a foreign military occupation, supported by sea power only, cannot indefinitely maintain itself against a home-rule rebellion. Morally incapable, because the imperialism which established the West-European Powers in the Mediterranean was an imperialism that was almost an internationalism. Its main object was to secure peace and safe passage in the borderland of East and West; and the Eastern empire, being no longer able to police its borders and seas, the Western empire had to take over the duty in the interest of international society. The *condominium* of the Naval Powers in the Mediterranean had the same *raison d'être* as the joint control of customs, quarantines, and navigation at Constantinople, and only in the second phase became imperial and sole for greater convenience of administration. This explains how it came about that Great Britain, against the policy of the Government of the time, became the administrator and mandatory of Europe on the southern isthmus at Cairo; and how Russia, in spite of three centuries of persistence, has never succeeded in securing the same office on the northern isthmus at Constantinople. For international interests were well enough served by a British occupation and administration of Egypt, and suffered no prejudice, but rather the contrary, from the gradual change of an international receivership into an imperial directorship. Whereas in Constantinople international interests are best served for the present by international institutions, and their development into an imperial domination by a military and monopolist empire would be worked against by all the influence of international commerce and capital.

But the question does not lie entirely between internationalism and imperialism, for nationalism has been for some time a ruling factor wherever Greek communities were concerned. The British occupation of Cyprus was in its policy partly imperial, as being strategic, and partly international, as being humanitarian. The Balkan wars have deprived it of such *raison d'être* as remained to it on either count; and, what is more important, have placed Cyprus next but one on the rota of Greek *irredentist* agitations. The Cyprus question has suddenly and unexpectedly become actual owing to the settlement by the Balkan wars of the Macedonian, Epirote, Cretan, Aegean, and Samian questions, all of which had political precedence. Those who have observed the resolute repression by Athens of the Cretan question in the interests of the more crucial Macedonian questions, and of the Samian and Cypriote agitations in deference to similar diplomatic considerations, will realize that Great Britain and Italy will soon be having trouble; while those who recall the methods by which the Greeks recovered the Ionian Islands from British occupation will also realize that, sooner or later, the Sea Power will be worried and wearied into withdrawal. But there will of course be no ' war ' in any sense of the word between the Sea Powers and the Greeks—such as seems to be inevitable from the resistance of the military imperialism of Slav or Teuton to the nationalism of the Balkan States.[1]

Passing on now to the Metropolitan Question comprising the control of Constantinople and the Straits with the command of Asia Minor, we find the same three tendencies of imperialism, internationalism, and nationalism combining or competing with each other. What has been the result of

[1] The war between Austrian imperialism and Serb nationalism has now hurried Europe into a war in which the political developments that would have slowly but surely realized themselves under peace conditions may be fulfilled in six months or frustrated for a century.

the Balkan wars in this conflict of forces ? Will the destiny
of the capital of the Near East now develop under influences
that are international and neutral, or imperial and external,
or national and internal ? A century ago the answer would
have been that the fate of Constantinople was to be an
imperial appanage of a Great Power. At the present moment
an international and neutral solution seems to be indicated
by the course of events. A century hence, if the question
is still unsolved, the settlement will probably be on a national
basis and due to internal forces of Turkish, Bulgar, or Greek
national development. This much is evident from an
examination of the effect of the Balkan wars on this chapter
of the Eastern Question—effects that must be reviewed more
in detail, in view of their importance to the future of European and Asiatic civilization. For the whole future course
of civilization is involved in the question whether Constantinople will be the citadel of a military empire, the
clearing-house of international commerce, or the capital either
of an East-European or West-Asiatic national culture.

In an earlier chapter the idea was advanced that Constantinople, through its Byzantinism, ruined the Ottoman
Empire. If this is so, the Ottoman Empire has had its
revenge, for by its barbarism it has temporarily ruined
Constantinople. Though it was inevitable that there should
be a great diversion of trade and traffic between East and
West from the land route by the Thracian isthmus to
the sea route across the Egyptian isthmus, yet Constantinople in the hands of a commercial and progressive community such as the Greeks would never have lost its position
as the economic and financial centre of eastern Europe and
western Asia. As it is, it became evident in the course of
the nineteenth century that whatever its strategic value
might still be for imperialist purposes, its economic value
to western commercial Powers had been much overrated.
As the Ottoman Empire dropped further into arrears in
developing its direct economic relations with the western and

the far-eastern peoples, Sea Powers, such as Great Britain, left the dead or dormant demands of the Levant to be dealt with out of the growing surplus supplies of the Land Powers, such as Austria. British mariners, merchants, and manufacturers had their energies occupied with the Far East, and the Levant was no longer indispensable to them either as a centre of distribution or a source of demand. Provided the sea route to the Far East through the Mediterranean and the Suez Canal was internationalized by the adjacent territories being in the control of the Sea Powers, those Powers had only a secondary interest in the control of the land route through the Roumelian and Anatolian isthmuses. Accordingly, throughout the nineteenth century we find the Metropolitan Question, the question of the control of Constantinople, declining in importance. With the establishment of Great Britain in territorial command of the Suez isthmus between Asia and Africa and of the main sea-route to the Far East, and with Russia in command of the main land-route through Siberia, the control of the isthmus between Europe and Asia and of the intervening land routes has become of less importance to both. For the present-day imperialist, Cairo and the African railway to the Cape takes the place held a half-century ago by Constantinople and an Anatolian railway to India. The practical Briton asks only that the Straits be kept open to the Black Sea grain and oil trade, and that the future railway connexion between Europe and Asia across the isthmus be kept open for British mails and passengers. French interests are mainly financial, and will be satisfied with any improvement in security for the returns from, and the redemption of, its vast investments in the Levant. Therefore both British and French interests in Constantinople are not such as to make it worth while for those Powers to resist at all costs a Russo-German *condominium* there ; though they might still risk a good deal to prevent a sole control by either of these empires.

Western sea power now counts for less in the future of

Constantinople; and that future, if it were to be decided
on the old imperialist lines, would be the result of a duel
between the Slavonic and the Teutonic empires.   Indeed
at first sight it might be feared that the Balkan wars
had so cleared the lists for this duel that the encounter
could not be long delayed.[1] The situation created by the
wars has already enabled Germany to give a political form
to the economic and diplomatic supremacy acquired over
Turkey in recent years, in that a German general officer
with a German staff has been given supreme command in
the capital.[2] Meantime the economic grasp of Germany has
tightened.   The Bagdad railway has finally imposed itself
on Europe and on Asia as the main land route between
central Europe and the middle East, and as an enterprise
which is to be under exclusively German control.   In the
diplomatic field Germany has advanced no less swiftly.   In
Anatolia, the Russian supremacy over Armenia has been
challenged, and a Prusso-Russian scheme of administrative
reform inaugurates there a new chapter of imperialism and
nationalism in Asia Minor.   This new development means
that as the Ottoman Empire gets too weak to make head
against Slavonic imperialism, it will be gradually reinforced
and replaced by a Teutonic imperialism, as it was in the
Balkan peninsula.   The position of Austro-German imperialism in Bulgaria and Turkey is strong enough to bar the road
to Constantinople by either the Balkans or the Caucasus,
and the strength of Russia does not and cannot lie in sea
power.   There is consequently nothing left to the Slavs but
either to accept the economic establishment of the Teutons
in Asia Minor, or to exclude their expansion from that
region by force of arms.   This trial by battle may come,

[1] Nor was it.
[2] This is a different thing from the educational functions hitherto held
by German officers in Turkey.   The demand for these new powers is
explained by Berlin as being indispensable to effective education and
the reputation of the German military system, and is excused by adducing
the British naval mission.

and if it does,[1] we shall owe it largely to the Balkan wars, which have so weakened Bulgaria and the Ottoman Empire as to make them no longer effective buffer states. But if it does not come in the next few years Russia may have to be content to renounce for ever its imperial interests in 'Tsargrad' in return for some form of internationalization of the Imperial City.

The basis of this international control would be right of free passage through the Straits under sanction of the Sea Powers commanding the Mediterranean and Black Seas, and rights of free trade and free port under sanction of the Land Powers controlling the railway systems of Anatolia and Roumelia. Such an international solution of the Metropolitan Question would require no dangerous or delicate diplomacy, but might almost grow naturally out of the various international institutions which already administer the less national services at the Turkish capital— out of the influence of the various foreign missions to whom the Turks are entrusting different branches of administration—and out of the ancient servitudes imposed on the Empire by the Capitulations. To take an example only of recent developments in this direction. The compensation claimed by Russia for the concessions to Germany is the addition of a Russian representative to the Council of the Ottoman Debt, in which Russia has practically no financial interest. This would be a long step towards making the Council a financial Board of Control. Moreover, an international solution of the Straits Question is facilitated by the policy of the Turkish Government itself, which is seeking in such international institutions protection for its own imperial rights against Teutonic economic penetrations, or Slavonic military pressure. To bring Germany into Armenia and Russia on to the Debt Council is obvious policy; while British Naval Missions and Customs Missions, and French Harbour and Lights Administrations all contribute to this same end—the

[1] It has now come, and on a scale which makes the effect of its issue in the Near East merely a secondary anxiety.

putting of Constantinople safely into commission. The Turkish intention is, of course, that such internationalization shall be *ad interim* until Ottoman nationalism is strong enough to take its place. The calculation is correct so far as it results from a realization that whereas imperial institutions could maintain themselves for long against national insurrection, such exotic international institutions could not— with the result that an international settlement will probably be replaced in the end by a national solution. But it is another question whether there is such a thing as Ottoman nationality and whether it is the Turkish or the Greek race that is the heir of the ages in Byzantium. In any case it is certain that the time for a settlement of the Metropolitan Question on nationalist lines is not yet:—as is shown by the general approbation that would have been accorded to the veto imposed from Petersburg on any conquest of Constantinople by the Allies in the War of Coalition—and by the general approbation that would have been accorded to the Turks had they transferred their capital to Brusa or Smyrna, and entrusted Constantinople to an Internal Administration in full and final payment of their debts. The future of Constantinople may of course also be decided as a result of a collision between the imperialisms of the Great Powers resulting in a general European and Balkan war, and a general readjustment. Whether this readjustment would result in a national or international solution would depend on the course of the war. Success for the German interest would mean a national settlement of Constantinople in favour of Turkey, carrying with it abolition of the capitulations and other international institutions and the substitution of a German protectorate for them. Success for the Russian interest would mean a combination of international institutions with a Russian predominance. In any event Constantinople, and Adrianople therewith, will probably be subjects for settlement in any future Continental Congress.

But it is to be feared that in respect of the future of the

Metropolitan Question and the possibility of promoting
Balkan peace by internationalizing and neutralizing Constantinople and Salonica, the Balkan wars have tended rather
to submit the future to the imperialism of the Great Land
Powers than to strengthen the internationalism of the Sea
Powers. While Macedonia was still subject to the Ottoman
Empire and not yet partitioned between the Balkan nations,
the internationalism of the philanthropic and pacific western
Powers, France and England, was still a factor in the future
of the provinces. A neutral Macedonia would no doubt
have been a more pacific and permanent solution than
a partition such as that of Bucharest. But to be successful
such an international settlement could only have been carried
out by France or England, and it was courting failure to
leave its execution to imperialist Austrian and Russian
agencies. When Austria and Russia were given a mandate
to prevent Macedonia becoming a menace to the peace of
Europe and a scandal to civilization, their mission was not
accepted by the Balkan nations because these Powers were
suspected of pursuing their own imperial motives rather than
the international mission they professed. Austria, which
had a land access to Macedonia, was most suspect of imperial
intentions ; Russia was an *instans tyrannus* less menacing
than Austria, only because of its greater remoteness and
more democratic relationship. In these conditions, as we
have seen, such internationalism as might with advantage
have been introduced into the situation by the Sea Powers,
could find no place ; and the conflict became a struggle of
the Balkan nations against the institutions of the Ottoman
Empire on the east, and the imperialist intentions of the
Austrian and Russian Empires on the north and west. The
combination of the two latter Empires ended by Austria
going out of partnership with Russia in 1908 and exchanging
all pretence of internationalism for an aggressive imperialist
Realpolitik against Balkan nationalism. This Russia met
with an astute diplomacy which furthered Russian imperialist

predominance in accord with Balkan nationalism. The side
that exploits popular forces will always win as against the
side that excludes them; and the political result of the
Balkan wars was a strengthening of the Russian position in
the Balkans amounting almost to Russian predominance
there.

The result of the earlier Balkan wars was to bring Teutonic
and Slav interests in the Balkans out of combination and
into competition. The result of the wars of the Coalition
and of Partition was to put the Slav interests in a position
of superiority which seems likely to be permanent.

It has been shown that the pacification at Bucharest was no
real peace so far as the Balkans were concerned. For while
avowedly built on a basis of balance of power there was no true
balance of forces, and the structure was submitted to a strain
which must in the end prove stronger than the struts resisting
it; so that the only doubtful question seemed to be whether the
breaking-point would come in the sea line of friction between
Turkey and Greece or on the land line of pressure round Bulgaria.
We shall now see that this settlement has been no help to the
peace of Europe, and that the Macedonian question remains as
a menace to the civilized world though it has taken on a different
form. In the old days the danger from Macedonia to European
peace lay in the fears and ambitions of European governments
as to each other's expansions at the expense of the Ottoman
Empire, and in the effect of Balkan nationalism in breaking
up the integrity of the Ottoman Empire and weakening its
guarantees. Thus the pacific Powers, England and France,
found their forces divided between a policy of supporting the
Empire against Russian and Austro-Hungarian imperialism so
as to prop up a precarious peace and a policy of subverting
the Empire to Balkan nationalism so as to make a more permanent and progressive provision against war. But no sooner had
Balkan nationalism begun to free itself from the control of
Turkish imperialism than it began itself to take a part in the
imperialist policies of Europe. The Balkan States had all of

them national expansions to pursue which forbade them becoming neutral nonentities in international politics such as Switzerland or Scandinavia. Balkan nationalism is still in active eruption—it is hot enough and fluid enough to penetrate any crack and ignite any combustible. Moreover, the War of Partition, by preventing the joint growth of the Balkan nations in co-operation had forced them to seek growth in competition by entering the field of European politics. They accordingly divided themselves between the two armed camps of Europe—the Triple Agreement and the Triple Alliance. Roumania, Greece, and Serbia ranged themselves with France, Great Britain and Russia; Turkey, Bulgaria, and Albania with Austria, Germany, and Italy. This arrangement is, at first glance, one of an equipoise of Balkan balance of power added to a European balance of power in stable equilibrium. But it will be suggested that just as we have already seen that the Balkan balance was no balance but a boiler under pressure, so we may suspect that the European balance of power is also a compression of living forces by dead weight rather than a counterpoise of equal national energies.

The development of the European balance of power and of the counterpoise of the Triple Agreement to the Triple Alliance cannot be dealt with here. It would require at least as long an inquiry as that which has been given to the forces which have brought about the Balkan balance of power. It must be enough to point out the curious resemblance between the European and the Balkan equations—not only in the nature of the equations themselves but also in that of the factors which compose each of them—a resemblance not altogether fortuitous owing to the same forces having been at work in both cases. The feature in this resemblance that most concerns us is that the Triple Agreement in Europe of France, Great Britain, and Russia has the same purpose towards, and has acquired the same preponderance over, the so-called Triple Alliance as the Triple Agreement of Roumania, Greece, and Serbia has in respect of the remaining three Balkan States.

It is no doubt rather a coincidence than any community of circumstances that makes the dominating Triple Coalition in both Europe and the Balkans contain the two leading culture powers—in Europe France and England, in the Balkans Roumania and Greece. France and Roumania have the most scientific soldiery in Europe and the Balkans respectively, animated in each case by a strong nationalist grievance ; whilst Great Britain and Greece have an almost incontestable superiority in sea power and an imperial position dependent on that superiority. Although in the Balkan Triple Agreement the South Slavs of Serbia do not bulk so large as the Russians in that of Europe, the big battalions and mediaeval policy of the two Slav Powers do play much the same part in either case. Moreover, if the European and Balkan Triple Agreements are to be combinations for the maintenance of peace and the furtherance of progress, the Slav partner is in either case a perilous associate; since the policy of such a partnership will always be at the mercy of the least pacific partner. It is no doubt also chiefly coincidence that the opposing Three-Powers group should in either case consist of the most formidable military machine and the most warlike race in the region concerned—in the one case the Prusso-German, in the other case the Bulgar nation :—supported in either case by States controlled by a similar and sympathetic race—the Austro-German and the Turk —but containing so many alien and antipathetic elements as much to neutralize their support; for neither the Slav elements of the Austrian Empire nor the Greek elements of the Ottoman Empire would ever be willing allies of Prussia or Bulgaria respectively. Finally, the third partner in each group, namely, Italy and Albania, is too much divided against itself to add any strength at present to the group policy. Italy cannot, as things are, join Austria in fighting France and England, and Albania can bring little effective assistance at present against Greece and Serbia. Therefore already before the Balkan wars there was a strong preponderance of power in favour of the European Triple Agreement, and as the first result of the Balkan wars there has been an even greater preponderance of the Balkan Allies over Bulgaria, Turkey, and Albania. Now as a second result that Balkan preponderance has been added to the already existing preponderance of the Triple Agreement over the Triple Alliance. The inequitable partition of Bucharest and the unenlightened policy of the Balkan States has dangerously added to the overweight in one scale of the so-called European balance of power.

But there is an even more dangerous consequence of the Balkan wars and of the Treaty of Bucharest than a mere throwing of the military preponderance of the Balkan Triple Agreement into the scale of the European Triple Agreement. The European balance of power is not really an equilibrium of static forces—a balance of deadweight of armaments and allies—any more than is the Balkan balance. It is really like the Balkan system, a coalition of conservative factors that have as much or almost as much as they think they can get, against one corporate force for change—an accumulation of static interests against a dynamic influence —an enclosing and repressing restraint upon an explosive and expansive energy. The energy in either case is the national expansion and racial efficiency of the Teutonic and Bulgar stock. The compression which seems bound to produce an explosion in either case is that of Serbs and Greeks on Bulgars, which has cut them off from Macedonia, and the pressure of British and Slavs on Teutons, which has checked the expansion of the German Empire.

The economic importance of the outlet for German energies through eastern Europe into Asia Minor has already been dealt with. But the political importance of this safety valve can only be understood if we remember the immense national energy developed by Germany in the present and past generations, and the impermeable barrier presented to its expansion in every other direction. German nationalism, considered as an underlying current too strong and deep to be affected by political distinctions between Austro-

Germans and Prusso-Germans, or even by racial differences between north and south, is perhaps the greatest political force now operative. German nationalism in the form of militarism is perhaps the most dynamic force for political disturbance that at present exists—just as in the form of socialism it is perhaps the most dynamic force for political development. It is this force which, having developed too late to expend itself either on developing waste places of the earth or on destroying its less warlike neighbours, is now cut off on the west from possible expansion overseas by British sea-power, and on the east from expansion overland by Slav land-power. Pressure of sea power is no menace to Germany though it may be a marplot to Prussia —the pressure of the Slavs on the Teutons is another matter. Slav expansion in the Balkan wars has now not only cut off Prussian imperialism from its eastern expansion into Asia Minor but has closed in upon the racial frontiers of German nationalism in Serbia and Croatia. The detachment of Roumania from its political allegiance to Germany and the downfall of Turkey have closed the Prussian outlet to the East by Galicia and the Black Sea, while the aggrandizement of Serbia and Greece and the debilitation of Bulgaria have closed the Austrian outlet by the Vardar valley and the Aegean. It has already been shown that the Slav power may well think that the time has come to meet the economic expansion of German nationalism in the Near East by war; and it is now suggested that the Teutonic Powers may also think that the time has come to reopen by war the outlet to the Near East that war has just closed. Compared with this aggravation of the tension between Berlin and Petersburg, the alleviation of the strain between Berlin and London, due to the co-operation of the British and German Governments in the Balkan crisis, is but a slight and superficial relief. Even should this improvement in Anglo-German relations result in opening up for Germany new outlets in Africa, such remote and unreal relaxation of the pressure on German nationalism overseas will not distract it from reopening its only overland outlet in the Near East.

The political result of the Balkan wars on Europe has already caused a heavy addition to the armaments of Germany, France, and Russia. Every slow movement of the Slavonic hordes is met by some swift manœuvre of the Teutonic hosts. Only the restraining influences of the Western Powers can prevent the Balkan wars infecting European nationalism with the war fever of its younger days.[1]

§ 24. MORAL RESULTS

The moral effect of the Balkan wars is a matter of even more moment than their economic and political effect; for it is the moral aversion of the civilized mind for war that is the main protection of society against it. If the effect of a war has been to lessen that moral aversion, then, however beneficial the war may have been in its political results, and however advantageous economically, in the main it will have been harmful. Wars of liberation are the more morally harmful the more distinctly they are rebellions and not revolutions.[2] Thus American foreign relations suffered for nearly a century from the bellicose tone given to them by the fact that American territories were acquired by foreign war against France, and American liberties by foreign war against Great Britain. In the same way, German foreign relationships still suffer in tone from the foundations of the Empire having

---

[1] There is nothing to alter in this prediction in consequence of the European war which has since broken out. It may even serve to explain the genesis of this war in the race rivalry of Teuton and Slav.

[2] This may seem a hard saying, and the hero-worship of great rebels such as Washington, Garibaldi, and Cromwell is certainly a strong moral influence. But it may be illustrated by comparing the moral reactions in England after the Great Rebellion with those which followed the Revolution a half-century later; and by comparing the War of Partition itself, looked at as a moral result of the War of Coalition, with the moral results of the Turkish revolution.

been laid by successful foreign war ; while the imperialism of the Napoleonic policy still obscures in France the internationalism of the principles of the Revolution. The British Empire, on the other hand, though the title to most of its territories is one of conquest, derives its character and constitution from peace ; and consequently its part in the politics of the world has been for some time pacific—if not so pacificist as the United States has recently become. It requires a century of progress by peace to eradicate the demoralizations of a few months' progress by war.

Turning to the Balkan States we find that, with the exception of Montenegro and Albania, both still in the stage where private war is still a normal social relationship, all of them were, morally speaking, pacific peoples.[1] They were of course prepared for war and prompt to seize an opportunity of forwarding their national development by war ; but for war as a political procedure they had no predilection, and they would have preferred any other means of attaining their end. This is natural enough in peoples who have emerged only one generation or so from such a waste of war as was Turkey in Europe. Newly emancipated democracies are not eager to risk the first laborious accumulations of peaceful effort in warlike adventures. We have already said that it takes a century for the glamour of wars of conquest or emancipation to die out, and it may be added that it is at least three generations after an epoch of war before the taste for it revives.[2] If this is so, we would expect to find, as is the case, that the belligerency of the Balkan nations was in proportion both to the length of the period of war, by which they emancipated themselves, and to the

[1] The people are here referred to as a whole. The public opinion of the ' politicals ' in the capital is a small though noisy element in the public opinion of these populations which consist almost entirely of peasantry.

[2] The reader is probably more ready to believe now that the British generation of to-day is more bellicose than the Bulgar, than he would have been when this was written.

length of the period of peace succeeding that war. For example, Bulgaria achieved emancipation last of the Allies and with the least fighting, and we accordingly find that before these Balkan wars the Bulgar people was distinctly more pacific than the Serbians or the Greeks—especially if the greater provocation to Bulgar national sentiment be discounted. It is to be feared, however, that one result of these wars will be to change this. Henceforward, Balkan opinion will draw its inspiration, not from a comparison of their social abjection under Ottoman rule with the social achievements of peaceful progress that followed it, but rather from a comparison of the national expansion that has been, or might have been, achieved by war with such as had, or had not, been acquired by peace. Those nations, like Greece and Serbia, that have gained more by war than they ever had ventured to claim in time of peace, will be strongly tempted to try their luck again. Serbia in the hope of becoming the centre of an Empire of the Southern Slavs, Greece hoping to restore the Greek Empire at Constantinople —both legitimate national aspirations. Those who have fared badly, like Bulgaria and Turkey, will attribute their failure, as they both justly may, to the effect of disadvantageous diplomatic or strategic conditions, and not to war being wrong policy for the world in general or for them in particular. They will be all the more determined to retrieve their reputation, restore their fortunes, and reassert their rights, by waging war as soon as war can again be waged. The War of Liberation by itself would in any case have given public opinion in the Balkan Peninsula a permanent bias towards war; which would, however, have been partly counteracted by the pacific and fraternal relations established by the Alliance. Then when the inevitable friction came between Bulgaria and Serbia, public opinion would have been restrained by the recollection that the two countries had been brothers in arms in the Great War. As it was, the War of Partition followed so close on the War of Coalition that the moral and sentimental ties created by the former had had no time to establish themselves in the public point of view. As things now are, the War of Partition has left the moral relationships between the two groups of Balkan democracies stripped of every sentiment of solidarity and full of ' raw wounds that bleed whene'er they see the hand that gave them '. It has been said in a previous chapter that the measure of pacificism in a State is almost a measure of the degree of popular government ; but this is not applicable to the period affected by the passions of war. Balkan democracy is still under the influence of such passions, and it will be found that war, whether successful or unsuccessful, has in the case of each people somewhat deteriorated the national character and brought out its defects.

The differences in character of the Balkan nationalities were summarily sketched in a previous chapter ; and it was there suggested that each nation emerged from the warfare of Turkish misrule with their virtues their own, but with defects in common that were due to that rule. They now, however, would seem to have emerged from these wars with a strong dose of the vices peculiar to their virtues. This can best be seen by taking their moral attitude on entering the War of Coalition against Turkey, a war entered into in the same spirit as that in which they had emerged from previous wars of liberation, and then contrasting it with their attitude towards the War of Partition. Observers of the behaviour of the general public in the Balkan States during the early days of the War of Coalition noted with surprise the good effect of a war crisis on general behaviour. The tone of public opinion in Athens became reserved and self-reliant—that of Sofia became expansive and European—that of Belgrade practical and purposeful : it seemed as though a common national cause had moulded the various characteristics into a common national character. It was, of course, no more than the effect of a great crisis, which had brought to the control of the public mind and voice the best elements in the public character. But it is the curse of war that while it may call such good elements to the front, it will recklessly use them up and rashly throw them aside. When, six months later, the War of Partition was the question of the day, the same observers were no less struck by the change for the worse in the tone taken by the press and the public at the Balkan capitals. The defects in the national character of each people were exhibited at their worst. From Athens arose a clamour of chauvinism, which was followed by a press campaign of such mendacious mendicity as the Greek character at its worst has ever shown itself capable of. Sofia, for its part, contributed to the War of Partition by developing, in a delicate diplomatic situation, a stubborn stupidity such as has made the Bulgar character at its worst through all ages the bugbear of the Balkans. At Belgrade when all the strength of Serbian statesmanship was being strained to make the Serbian army keep bounds and respect treaty rights, the press flung itself into a fanatical frenzy of rhodomontade and romance. The lamentable loss of tone in public opinion at each capital can be easily verified by comparing leading articles dating from October 1912 with those of six months later.

No doubt the harm is not permanent and, as passion cools, the balance will be restored and the national characteristics will revert to a condition in which there is more of virtue than of vice ; but the convalescence will be slow and a relapse easy. On the other hand, the effect of this deplorable exhibition on the moral relations between the Western and the Near-Eastern peoples has been lamentable and will be lasting. The injury affects that sphere of democratic relationships between peoples which, as earlier chapters have shown, is the only form of foreign alliance on which Balkan democracy can safely rely. But the community of religion which informs the fellow feeling of Russia for these Balkan peoples, and the community in civil and constitutional systems which inspire British and French sympathies for them, have both received a fatal blow from the War of Partition. The shock was all the worse that it came short and sharp in the middle of European enthusiasm over the ' crusade' of the Coalition. Europe felt it had made a fool of itself over the Alliance, and had then been made a fool of by the Allies. Its indignation was not unmixed with irritation and was forcibly expressed.

> Themselves the conquerors
> Make war upon themselves, brother to brother,
> Blood to blood, self against self : O preposterous
> And frantic outrage—

And it is as perpetrators of an outrage to civilization that the participants in the War of Partition are at present considered by Europe.

This is one of the most unfortunate moral results of these wars. It has already exhibited itself in a restricting of existing international relations and a reluctance to enter new engagements, with resulting bad effects on the financial and political position of the Balkans such as have already been noted. For, unfortunately, the disapproval of Europe has been visited on the character of the Balkan peoples in the first place, and, in the second place, on the working of democratic principles; whereas the true cause of the trouble, the work of war on nationalism, has almost escaped notice. The brutalities and treacheries of the War of Partition are, it must be repeated, merely a relapse into those conditions of social warfare which had been preserved by Europe in Macedonia.[1]

One democratic relationship fortunately remains unaffected by these wars, and that is the relationship, which has already been suggested as being the most important—the relationship with the United States. The Balkan nations can still count on emigration to America for political education and financial support. The American Immigration Act will not exclude the ex-soldier from the Balkans for having committed murder wholesale in Macedonia : the

[1] The relapse of Europe into conditions of the bitterest and most barbarous warfare makes this defence of the Balkan States sadly unnecessary.

American employer will not pay him any the less wages
for having pillaged and burnt: nor will he send any less
of his wages home; for there will be scarcely one of such
emigrants whose character will be any the worse for what
he has done, and of whom it could not be said that—

> S'il ne tuait, violait, brûlait,
> Ne fût assez bonne personne.

It has been the rôle of the New World to maintain democratic relationship with the Old World based principally
on the demand for masses of the raw human material of
Europe and the re-exportation of a small proportion of it
as a manufactured product. The relationship with Western
Europe has, on these lines, been productive of some benefit
to both societies : the relationship with Africa, in the form
of the slave trade, was a source of unmixed evil to both
continents. But the relationship with Eastern Europe will,
it seems likely, avoid the disadvantages and dangers of
both these precedents. There will be no Slave States on
the one side, and there will be no Liberia on the other :
there will be no fields and factories empty in Europe, and
no over-filled pockets in America; but men will go where
they are most wanted, and money will flow to where it is
most needed. It can at least be said for the Balkan wars
that they did not deteriorate the relationship between the
peoples of the Balkan peninsula and the peoples of the
American continent.

In another moral region, however, there is a serious
indictment to be brought against these wars. Every advance
has its corresponding disadvantages, and the development
of democratic control over foreign relations has undoubtedly
had the effect of weakening the moral obligation of treaties.
It is curious that it should be so, for the democratic influence,
in other respects, exercises a moral restraint on foreign policy
in time of peace. A democratic diplomacy is less likely to
make the moral mistakes into which despotic imperialism,

or diplomatic opportunism, fall so easily; and therefore, though it is less sensational in tactics, it is, as a rule, sounder in strategy. But the very vitality and humanity which keep a democratic Government in touch, by instinct and by imagination, with another democracy through every change of condition in their relationship, only too often make hard-and-fast obligations, contracted under other conditions, too irksome to be borne. Whereas the more conservative character of the despotic or diplomatic Government enables it to maintain, artificially, if necessary, the same relationship under which the obligation was contracted, even though the conditions have completely changed. The avoidance of ' entangling alliances ' by the United States is sound, because of the great difficulty imposed on the nation of observing such obligations, owing to the democratic character of its diplomacy. The ' continuity of foreign policy ' on which the United Kingdom prides itself, is achieved by the exclusion of the more democratic factors in foreign policy. The most scrupulous observance of the point of honour and of the precept that honesty is the best policy, admits that treaty obligations may be nullified by a complete change of the conditions with which the *casus foederis* was concerned; although even so, when there is any advantage accruing from the breach, the defaulting party will not escape odium.[1] The Governments concerned in these wars were very democratic in character, even when not so in constitution, as in the case of the Ottoman Government; and the conditions of the last few years in the Near East have, moreover, been those of a crisis in which fundamental changes have been continually occurring in the whole region of treaty right. Repudiations of treaty obligations were therefore to be expected, and, within reason, would have been covered by general approbation of the progress made or condoned by special considerations. Thus general appro-

---

[1] It would remove a danger from international relations if every country published annually a list of the treaties it considered as ' alive '.

bation of the partition of Macedonia would have covered
the nullification of the Treaty of Berlin; and the abolition
there of the Ottoman capitulations would have been condoned in view of the termination of Turkish rule. But,
unfortunately, Bulgarian policy put that State into a false
position, in which it could proceed only by straining to
breaking-point a whole structure of very recent compacts.
The first of these to break was the partition settlement
embodied in the solemn Treaty of Alliance between the
Serbian and Bulgarian sovereigns, under sanction of the
Tsar. The next was the partition settlement imposed by
the so-called ' award ' between Roumania and Bulgaria,
also under Russian sanction. The third was the partition
between Turkey and Bulgaria in the Treaty of London,
signed under Anglo-Russian pressure. The almost simul-
taneous repudiation of all these engagements could not but
profoundly impress European opinion; which in this case
has shown an inclination to argue from it the inefficacy of
international arrangements for the preservation of peace.
Of what use are vague arbitration obligations, it is argued,
when the precise procedure and strong sanction of the
Serbo-Bulgar Treaty was of no avail : of what use arbitration awards when that of Petersburg was so swiftly and
cynically repudiated : of what use international interventions in the interest of peace when bankrupt and beaten
Turkey could re-establish itself in Europe by tearing up the
Treaty of London while the ink was still wet, and do it,
moreover, on the strength of financial support from one
western capital and of moral support from another ? The
answer is that no arbitration agreement or award would
stop a people going to war when it is determined to do so;
though such provisions will hinder a bellicose Government in
working up war, and will help a pacific Government in dealing with a war fever. For this purpose, the more general
and purely abstract the agreements and awards are, the
better—in that such general provisions have an equal moral

obligation, while they encounter less practical obstacles to their enforcement or execution. For instance, if the arbitral agreement in the Serbo-Bulgar treaty had provided any alternative to a Russian arbitration, such arbitration might have been carried out and might have preserved the peace. If the Petersburg award and the Treaty of London had had a purely moral sanction and had offered no presumption of political support from Petersburg or London, Bulgaria would never have uncovered Silistria and Adrianople so as to concentrate against Serbia. But just as Bulgarian nationalism failed because it tried to combine the incompatible, namely, the static political forces of peace and the dynamic popular forces of war, so European internationalism failed because it allowed the moral sanction of neutral arbitration and impartial award to become dependent on the material sanction of national armies and imperial navies which it could not employ. It is not the new principle of international arbitration that has been discredited by these breaches of treaty and relapses into war, but the old practice of diplomatic intervention with no democratic driving power or direction. But public opinion, or rather the opinion of publicists, will continue to ascribe the failure to insufficiencies in the principle of arbitration instead of to defects in the diplomatic application of it—just as they ascribe the ' atrocities ' to the principle of nationality instead of to the action of war upon nationalism.

But the region in which war has worked most harm is in the moral atmosphere of the Near-Eastern renascence. It has not been possible in this short review to do full justice to the extraordinary significance of the Ottoman revolution, which, morally speaking, is as epoch-making an event for Asia as was the French Revolution for Europe—that French Revolution whose main features it has unfortunately been compelled by war to reproduce. Excluding China and Japan as Far-Eastern and of different development, this Ottoman revolution may be considered as the beginning of the true

Asiatic national renascence. Though the seed has fallen on
stony ground in Persia, even as it has fallen by the wayside in
Macedonia, yet it was none the less good seed. It is the
self-same impetus which made the history of the nineteenth
century in Europe a record of progress in economic science
and in national democracy that has now spread to Asia.
What it will there produce is a question of transcendent
importance to us all. Will it be merely an Asiatic adaptation
of European industrialism, militarism, socialism, and all the
other ' isms ' with which the Western world is already weary
and heavy laden? Will the Asiatic revolutions have the
same moral history as the French Revolution—and, after
imperialist warfares, will they end only in establishing a rather
better form of government? Will the Asiatic renascence, like
the Protestant Reformation, do no more than bring the
Islamic religion into conformity with scientific reasoning?
It would seem indeed that it can do no more than this if
we are to judge by the results in Persia and Turkey, where
war has perverted or suppressed the new consciousness of
liberty, equality, and fraternity, and brought it crippled to
the ground. But the leaders of the new age in Asia have a
higher view of their mission than a mere raising of their state
to the materialist standards of modern civilization. Exploitation, efficiency, and education are for them only means to
an end. They believe, as do many of us, that the European
social systems and standards of civilization have in themselves
no long life left to them, but are awaiting a reanimation—
a reinspiration, from outside, and that the social mind and
body have developed until the communal soul is dead and
can only be revived by a spiritual reawakening. Where now
could such reawakening come from if not from the birthplace of all great spiritual revivals in the Near East? Might
it not have been forthcoming from the simple virtues and
strong faith of such a race as the Turks when stimulated by
contact with Jewish, Greek, and European thought?
This Messianic vision of the Young Turks has been blown

from the guns; and the renascence in so far as the Near East
is concerned has become no more than, at best, a reformation
and will never bring us a revelation. Not that there will be
no gain from these Balkan Wars. They will open the way
for revivals of European arts by the South Slavs, of
European sciences by Greeks and Armenians, of European
socialism by Bulgars and Turks. Yet, great as these gains
will be, they will be no more than contributions to European
culture as it is; they will not convert Christian civilization
to what it should be. The new revelation will not now come
in our time, nor will it come now from the Near East. We
must look for the dawn over a farther horizon, and who can
say that the Asiatic peoples are altogether wrong in believing
that the truth is in their life and not in the European industrialism and capitalism that threaten it? They believe that
the only salvation for us lies in recovering what they still
keep hold of;—but they have not as yet found words to
tell us so.

> I perceive not he affects to preach
> The doctrine of his sect whate'er it be,
> Make proselytes as madmen thirst to do;
> How can he give his neighbour the real ground,
> His own conviction? Ardent as he is—
> Call his great truth a lie, why still the old
> ' Be it as God please ' reassureth him.
> ' How, beast,' said I, ' this stolid carelessness
> Sufficeth thee, when Rome is on her march
> To stamp out like a little spark thy town,
> Thy tribe, thy crazy tale and thee at once? '

But that little spark was not stamped out by war.

The work of war upon Near Eastern nationalism has now
been explored through a hundred years of history, and
examined in detail in its effects on the events of the last
few months. Repeated recourse to war has been shown
to have been responsible for the failure of a whole series

of possible solutions of the Near-Eastern Question. First
it was the wars caused by the imperialist policies of the
Great Powers that prevented an international trusteeship
for Macedonia. War, then, wrecked the imperialist solution
that would have been afforded by a constitutional Ottoman
Empire ; for it was wars between the nationalist parties in
the Empire that made representative institutions unworkable. War, finally, has injured the present nationalist settlement by making it non-national in certain respects to an
extent which will require remedy. That remedy is being
effected by ' suppressed' race wars which have already
almost resulted in an open race war between Greece and
Turkey, and which have established a warlike relationship
between the Balkan nations that will make them mortgage
for armaments much of their newly-won liberties.

It has been shown that by allowing a region in Europe to
remain in a condition of endemic war Europe has been exposed
to epidemics of war ; and it is suggested that the best
precaution against the danger is an immediate inoculation
of the governments of Europe with a strong dose of democratic
diplomacy.

> All may be well, tho' if God sort it so
> 'Tis more than we deserve or I expect.

APPENDIX

No. 1

TREATY OF COALITION

SERBIA AND BULGARIA

Signed February 29, 1912

(Text as published in the *Matin* of November 24, 1913)

S. M. Ferdinand Ier, roi des Bulgares, et S. M. Pierre Ier, roi de Serbie, pénétrés de la conviction de la communauté d'intérêts et de la similitude des destinées de leurs États et des deux peuples frères, bulgare et serbe, et décidés à défendre solidairement, avec des forces communes, ces intérêts et à s'efforcer de les mener à bonne fin, sont convenus de ce qui suit :

ARTICLE PREMIER. — Le royaume de Bulgarie et le royaume de Serbie se garantissent mutuellement leur indépendance politique et l'intégrité de leur territoire, en s'engageant d'une manière absolue et sans restriction d'aucune sorte à se porter réciproquement secours, avec la totalité de leurs forces, dans tout cas où l'un des deux royaumes serait attaqué par un ou plusieurs États.

ART. 2. — Les deux parties contractantes s'engagent de même à se porter mutuellement secours, avec la totalité de leurs forces, au cas où l'une quelconque des grandes Puissances tenterait de s'annexer, ou d'occuper, ou de prendre possession avec ses troupes, même provisoirement, de n'importe quelle partie des territoires de la péninsule des Balkans se trouvant actuellement sous la domination turque, si l'une des parties contractantes estime ce fait contraire à ses intérêts vitaux et constituant un *casus belli*.

ART. 3. — Les deux parties contractantes s'engagent à ne conclure la paix que conjointement et après entente préalable.

ART. 4. — Une convention militaire sera conclue à l'effet d'assurer l'exécution du présent traité d'une manière complète et la plus conforme au but poursuivi. Cette convention stipulera aussi bien que tout ce qu'il y aura lieu d'entreprendre de part et d'autre en cas de guerre, ayant trait à l'organisation militaire, la dislocation et la mobilisation des troupes, les rapports des hauts commandements, devra être établi, dès le temps de paix, pour la préparation et la bonne conduite de la guerre.

La convention militaire fera partie intégrante du présent traité. Son élaboration devra commencer au plus tard quinze jours après la signature du présent traité et être terminée dans le délai suivant de deux mois.

Art. 5. — Le présent traité et la convention militaire seront en vigueur du jour de leur signature jusqu'au 31 décembre 1920 inclusivement. Ils ne pourront être prorogés au delà de ce délai qu'après une entente complémentaire, expressément sanctionnée des deux parties contractantes. Toutefois, au cas où au jour de l'expiration du traité et de la convention militaire les deux parties se trouveraient être en guerre ou sans avoir liquidé encore la situation résultant de la guerre, le traité et la convention seront maintenus en vigueur jusqu'à la signature de la paix ou à la liquidation de l'état de choses amené par la guerre.

Art. 6. — Le présent traité sera établi en deux exemplaires uniformes, rédigés tous les deux en langue serbe et bulgare. Il sera signé par les souverains et les ministres des Affaires étrangères des deux États. La convention militaire également en deux exemplaires, rédigés en bulgare et en serbe, sera signée par les souverains, les ministres des Affaires étrangères et les plénipotentiaires militaires spéciaux.

Art. 7. — Le présent traité et la convention militaire ne pourront être publiés ou communiqués à d'autres États qu'après entente préalable des deux parties contractantes, et ce conjointement et simultanément.

Une entente préalable sera de même nécessaire pour l'admission d'un tiers État dans l'alliance.

Fait à Sofia, le 29 février 1912.

Secret Annexe to the Treaty

Article premier. — Au cas où des troubles intérieurs, de nature à mettre en danger les intérêts nationaux ou d'État des parties contractantes ou de l'une d'elles, survenaient en Turquie, comme au cas où des difficultés intérieures ou extérieures avec lesquelles la Turquie se verrait aux prises mettraient en cause le maintien du *statu quo* dans la péninsule des Balkans, celle des deux parties contractantes qui aboutirait la première à la conviction qu'une action militaire doit être engagée de ce fait s'adressera, par une proposition motivée, à l'autre partie qui sera tenue d'entrer immédiatement dans un échange de vues, et si elle ne tombe pas d'accord avec son alliée, de lui donner une réponse motivée.

Si une entente en vue d'une action intervient, cette entente devra être communiquée à la Russie, et au cas où cette Puissance

ne s'y opposerait pas l'action sera engagée, conformément à l'entente
établie et en s'inspirant en tout des sentiments de solidarité et de
communauté d'intérêts. Dans le cas contraire — soit si une entente
n'intervient pas — les deux États feront appel à l'opinion de la
Russie, laquelle opinion sera, si et dans la mesure dans laquelle la
Russie se prononcera, obligatoire pour les deux parties.

Au cas où, la Russie s'abstenant de donner son opinion et l'entente
entre les deux parties contractantes ne pouvant, même après cela,
être obtenue, celle des deux parties qui est pour une action décide
d'engager cette dernière à elle seule et à ses risques, l'autre partie
sera tenue d'observer une neutralité amicale vis-à-vis de son alliée,
de procéder sur-le-champ à une mobilisation dans les limites prévues
par la convention militaire, et de se porter, avec toutes ses forces,
au secours de son alliée, si un tiers État prenait le parti de la Turquie.

ART. 2. — Tous les accroissements territoriaux qui seraient
réalisés par une action commune dans le sens des articles premier
et second du traité et de l'article premier de la présente annexe
secrète tombent sous la domination commune (condominium) des
deux États alliés. Leur liquidation aura lieu sans retard, dans un
délai maximum de trois mois après le rétablissement de la paix, et
sur les bases suivantes :

La Serbie reconnaît à la Bulgarie le droit sur les territoires à l'est
des Rhodopes et de la rivière Strouma : la Bulgarie reconnaît le
droit de la Serbie sur ceux situés au nord et à l'ouest du Char-
Planina.

Quant aux territoires compris entre le Char, les Rhodopes, la
mer Égée et le lac d'Ochrida, si les deux parties acquièrent la
conviction que leur organisation en province autonome distincte est
impossible en vue des intérêts communs des nationalités bulgare
et serbe ou pour d'autres raisons d'ordre intérieur ou extérieur, il
sera disposé de ces territoires conformément aux stipulations ci-
dessous :

La Serbie s'engage à ne formuler aucune revendication en ce qui
concerne les territoires situés au delà de la ligne tracée sur la carte
ci-annexée et qui, ayant son point de départ à la frontière turco-
bulgare, au mont Golem (au nord de Kr Palanka), suit la direction
générale du sud-ouest jusqu'au lac d'Ochrida, en passant par le
mont Kitka, entre les villages de Metejevo et Podarji-Kon, par le
sommet à l'est du village Nerav, en suivant la ligne de partage des
eaux jusqu'au sommet 1,000, au nord du village de Baschtévo,
entre les villages de Liubentzi et Petarlitza, par le sommet Ostritch
1,000 (Lissetz-Planina), le sommet 1,050 entre les villages de Dratch
et Opila, par les villages de Talichmantzi et Jivalevo, le sommet

1,050, le sommet 1,000, le village Kichali, la ligne principale de partage des eaux Gradichté-Planina jusqu'au sommet Gorichté, vers le sommet 1,023, suivant ensuite la ligne de partage des eaux entre les villages Ivankovtzi et Loghintzi, par Vetersko et Sopot sur le Vardar. Traversant le Vardar, elle suit les crêtes vers le sommet 2,550 et jusqu'à la montagne Petropole, par la ligne de partage des eaux de cette montagne entre les villages de Krapa et Barbarès jusqu'au sommet 1,200, entre les villages de Yakryenovo et Drenovo, jusqu'au mont Tchesma (1,254), par la ligne de partage des eaux des montagnes Babanina et Krouchka-Tepessi, entre les villages de Salp et Tzerske, jusqu'au sommet de la Protoyska-Planina, à l'est du village de Belitza, par Bréjani, jusqu'au sommet 1,200 (Ilinska-Planina), par la ligne de partage des eaux passant par le sommet 1,330 jusqu'au sommet 1,217 et entre les villages de Livoitcha et Gorentzi jusqu'au lac d'Ochrida près du monastère de Gabovtzi.

La Bulgarie s'engage à accepter cette frontière si S. M. l'empereur de Russie, qui sera sollicité d'être l'arbitre suprême en cette question, se prononce en faveur de cette ligne.

Il va de soi que les deux parties contractantes s'engagent à accepter comme frontière définitive la ligne que S. M. l'empereur de Russie, dans les limites susindiquées, aurait trouvé correspondre le plus aux droits et aux intérêts des deux parties.

ART. 3. — Copie du traité et de la présente annexe secrète sera communiquée conjointement au gouvernement impérial de Russie, qui sera prié en même temps d'en prendre acte, de faire preuve de bienveillance à l'égard des buts qu'ils poursuivent, et de prier S. M. l'empereur de Russie de daigner accepter et approuver les attributions désignées pour sa personne et son gouvernement, par les clauses de ces deux actes.

ART. 4. — Tout différend qui surgirait touchant l'interprétation et l'exécution d'une quelconque des clauses du traité, de la présente annexe secrète et de la convention militaire sera soumis à la décision définitive de la Russie, dès lors que l'une des deux parties aura déclaré qu'elle estime impossible une entente par des pourparlers directs.

ART. 5. — Aucune des dispositions de la présente annexe secrète ne pourra être publiée ou communiquée à un autre État sans une entente préalable des deux parties et l'assentiment de la Russie.

Fait à Sofia, le 29 février 1912.

MILITARY CONVENTION

Serbia and Bulgaria

Signed June 12, 1912

Conformément à l'esprit et sur la base de l'article 3 du traité d'amitié et d'alliance entre le royaume de Bulgarie et le royaume de Serbie et afin de mieux assurer la conduite de la guerre avec succès et la réalisation plus complète des buts que l'alliance a en vue, les deux parties contractantes conviennent des stipulations ci-dessous, qui auront en tout même force et valeur que les dispositions du traité lui-même.

' Art. 1er. — Le royaume de Bulgarie et le royaume de Serbie s'engagent, dans les cas prévus par les articles 1 et 2 du traité d'alliance et par l'article 1 de l'annexe secrète à ce traité, à se porter mutuellement secours, la Bulgarie avec une force armée qui ne devra pas être inférieure à deux cent mille combattants et la Serbie avec une force d'au moins cent cinquante mille combattants, en mesure aussi bien de combattre à la frontière que de prendre part à des opérations militaires hors du territoire national.

' Dans ce nombre ne sauraient être compris ni les combattants de formations surnuméraires, ni ceux du troisième ban serbe, ni les troupes territoriales bulgares.

' Ce contingent de combattants devra être rendu à la frontière ou au delà des frontières de son territoire national — dans la direction où il devra être dirigé suivant les causes et le but de la guerre, et d'après le développement des opérations militaires — au plus tard le 21e jour après la déclaration de la guerre ou la communication de l'État allié que le *casus foederis* s'est produit. Toutefois, même avant l'expiration de ce délai, les deux parties considéreront comme leur devoir d'alliée — et si cela est conforme à la nature des opérations militaires et peut contribuer à l'issue favorable de la guerre — d'envoyer, même partiellement et dans les limites de la mobilisation et de la concentration, leurs troupes sur le champ de bataille dès le septième jour à partir de la déclaration de la guerre ou de la survenance du *casus foederis*.

' Art. 2. — Si la Roumanie attaque la Bulgarie, la Serbie est tenue de lui déclarer immédiatement la guerre et de diriger contre elle ses forces, d'au moins cent mille combattants, soit sur le moyen Danube, soit sur le théâtre d'opérations de la Dobroudja.

' Au cas où la Turquie attaquerait la Bulgarie, la Serbie s'engage à pénétrer en Turquie et à distraire de ses troupes mobilisées cent mille combattants au moins pour les diriger sur le théâtre d'opérations du Vardar.

' Si la Serbie se trouve être à ce moment seule ou conjointement avec la Bulgarie, déjà en guerre avec un tiers État, elle engagera contre la Roumanie ou la Turquie toutes les troupes dont elle conservera la libre disposition.

' Art. 3. — Si l'Autriche-Hongrie attaque la Serbie, la Bulgarie est tenue de déclarer immédiatement la guerre à l'Autriche-Hongrie et de diriger ses troupes, d'au moins deux cent mille combattants, en Serbie, de telle sorte que, unies à l'armée serbe, elles opèrent soit offensivement, soit défensivement, contre l'Autriche-Hongrie.

' La même obligation incombera à la Bulgarie vis-à-vis de la Serbie au cas où l'Autriche-Hongrie, sous quelque prétexte que ce soit, d'accord ou sans le consentement de la Turquie, fait pénétrer ses troupes dans le sandjak de Novi-Bazar et que par suite la Serbie lui déclare la guerre ou, pour la défense de ses intérêts, dirige ses troupes dans le sandjak et par là provoque un conflit armé entre elle et l'Autriche-Hongrie.

' Au cas où la Turquie attaquerait la Serbie, la Bulgarie s'engage à franchir immédiatement la frontière turque et à prélever sur ses troupes, mobilisées conformément à l'article premier de la présente convention, une armée forte d'au moins cent mille combattants, qui sera dirigée sur le théâtre d'opérations du Vardar.

' Si la Roumanie attaque la Serbie, la Bulgarie est tenue d'attaquer les troupes roumaines dès qu'elles auront pénétré, en traversant le Danube, sur le territoire serbe.

' Si la Bulgarie, dans l'un quelconque des cas envisagés par le présent article, se trouve déjà, seule ou conjointement avec la Serbie, en guerre avec un tiers État, elle est tenue de porter au secours de la Serbie toutes les troupes dont elle conserverait la libre disposition.

' Art. 4. — Si la Bulgarie et la Serbie, suivant une entente préalable, déclarent la guerre à la Turquie, l'une et l'autre seront tenues, s'il n'en est disposé autrement par un arrangement spécial, de prélever sur leurs troupes, mobilisées conformément à l'article premier de la présente convention, et de diriger sur le théâtre d'opérations du Vardar une armée d'au moins cent mille combattants.

' Art. 5. — Au cas où l'une des parties contractantes déclarerait la guerre à un tiers État sans entente préalable et sans le consentement de l'autre partie contractante, cette dernière sera déliée des obligations prévues à l'article premier de la présente convention, mais sera tenue d'observer, pendant la durée de la guerre, une neutralité amicale vis-à-vis de son alliée, ainsi que de mobiliser sans retard une force d'au moins cinquante mille combattants qui sera concentrée de manière à assurer au mieux la liberté des mouvements de son alliée.

' Art. 6. — En cas de guerre conjointe, aucune des parties contractantes ne pourra conclure avec l'ennemi d'armistice plus long que vingt-quatre heures, sans une entente préalable et sans le consentement de l'autre partie.

' Une entente préalable et par écrit sera de même nécessaire pour que des pourparlers de paix puissent être engagés et un traité de paix signé.

' Art. 7. — Pendant la durée de la guerre, les troupes de chacune des parties contractantes seront commandées et toutes leurs opérations seront dirigées par leurs propres commandements.

' Lorsque des corps de troupes appartenant aux armées des deux États opéreront contre un même objectif, le commandement commun sera pris, pour des unités de même importance, par le chef le plus ancìen en grade, et pour des unités d'importance différente par le chef le plus ancien au point de vue du commandement exercé.

' Lorsqu'une ou plusieurs armées distinctes appartenant à une des parties contractantes seront mises à la disposition de l'autre partie, elles se trouveront sous les ordres de leurs propres commandants qui, pour la conduite stratégique des opérations, seront soumis au commandant en chef de l'armée à la disposition de laquelle elles sont mises.

' En cas de guerre conjointe contre la Turquie, le commandement en chef sur le théâtre d'opérations du Vardar appartiendra à la Serbie si l'armée principale serbe opère sur ce théâtre et si elle est numériquement plus forte que les troupes bulgares sur ce théâtre, conformément à l'article 4 de la présente convention. Toutefois si l'armée principale serbe n'opère pas sur ce théâtre, et lorsqu'elle y sera numériquement plus faible que les troupes bulgares, le commandement en chef sur ce théâtre appartiendra à la Bulgarie.

' Art. 8. — Au cas où les troupes des deux parties contractantes se trouveraient placées sous les ordres d'un même commandement, tous les ordres et toutes les prescriptions se rapportant à la conduite stratégique des opérations tactiques communes seront rédigées dans les deux langues — en bulgare et en serbe.

' Art. 9. — En ce qui concerne le ravitaillement et les subsistances en général, le logement, le service médical, le transport des blessés et malades ou l'inhumation des morts, le transport du matériel de guerre et autres objets similaires, l'armée de chacune des parties contractantes jouira des mêmes droits et facilités sur le territoire de l'autre partie et par les mêmes procédés que les troupes de cette dernière partie, conformément aux lois et règles locales. Toutes les autorités locales doivent, dans le même but, prêter leur appui aux troupes alliées.

' Le paiement de toutes les subsistances sera réglé par chaque partie pour son compte aux prix locaux, de préférence en espèces et dans des cas exceptionnels contre bons délivrés spécialement.

' Le transport des troupes et de tout le matériel de guerre, subsistances et autres objets en chemin de fer et les frais y relatifs seront à la charge de la partie sur le territoire de laquelle ce transport a lieu.

' Art. 10. — Les trophées appartiennent à l'armée qui les aura pris.

' Dans le cas où la prise a lieu par l'effet d'un combat en commun sur le même terrain, les deux armées partageront les trophées proportionnellement aux forces des combattants qui y auront directement participé.

' Art. 11. — Durant la guerre, chaque partie contractante aura un délégué dans l'état-major du commandement en chef ou dans les commandements des armées, lesquels délégués entretiendront les liens entre les deux armées sous tous les rapports.

' Art. 12. — Les opérations stratégiques et les cas qui ne sont pas prévus, ainsi que les contestations qui pourraient surgir, seront réglés d'un commun accord par les deux commandements en chef.

' Art. 13. — Les chefs des états-majors des armées alliées s'entendront, immédiatement après la conclusion de la présente convention, sur la distribution des troupes mobilisées d'après l'article premier de cette convention et leur groupement dans la zone de concentration dans les cas exposés ci-dessus, et sur les routes qui devront être réparées ou construites de nouveau en vue de la concentration rapide sur la frontière et les opérations ultérieures.

' Art. 14. — La présente convention sera en vigueur à partir du jour de sa signature et durera tant qu'aura force le traité d'amitié et d'alliance auquel elle est annexée à titre de partie intégrante.'

ARRANGEMENT ENTRE LES ÉTATS-MAJORS DE BULGARIE ET DE SERBIE

Conformément à l'article 13 de la convention militaire existant entre le royaume de Bulgarie et le royaume de Serbie, les délégués désignés par les deux parties ont, sur la base des plans d'opérations respectifs, convenu de ce qui suit :

' *Au cas d'une guerre entre la Bulgarie et la Serbie d'une part et la Turquie de l'autre :*

' Dans l'hypothèse où la principale armée turque serait concentrée dans la région d'Uskub, Koumanovo, Kratovo, Kotchani, Velès, les troupes alliées destinées à agir sur le théâtre d'opérations du Vardar seront réparties comme suit :

' 1º Une armée serbe de deux divisions marchera, par le Kara-Dagh, sur Uskub. Cette armée formera l'aile droite des troupes alliées ;

' 2º Une armée serbe de cinq divisions d'infanterie et une division de cavalerie avancera, par la vallée de la Moravitza et de la Ptchinia, sur le front Koumanovo-Kratovo. Cette armée constituera le centre des troupes alliées avec la mission d'opérer de front contre l'ennemi ;

' 3º Une armée bulgare de trois divisions formera l'aile gauche des troupes alliées, avec la mission d'opérer contre l'aile droite et sur les derrières de l'ennemi, dans les directions de Kustendil-Egri-Palanka-Uskub et Kustendil-Tzarévo-Sélo-Kotchani ;

' 4º Les deux chefs d'état-major général reconnaîtront ensemble la région entre Kustendil et Vrania, et si cette reconnaissance démontre la possibilité d'employer de grandes masses dans la direction Kustendil-Egri-Palanka-Uskub, les deux divisions serbes destinées à opérer, par le Kara-Dagh, contre Uskub, seront, si la situation générale le permet, employées à renforcer l'aile gauche des troupes alliées et seront concentrées à cet effet près de Kustendil ;

' 5º Pour couvrir le flanc droit des troupes alliées, le chef d'état-major de l'armée serbe disposera à sa convenance des trois divisions restantes du deuxième ban ;

' 6º Le chef d'état-major de l'armée bulgare s'engage à agir pour la prompte mise en état de la route de Bossilegrad à Vlassina ;

' 7º Si la situation exige le renforcement des troupes bulgares sur le théâtre d'opérations de la Maritza et si, pour le théâtre d'opérations du Vardar, toutes les troupes ci-dessus énumérées ne sont point indispensables, les unités nécessaires seront transportées de ce dernier théâtre d'opérations sur celui de la Maritza. A l'inverse, si la situation exige le renforcement des troupes alliées sur le théâtre d'opérations du Vardar et si le maintien de toutes les troupes désignées pour les opérations sur le théâtre de la Maritza n'est pas indispensable, les unités nécessaires seront transportées de ce théâtre sur celui du Vardar.

ANNEXE

' Les deux états-majors généraux s'engagent :

' a) A échanger tous leurs renseignements sur les armees des pays limitrophes ;

' b) A se procurer mutuellement le nombre voulu d'exemplaires de tous les règlements, instructions, cartes, etc., tant officiels que secrets

' *c*) A envoyer chacun dans l'armée alliée un certain nombre d'officiers chargés de se familiariser avec son organisation et d'en étudier la langue, conformément à l'article 2 de la convention militaire ;

' *d*) Les chefs d'état-major des armées serbe et bulgare se rencontreront chaque automne pour se mettre au courant de la situation générale et pour introduire dans les arrangements conclus les modifications rendues nécessaires par les changements de la situation.

' Varna, 19 juin 1912.

' Général R. POUTNIK,
' Général FITCHEFF.'

No. 2

TREATY OF COALITION

GREECE AND BULGARIA

Signed May 16, 1912
(Text published by the *Matin*, November 26, 1913)

Considérant que les deux royaumes désirent fermement la conservation de la paix dans la péninsule balkanique et peuvent, par une alliance défensive solide, mieux répondre à ce besoin :

Considérant, dans ce même ordre d'idées, que la coexistence pacifique des différentes nationalités en Turquie, sur la base d'une égalité politique réelle et véritable et le respect des droits découlant des traités ou autrement concédés aux nationalités chrétiennes de l'empire, constitue des conditions nécessaires pour la consolidation de l'état de choses en Orient ;

Considérant enfin qu'une coopération des deux royaumes, dans le sens indiqué, est de nature, dans l'intérêt même de leurs bons rapports avec l'empire ottoman, à faciliter et à corroborer l'entente des éléments grec et bulgare en Turquie :

Le gouvernement de Sa Majesté le roi des Bulgares et le gouvernement de Sa Majesté le roi des Hellènes se promettent de ne pas donner une tendance agressive quelconque à leur accord purement défensif et ayant résolu de conclure une alliance de paix et de protection réciproque dans les termes ci-dessous indiqués, ont nommé pour leurs plénipotentiaires . . .

Lesquels, après avoir échangé leurs pleins pouvoirs, ont arrêté ce qui suit :

ARTICLE PREMIER. — Si, contrairement au sincère désir des deux hautes parties contractantes, et en dépit d'une attitude de leur gouvernement évitant tout acte d'agression et toute provocation vis-à-vis de l'empire ottoman, l'un des deux États venait à être attaqué par la Turquie, soit dans son territoire, soit par une atteinte systématique aux droits découlant des traités ou des principes fondamentaux du droit des gens, les deux hautes parties contractantes sont tenues à se prêter réciproquement secours avec la totalité de leurs forces armées et par suite à ne conclure la paix que conjointement et d'accord.

ART. 2. — Les deux hautes parties contractantes se promettent mutuellement, d'un côté d'user de leur influence morale auprès de leurs congénères en Turquie afin qu'ils contribuent sincèrement à la coexistence pacifique des éléments constituant la population de l'empire, et de l'autre côté de se prêter une assistance réciproque et de marcher d'accord, dans toute action, auprès du gouvernement ottoman ou auprès des grandes puissances, qui aurait pour but d'obtenir ou d'assurer la réalisation des droits découlant des traités ou autrement concédés aux nationalités grecque et bulgare, l'application de l'égalité politique et des garanties constitutionnelles.

ART. 3. — Le présent traité aura une durée de trois ans à partir du jour de sa signature et sera renouvelé tacitement pour une année sauf dénonciation. Sa dénonciation doit être notifiée au moins six mois avant l'expiration de la troisième année à partir de la signature du traité.

ART. 4. — Le présent traité sera gardé secret. Il ne pourra être communiqué à une tierce puissance soit intégralement, soit en partie, ni divulgué en partie ou en tout qu'avec le consentement des deux hautes parties contractantes.

Le présent traité sera ratifié le plus tôt que faire se pourra. Les ratifications seront échangées à Sofia (ou à Athènes).

En foi de quoi, les plénipotentiaires respectifs ont signé le présent traité et y ont apposé leurs cachets.

Fait à Sofia, en double expédition, le 16 mai 1912.

I. E. GUÉCHOFF, D. PANAS.

DÉCLARATION

L'article 1er ne se rapporte notamment pas au cas où une guerre viendrait à éclater entre la Grèce et la Turquie par suite de l'admission dans le Parlement grec des députés crétois contre la volonté du gouvernement ottoman ; dans ce cas, la Bulgarie n'est tenue qu'à garder vis-à-vis de la Grèce une neutralité bienveillante. Et comme la liquidation de la crise des affaires d'Orient, née des événements de 1908, aussi quant à la question crétoise, correspond à l'intérêt général, et est même de nature, sans troubler l'équilibre dans la péninsule balkanique, à y consolider dans l'intérêt de la paix la situation internationale, la Bulgarie (indépendamment des engagements assumés par le présent traité) promet de ne gêner d'aucune façon une action éventuelle de la Grèce qui tendrait à la solution de cette question.

I. E. Guéchoff, D. Panas.

MILITARY CONVENTION
Greece and Bulgaria
Signed September 22, 1912

S. M. le roi des Bulgares et S. M. le roi des Hellènes, désirant compléter par une convention militaire le traité d'alliance défensive conclu à Sofia le 16 mai 1912 entre le royaume de Bulgarie et le royaume de Grèce ont, dans ce but, nommé pour leurs plénipotentiaires :

Sa Majesté le roi des Bulgares :
Son Exc. M. Iv. Ev. Guéchoff, etc., etc.
Sa Majesté le roi des Hellènes :
Son Exc. M. D. Panas, etc., etc.

Lesquels, après s'être communiqué leurs pleins pouvoirs trouvés en bonne et due forme, sont convenus de ce qui suit :

ARTICLE PREMIER. — Dans le cas où, conformément aux obligations découlant du traité d'alliance défensive conclu à Sofia le 16 mai 1912 entre la Bulgarie et la Grèce, la Grèce interviendrait militairement contre la Turquie dans une guerre bulgaro-turque, ou bien la Bulgarie contre la Turquie dans une guerre turco-grecque, les deux États, bulgare et grec, s'engagent à se prêter mutuellement secours, soit la Grèce avec un effectif atteignant au minimum cent vingt mille hommes, et la Bulgarie avec un effectif d'au moins trois cent mille hommes ; ces forces devront être aptes aussi bien à entrer en campagne sur la frontière qu'à prendre part à des opérations militaires en dehors des limites du territoire national.

Les troupes susindiquées devront être concentrées à la frontière et à même de la franchir au plus tard le vingtième jour qui aura suivi la mobilisation ou l'avis donné par l'une des parties contractantes que le *casus foederis* s'est produit.

ART. 2. — Au cas où la Grèce viendrait à être attaquée par la Turquie, la Bulgarie s'engage à déclarer la guerre à cette dernière puissance et à entrer en campagne contre elle avec l'ensemble de ses forces, fixées, aux termes de l'article premier, à un minimum de trois cent mille hommes, en conformant ses opérations militaires au plan élaboré par l'état-major bulgare.

Au cas où la Bulgarie viendrait à être attaquée par la Turquie, la Grèce s'engage à déclarer la guerre à cette dernière puissance et à entrer en campagne contre elle avec l'ensemble de ses forces, fixées, aux termes de l'article premier, à un minimum de cent vingt mille hommes, en conformant ses opérations militaires au plan élaboré par l'état-major grec. L'objectif principal de la flotte hellénique devra toutefois être de se rendre maîtresse de la mer Égée et d'interrompre les communications par cette voie entre l'Asie Mineure et la Turquie d'Europe.

Dans les cas prévus aux deux paragraphes précédents, la Bulgarie s'engage à opérer offensivement avec une partie importante de son armée contre les forces turques concentrées dans la région des vilayets de Kossovo, Monastir et Salonique. Si la Serbie, en vertu de ses accords avec la Bulgarie, prend part à la guerre, la Bulgarie pourra disposer de la totalité de ses forces militaires en Thrace, mais dans ce cas elle prend par le présent acte l'engagement envers la Grèce que des forces militaires serbes d'un effectif d'au moins cent vingt mille combattants opéreront offensivement contre les forces turques concentrées dans la région des trois vilayets susmentionnés.

Art. 3. — Si la Bulgarie et la Grèce, aux termes d'une entente préalable, déclarent la guerre à la Turquie, elles sont l'une et l'autre tenues — à moins qu'il n'en soit disposé autrement par un accord spécial — de faire entrer en campagne les effectifs prévus à l'article premier de la présente convention.

Les dispositions des deux derniers paragraphes de l'article 2 sont dans ce cas aussi applicables.

Art. 4. — Au cas où l'un des gouvernements contractants déclarerait la guerre à un État autre que la Turquie, sans une entente préalable et sans le consentement de l'autre gouvernement, ce dernier est délié des obligations exposées à l'article premier, mais reste néanmoins tenu d'observer, pendant toute la durée de la guerre, une neutralité amicale à l'égard de son allié.

Art. 5. — En cas de guerre conjointe, aucun des États alliés ne pourra conclure d'armistice d'une durée supérieure à vingt-quatre heures sans une entente préalable et sans le consentement de l'autre État allié.

L'entente des deux parties contractantes, contenue dans un accord écrit, sera de même nécessaire pour que l'une d'elles puisse engager des négociations en vue de la paix ou conclure un traité de paix.

Art. 6. — Dans le cas où, la Bulgarie et la Grèce ayant mobilisé leurs forces armées ou étant entrées en campagne, la Grèce se verra obligée de régler la question crétoise suivant les vœux des populations de l'île et serait pour cela attaquée par la Turquie, la Bulgarie s'engage à se porter à son secours, conformément à l'article premier de la présente convention.

ART. 7. — Les chefs d'état-major général des armées bulgare et grecque devront se renseigner mutuellement et en temps opportun sur leurs plans d'opérations en cas d'une guerre. Ils devront en outre faire connaître tous les ans les modifications apportées à ces plans du fait de circonstances nouvelles.

ART. 8. — La présente convention deviendra obligatoire pour les deux parties contractantes sitôt après avoir été signée ; elle demeurera en vigueur pendant toute la durée du traité d'alliance défensive du 16 mai 1912, auquel elle est incorporée à titre de partie intégrante.

Fait à Sofia, en double exemplaire, le 22 septembre 1912.

> I. E. GUÉCHOFF, D. PANAS,
> Général FITCHEFF. J. P. MÉTAXAS, *capitaine.*

No. 3
TREATY OF LONDON
Signed May 17 (30), 1913, but never ratified

ARTICLE PREMIER. — Il y aura, à dater de l'échange des ratifications du présent traité, paix et amitié entre Sa Majesté l'Empereur des Ottomans d'une part, et leurs Majestés les Souverains alliés d'autre part, ainsi qu'entre leurs héritiers et successeurs, leurs États et sujets respectifs, à perpétuité.

ART. 2. — Sa Majesté l'Empereur des Ottomans cède à leurs Majestés les Souverains alliés tous les territoires de son Empire sur le continent européen à l'ouest d'une ligne tirée d'Énos sur la mer Égée à Midia sur la mer Noire, à l'exception de l'Albanie.

Le tracé exact de la frontière d'Énos à Midia sera déterminé par une commission internationale.

ART. 3. — Sa Majesté l'Empereur des Ottomans et leurs Majestés les Souverains alliés déclarent remettre à Sa Majesté l'Empereur d'Allemagne, à Sa Majesté l'Empereur d'Autriche, Roi de Bohême, etc., et Roi Apostolique de Hongrie, à M. le Président de la République française, à Sa Majesté le Roi de Grande-Bretagne et d'Irlande et des Territoires britanniques au delà des mers, Empereur des Indes, à Sa Majesté le Roi d'Italie et à Sa Majesté l'Empereur de toutes les Russies, le soin de régler la délimitation des frontières de l'Albanie et toutes autres questions concernant l'Albanie.

Art. 4. — Sa Majesté l'Empereur des Ottomans déclare céder à leurs Majestés les Souverains alliés l'île de Crète et renoncer en leur faveur à tous les droits de souveraineté et autres qu'il possédait sur cette île.

Art. 5. — Sa Majesté l'Empereur des Ottomans et leurs Majestés les Souverains alliés déclarent confier à Sa Majesté l'Empereur d'Allemagne, à Sa Majesté l'Empereur d'Autriche, Roi de Bohême, etc., et Roi Apostolique de Hongrie, à M. le Président de la République française, à Sa Majesté le Roi de Grande-Bretagne et d'Irlande et des Territoires Britanniques au delà des Mers, Empereur des Indes, à Sa Majesté le Roi d'Italie et à Sa Majesté l'Empereur de toutes les Russies, le soin de statuer sur le sort de toutes les îles ottomanes de la mer Égée, l'île de Crète exceptée, et de la péninsule du mont Athos.

Art. 6. — Sa Majesté l'Empereur des Ottomans et leurs Majestés les Souverains alliés déclarent remettre le soin de régler les questions d'ordre financier résultant de l'état de guerre qui prend fin et des cessions territoriales ci-dessus mentionnées à la commission internationale convoquée à Paris, à laquelle ils ont délégué leurs représentants.

Art. 7. — Les questions concernant les prisonniers de guerre, juridiction, nationalité et commerce seront réglées par des conventions spéciales.

Article final. — Le présent traité sera ratifié et les ratifications seront échangées à Londres dans le plus bref délai possible.

En foi de quoi les Plénipotentiaires des Hautes Parties contractantes ont signé le présent traité et y ont apposé leurs sceaux.

Fait à Londres, le 17/30 mai 1913, à midi 35 (heure de Greenwich).

Dr. St. Daneff.
M. Iv. Madjaroff.

Étienne Skouloudis.
J. Gennadius.
G. Streit.
J. Popovitch.
L. de Voinovich.
Stojan Novakovitch.
And. Nikolitch.
Mil. R. Vesnitch.
Ivan Paplovitch.
Osman Nizamy.
N. Batztaria.
Ahmed Rechid.

No. 4

TREATY OF PEACE

Signed at Bucharest August 10, 1913
(ratified August 25)

LL. MM. le Roi de Roumanie, le Roi des Hellènes, le Roi de Monténégro et le Roi de Serbie, d'une part, et S. M. le Roi des Bulgares, d'autre part, animés du désir de mettre fin à l'état de guerre actuellement existant entre leurs pays respectifs, voulant, dans une pensée d'ordre, établir la paix entre leurs peuples si longtemps éprouvés, ont résolu de conclure un Traité définitif de paix. Leurs dites Majestés ont, en conséquence, nommé pour leurs Plénipotentiaires, savoir (suit la liste des Délégués).

Lesquels, suivant la proposition du Gouvernement Royal de Roumanie, se sont réunis en Conférence à Bucarest, munis de pleins pouvoirs, qui ont été trouvés en bonne et due forme.

L'accord s'étant heureusement établi entre eux, ils sont convenus des stipulations suivantes :

ART. 1er. — Il y aura, à dater du jour de l'échange des ratifications du présent Traité, paix et amitié entre S. M. le Roi de Roumanie, S. M. le Roi des Bulgares, S. M. le Roi des Hellènes, S. M. le Roi de Monténégro et S. M. le Roi de Serbie, ainsi qu'entre leurs héritiers et successeurs, leurs États et sujets respectifs.

ART. 2. — Entre le Royaume de Bulgarie et le Royaume de Roumanie, l'ancienne frontière entre le Danube et la mer Noire est, conformément au procès-verbal arrêté par les Délégués militaires respectifs et annexé au Protocole no 5 du 22 juillet (4 août) 1913 de la Conférence de Bucarest, rectifiée de la manière suivante :

La nouvelle frontière partira du Danube, en amont de Turtukaïa, pour aboutir à la mer Noire au sud d'Ekrene.

Entre ces deux points extrêmes, la ligne frontière suivra le tracé indiqué sur les cartes 1/100,000e et 1/200,000e de l'état-major roumain et selon la description annexée au présent article.

Il est formellement entendu que la Bulgarie démantèlera, au plus tard dans un délai de deux années, les ouvrages de fortifications existants et n'en construira pas d'autres à Roustchouk, à Schoumla, dans le pays intermédiaire et dans une zone de vingt kilomètres autour de Baltchik.

Une commission mixte, composée de représentants des deux Hautes Parties contractantes, en nombre égal des deux côtés, sera

chargée, dans les quinze jours qui suivront la signature du présent
Traité, d'exécuter sur le terrain le tracé de la nouvelle frontière,
conformément aux stipulations précédentes. Cette commission
présidera au partage des biens-fonds et capitaux qui ont pu jusqu'ici
appartenir en commun à des districts, des communes ou des communautés d'habitants séparés par la nouvelle frontière. En cas de
désaccord sur le tracé et les mesures d'exécution, les deux Hautes
Parties contractantes s'engagent à s'adresser à un Gouvernement
tiers ami pour le prier de désigner un arbitre dont la décision sur
les points en litige sera considérée comme définitive.

ART. 3. — Entre le Royaume de Bulgarie et le Royaume de
Serbie, la frontière suivra, conformément au procès-verbal arrêté
par les Délégués militaires respectifs et annexé au Protocole n° 9
du 25 juillet (7 août) 1913 de la Conférence de Bucarest, le tracé
suivant :

La ligne frontière partira de l'ancienne frontière du sommet
Patarica, suivra l'ancienne frontière turco-bulgare et la ligne de
partage des eaux entre le Vardar et la Struma, avec l'exception
que la haute vallée de la Strumitza restera sur territoire serbe ;
elle aboutira à la montagne Belasica, où elle se reliera à la frontière
bulgaro-grecque. Une description détaillée de cette frontière et
son tracé sur la carte 1/200,000e de l'état-major autrichien sont
annexés au présent article.

Une commission mixte, composée de représentants des deux
Hautes Parties contractantes, en nombre égal des deux côtés, sera
chargée, dans les quinze jours qui suivront la signature du présent
Traité, d'exécuter sur le terrain le tracé de la nouvelle frontière,
conformément aux stipulations précédentes.

Cette commission présidera au partage des biens-fonds et capitaux
qui ont pu jusqu'ici appartenir en commun à des districts, des
communes ou des communautés d'habitants séparés par la nouvelle
frontière. En cas de désaccord sur le tracé et les mesures d'exécution,
les deux Hautes Parties contractantes s'engagent à s'adresser à un
Gouvernement tiers ami pour le prier de désigner un arbitre dont
la décision sur les points en litige sera considérée comme définitive.

ART. 4. — Les questions relatives à l'ancienne frontière serbo-
bulgare seront réglées suivant l'entente intervenue entre les deux
Hautes Parties contractantes, constatée dans le Protocole annexé au
présent article.

ART. 5. — Entre le Royaume de Grèce et le Royaume de Bulgarie,
la frontière suivra, conformément au procès-verbal arrêté par les
Délégués militaires respectifs et annexé au Protocole n° 9 du 25
juillet (7 août) 1913 de la Conférence de Bucarest, le tracé suivant :

La ligne frontière partira de la nouvelle frontière bulgaro-serbe sur la crête de Belasica Planina, pour aboutir à l'embouchure de la Mesta à la mer Égée.

Entre ces deux points extrêmes, la ligne frontière suivra le tracé indiqué sur la carte 1/200,000e de l'état-major autrichien et selon la description annexée au présent article.

Une commission mixte, composée de représentants des deux Hautes Parties contractantes, en nombre égal des deux côtés, sera chargée, dans les quinze jours qui suivront la signature du présent Traité, d'exécuter sur le terrain le tracé de la frontière conformément aux stipulations précédentes.

Cette commission présidera au partage des biens-fonds et capitaux qui ont pu jusqu'ici appartenir en commun à des districts, des communes, ou des communautés d'habitants séparés par la nouvelle frontière. En cas de désaccord sur le tracé et les mesures d'exécution, les deux Hautes Parties contractantes s'engagent à s'adresser à un Gouvernement tiers ami pour le prier de désigner un arbitre dont la décision sur les points en litige sera considérée comme définitive.

Il est formellement entendu que la Bulgarie se désiste, dès maintenant, de toute prétention sur l'île de Crète.

Art. 6. — Les quartiers généraux des armées respectives seront aussitôt informés de la signature du présent Traité. Le Gouvernement bulgare s'engage à ramener son armée, dès le lendemain de cette signification, sur le pied de paix. Il dirigera les troupes sur leurs garnisons où l'on procédera, dans le plus bref délai, au renvoi des diverses réserves dans leurs foyers.

Les troupes dont la garnison se trouve située dans la zone d'occupation de l'armée de l'une des Hautes Parties contractantes seront dirigées sur un autre point de l'ancien territoire bulgare et ne pourront gagner leurs garnisons habituelles qu'après l'évacuation de la zone d'occupation sus-visée.

Art. 7. — L'évacuation du territoire bulgare, tant ancien que nouveau, commencera aussitôt après la démobilisation de l'armée bulgare, et sera achevée au plus tard dans la quinzaine.

Durant ce délai, pour l'armée d'opération roumaine, la zone de démarcation sera indiquée par la ligne Sistov-Lovcea-Turski-Izvor-Glozene-Zlatitza-Mirkovo-Araba-Konak-Orchania-Mesdra-Vratza-Berkovitza-Lom-Danube.

Art. 8. — Durant l'occupation des territoires bulgares, les différentes armées conserveront le droit de réquisition, moyennant paiement en espèces.

Elles y auront le libre usage des lignes de chemin de fer pour les transports de troupes et les approvisionnements de toute nature, sans qu'il y ait lieu à indemnité au profit de l'autorité locale.

Les malades et les blessés y seront sous la sauvegarde desdites armées.

Art. 9. — Aussitôt que possible après l'échange des ratifications du présent Traité, tous les prisonniers de guerre seront réciproquement rendus.

Les Gouvernements des Hautes Parties contractantes désigneront chacun des Commissaires spéciaux chargés de recevoir les prisonniers.

Tous les prisonniers aux mains d'un des Gouvernements seront livrés au commissaire du Gouvernement auquel ils appartiennent ou à son représentant dûment autorisé, à l'endroit qui sera fixé par les parties intéressées.

Les Gouvernements des Hautes Parties contractantes présenteront respectivement l'un à l'autre, et aussitôt que possible après la remise de tous les prisonniers, un état des dépenses directes supportées par lui pour le soin et l'entretien des prisonniers depuis la date de la capture ou de la reddition jusqu'à celle de la mort ou de la remise. Compensation sera faite entre les sommes dues par la Bulgarie à l'une des autres Hautes Parties contractantes et celles dues par celles-ci à la Bulgarie et la différence sera payée au Gouvernement créancier aussitôt que possible après l'échange des états de dépenses sus-visés.

Art. 10. — Le présent traité sera ratifié et les ratifications en seront échangées à Bucarest dans le délai de quinze jours ou plus tôt si faire se peut.

En foi de quoi, les Plénipotentiaires respectifs l'ont signé et y ont apposé leurs sceaux.

Fait à Bucarest le vingt-huitième jour du mois de juillet (dixième jour du mois d'août) de l'an mil neuf cent treize.

(Signatures follow.)

Protocols

(Protocols annexed to Arts. 2, 3, 4, and 5 delimit respectively the Bulgar-Roumanian, new Bulgar-Serb, old Bulgar-Serb, and Bulgar-Greek frontiers.)

No. 5

TREATY OF PEACE

Signed at Constantinople, September 29, 1913

S. M. l'Empereur des Ottomans et S. M. le Roi des Bulgares, animés du désir de régler à l'amiable et sur une base durable l'état de choses créé par les événements qui se sont produits depuis la conclusion du Traité de Londres, de rétablir les relations d'amitié et de bon voisinage si nécessaires pour le bien-être de leurs Peuples, ont résolu de conclure le présent Traité et ont choisi respectivement, à cet effet, pour leurs Plénipotentiaires :

S. M. l'Empereur des Ottomans : S. E. Talaat Bey, Ministre de l'Intérieur, S. E. le Général Mahmoud Pacha, Ministre de la Marine, S. E. Halil Bey, Président du Conseil d'État ;

S. M. le Roi des Bulgares : S. E. le Général Savoff, ancien Ministre, S. E. Monsieur Natchévitch, ancien Ministre, S. E. Monsieur Tocheff, Ministre plénipotentiaire, lesquels, après s'être communiqué leurs pleins pouvoirs, trouvés en bonne et due forme, sont convenus de ce qui suit :

ART. PREMIER. — La frontière entre les deux pays prend son point de départ à l'embouchure de la rivière Rezvaja, au Sud du monastère San Ivan, se trouvant sur la mer Noire ; elle suit le cours de cette rivière jusqu'au point de jonction des rivières Pirogu et Déliva, à l'Ouest de Kamila-köj. Entre l'embouchure et le point de jonction plus haut mentionné, la rivière Rezvaja, à partir de l'embouchure, suit d'abord la direction du Sud-Ouest et, laissant à la Turquie Placa, forme un coude et se dirige vers le Nord-Ouest et puis vers le Sud-Ouest ; les villages Madzura et Pirgoplo restent en territoire ottoman. La rivière Rezvaja, après avoir suivi, à partir de Pirgoplo, la direction du Sud sur une longueur approximative de cinq kilomètres et demi, forme un coude vers l'Ouest et le Nord et se prolonge ensuite, légèrement incurvée vers le Nord, dans la direction générale de l'Ouest. Dans cette partie, les villages Likudi, Kladara restent en territoire bulgare et les villages Ciknigori, Mavrodio et Lafva reviennent à la Turquie ; ensuite, la frontière, suivant toujours la rivière Rezvaja, laisse Torfu-ciflik à la Bulgarie, se dirige vers le Sud-Est et, laissant le village Radoslavci en territoire ottoman, oblique vers l'Ouest à huit cents mètres environ au Sud de ce village ; elle laisse le village Kamila-köj en territoire ottoman et arrive à une distance de quatre cents mètres environ à l'Ouest de ce village, au point de jonction des rivières Pirogu et Déliva.

La ligne frontière suit, à partir du point de jonction des rivières Pirogu et Déliva, le cours du Déliva et, se prolongeant avec ladite

rivière dans la direction générale du Nord-Ouest, laisse à la Turquie
les villages Paspala, Kandildzik et Déli et se termine à l'Est de
Souk Sou; ce dernier village reste à la Turquie, tandis que Sévéligu
revient à la Bulgarie. La ligne frontière, après avoir passé entre
Souk Sou et Sévéligu, continue dans la direction du Nord-Ouest, en
suivant la crête qui passe sur les cotes 687, 619 et 563 ; au delà de la
cote 563, elle laisse le village Caglaïk (Cajirlik) en territoire ottoman
et, contournant ce dernier village à trois kilomètres à l'Est et au Nord,
gagne le ruisseau Goléma. La frontière suit le cours du Goléma sur
une longueur de deux kilomètres environ et arrive au point de
jonction de ce ruisseau avec l'autre bras de la même rivière, qui vient
du Sud de Karabanlar (Karabaalar). A partir de ce point de jonction,
la ligne frontière passe sur la crête au Nord du ruisseau venant de
Türk-Alatli pour aboutir à l'ancienne frontière turco-bulgare.

Le point de jonction de la nouvelle ligne et de l'ancienne frontière
se trouve à quatre kilomètres à l'Est de Türk-Alatli, au point où
l'ancienne frontière turco-bulgare forme un coude vers le Nord,
dans la direction de Ajkiri-Jol.

A partir de ce point, elle suit exactement l'ancienne frontière
turco-bulgare jusqu'à Balaban-Basi, à l'Ouest de la Tundja et au
Nord du village Derviska-Mog.

La nouvelle ligne frontière se sépare de l'ancienne frontière aux
environs de Balaban-Basi et descend en ligne droite vers Dermen-
Déré. Le point où la nouvelle frontière se sépare de l'ancienne se
trouve à deux kilomètres de distance de l'église du village Derviska-
Mog. La frontière, après avoir laissé le village Derviska-Mog dans
le territoire ottoman, suit le cours du Dermen-Déré jusqu'au village
Bulgar-Lefké et laisse ce village en territoire bulgare. A partir des
lisières Est et Sud de Bulgar-Lefké, la ligne frontière abandonne le
cours du Dermen-Déré et se dirige vers l'Ouest, laisse en territoire
ottoman les villages Türk-Lefké et Dimitri-köj et, en suivant la
ligne de partage des eaux entre Bük-Déré et Démirhan-Déré (c. 241),
arrive au point le plus septentrional du coude formé par la Marica
vers le Nord, à l'Est de Mustafa-Pasa. Cette partie du coude se
trouve à trois kilomètres et demi de distance de l'entrée Est du
pont de Mustafa-Pasa. La frontière suit la partie Ouest du coude
de la Marica jusqu'au moulin et, de là, arrive en ligne droite,
atteignant Cermen-Déré, au Nord du pont du chemin de fer
(Cermen-Déré est la rivière qui se jette dans la Marica à trois kilomètres à l'Est du village Cermen), et puis, contournant Cermen au
Nord, va à Tazi-Tépési. La frontière laisse Cermen à la Turquie et,
suivant le cours de Cermen-Déré, coupe la ligne de chemin de fer
au Nord-Ouest de Cermen ; elle suit toujours la même rivière et

monte à Tazi-Tépési (c. 613). (Le point où Cermen-Déré coupe la
ligne du chemin de fer au Nord-Ouest de Cermen se trouve à une
distance de cinq kilomètres du centre du village de Cermen et à trois
mille deux cents mètres de la sortie Ouest du pont de Mustafa-Pasa.)

La frontière laisse en territoire ottoman le point le plus élevé
de Tazi-Tépési et, à partir de ce point, suit la ligne de partage des
eaux entre l'Arda et la Marica en passant par les villages Jajladzik
et Gjuldzuk (Goldzik), qui restent en territoire ottoman.

A partir de Goldzik, la frontière passe par la cote 449 et ensuite
descend à la cote 367 et, à partir de cette cote, se dirige vers l'Arda
dans la direction Sud, à peu près en ligne droite. Cette ligne droite
passe à un kilomètre à l'Ouest de Bektasli, qui reste en territoire
ottoman.

La ligne frontière, après être arrivée de la cote 367 à l'Arda, suit
vers l'Est la rive droite de l'Arda et arrive au moulin qui se trouve à
un kilomètre au Sud du village de Cingirli ; à partir de ce moulin
elle suit la ligne de partage des eaux se trouvant à l'Est de Gajdohor-
Déré ; elle passe à un kilomètre à l'Est du village Gajdohor et,
laissant le village Drébisna à la Bulgarie, en passant à peu près
à un kilomètre à l'Est de ce village, descend à Atéren-Déré à un
kilomètre au Sud du susdit village ; de là, elle va dans la direction
du Sud-Ouest, par le plus court chemin, à la source du ruisseau
qui coule entre les villages Akalan et Kajlikliköj et suit le thalweg de ce cours d'eau pour descendre à la rivière Kizil-Déli. A
partir du susdit ruisseau, la frontière, laissant Gökcebunar en
Bulgarie, emprunte le cours de Kizil-Déli-Déré et, de là, en suivant
le thalweg du ruisseau qui se sépare vers le Sud en un point se
trouvant à quatre kilomètres au Sud de Mandrica et à trois kilomètres à l'Est de Soganliki-Bala, va à la source du même ruisseau ;
elle descend ensuite par le plus court chemin à la source du Mandra-
Déré ; elle suit le thalweg du Mandra-Déré, à partir de sa source,
pour joindre la Marica à l'Ouest de Mandra. Dans cette partie,
le village Krantu reste en territoire bulgare et les villages Bas-
Klisa, Ahirjanbunar et Mandra reviennent à la Turquie.

A partir de ce point, la frontière suit le thalweg de la Marica
jusqu'au point où le fleuve se sépare en deux branches, à trois
kilomètres et demi au Sud du village de Kaldirkoz ; de là, elle
suit le thalweg de la branche droite, qui passe non loin de Férédzik,
pour aboutir à la mer Égée. Dans cette partie, les marais d'Ak-Sou,
ainsi que les lacs de Quénéli-Gheul et de Kazikli-Gheul, restent
à la Turquie et les lacs de Touzla-Gheul et de Drana-Gheul reviennent
à la Bulgarie.

ART. 2. — Dix jours après la signature du present Traité par les

Plénipotentiaires susmentionnés, les armées des deux Parties contractantes qui, en ce moment, occuperaient des territoires revenant à l'autre Partie s'empresseront de les évacuer et, dans l'espace des quinze jours suivants, de les remettre, conformément aux règles et aux usages, aux autorités de l'autre Partie.

Il est en outre entendu que les deux États démobiliseront leurs armées dans l'espace de trois semaines, à partir de la date du présent Traité.

ART. 3. — Les relations diplomatiques, ainsi que les communications postales, télégraphiques et de chemin de fer, reprendront entre les Hautes Parties contractantes immédiatement après la signature du présent Traité.

L'Arrangement sur les Muftis, formant l'Annexe II du présent Traité, sera applicable dans tous les territoires de la Bulgarie.

ART. 4. — En vue de favoriser les relations économiques entre les deux pays, les Hautes Parties contractantes s'engagent à remettre en vigueur, aussitôt après la signature du présent Traité et pour un délai d'un an à dater de ce jour, la Convention pour le Commerce et la Navigation conclue le 6–19 février 1911, et à accorder à leurs produits industriels, agricoles et autres toutes les facilités douanières compatibles avec leurs engagements existant à l'égard des Puissances tierces.

La Déclaration consulaire du 18 novembre 2 décembre 1909 sera également remise en vigueur pendant le même délai.

Toutefois, chacune des Hautes Parties contractantes pourra créer des Consulats Généraux, Consulats, Vice-Consulats de carrière dans toutes les localités de leurs territoires où des agents de Puissances tierces sont admis.

Les Hautes Parties contractantes s'engagent en outre à procéder, dans le plus bref délai possible, à la nomination de Commissions mixtes pour négocier un Traité de Commerce et une Convention consulaire.

ART. 5. — Les prisonniers de guerre et otages seront échangés dans le délai d'un mois à partir de la signature du présent Traité, ou plus tôt, si faire se peut.

Cet échange aura lieu par les soins de commissaires spéciaux nommés de part et d'autre.

Les frais d'entretien desdits prisonniers de guerre et otages seront à la charge du Gouvernement au pouvoir duquel ils se trouvent.

Toutefois, la solde des officiers payée par ce Gouvernement sera remboursée par l'État dont ils relèvent.

ART. 6. — Une amnistie pleine et entière est accordée par les Hautes Parties contractantes à toutes les personnes qui ont pris part aux hostilités ou qui se sont compromises dans les événements politiques antérieurs au présent Traité.

Les habitants des territoires cédés jouiront de la même amnistie pour les événements politiques y survenus.

Le bénéfice de cette amnistie cessera à l'expiration du délai de deux semaines fixé par les autorités légalement constituées lors de la réoccupation des territoires revenant à la Bulgarie et dûment porté à la connaissance des populations.

Art. 7. — Les originaires des territoires cédés par l'Empire Ottoman au Gouvernement Royal de Bulgarie et qui y sont domiciliés deviendront sujets bulgares.

Ces originaires devenus sujets bulgares auront, pendant un délai de quatre ans, la faculté d'opter sur place en faveur de la nationalité ottomane, par une simple déclaration aux autorités locales bulgares et un enregistrement aux Consulats impériaux ottomans. Cette déclaration sera remise, à l'étranger, aux chancelleries des Consulats bulgares et enregistrée par les Consulats ottomans. L'option sera individuelle et n'est pas obligatoire pour le Gouvernement Impérial Ottoman.

Les mineurs actuels useront de l'option dans les quatre ans qui suivent leur majorité.

Les Musulmans des territoires cédés devenus sujets bulgares ne seront pas assujettis pendant ce délai au service militaire, ni ne payeront aucune taxe militaire.

Après avoir usé de leur faculté d'option, ces Musulmans quitteront les territoires cédés, et cela jusqu'à échéance du délai de quatre ans prévu plus haut, en ayant la faculté de faire passer en franchise de droits de sortie leurs biens meubles. Ils peuvent toutefois conserver leurs biens immeubles de toutes catégories, urbains et ruraux, et les faire administrer par des tiers.

Art. 8. — Les sujets bulgares musulmans de tous les territoires de la Bulgarie jouiront des mêmes droits civils et politiques que les sujets d'origine bulgare.

Ils jouiront de la liberté de conscience, de la liberté et de la pratique extérieure du culte. Les coutumes des Musulmans seront respectées.

Le nom de Sa Majesté impériale le Sultan, comme Khalife, continuera à être prononcé dans les prières publiques des Musulmans.

Les communautés musulmanes, constituées actuellement ou qui se constitueront à l'avenir, leur organisation hiérarchique, leurs patrimoines seront reconnus et respectés ; elles relèveront sans entraves de leurs chefs spirituels.

Art. 9. — Les communautés bulgares en Turquie jouiront des mêmes droits dont jouissent actuellement les autres communautés chrétiennes de l'Empire Ottoman.

Les Bulgares sujets ottomans conserveront leurs biens meubles et immeubles et ne seront aucunement inquiétés dans l'exercice et la jouissance de leurs droits de l'homme et de propriété. Ceux qui ont quitté leurs foyers lors des derniers événements pourront retourner dans un délai de deux ans au plus tard.

ART. 10. — Les droits acquis antérieurement à l'annexion des territoires, ainsi que les actes judiciaires et titres officiels émanant des autorités ottomanes compétentes, seront respectés et inviolables jusqu'à la preuve légale du contraire.

ART. 11. — Ce droit de propriété foncière dans les territoires cédés, tel qu'il résulte de la loi ottomane sur les immeubles urbains et ruraux, sera reconnu sans aucune restriction.

Les propriétaires d'immeubles ou de meubles dans lesdits territoires continueront à jouir de tous leurs droits de propriété, même s'ils fixent, à titre provisoire ou définitif, leur résidence personnelle hors de la Bulgarie. Ils pourront affermer leurs biens ou les administrer par des tiers.

ART. 12. — Les vakoufs Mustesna, Mulhaka, Idjarétein, Moukataa, Idjaréi-Vahidé, ainsi que les dîmes vakoufs, dans les territoires cédés, tels qu'ils résultent actuellement des lois ottomanes, seront respectés.

Ils seront gérés par qui de droit.

Leurs régimes ne pourront être modifiés que par indemnisation juste et préalable.

Les droits des établissements religieux et de bienfaisance de l'Empire Ottoman sur les revenus vakoufs dans les territoires cédés, à titre d'Idjaréi-Vahidé, de Moukataa, de droits divers, de contrevaleur de dîmes vakoufs et autres, sur les vakoufs bâtis ou non bâtis seront respectés.

ART. 13. — Les biens particuliers de Sa Majesté impériale le Sultan, ainsi que ceux des Membres de la Dynastie impériale, seront maintenus et respectés. Sa Majesté et les Membres de la Dynastie impériale pourront les vendre ou les affermer par des fondés de pouvoir.

Il en sera de même pour les biens du domaine privé qui appartiendraient à l'État.

En cas d'aliénation, préférence sera accordée, à conditions égales, aux sujets bulgares.

ART. 14. — Les Hautes Parties contractantes s'engagent à donner à leurs autorités provinciales des ordres afin de faire respecter les cimetières et particulièrement les tombeaux des soldats tombés sur le champ d'honneur.

Les autorités n'empêcheront pas les parents et amis d'enlever les ossements des victimes inhumées en terre étrangère.

ART. 15. — Les sujets de chacun des États contractants pourront séjourner et circuler librement, comme par le passé, sur le territoire de l'autre État contractant.

ART. 16. — Le Gouvernement Royal de Bulgarie est subrogé aux droits, charges et obligations du Gouvernement Impérial Ottoman à l'égard de la Compagnie des Chemins de fer orientaux, pour la partie de la ligne à elle concédée et située dans les territoires cédés.

Le Gouvernement Royal de Bulgarie s'oblige à rendre sans retard le matériel roulant et les autres objets appartenant à ladite Compagnie et saisis par lui.

ART. 17. — Tous les différends et litiges qui surviendraient dans l'interprétation ou l'application des Articles 11, 12, 13 et 16 du présent Traité seront réglés par l'Arbitrage à La Haye, conformément au compromis formant l'Annexe III du présent Traité.

ART. 18. — Le Protocole relatif à la frontière (Annexe I); l'Arrangement concernant les Muftis (Annexe II); le Compromis d'Arbitrage (Annexe III); le Protocole relatif au Chemin de fer et à la Maritza (Annexe IV) et la Déclaration se rapportant à l'Article 10 (Annexe V) sont annexés au présent Traité dont ils font partie intégrante.

ART. 19. — Les dispositions du Traité de Londres sont maintenues en ce qui concerne le Gouvernement Impérial Ottoman et le Royaume de Bulgarie pour autant qu'elles ne sont pas abrogées ou modifiées par les stipulations qui précèdent.

ART. 20. — Le présent Traité entrera en vigueur immédiatement après sa signature.

Les ratifications en seront échangées dans la quinzaine à dater de ce jour.

En foi de quoi, les Plénipotentiaires respectifs l'ont signé et y ont apposé leurs cachets.

Fait en double exemplaire à Constantinople, le 16/29 septembre 1913.

ANNEXE I

PROTOCOLE No 1

A. — Les Hautes Parties contractantes ont convenu d'ajouter à la description de la frontière insérée à l'article premier du Traité les remarques suivantes :

1o La frontière est décrite d'après la carte de l'état-major autrichien à l'échelle de 1/200,000e et le tracé en est marqué sur un croquis annexe, copié sur cette carte.

Les indications se rapportant à la partie inférieure et à l'affluent de la Maritza sont enregistrées d'après la carte topographique à l'échelle de 1/50,000ᵉ et elles sont portées sur une carte détaillée et complète de cette partie, indiquant la frontière définitive de Mandra à l'embouchure.

2º Des Commissions mixtes composées d'officiers ottomans et bulgares traceront la carte de la nouvelle ligne frontière sur un espace de deux kilomètres de chaque côté de cette ligne, à l'échelle de 1/25,000ᵉ ; la frontière définitive sera marquée sur cette carte. Ces Commissions seront divisées en trois sections et commenceront leurs travaux simultanément dans les parties suivantes : la côte de la mer Noire, le territoire situé entre la Maritza et l'Arda et celui compris entre l'Arda et Mandra.

Après cette opération, la ligne frontière sera appliquée sur le terrain et des pyramides y seront élevées par les soins desdites Commissions mixtes. Les protocoles de la frontière définitive seront dressés par les Commissions.

3º Lors du tracé de la ligne frontière, les Commissions relèveront le plan des propriétés privées ou publiques restant en deçà ou au delà de la ligne.

Les deux Hauts Gouvernements examineront les mesures à prendre pour éviter des conflits qui pourraient éventuellement surgir de l'exploitation de pareilles propriétés.

Il est bien entendu que jusqu'à ce qu'une entente intervienne à ce sujet les propriétaires continueront à jouir librement de leurs biens, comme par le passé.

4º Les protocoles antérieurement dressés par les deux parties en ce qui concerne les parties de l'ancienne frontière turco-bulgare maintenues actuellement telles quelles resteront en vigueur.

Si les bornes-frontière ou Koulés, se trouvant dans ces parties, sont détruites ou endommagées, il sera procédé à leur reconstruction ou restauration.

5º Pour les rivières et les ruisseaux, sauf la Toundja, la Maritza et l'Arda, la ligne frontière suivra le thalweg des cours d'eau. Pour les trois susdites rivières, la ligne frontière est indiquée exactement dans le protocole.

B. — La délimitation en ce qui concerne les îles situées dans le lit de la Maritza sera confiée à une commission spéciale.

Il a été également convenu que les deux Gouvernements s'engagent à s'entendre, le moment venu, pour la canalisation de la Maritza.

C. — Les deux Gouvernements sont d'accord pour faciliter l'échange facultatif mutuel des populations bulgare et musulmane de part et d'autre ainsi que de leurs propriétés dans une zone de 15 kilomètres au plus, le long de toute la frontière commune.

L'échange aura lieu par des villages entiers.

L'échange des propriétés rurales et urbaines aura lieu sous les auspices des deux Gouvernements et avec la participation des anciens des villages à échanger.

Des Commissions mixtes nommées par les deux Gouvernements procéderont à l'échange et à l'indemnisation, s'il y a lieu, de différences résultant de l'échange de biens entre villages et particuliers en question.

Fait en double exemplaire, à Constantinople, le 16/29 septembre 1913.

ANNEXE II

Arrangement concernant les Muftis

Art. premier. — Un Mufti en Chef résidera à Sofia et servira d'intermédiaire entre les Muftis de la Bulgarie dans leurs relations avec le Cheikh-ul-Islamat, pour les affaires religieuses et civiles relevant du Chéri, et avec le Ministère bulgare des Cultes.

Il sera élu par les Muftis de la Bulgarie et parmi ceux-ci, réunis spécialement à cet effet. Les Mufti-Vékilis prendront part à cette réunion, mais seulement en qualité d'électeurs.

Le Ministère bulgare des Cultes notera l'élection du Mufti en Chef, par l'entremise de la Légation impériale à Sofia, au Cheikh-ul-Islamat, qui lui fera parvenir un Menchour et le Murassélé l'autorisant à exercer ses fonctions et à accorder, de son côté, le même pouvoir aux autres Muftis de la Bulgarie.

Le Mufti en Chef aura, dans les limites des prescriptions du Chéri, le droit de surveillance et de contrôle sur les Muftis de la Bulgarie, sur les établissements religieux et de bienfaisance musulmans, ainsi que sur leurs desservants et leurs Mutévellis.

Art. 2. — Les Muftis sont élus par les électeurs musulmans de la Bulgarie.

Le Mufti en Chef vérifie si le Mufti élu réunit toutes les qualités requises par la loi du Chéri et, en cas d'affirmative, il informe le Cheikh-ul-Islamat de la nécessité de lui délivrer l'autorisation nécessaire pour les Fetvas (Menchour). Il délivre au nouveau Mufti, en même temps que le Menchour ainsi obtenu, le Murassélé nécessaire pour lui conférer le droit de juridiction religieuse entre les Musulmans.

Les Muftis peuvent, à condition de faire ratifier leur choix au Mufti en Chef, proposer la nomination, dans les limites de leurs circonscriptions et dans les localités où on en verrait la nécessité, des Mufti-Vékilis, qui auront à y remplir les fonctions déterminées par le présent arrangement, sous la surveillance directe des Muftis locaux.

Art. 3. — La rétribution du Mufti en Chef, des Muftis et des

Mufti-Vékilis, ainsi que du personnel de leurs bureaux, sera à la charge du Gouvernement Royal Bulgare et sera fixée en considération de leur dignité et de l'importance de leur poste.

L'organisation du Bach-Muftilik sera fixée par un règlement élaboré par le Mufti en Chef et dûment publié.

Le Mufti en Chef, Muftis et Mufti-Vékilis, ainsi que leur personnel, jouiront de tous les droits que les lois assurent aux fonctionnaires bulgares.

ART. 4. — La révocation des Muftis et de leurs Vékilis aura lieu conformément à la loi sur les fonctionnaires publics.

Le Mufti en Chef, ou son délégué, sera appelé à siéger au Conseil disciplinaire, toutes les fois que ce dernier aura à se prononcer sur la révocation d'un Mufti ou d'un Mufti-Vékili. Toutefois, l'avis du Mufti en Chef ou de son délégué servira audit conseil de base à l'appréciation des plaintes de caractère purement religieux.

L'acte de révocation d'un Mufti ou d'un Mufti-Vékili fixera le jour de l'élection de son remplaçant.

ART. 5. — Les Heudjets et jugements rendus par les Muftis seront examinés par le Mufti en Chef, qui les confirmera, s'il les trouve conformes aux prescriptions de la Loi du Chéri, et les remettra au Département compétent afin d'être mis à exécution.

Les Heudjets et jugements qui ne seront pas confirmés pour cause de non-conformité à la Loi du Chéri seront retournés aux Muftis qui les auraient rendus et les affaires auxquelles ils ont trait seront examinées et réglées de nouveau suivant les prescriptions de ladite loi. Les Heudjets et jugements qui ne seront pas trouvés conformes aux prescriptions de la Loi du Chéri ou ceux dont l'examen au Cheikh-ul-Islamat aura été demandé par les intéressés seront envoyés par le Mufti en Chef à son Altesse le Cheikh-ul-Islam.

Les Heudjets et jugements confirmés par le Mufti en Chef ou sanctionnés par le Cheikh-ul-Islamat seront mis à exécution par les autorités bulgares compétentes. Dans ce cas, ils seront accompagnés d'une traduction en langue bulgare.

ART. 6. — Le Mufti en Chef fera, le cas échéant, aux autres Muftis les recommandations et communications nécessaires en matière de mariage, divorce, testaments, successions et tutelle, pension alimentaire (nafaka) et autres matières du Chéri, ainsi qu'en ce qui concerne la gestion des biens des orphelins. En outre, il examinera les plaintes et réclamations se rapportant aux affaires susmentionnées et fera connaître au Département compétent ce qu'il y aurait lieu de faire conformément à la loi du Chéri.

Les Muftis étant aussi chargés de la surveillance et de l'administration des Vakoufs, le Mufti en Chef aura, parmi ses attributions principales, celle de leur demander la reddition de leurs comptes et de faire préparer les états de comptabilité y relatifs.

Les livres relatifs aux comptes des Vakoufs pourront être tenus en langue turque.

Art. 7. — Le Mufti en Chef et les Muftis inspecteront, au besoin, les conseils d'instruction publique et les écoles musulmanes ainsi que les Médressés de la Bulgarie et adopteront des dispositions pour la création d'établissements scolaires dans les localités où le besoin s'en ferait sentir ; le Mufti en Chef s'adressera, s'il y a lieu, au Département compétent pour les affaires concernant l'instruction publique musulmane.

Le Gouvernement Royal créera à ses frais des écoles primaires et secondaires musulmanes dans la proportion établie par la loi sur l'instruction publique bulgare. L'enseignement aura lieu en langue turque et en conformité du programme officiel, avec enseignement obligatoire de la langue bulgare.

Toutes les lois relatives à l'enseignement obligatoire ainsi qu'au nombre et aux droits des instituteurs continueront à être appliquées au corps enseignant des communautés musulmanes. Les appointements du personnel enseignant ou autre de ces institutions seront réglés par le Trésor bulgare dans les mêmes conditions que ceux des corps enseignants des institutions bulgares.

Une institution spéciale sera également fondée pour former des Naïbs.

Art. 8. — Dans chaque chef-lieu ou ville ayant une nombreuse population musulmane, il sera procédé à l'élection d'une communauté musulmane, chargée des affaires vakoufs et d'instruction publique secondaire. La personnalité morale de ces communautés sera reconnue en toute circonstance et par toutes les autorités.

Les vakoufs de chaque district devant être administrés, selon les lois et dispositions du Chéri, par la communauté musulmane respective, c'est la personnalité morale de cette dernière qui sera considérée comme propriétaire de ces vakoufs.

Les cimetières publics musulmans et ceux sis à proximité des mosquées sont compris dans le domaine des biens vakoufs appartenant aux communautés musulmanes, qui en disposeront à leur convenance et conformément aux lois de l'hygiène.

Aucun bien vakouf ne peut en aucun cas être exproprié sans que sa contre-valeur soit versée à la communauté respective.

On veillera à la bonne conservation des immeubles vakoufs sis en Bulgarie. Aucun édifice du culte ou de bienfaisance ne pourra être démoli que pour une nécessité impérieuse et conformément aux lois et aux règlements en vigueur.

Dans le cas où un édifice vakouf devrait être exproprié pour des causes impérieuses, on ne pourra y procéder qu'après la désignation d'un autre terrain ayant la même valeur par rapport à l'endroit où il se trouve situé, ainsi qu'après le paiement de la contre-valeur de la bâtisse.

Les sommes à payer comme prix des immeubles vakoufs qui seront expropriés pour des causes impérieuses seront remises aux communautés musulmanes pour être entièrement affectées à l'entretien des édifices vakoufs.

ART. 9. — Dans les six mois qui suivront la signature du présent Arrangement, une commission spéciale, dont le Mufti en Chef fera partie de droit, sera nommée par le Gouvernement bulgare et aura pour but, dans une période de trois ans à partir de la date de sa constitution, d'examiner et de vérifier les réclamations qui seront formulées par les Mutévellis ou leurs ayants droit.

Ceux des intéressés qui ne seraient pas contents des décisions de la commission pourront recourir aux tribunaux compétents du pays.

Fait en double exemplaire à Constantinople, le 16/29 septembre 1913.

ANNEXE III

COMPROMIS D'ARBITRAGE

ART. PREMIER. — Au cas où quelque différend ou litige surviendrait, d'après les prévisions de l'Article 17 du Traité conclu en date de ce jour entre le Gouvernement Impérial Ottoman d'une part, et le Gouvernement Royal de Bulgarie de l'autre, ce différend ou ce litige sera déféré à l'Arbitrage à La Haye, conformément aux dispositions ci-après.

ART. 2. — Le Gouvernement demandeur notifiera au Gouvernement défendeur la ou les questions qu'il entendra soumettre à l'arbitrage, au fur et à mesure qu'elles surgiront, et donnera à leur sujet des indications succinctes, mais précises.

ART. 3. — Le Tribunal Arbitral auquel la ou lesdites questions seront soumises sera composé de cinq membres, lesquels seront désignés de la manière suivante :

Chaque partie, aussitôt que possible et dans un délai qui n'excédera pas deux mois à partir de la date de la notification spécifiée dans l'Article précédent, devra nommer deux Arbitres.

Le Sur-Arbitre sera choisi parmi les Souverains de Suède, Norvège et Hollande. Si on ne tombe pas d'accord sur le choix de l'un de ces trois Souverains, le sort en décidera. Si la partie défenderesse ne nomme pas ses arbitres dans le délai précité de deux mois, elle pourra le faire jusqu'au jour de la première réunion du Tribunal Arbitral. Passé ce délai, la Partie demanderesse indiquera le Souverain qui aura à choisir le Sur-Arbitre. Après le choix dudit Sur-Arbitre, le Tribunal se constituera valablement par le Sur-Arbitre et par les deux Arbitres choisis par la Partie demanderesse.

ART. 4. — Les Puissances en litige se feront représenter auprès du Tribunal Arbitral par des Agents, Conseils ou Avocats, en conformité des prévisions de l'Article 62 de la Convention de La Haye pour le règlement pacifique des conflits internationaux.

Ces Agents, Conseils ou Avocats seront désignés à temps par les Parties pour que le fonctionnement de l'Arbitrage ne subisse aucun retard.

Toutefois, si la Partie défenderesse s'en abstient, il sera procédé à son égard par défaut.

ART. 5. — Le Tribunal Arbitral, une fois constitué, se réunira à La Haye à une date qui sera fixée par les Arbitres et dans le délai d'un mois à partir de la nomination du Sur-Arbitre. Après le règlement en conformité avec le texte et l'esprit de la Convention de La Haye de 1907 de toutes les questions de procédure qui pourraient surgir et qui ne seraient pas prévues par le présent Compromis, ledit Tribunal ajournera sa prochaine séance à la date qu'il fixera.

Toutefois, il reste convenu que le Tribunal ne pourra ouvrir les débats sur les questions en litige ni avant les deux mois, ni plus tard que les trois mois qui suivront la remise du Contre-mémoire ou de la Contre-réplique prévue par l'Article 7.

ART. 6. — La procédure arbitrale comprendra deux phases distinctes : l'instruction écrite et les débats, qui consisteront dans le développement oral des moyens des Parties devant le Tribunal.

La seule langue dont fera usage le Tribunal et dont l'emploi sera autorisé devant lui sera la langue française.

ART. 7. — Dans le délai de dix mois au plus tard à dater de la notification prévue à l'Article 2, la Partie demanderesse devra remettre à chacun des membres du Tribunal Arbitral, en cinq exemplaires, et à la Partie défenderesse, en trente exemplaires, les copies complètes, écrites ou imprimées, de son Mémoire, contenant toutes pièces à l'appui de sa demande, lesquelles se référeraient à la ou aux questions en litige.

Dans un délai de dix mois au plus tard après cette remise, la Partie défenderesse devra remettre à chacun des membres du Tribunal, ainsi qu'à la Partie demanderesse, en autant d'exemplaires que ci-dessus, les copies complètes, manuscrites ou imprimées, de son Contre-mémoire avec toutes les pièces à l'appui.

Dans le délai d'un mois après cette remise, la Partie demande-resse notifiera au Président du Tribunal Arbitral si elle a l'intention de présenter une Réplique. Dans ce cas, elle aura quatre mois au plus, à compter de cette notification, pour communiquer ladite Réplique dans les mêmes conditions que le Mémoire. La Partie défenderesse aura alors cinq mois, à compter de cette communication, pour présenter sa Contre-réplique dans les mêmes conditions que le Contre-mémoire.

Les délais fixés par le présent Article pourront être prolongés de commun accord par les Parties ou par le Tribunal, quand il le jugera nécessaire pour arriver à une décision juste.

Mais le Tribunal ne prendra pas en considération les Mémoires, Contre-mémoires et autres communications qui lui seront présentées par les Parties après l'expiration du dernier délai fixé par lui.

ART. 8. — Si dans les Mémoires ou autres pièces échangées l'une ou l'autre Partie s'est référée ou a fait allusion à un document ou papier en sa possession exclusive, et dont elle n'aura pas joint la copie, elle sera tenue, si l'autre partie le demande, de lui en donner copie au plus tard dans les trente jours.

ART. 9. — Les décisions du Tribunal Arbitral sur la ou les questions en litige seront prononcées dans le délai maximum d'un mois après la clôture, par le Président des débats relatifs à cette ou ces questions.

ART. 10. — Le jugement du Tribunal Arbitral sera définitif et devra être exécuté strictement, sans aucun retard.

ART. 11. — Chaque Partie supporte ses propres frais et une part égale des frais du Tribunal.

ART. 12. — En tout ce qui n'est pas prévu par le présent Com-promis, les stipulations de la Convention de La Haye de 1907 pour le règlement pacifique des conflits internationaux seront appliquées aux Arbitrages résultant du présent Compromis, à l'exception, toutefois, des Articles qui ont été réservés par les Parties contrac-tantes.

Fait en double exemplaire à Constantinople, le 16/29 septembre 1913.

ANNEXE IV

PROTOCOLE N° 2

Le tracé de la frontière coupant le fleuve Maritza et le chemin de fer Moustafa-Pacha-Andrinople-Dédéagatch, qui desservent les territoires ottomans et bulgares, il a été convenu entre les deux Parties contractantes que, pour préserver les relations commerciales et autres des moindres entraves, les règlements et les usages qui régissent actuellement les mouvements commerciaux, tant sur le fleuve Maritza que sur ladite ligne ferrée, ainsi que tous les droits, taxes et autres découlant desdits règlements, seront maintenus dans leur plénitude et que toutes facilités compatibles avec lesdits règlements et usages seront accordées. Aucune modification ne pourra y être introduite sans un accord préalable entre les deux États contractants et les Administrations desdits chemin de fer et fleuve. Le transit direct des marchandises sera exempt de droits et taxes quelconques ; toutefois, chaque Gouvernement pourra réglementer la surveillance dudit transit.

Les dispositions ci-dessus ne s'appliqueront pour le chemin de fer que jusqu'au jour où les deux Hautes Parties contractantes auront déjà construit simultanément, la Bulgarie une ligne de raccordement à la mer Égée, dans son territoire, et la Turquie une ligne aboutissant à ladite mer.

Il est bien entendu qu'en temps de paix la Bulgarie sera libre, jusqu'à la construction de la ligne prévue, qui aura lieu au plus tard dans dix ans, de faire transporter sur ledit chemin de fer, ainsi que sur le fleuve, des recrues, des troupes, des armes, des munitions, des vivres, etc.

L'État Ottoman aura toujours le droit de prendre les mesures de surveillance nécessaires.

Toutefois, ce transport de troupes et autre ne pourra commencer qu'à partir de trois mois à dater de ce jour.

Fait en double exemplaire à Constantinople, le 16/29 septembre 1913.

ANNEXE V

Déclaration

En ce qui concerne l'Article 10 du Traité, le Gouvernement Impérial Ottoman déclare qu'il n'a point consenti, depuis l'occupation par les forces bulgares des territoires cédés, à des cessions de droits à des particuliers, en vue de restreindre les droits souverains de l'État Bulgare.

Fait en double exemplaire à Constantinople, le 16/29 septembre 1913.

No. 6

TREATY OF PEACE

Turkey and Greece

Signed November 14, 1913

S. M. l'Empereur des Ottomans et S. M. le Roi des Hellènes, animés d'un égal désir de consolider les liens de paix et d'amitié heureusement rétablis entre Eux et de faciliter la reprise des relations normales entre les deux Pays, ont résolu de conclure une convention à cet effet et ont nommé pour Leủrs Plénipotentiaires, savoir :

S. M. l'Empereur des Ottomans : S. E. Ghalib Kémal Bey, plénipotentiaire ottoman ;

S. M. le Roi des Hellènes : S. E. M. D. Panas, Ministre des Affaires étrangères.

Lesquels, après s'être communiqué leurs pleins pouvoirs, trouvés en bonne et due forme, sont convenus de ce qui suit :

Article premier. — Dès que le présent acte aura été signé, les relations diplomatiques entre la Turquie et la Grèce seront reprises et les consulats respectifs pourront être rétablis et fonctionner dans les deux pays.

Le Gouvernement Impérial Ottoman pourra instituer des consulats dans les localités des territoires cédés où se trouvent déjà des agents des Puissances étrangères, ainsi que dans toutes celles où le Gouvernement Royal de Grèce ne verrait pas inconvénient à les admettre.

Art. 2. — Les traités, conventions et actes conclus ou en vigueur entre les deux pays au moment de la rupture des relations diplomatiques seront remis intégralement en vigueur à partir de la signature de la présente convention et les deux gouvernements seront placés, l'un vis-à-vis de l'autre, ainsi que les sujets respectifs, dans la même situation où ils se trouvaient avant les hostilités.

Le protocole n⁰ 3 annexé à la présente convention sera applicable dans tous les territoires de la Grèce.

Art. 3. — Les deux Hautes Parties contractantes accordent pleine et entière amnistie à toutes les personnes compromises dans les événements politiques antérieurs au présent traité.

En conséquence, aucun individu ne pourra être poursuivi, inquiété ni troublé dans sa personne ou sa propriété, ou dans l'exercice de ses droits, en raison d'actes ayant une relation quelconque avec la guerre, et toutes condamnations judiciaires et mesures administratives motivées par des faits de cette nature seront *ipso facto* annulées.

Art. 4. — Les individus domiciliés dans les territoires de l'Empire

Ottoman passant sous la domination de la Grèce deviendront sujets hellènes.

Ils auront le droit d'opter pour la nationalité ottomane, moyennant une déclaration à l'autorité hellénique compétente, dans l'espace de trois ans à partir de la date de ce jour, déclaration qui sera suivie d'un enregistrement aux consulats impériaux ottomans. Cette déclaration sera remise à l'étranger aux chancelleries des consulats helléniques et enregistrée par les consulats ottomans. Toutefois, l'exercice de ce droit d'option est subordonné au transfert du domicile des intéressés et à leur établissement hors de Grèce.

Les personnes qui, pendant ce délai, auront émigré dans l'Empire Ottoman ou à l'étranger, ou y auront fixé leur domicile, resteront ottomanes. Elles jouiront de la franchise des droits de sortie pour leurs biens meubles.

L'option sera individuelle.

Pendant le même espace de trois ans, les musulmans ne seront pas astreints au service militaire ni ne payeront aucune taxe militaire.

En ce qui concerne les enfants mineurs, le délai d'option commencera à courir à partir de la date où ils auront atteint l'âge de la majorité.

Art. 5. — Les droits acquis jusqu'à l'occupation des territoires cédés, ainsi que les actes judiciaires et titres officiels émanant des autorités ottomanes compétentes, seront respectés et inviolables jusqu'à preuve légale du contraire.

Cet article ne préjuge en rien les décisions que pourrait prendre la commission financière des affaires balkaniques siégeant à Paris.

Art. 6. — Les habitants des territoires cédés, qui, se conformant aux dispositions de l'article 4 de la présente convention et conservant la nationalité ottomane, auraient émigré dans l'Empire Ottoman ou à l'étranger, ou qui y auraient fixé leur domicile, continueront à conserver leurs propriétés immobilières sises dans ces territoires, à les affermer ou à les faire administrer par des tiers.

Les droits de propriété sur les immeubles urbains et ruraux possédés par des particuliers en vertu de titres émanant de l'État Ottoman, ou bien de par la loi ottomane dans les localités cédées à la Grèce et antérieurs à l'occupation, seront reconnus par le Gouvernement Royal Hellénique.

Il en sera de même des droits de propriété sur lesdits immeubles inscrits au nom de personnes morales ou possédés par elles en vertu des lois ottomanes antérieures à l'occupation précitée.

Nul ne pourra être privé de sa propriété, partiellement ou totalement, directement ou indirectement, que pour cause d'utilité publique dûment constatée, moyennant une juste et préalable indemnité.

ART. 7. — Les biens particuliers de S. M. le Sultan, ainsi que ceux des membres de la Dynastie impériale, seront maintenus et respectés. Sa Majesté Impériale et les membres de la Dynastie Impériale pourront les vendre ou les affermer par des fondés de pouvoirs.

Tous les différends ou litiges qui surviendraient dans l'interprétation ou l'application du présent article seront réglés par un arbitrage à La Haye, en vertu d'un compromis à conclure.

ART. 8. — Les prisonniers de guerre ainsi que toutes autres personnes arrêtées par mesure militaire ou d'ordre public seront échangés dans le délai d'un mois à partir de la signature du présent Traité ou plus tôt si faire se peut.

Cet échange aura lieu par les soins de commissaires spéciaux nommés de part et d'autre.

Les réclamations réciproques des deux Hautes Parties contractantes relatives aux prisonniers de guerre seront déférées à un arbitrage à La Haye, en vertu d'un compromis à conclure.

Toutefois la solde des officiers payés par le Gouvernement Royal Hellénique sera remboursée par l'État dont ils relèvent.

ART. 9. — Immédiatement après la signature de la présente Convention, le Gouvernement Impérial Ottoman relâchera tous les navires et toutes les embarcations sous pavillon hellénique qui, saisis avant la déclaration de la guerre, sont détenus par lui.

Les demandes en réparations des dommages et des pertes des intéressés, du fait de l'embargo et de la saisie mis sur les navires et les cargaisons helléniques, seront soumises, conformément à un compromis qui sera arrêté d'un commun accord, à un Tribunal arbitral formé par quatre arbitres nommés de part et d'autre et de trois arbitres qui seront choisis parmi les sujets des nations maritimes par les deux Parties, ou, en cas de désaccord, par le Conseil Fédéral Suisse.

ART. 10. — Les deux Gouvernements s'engagent également de s'adresser, en vertu d'un compromis à conclure, à un Tribunal arbitral à La Haye, pour le règlement du différend surgi au sujet de l'interprétation des clauses du Protocole de reddition de Salonique, en date du 23 octobre 1912 (v. st.), et du Protocole-Annexe, signé le jour suivant, relatifs aux armes des soldats ottomans de la garnison de cette ville, dont le Gouvernement Impérial Ottoman réclame la restitution.

ART. 11. — La vie, les biens, l'honneur, la religion et les coutumes de ceux des habitants des localités cédées à la Grèce qui resteront sous l'Administration hellénique seront scrupuleusement respectés.

Ils jouiront entièrement des mêmes droits civils et politiques que les sujets hellènes d'origine. La liberté, la pratique extérieure du culte, seront assurées aux Musulmans.

Le nom de Sa Majesté Impériale le Sultan, comme Khalife, continuera à être prononcé dans les prières publiques des Musulmans.

Aucune atteinte ne pourra être portée à l'autonomie et à l'organisation hiérarchique des communautés musulmanes existantes ou qui pourraient se former, ni à l'administration des fonds et immeubles qui leur appartiennent.

Aucune entrave ne pourra également être apportée aux rapports des particuliers et des communautés musulmanes avec leurs chefs spirituels qui dépendront du Cheikh-ul-Islamat à Constantinople, lequel donnera l'investiture au Mufti en chef.

Les muftis, chacun dans sa circonscription, seront élus par les électeurs musulmans.

Le Mufti en chef est nommé par Sa Majesté le Roi des Hellènes parmi trois candidats élus et présentés par une assemblée électorale composée de tous les Muftis de Grèce.

Le Gouvernement Hellénique notifiera l'élection du Mufti en chef par l'intermédiaire de la Légation Royale de Grèce à Constantinople au Cheikh-ul-Islamat qui lui fera parvenir un menchour et le murassélé l'autorisant à exercer ses fonctions et à accorder, de son côté, aux autres muftis de Grèce le droit de juridiction et celui de rendre les fetvas.

Les Muftis, outre leur compétence sur les affaires purement religieuses et leur surveillance sur l'administration des biens vakoufs, exerceront leur juridiction entre musulmans en matière de mariage, divorce, pensions alimentaires (nefaca), tutelle, curetelle, émancipation de mineurs, testaments islamiques et successions au poste de mutévelli (tevliet).

Les jugements rendus par les muftis seront mis à exécution par les autorités helléniques compétentes.

Quant aux successions, les parties musulmanes intéressées pourront, après accord préalable, avoir recours au mufti, en qualité d'arbitre.

Contre le jugement arbitral ainsi rendu, toutes les voies de recours devant les tribunaux du pays seront admises, à moins d'une clause contraire expressément stipulée.

ART. 12. — Les vakoufs Idjaréi, Vahidé, Idjaretéin, Moukataa, qu'ils soient Mazbouta, Mulhaka ou Mustesna, dans les territoires cédés, tels qu'ils résultaient des lois ottomanes au moment de l'occupation militaire, seront respectés.

Ils seront gérés par les communautés musulmanes des territoires cédés, qui respecteront les droits des mutévélis et des gallédars.

Tous les immeubles vakoufs urbains et ruraux, mazbouta ou

mulhaka, sis dans les territoires cédés à la Grèce et dont les revenus appartiennent à des fondations pieuses et de bienfaisance se trouvant en Turquie seront également administrés par lesdites communautés musulmanes jusqu'à ce qu'ils soient vendus par le ministère de l'Evkaf.

Il est bien entendu que les droits des gallédars sur les vakoufs précités seront respectés par ledit ministère.

Le régime des vakoufs ne pourra être modifié que par indemnisation juste et préalable.

Les dîmes vakoufs étant supprimées, si, à la suite de cette suppression, certains tekkès, mosquées, écoles, hôpitaux et autres institutions religieuses et de bienfaisance des territoires cédés à la Grèce n'ont pas, à l'avenir, des revenus suffisants pour leur entretien, le Gouvernement Royal Hellénique accordera des subventions nécessaires à cet effet.

Toutes contestations au sujet de l'interprétation ou de l'application du présent article seront tranchées par voie d'arbitrage à La Haye.

ART. 13. — Les Hautes Parties contractantes s'engagent à donner à leurs autorités provinciales des ordres afin de faire respecter les cimetières et particulièrement les tombeaux des soldats tombés sur le champ d'honneur.

Les autorités n'empêcheront pas les parents et amis d'enlever les ossements des victimes inhumées en terre étrangère.

ART. 14. — Le Gouvernement Royal de Grèce étant subrogé aux droits, charges et obligations du Gouvernement Impérial Ottoman à l'égard des Compagnies de chemins de fer Salonique-Monastir, des chemins de fer Orientaux et des chemins de fer de jonction Salonique-Dédéagatch, pour les parties de ces chemins de fer dans les territoires cédés à la Grèce, toutes les questions y relatives seront déférées à la Commission financière des Affaires balkaniques siégeant à Paris.

ART. 15. — Les deux Hautes Parties contractantes s'engagent à maintenir, en ce qui les concerne, les dispositions du Traité de Londres du 30 mai 1913, y compris les stipulations de l'article 5 dudit Traité.

ART. 16. — Le présent Traité entrera en vigueur immédiatement après sa signature.

Les ratifications en seront échangées dans la quinzaine à dater de ce jour.

En foi de quoi les Plénipotentiaires respectifs l'ont signé et y ont apposé leurs cachets.

Fait en double exemplaire à Athènes, le 1/14 novembre 1913.

(L. S.) D. PANAS.   (L. S.) GHALIB KÉMALY BEY.

Protocole n° 1

Les originaires des territoires cédés, domiciliés hors de l'Empire ottoman, auront un délai de six mois pour opter en faveur de la nationalité hellénique.

La déclaration et les conséquences en seront les mêmes que celles prévues dans l'article 4.

Protocole spécial n° 2

Le Gouvernement impérial ottoman prétendant que les propriétés du domaine privé de l'État sises dans les territoires cédés doivent lui rester et le Gouvernement royal hellénique n'acceptant pas et prétendant que ces propriétés doivent lui appartenir, les deux Parties contractantes sont convenues de soumettre cette question à un Tribunal arbitral à La Haye, en vertu d'un compromis à conclure.

Le nombre et l'étendue des propriétés en question se trouvent dans la liste jointe à ce protocole.

BIENS DU DOMAINE PRIVÉ DE L'ÉTAT

I. — VILAYET DE SALONIQUE

A. *Biens qui ont passé successivement à l'État.*

Le nombre de ces biens n'est pas encore relevé ; mais ils sont de peu d'importance, d'une valeur approximative de 2.000 L. T., soit . . . . L. T. 2.000

B. *Biens qui ont passé de la Liste Civile à l'État.*

1 ferme, 46.210 deunumes . . . . L. T. 450

93 terrains, y compris les 288.290 mètres sis à Salonique et où ont été construites des bâtisses, 188.024 deunumes . . . . L. T. 312.139

Terrain situé sur le port de Salonique, 6.410 m. . L. T. 30.300

II. — VILAYET DE JANINA

A. *Biens qui ont passé successivement à l'État.*

916 terrains, 109.732 deunumes . . . L. T. 15.175

319 immeubles bâtis, 48 deunumes . . . L. T. 12.105

B. *Biens qui ont passé de la Liste Civile à l'État.*

119 terrains, 2.672 deunumes . . . . L. T. 235

193 fermes, 550.380 ,, ... L. T. 200.000

48 bâtisses, pas évaluées.

III

14 pêcheries dans le Vilayet de Salonique . . L. T. 12.506

CONCESSIONS DE MINES ET ENTREPRISES
QUI ONT PASSÉ DE LA LISTE CIVILE A L'ÉTAT

I. — Vilayet de Salonique

Mines, village de Lania, Nahié de Vardar.
Mines, fermes Bochanak et Stanova, même Nahié.
Mines d'or, Caza d'Avret Hissar.
Dépôts de pétrole, Salonique.
Desséchement de marais ' Ladova '.
Terrains à gagner sur la mer, côte orientale de Salonique.
Constructions de quai et port dans le golfe de Salonique.
Navigation à vapeur, golfes de Cassandra, de Salonique.

II. — Vilayet de Janina

Mine de bitume, Lenitché.
Mine de pétrole, ferme de Lenitché.
Données à bail pour quarante ans à M. Frédéric Spadell. La mine de zinc est seule exploitée.

(S.) D. Panas.   (S.) Ghalib Kémaly Bey.

Protocole n⁰ 3

1. — Aucune réclamation, de quelque nature qu'elle soit, ne pourra être élevée de la part du Gouvernement impérial ottoman pour les anciennes églises chrétiennes converties dans le temps en mosquées et rendues dans le cours des hostilités à leur premier culte.

2. — Toute demande du Gouvernement impérial ottoman, d'après laquelle les mosquées converties n'auraient pas été autrefois des églises, sera examinée par le Gouvernement hellénique.

3. — Toutefois, les revenus des propriétés vakoufs, appartenant aux mosquées mentionnées dans le paragraphe 1, seront, s'il en existe, respectés et remis aux communautés musulmanes des nouveaux territoires annexés afin d'être employés librement par elles pour des fins identiques à celles pour lesquelles ils avaient été créés à l'origine.

4. — Le Gouvernement royal hellénique fera construire, à ses frais, une mosquée dans la capitale et quatre autres mosquées dans les villages pauvres où le besoin s'en ferait sentir.

5. — Toutes contestations relatives à l'interprétation ou à l'application des dispositions qui précèdent seront réglées par un arbitrage à La Haye, en vertu d'un compromis à conclure.

6. — Une institution spéciale sera également créée pour former des naïbs.

7. — Le mufti en chef et les muftis, ainsi que le personnel de leurs bureaux, auront les mêmes droits et les mêmes devoirs que les autres fonctionnaires publics hellènes.

8. — Le mufti en chef vérifie si le mufti élu réunit toutes les qualités requises par la loi du Chéri.

9. — Les muftis ne pourront être révoqués que conformément aux dispositions de l'article 88 de la Constitution du Royaume hellénique.

10. — Les communautés musulmanes étant aussi chargées de l'administration et de la surveillance des vakoufs, le mufti en chef aura, parmi ses attributions principales, celle de leur demander la reddition de leurs comptes et de faire préparer les états de comptabilité y relatifs.

11. — Aucun bien vakouf ne pourra être exproprié que pour cause d'utilité publique, dûment constatée, moyennant une indemnité juste et préalable.

12. — Les cimetières publics musulmans seront reconnus comme biens vakoufs.

13. — La personnalité morale des communautés musulmanes est reconnue.

14. — Les heudjets et jugements rendus par les muftis seront examinés par le mufti en chef, qui les confirmera s'il les trouve conformes aux prescriptions de la loi du Chéri. Lorsque ces heudjets et jugements portent sur des questions religieuses autres que les testaments islamiques, ou qui concernent des intérêts exclusivement matériels, tant le mufti en chef que les parties pourront s'adresser au Cheikh-ul-Islamat.

15. — Les écoles privées musulmanes, entre autres l'École des Arts et Métiers Midhat Pacha à Salonique, seront reconnues, et les biens de rapport, dont elles disposent depuis leur création pour subvenir à leurs frais, seront respectés.

Il en sera de même de toutes les écoles privées musulmanes existantes ou qui seront créées par des particuliers ou des commissions locales composées de notables musulmans.

Le mufti en chef, les muftis et les inspecteurs de l'Instruction publique de l'État hellénique pourront inspecter ces écoles. L'enseignement aura lieu en langue turque et en conformité du programme officiel avec enseignement obligatoire de la langue grecque.

Déclaration du Délégué ottoman.

Le soussigné Délégué ottoman, chargé de négocier et de signer la Convention turco-hellénique, conclue en date de ce jour, a l'honneur de déclarer qu'aucun des navires sous pavillon hellénique, saisis avant la déclaration de la guerre, n'a été confisqué.

GENERAL APPENDIX

PUBLICATIONS OF THE DIVISION OF ECONOMICS AND HISTORY

THE Conference, which met at Berne in 1911, under the auspices of the Division of Economics and History of the Carnegie Endowment for International Peace, appointed three Commissions to draft the questions and problems to be dealt with by competent authorities in all countries. The first Commission was entrusted with *The Economic and Historical Causes and Effects of War*; the second with *Armaments in Time of Peace*; the third with *The Unifying Influences in International Life*. Subsequently the suggestions of the three Commissions were considered and approved by the entire Conference.

The questions are to be discussed scientifically, and as far as possible without prejudice either for or against war; and their discussion may have such important consequences that the questions are presented below *in extenso*.

Report of the First Commission

THE ECONOMIC AND HISTORICAL CAUSES AND EFFECTS OF WAR

The Conference recommends the following researches :

1. Historical presentation of the causes of war in modern times, tracing especially the influence exercised by the striving for greater political power, by the growth of the national idea, by the political aspirations of races and by economic interests.

2. Conflicts of economic interests in the present age :

(*a*) The influence of the growth of population and of the industrial development upon the expansion of States.

(*b*) The protectionist policy; its origin and basis; its method of application and its influence upon the relations between countries; bounties (open and disguised, public and private); most favoured nation treatment; the attitude towards foreign goods and foreign capital; the boycott; discouragement of foreign immigration.

GENERAL APPENDIX

(c) International loans ; the policy of guarantees ; the relations of the creditor to the debtor States ; the use of loans for gaining influence over other States.

(d) Rivalry among States with respect to capitalist investments in foreign countries :

1. The endeavour to obtain a privileged position in banking enterprises, in the opening and development of mines, in the letting of public contracts, in the execution of public works, in the building of railways (Siberian, Manchurian, Persian Bagdad Railway, Adriatic Railway, &c.) ; in short, the organization of larger capitalistic enterprises in foreign countries.

2. The hindering of foreign countries by convention from executing productive enterprises on their own soil, e.g. from building railways in their own countries.

3. The anti-militarist movement, considered in its religious and political manifestations. (Only opposition to all military organization is here to be considered.)

4. The position of organized labour and the socialists in the various States on the questions of war and armaments.

5. Is it possible to determine a special interest of individual classes making for or against war, for or against standing armies ?

6. The influence of women and woman suffrage upon war and armaments.

7. The extension of obligatory military service in the different States, in times both of war and of peace.

(a) The conditions of military service ; the system of enlistment and of general obligatory service, the actual position of aliens.

(b) The ratio of the persons obliged to render military service to the entire population.

(c) The influence of the present system of military obligation and the organization of armies upon warfare and upon its duration.

8. The economic effects of the right of capture and its influence upon the development of navies.

9. War loans provided by neutral countries ; their extent and influence on recent warfare.

10. The effects of war :

(a) Financial cost of war. The methods of meeting it : Taxation ; International Loans ; External Loans.

(b) Losses and gains from the point of view of public and private economic interests ; checks to production and the destruction of productive forces ; reduction of opportunities for business enter-

2

prises; interruption of foreign trade and of the imports of food; the destruction of property; shrinkage of values of property, including securities; financial burden caused by new taxes, debts, and war indemnities; effects upon private credit and upon savings banks; advantages to those industries which furnish military materials; advantages and disadvantages to neutral countries.

(c) The effects of war upon the supply of the world with food and raw materials, with special reference to those States which are in large degree dependent upon other countries for such supplies, e.g. Great Britain and Germany; by diversion of capital from those countries which produce food and raw materials (especially the stoppage of railway building and of new investments in agriculture and other industries).

(d) The condition of the victorious State: manner of levy and use of contributions and war indemnities; influence upon industry and social life.

(e) The manner in which the energy of nations is stimulated or depressed by war.

11. Loss of human life in war and as a result of war: influence upon population (birth-rate, relation between the sexes, ratio of the various ages, sanitary conditions).

12. The influence of war and of the possibility of war upon the protective policy, upon banking conditions (especially upon banks of issue), and upon monetary systems.

13. The influence of annexation upon the economic life of the annexing States, and upon the State whose territory has been annexed.

14. The annexation of half-civilized or uncivilized peoples, considered especially from the point of view of the economic interests, which act as motive powers; the methods through which private enterprises take root in such regions and through which they bring influence to bear upon their own governments; the effects of such annexations upon the development of trade with the annexing State and with other countries, as well as upon the economic and social life of the natives.

15. The progressive exemption of commercial and industrial activities from losses and interferences through war.

16. Influence of the open door policy upon war and peace.

3

GENERAL APPENDIX

Report of the Second Commission

ARMAMENTS IN TIME OF PEACE. MILITARY AND NAVAL ESTABLISH-
MENTS. THE THEORY, PRACTICE, AND HISTORY OF MODERN
ARMAMENTS.

1. Definition. Armaments might be described as ' the preparations made by a State either for defence or for attack '. These would include the provision of food, financial preparations, and also semi-military railways, canals, docks, &c.

2. Causes of armaments. Motives for increasing or commencing them, distinguishing the great from the small powers.

3. Rivalry and competition in armaments. Motives and consequences of rivalry, with the possibilities of limitation.

4. Modern history of armaments, with special fullness from 1872. To be noted as important landmarks :

    (a) The introduction of conscription into Germany, France, Austria, Italy, Japan, &c.

    (b) Modern inventions affecting war.

    (c) The question of privateering and private property at sea.

    (d) Duration of military service.

    (e) The traffic in arms.

5. Military budgets from 1872 (distinguishing ordinary from extraordinary expenditures).

6. The burden of armaments in recent times.

    (a) The proportion of military to civil expenditure.

    (b) Military expenditure per capita.

    (c) Military expenditure from loans in time of peace, i.e. a comparison of expenditure from taxes with expenditure from borrowed money.

    (d) Comparative burdens of individual taxpayers in different countries and the extent to which the differences are due to armaments.

    (e) Military pensions.

    (f) It is desirable to ascertain where possible the ratio between the total income of each nation and the total expenditure on armament at various times.

7. The effects of war preparations upon the economic and social life of a nation :

    (a) On the sustenance of the entire population of a country at war.

GENERAL APPENDIX

(*b*) On railway policy.

(*c*) On public administration and on social legislation.

8. The economic effects of withdrawing young men from industrial pursuits, into the army and navy :

(*a*) Compulsory.

(*b*) Of non-compulsory service (specially in the case of mercenary troops).

(Allowance being made for the industrial value of military education and training.)

9. The influence of changes in the occupations of a people upon the composition and efficiency of armies, and the influence of the changes in the composition of armies on the economic life.

10. Loans for armaments (participation of domestic and foreign capital).

11. The industries of war, i.e. the various manufactures and other industries which are promoted and encouraged by military and naval establishments, distinguishing between :

(*a*) Government undertakings (arsenals, dockyards, &c.).

(*b*) Private undertakings, including the history and working of the great armament firms, which sell to foreign customers as well as to their own governments.

12. War materials (munitions of war). Their recent development and their cost. This includes arms, ammunition, armour-plate, warships, guns of all kinds, military airships, &c. So far as possible the effect of recent inventions upon offensive and defensive war should be indicated.

Report of the Third Commission

THE UNIFYING INFLUENCES IN INTERNATIONAL LIFE

1. The Conference is of the opinion that the economic life of individual countries has definitely ceased to be self-contained ; and that, notwithstanding the barriers raised by fiscal duties, it is becoming in ever increasing measure a part of an economic life in which the whole world participates.

2. It desires that this change be studied with the object of ascertaining to what extent the economic life of individual nations has ceased to be self-contained, and the causes which are bringing about the greater interdependence of nations.

3. Special attention should be paid to the following factors :

(*a*) How far the growth of population is responsible for the changes that have occurred and are in progress.

5

GENERAL APPENDIX

(*b*) The extent to which the insufficiency of the natural resources of individual countries for their own requirements has contributed to it.

(*c*) Whether the increasing economic unity of the world is the cause or the result of the rising in the standard of living, and how far the increasing welfare of nations has been caused by the growing unity.

(*d*) In what measure the need of individual countries to obtain materials of production from other lands and to find new markets for their own products is responsible for the growth of international dependence.

4. The Conference desires that investigations be made into :

(*a*) The volume of the world's production of all the many articles of food, of the various raw materials and of the principal manufactures.

(*b*) The productions of individual countries, and the extent to which they are retained for home consumption or are exported.

(*c*) The consumption of individual countries, and the extent to which the various articles are supplied from home productions or are imported.

5. The Conference wishes to ascertain to what extent the economy of production by large units, instead of by small units, has contributed to the international dependence of nations.

6. The development of this world-embracing economy has taken place in great measure in consequence of the investment of capital by rich countries in less developed lands. Through this there have arisen close relations and a great increase of wealth, not only for the lending and the borrowing countries, but for all nations. The Conference is of the opinion that researches should be made into the extent of the interdependence of the nations in the matter of capital.

7. The Conference desires to institute inquiries into the interdependence of the financial centres of the world.

8. The Conference desires to make the unifying effects of international trade, the building of railways, the progress of shipping, the improvement and extension of all means of communication and the progress of inventions, the subjects of careful investigation.

9. The Conference is in favour of making a comprehensive study of the various international unions and associations, in which the social and economic interests of all classes of society are now either organized or in process of organization, through official or private action.